Laansma has used his extensive knowledge of the New Testament and careful exegetical judgment to give us an insightful interpretation of this crucial Biblical book. His work will contribute to the use of Hebrews for the edification of the people of God.

> —**Gareth Lee Cockerill**, Professor of Biblical Interpretation and Theology, Wesley Biblical Seminary, Jackson, Mississippi

Jon Laansma's new commentary on Hebrews is an ideal resource for serious expositors, full of practical themes for teaching and preaching. As a gifted scholar with a heart for the local church and for global evangelism, Dr. Laansma has an intuitive grasp of the epistle's missional context and homiletical structure. His scholarship—which is thoroughly up to date—is presented in a fresh, accessible style and animated throughout by a dramatic encounter with Jesus Christ as the Son of God and the Great High Priest of our salvation.

> —**Philip Ryken**, President, Wheaton College

# The Letter to the Hebrews

# The Letter to the Hebrews

A Commentary for Preaching, Teaching, and Bible Study

Jon C. Laansma

CASCADE *Books* • Eugene, Oregon

THE LETTER TO THE HEBREWS
A Commentary for Preaching, Teaching, and Bible Study

Copyright © 2017 Jon C. Laansma. All rights reserved. Except for brief quotations in critical publications or reviews, no part of this book may be reproduced in any manner without prior written permission from the publisher. Write: Permissions, Wipf and Stock Publishers, 199 W. 8th Ave., Suite 3, Eugene, OR 97401.

Cascade Books
An Imprint of Wipf and Stock Publishers
199 W. 8th Ave., Suite 3
Eugene, OR 97401

www.wipfandstock.com

PAPERBACK ISBN: 978-1-4982-9321-1
HARDCOVER ISBN: 978-1-4982-9323-5
EBOOK ISBN: 978-1-4982-9322-8

*Cataloguing-in-Publication data:*

Names: Laansma, Jon C.

Title: The letter to the Hebrews : a commentary for preaching, teaching, and bible study / by Jon C. Laansma.

Description: Eugene, OR: Cascade Books, 2017 | Includes bibliographical references and index.

Identifiers: ISBN 978-1-4982-9321-1 (paperback) | ISBN 978-1-4982-9323-5 (hardcover) | ISBN 978-1-4982-9322-8 (ebook)

Subjects: LCSH: Bible—Hebrews—Commentary.

Classification: LCC BS2775.53 L1 2017 (print) | LCC BS2775.53 (ebook)

Manufactured in the U.S.A.                              07/10/17

Unless otherwise indicated, all Scripture quotations are from the ESV® Bible (The Holy Bible, English Standard Version®), copyright © 2001 by Crossway, a publishing ministry of Good News Publishers. Used by permission. All rights reserved.

Scripture quotations marked NRSV are from New Revised Standard Version Bible, copyright © 1989 National Council of the Churches of Christ in the United States of America. Used by permission. All rights reserved.

Greek Bible text from: Novum Testamentum Graece, 28th revised edition, edited by Barbara Aland and others, © 2012 Deutsche Bibelgesellschaft, Stuttgart.

For John Wilson and Carl B. Hoch, Jr.†, in gratitude for
their exposition of this letter and example of life.

And for Marvin J. Laansma, our beloved father who has
rested from his works,

ὃς ἐλάλησέν μοι τὸν λόγον τοῦ θεοῦ, οὗ ἀναθεωρῶν
τὴν ἔκβασιν τῆς ἀναστροφῆς μιμήσομαι τὴν πίστιν.

We believe in one God the Father all-powerful, Maker of heaven and of earth, and of all things both seen and unseen.

And in one Lord Jesus Christ, the only-begotten Son of God, begotten from the Father before all the ages, light from light, true God from true God, begotten not made, consubstantial with the Father, through whom all things came to be; for us humans and for our salvation he came down from the heavens and became incarnate from the Holy Spirit and the Virgin Mary, became human and was crucified on our behalf under Pontius Pilate; he suffered and was buried and rose up on the third day in accordance with the Scriptures; he is coming again with glory to judge the living and the dead; his kingdom will have no end.

And in the Spirit, the holy, the lordly, the life-giving one, proceeding forth from the Father, co-worshiped and co-glorified with Father and Son, the one who spoke through the prophets; in one, holy, catholic, and apostolic church. We confess one baptism for the forgiving of sins. We look forward to a resurrection of the dead and life in the age to come. Amen.[1]

---

1. Pelikan and Hotchkiss, *Creeds and Confessions*, 1:163.

The achievements of the Savior, effected by his incarnation, are of such a kind and number that if anyone should wish to expound them he would be like those who gaze at the expanse of the sea and wish to count its waves.

—Athanasius (*On the Incarnation* 54 [PG 25, 192 BC])

# Contents

*Illustrations or Tables* | xi
*Preface* | xiii
*Abbreviations* | xvii

**Introduction** | 1

    An Invitation to the Text | 1
    Approaching the Text: The Genre and Argument of Hebrews | 4
    Looking Behind the Text: The Original Setting | 8
    Looking in Front of the Text: Hebrews' Reception (Canonicity) | 11
    Looking Through the Text: The Preacher's Strategy | 12
    The Preacher and the Philosopher | 16
    Meeting Jesus Again | 19
    Jesus and the Old Testament Witness | 25
    Jesus and the Heavenly Tabernacle | 27
    The Great Salvation | 32
    Salvation as Gift | 35
    Salvation as Covenant | 41
    The Wrinkles in the Plot | 42
    The Hope of Salvation | 44
    Encountering the Holy | 45
    The Summons | 46

## The Letter to the Hebrews

| | | | |
|---|---|---|---|
| 1:1–4 | 49 | 8:1–6 | 179 |
| 1:5–14 | 56 | 8:7–13 | 185 |
| 2:1–4 | 63 | 9:1–10 | 191 |
| 2:5–9 | 70 | 9:11–14 | 201 |
| 2:10–18 | 78 | 9:15–22 | 212 |
| 3:1–6 | 87 | 9:23–28 | 220 |
| 3:7–19 | 94 | 10:1–10 | 227 |
| 4:1–11 | 102 | 10:11–18 | 236 |

Excursus: The Sabbath Celebration in God's Resting Place | 109

| | | | |
|---|---|---|---|
| | | 10:19–25 | 242 |
| | | 10:26–31 | 249 |
| | | 10:32–39 | 255 |
| 4:12–13 | 112 | 11:1–7 | 263 |
| 4:14–16 | 117 | 11:8–22 | 272 |
| 5:1–10 | 126 | 11:23–31 | 279 |
| 5:11—6:3 | 137 | 11:32–40 | 285 |
| 6:4–8 | 143 | 12:1–3 | 294 |
| 6:9–12 | 150 | 12:4–17 | 302 |
| 6:13–20 | 156 | 12:18–29 | 311 |
| 7:1–10 | 162 | 13:1–17 | 321 |
| 7:11–28 | 170 | 13:18–25 | 330 |

*Bibliography* | 337
*Index* | 343

# Illustrations or Tables

Hebrews' Tabernacle and the Old Testament Tabernacle | 194
The Day of Atonement | 204
Old Testament Offerings | 205

# Preface

A FRIEND OF A friend wrote a commentary for, as it happened, a Chinese audience. When it was released a Chinese pastor said, maybe with a twinkle in his eye, "We wish you had added more helpful words, and that you had made it shorter." Indeed.

This commentary was originally undertaken at the invitation of the editors of Baker's Teach the Text Series. As I neared completion of the manuscript, however, the notice went out that the series had been terminated. I am deeply grateful to Cascade Books for the interest they showed in bringing this work to its conclusion. The substance of the commentary itself, including the sections suggesting lines for teachers, was all complete before the original series was terminated and remains largely shaped by the strictures imposed by that series. I could not undertake a complete revision of the project since that time and, in any event, I had already worked conscientiously to fit a meticulously wrought exegetical reading into the original series' guidelines and aims. Yet with the break from from the series, certain formal features have been abandoned—mostly to do with visual and homiletical aids—while I also took advantage of the freedom to expand the exposition at points.

This short description of this commentary's history is necessary in part to explain its contents and approach. Those seeking a technical defense of particular interpretations will not find that here, except by implication. The intended reader of this commentary is a motivated, curious, experienced reader of the Scriptures (in brief, the reader sought by Hebrews itself in 5:11—6:12), who wants a specialist to get straight to the bottom line with each passage. Just give them the meal; they can figure out for themselves how to make it. Hit the high points, and they can figure out what would fall in between. Those who are most fond of the details—specialists—are probably least in need of them, once the main thing has been said. And if some of it falls between the stools—asking too much of the non-specialist, supplying too little for the specialist—I am bound nevertheless to state my judgments and attempt to make Hebrews heard. One can do no more. The rest occurs only "if God permits."

For the same reason, references to both extra-canonical primary sources and secondary literature will be minimized. The assumption of this commentary is that most users will have limited personal holdings of secondary literature and might have no access to a good college library. For this reason among others I have attempted to restrict citations to a very limited number of other commentaries, one or two of which could serve as a resource alongside the present volume. Cockerill, Attridge, Lane, or C. Koester would serve this end well, though several others deserve to be named.[1] Going back a generation or more one would quickly name Westcott, Bruce,[2] and P. Hughes. In addition, a good study Bible, of which there are several, will be a useful complement to our notes.[3]

The steady flow of yet new commentaries in general needs no justification here; the gains outpace the costs; the organic progress and freshness outweigh the redundancy. This one was originally commissioned for a larger project that sought to serve the busy teacher and preacher by giving them the best of scholarship in a form most immediately serviceable for their churchly ends. That remains the spirit and intent of what follows. With this comes a desire by-and-large to refrain from polemics. Reference can be made to Calvin's comment on 1 Cor 5:9: ". . . because of its obscurity this passage is twisted to give different meanings. I think that we ought not to waste time in refuting these, but that I should simply state what seems to me to be the true meaning."[4] This choice has the unintended effect of failing to

---

1. For those interested in the Greek text, Ellingworth (*Epistle to the Hebrews*) is a dependable go-to. His volume is not the most readable, but he has done his homework, especially in conversation with Continental scholarship. The raw material for theological insight is present, though "assembly is required." For religious historical parallels, see especially Attridge (*Hebrews*). For situating Hebrews in the history of interpretation, see Koester (*Hebrews*) and Hughes (*Commentary on Hebrews*). For good general coverage in the interest of exposition, see Cockerill (*Epistle to the Hebrews*) and Lane (*Hebrews*), among others. For a convenient collection of charts and diagrams that distill interpretive options, background sources, and visual perspectives, see Bateman, *Charts*. The United Bible Society has prepared handbooks for translators that provide a running comparison of English (and other language) translations which are illuminating for any reader: Ellingworth and Nida, *Letter to the Hebrews*.

2. Westcott, *Epistle to the Hebrews*; and Bruce, *Epistle to the Hebrews*.

3. Especially helpful are *The ESV Study Bible*, *The NIV Zondervan Study Bible*, *The NLT Illustrated Study Bible*, *The HCSB Study Bible*, *The New Oxford Annotated Bible*, and *The NIV Cultural Backgrounds Study Bible*.

4. Calvin, *First Epistle to the Corinthians*, 111.

notify the reader where there are different but still-viable interpretations, but the hospital room, the grieving home, the counselor's office, and the pulpit are not the place to argue a thesis. I recall, too, a conversation with a masterful preacher who was responding to my encouragement to consider a newer theory about a key text of Scripture. Wisely, he preferred not to try out novel interpretations on his church, interpretations that had not been fully vetted by other scholars and that he himself had not yet had time to consider. I cannot claim that there is nothing novel in what follows. Hebrews is a book over which I have spent considerable time since my student days and my convictions have been forged in the fires of conversations with other specialists.[5] My ambition, however, has not been to advance a new theory and carve out my own interpretive niche, but rather to convey what I believe to be Hebrews' own voice—whether that aligns with well-established readings or not. If I have failed, it is to be measured by that standard, rather than the standard of new findings. We moderns do well to remember that there was a day when what was old was considered true. The word must become greater, the interpreter must become less.

While working on this introduction a former student visited who is presently working in advanced agricultural research. He found his work there fascinating and important in many ways, but his heart was less in exploring new ways to enhance the industrialized food production systems of North America than in assisting societies still struggling with providing what is essential. Likewise, the ongoing efforts of biblical scholars and academic theologians are vitally important (I share those values and interests!) but there are many who are simply hungry for the word. If in some way my work contributes to the feeding of the Great Shepherd's sheep my heart's prayers will have been answered.

While Hebrews claims that "God spoke in his Son" it never quotes the words of Jesus that we know from the Gospels. Its strategy is to present God's speech in the Son as a fusion of the OT Scriptures and the Son's person and work. Our decision to head each unit of our exposition with

---

5. The debt of what follows to the work of others goes far beyond what is explicitly acknowledged here and throughout this commentary. If, however, without my acknowledgment there are substantial verbal correspondences to things they have said, these are due to a memory that has forgotten the source of its thought. In general, the attempt was to document sparingly in the spirit of this commentary's aims. If I felt I had for some time already digested an idea, if it seemed common to several interpreters, if it seemed rather self-evident from the English version of Hebrews, if it was owing neither to the unique researches nor creative insight of a particular scholar, and if I was not relying on their wording for whole ideas, I probably let it go without a reference. I merely repeat my deep debt to my fellow interpreters, and in particular those already named. I have nothing I was not given.

a dominical saying does not ignore that strategy. Hebrews itself directs its audience's attention to the traditions of Jesus' life and references the great salvation announced through him (2:3). We believe that the preacher meant for his exposition to represent a faithful continuation of Jesus' work and teaching, making it fitting to juxtapose these formally different but materially coherent forms of God's speech in and as the Son.

Thanks are due to Wheaton College—administration, colleagues, students—for its support of this work, not least the partial release time in the spring of 2016 and a sabbatical during the fall of the same year. Friends who were willing to take a look at the work-in-progress and give feedback included Daniel Treier, Josh Moody, Peter Walters, Gregg Quiggle, and Brian Hillstrom. Alexa Marquardt and Stephen Wunrow provided essential help in technical style editing, checking references, finding literature, and matters of clarity in general. The privilege of working with this rich text of Scripture began under the guidance of John Wilson (Grand Rapids Baptist College), continued under that of Carl B. Hoch, Jr. (Grand Rapids Baptist Seminary), and advanced considerably during my doctoral research with I. H. Marshall and Paul Ellingworth (University of Aberdeen). That foundation has been strengthened immeasurably by the succeeding opportunities to discuss these things with students and colleagues at Moody Bible Institute and Wheaton College and Graduate School, as well as with colleagues from other institutions. Chairing the Hebrews Section of the Evangelical Theological Society these last several years has permitted me to learn from gifted fellow-exegetes and theologians. Lisa and I have been blessed with wonderful friends as we have made our way on the great Camino that is the subject matter of Hebrews: Among those more closely connected to this work are Andrew and Libby Lau, Mark and Ruth Brucato, Dan and Amy Treier, the Dead Theologians, Bob and Peg Carlson and the members of the College Church Greek Exegesis Sunday School class, and John and Kim Walton. We have also been blessed with supportive families and acknowledge with unspeakable gratitude the love of Marv (who, as this volume neared completion, finished the race) and Ann Laansma and Ed and Margaret Rysdyk. Our church fellowships—Highland Hills Baptist (Grand Rapids, MI), Gerrard Street Baptist (Aberdeen, Scotland), and College Church in Wheaton—have enabled us to walk within the world to which Hebrews witnesses. My love and thanks go to Lisa, and together we give our love to our daughter, Kiersten, who has veritably lived inside of Hebrews her entire life.

*Soli Deo gloria*
Wheaton
Fall 2016

| | |
|---|---|
| Hag | Haggai |
| Heb | Hebrews |
| *Her.* | *Quis rerum divinarum heres sit* (Philo) |
| Herm. *Sim.* | Shepherd of Hermas, *Similitude* |
| *Hist. eccl.* | *Historia ecclesiastica* (Eusebius) |
| Hos | Hosea |
| Ign. *Smyrn.* | Ignatius, *To the Smyrnaeans* |
| *Inst.* | *Institutio oratoria* (Quintilian) |
| *Inv.* | *De inventione rhetorica* (Cicero) |
| Isa | Isaiah |
| IVP | InterVarsity Press |
| Jas | James |
| *JBL* | *Journal of Biblial Literature* |
| *JCS* | *Journal of Cuneiform Studies* |
| Jer | Jeremiah |
| Josh | Joshua |
| *Jub.* | *Jubilees* |
| Judg | Judges |
| 1–2 Kgs | 1–2 Kings |
| KJV | King James Version |
| Lam | Lamentations |
| LCC | Library of Christian Classics |
| LCL | Loeb Classical Library |
| *Leg.* | *Legum allegoriae* (Philo) |
| Lev | Leviticus |
| *Lev. Rab.* | *Leviticus Rabbah* |
| LNTS | Library of New Testament Studies |
| LXX | Septuagint |
| *m. 'Abot* | *Mishnah 'Abot* |
| 1–4 Macc | 1–4 Maccabees |
| Mal | Malachi |
| *Mart. Ascen. Isa.* | *Martyrdom and Ascension of Isaiah* |
| *Mart. Pol.* | *Martyrdom of Polycarp* |

| | |
|---|---|
| Matt | Matthew |
| Mic | Micah |
| *Migr.* | *De migratione Abrahami* (Philo) |
| *Mos.* | *De vita Mosis* (Philo) |
| *Mut.* | *De mutatione nominum* (Philo) |
| Neh | Nehemiah |
| NICNT | New International Commentary on the New Testament |
| NIGTC | New International Greek Testament Commentary |
| NIV | New International Version |
| NovTSup | Novum Testamentum Supplements |
| NRSV | New Revised Standard Version |
| NT | New Testament |
| *NTS* | *New Testament Studies* |
| Num | Numbers |
| OT | Old Testament |
| OTP | Charlesworth, James H., ed. *The Old Testament Pseudepigrapha*. 2nd. ed. 2 vols. Peabody: Hendrickson, 2011. |
| 1–2 Pet | 1–2 Peter |
| Phil | Philippians |
| Phlm | Philemon |
| Prov | Proverbs |
| *Prov.* | *De providentia* (Philo) |
| Ps (*pl.* Pss) | Psalms |
| Ps-Eup. | Pseudo-Eupolemus |
| *Pss. Sol.* | *Psalms of Solomon* |
| 1QapGen XXII | Genesis Apocryphon |
| QE | *Quaestiones et solutiones in Exodum* (Philo) |
| 1 QHa | *Thanksgiving Hymns*a |
| 1QS | Rule of the Community |
| *Rep.* | *Republic* (Plato) |
| Rev | Revelation |
| *Rhet. Her.* | *Rhetorica ad Herennium* |
| Rom | Romans |

| | |
|---|---|
| *Sacr.* | *De sacrificiis Abelis et Caini* (Philo) |
| 1–2 Sam | 1–2 Samuel |
| SBL | Society of Biblical Literature |
| SBLDS | Society of Biblical Literature Dissertation Series |
| SBLMS | Society of Biblical Literature Monograph Series |
| SBLRBS | Society of Biblical Literature Resources for Biblical Study |
| *Scorp.* | *Scorpiace* (Tertullian) |
| *Sib. Or.* | *Sibylline Oracles* |
| Sir | Sirach |
| SNTSMS | Society for New Testament Studies Monograph Series |
| *Somn.* | *De somniis* (Philo) |
| Song | Song of Solomon |
| SPCK | Society for Promoting Christian Knowledge |
| *Spec.* | *De specialibus legibus* (Philo) |
| STDJ | *Studies on the Texts of the Desert of Judah* |
| TDNT | *Theological Dictionary of the New Testament.* Edited by G. Kittel and G. Friedrich. Translated by G. W. Bromiley. 10 vols. Grand Rapids, 1964–1976. |
| *Tg. Neof.* | *Targum Neofiti* |
| *Tg. Ps.-J.* | *Targum Pseudo-Jonathan* |
| 1–2 Thess | 1–2 Thessalonians |
| 1–2 Tim | 1–2 Timothy |
| TLevi | Testament of Levi |
| Tob | Tobit |
| *t. Sanh.* | *Tosefta Sanhedrin* |
| UBS | United Bible Societies |
| v./vv. | verse/verses |
| *Virt.* | *De virtutibus* (Philo) |
| WBC | Word Bible Commentary |
| Wis | Wisdom of Solomon |
| WUNT | Wissenschaftliche Untersuchungen zum Neuen Testament |
| YHWH | Yahweh, Jehovah, the Lord |
| Zech | Zechariah |

# Introduction

## An Invitation to the Text

IMAGINE THE SCRIPTURES AS a great river, the Mississippi, if you will, but any great river will do. Already as the Mississippi flows past St. Louis it is a wide expanse, and all the more so as it is joined by the Ohio downstream. The more northernly expanses are like the law and the prophets of Israel, deep and broad, moving inexorably down the bed. Imagine, then, that when it has reached its greatest volume all of its waters are forced at once through a gorge of only a few meters in width. This is Hebrews. Even on its surface one can see Hebrews' character as an exposition of the OT Scriptures that spans the Pentateuch, the historical writings, the psalms, the wisdom literature, and the prophets. When we dive into its substance, all the more do we appreciate that this sermon's dependence on the Scriptures is owing to a comprehensive retelling of Israel's history from the viewpoint of its conclusion in the new covenant brought to effect in Jesus the Son. The preacher is a master of allusion. Not for nothing does he pause mid-sermon to chide his listeners—"you need someone to teach you again the basic principles of the oracles of God." He does this not in order to stop and review but in order to stir them to remember what they should already know so as to grasp the teaching so necessary for the moment. If we think that Hebrews' reading of Pss 8, 95, and 110, or Prov 3, for example, can be understood by examining each citation in detail our attempt will end in puzzles and the whole will seem only a badly assembled mosaic. We will have to "think together" the stories of Israel, the Son, and our new covenant situation if we are to sense their harmony. Consider, then, that when Hebrews chides in this way, holding our feet to the fire with respect to deep biblical literacy, it is addressing the whole church—not merely a special group of scribes and lawyers, that is, biblical scholars—and it is arguing that our lives depend on paying attention to the story. God has been telling a story and he expects that we are not lazy listeners but interested and attentive ones. This is so because this story is our story and the story of the entire world whether or not we pay attention. We are inside this story and everything hangs on whether we embrace its script or resist it. And to those who have more is given. For those who do not treat this like some conceptual problem but who instead take up their place in its story by faith and inhabit its world the meat of this gospel's teaching becomes strengthening food.

Some passages in this book are among the most memorable of Scripture. Some speak almost immediately to believers of all times and places with transparent images, fear-inspiring warnings, and strong encouragement. Yet other passages leave us flat or confused, wondering if we have comprehended even what we thought we understood. Its teaching on Christ confronts us as directly with his full divinity as any NT writing, but just as uncompromisingly (almost uncomfortably) with his full humanity, as at once eternal and historical. Its teaching on the covenants seems to set gospel and law against each other but just as clearly views them in total continuity. Its gospel is recognizably that of Paul, John, Peter, and Luke but we question at times whether it has broken ranks by an attempt to conceptualize the gospel in terms of Greek philosophy or by pressing its warnings too far. Its imagery of blood and sacrifice seems worlds removed from our own scientific age. Maybe it really is the gospel to and for the Hebrews, not for the Gentiles, after all. But, no, it is the gospel for all peoples.

Hebrews requires us to view earth from the vantage point of heaven—not unlike Revelation. So completely is this true that we know nothing definite at all of the identity of writer and original readers. This is a pastor who believes that if we are not heavenly minded we can be of no earthly good. The preacher will therefore as a matter of urgency resist the temptation to translate the gospel into a form applicable to the lives of his readers and instead translate their lives into the heavenly drama of the Son. All history proceeds from heaven to earth so that when we see salvation's accomplishment there we know what is true, what must be true, and what will be true on earth. This is also a pastor who believes that the history of God's covenants is the history of the world. The viewpoint of many interpreters notwithstanding, this teacher has not applied a pre-conceived cosmology to the Scriptures as a way of understanding priesthoods and sacrifices. That understanding has it backwards. Rather, from the history of God's covenants he understands the history of creation. Already in the OT the temple is the center of the world. For Hebrews, as goes the tabernacle so goes the world. This is a teacher who believes that salvation is of the Jews; that the God who speaks as the Father of the Son is the same God who created heaven and earth, delivered his promise to Abraham, and established his covenant through

Moses. This teacher has long since come to grips with the implications of this truth for the understanding of divine speech, the person and work of the Son, and the great salvation worked. He now bends all these resources to the urgent need of his brothers and sisters to persevere to the obtaining of what was promised Abraham.[1]

In ways that probably have yet to be fathomed Hebrews has formed the confession and the life of the church and catalyzed her reading of the other prophetic and apostolic writings, even where its influence was unacknowledged or even felt.[2] Who can read any other part of the canon forgetting that Christ is our high priest and offering? Who does not feel the potency of its language of shadows and copies as a way of holding together the continuities and discontinuities of the covenants? Its imagery of pilgrimage, its promise of a resting place, its examples of faith, its vision of divine discipline—these and others of its teachings acquaint us with the salvation to which with greater understanding we then go on to hear Paul, Peter, John, and the others witness. Consider its logic: Without the pouring out of blood there is no forgiveness; it is impossible for the blood of animals to remove sin; the blood of Jesus, through the eternal Spirit, cleanses us; God did not desire sacrifices, though he commanded that they be offered; through the offering of the body of Jesus we have been made holy.

Alec Motyer reportedly characterized how Israelites under Moses would have summarized their experience: "We were in a foreign land, in bondage, under the sentence of death. But our mediator—the one who stands between us and God—came to us with the promise of deliverance. We trusted in the promises of God, took shelter under the blood of the lamb, and he led us out. Now we are on the way to the Promised Land. We are not there yet, of course, but we have the law to guide us, and through blood sacrifice we also have his presence in our midst. So he will stay with us until we get to our true country, our everlasting home."[3] It is hardly credible to think that the vision of Hebrews has not instructed such a reading as this, even if that reading purports to represent a *pre*-Christian viewpoint.

In part because Hebrews uttered more directly what was assumed by the other NT authors and their heirs and in part because its message has since worked itself so fully into the church's reading of all of Scripture, a theological understanding of the whole of the canon is impossible to imagine without this brief word of exhortation.[4]

1. This was an insight of Hughes, *Hebrews and Hermeneutics*.
2. Laansma, "Hebrews: Yesterday, Today, and Future," 1–6, 26–32.
3. Mesa, "Tim Keller and Don Carson?"
4. For other examples, see Laansma, "Hebrews: Yesterday, Today, and Future," 1–2.

## Approaching the Text: The Genre and Argument of Hebrews

There is finally no reason to doubt that Heb 13 was part of the original composition—the alternative theories of some notwithstanding—and no strong argument for assigning any of that chapter to a hand other than the author of the rest of the book. That said, Hebrews closes like a typical letter but is otherwise composed in the form of a direct address to the church from a known teacher. We have too little definite knowledge of ancient homilies to draw confident inferences about Hebrews' genre and structure based on that characterization, but the writer's own description of his work as a "word of exhortation" (13:22; cf. Acts 13:15), the nature of its contents, and the near-certainty that it was meant to be read to the gathered church and thus received orally justify styling it for moderns as a sermon. We will refer to the author as either a writer or as the "preacher," and to the book as either a letter or a sermon. If we refer to the recipients as "readers" it is to be understood that for the greater part they would have in fact been listeners.

That the preacher was not only highly educated but a masterful orator is plain. The power of his rhetoric has been universally felt and the intricacies of his argument have been endlessly studied and admired. The conclusions of those who have attempted to uncover the letter's structure, however, have led to no consensus.[5] We can say with confidence that the writer knew where he was going with his argument from beginning to end. There is nothing arbitrary about it. He employs a range of rhetorical devices to underscore, remind of, and anticipate ideas. But he also seems to have been working from pastoral instinct, seeking effect more than strict orderliness of presentation. Exchanges between intimates follow their own rules and rhythms. His effort, which was oriented on a particular audience known to him, was to bring to mind a divine drama of salvation and to convince the recipients of their place in it, impressing on them that they were in this drama whether they acknowledged this in faith or not. He is clarifying ideas but even more to the point he is situating us—we may as well include ourselves without further ado—in a story. The result for our outlines is that more than one approach can get it right, and those that get it right succeed in highlighting differing aspects rather than exhausting the whole.

Our view is that following the opening—the exordium of 1:1–4—the preacher draws on the resources of their existing confession to convey the

---

Calvin is a good exhibit (see *Institutes*, II.7.16; II.9.4); Barclay, *Paul and the Gift*, 120; Allen, "The Perfect Priest," 120–34.

5. Among the proposals, see Guthrie, *Structure of Hebrews*, and Westfall, *Discourse Analysis of Hebrews*.

glory of the Son, in and as whom God has spoken, and the urgency of perseverance in faith if entrance into the promised inheritance, God's resting place, is to be attained (1:5—4:13). In more than one way the whole drama of salvation, from creation to the end, is related. He then proceeds to his central exposition which revolves chiefly on Ps 110, Jer 31, Exod 24-25, and Ps 40 (4:14—10:25). Here the focus is on the pivotal moment of salvation in Christ's offering and the approach that it opens and necessitates. Finally, the sermon proceeds to a series of exhortations that call to a response of enduring faith in our identity as the new covenant family of God (10:26—12:29). After the climax of 12:18-29 there comes a peroration (13:1-17) and the epistolary closing (13:18-25).

1:1-4  Exordium: God has spoken in his Son

1:5—4:11  In praise of the Son who became high priest and the need to listen to what God says

   1:5-14  The Son in and as whom God speaks in relation to God's angels

   2:1-4  Exhortation

   2:5-18  The Son's way of salvation in relation to God's angels

   3:1-6  Moses and the Son in the history of God's house

   3:7—4:11  The need of faith for the entrance into God's promised inheritance

      3:7-19  Ps 95 as a warning not to repeat the rebellion of Israel

      4:1-11  Ps 95 as a promise that remains and the need to respond in faith

4:12-13  Conclusion to first movement, reprisal of exordium

4:14—10:25  Christ as high priest and offering

   *4:14-16  Transition, frame with 10:19-25

   5:1—7:28  Christ is high priest

      5:1-10  You are a priest

      (5:11—6:20  Warning, encouragement, exposition)

      7:1-10  According to the order of Melchizedek

      7:11-19  Forever

      7:20-25  The Lord has sworn and will not change his mind

7:26-28 Summary application

8:1—10:18 Christ's high priestly ministry

    8:1-6 Introduction: The tabernacles, priesthoods, and covenants

    8:7-13 The better promises of the new covenant

    9:1—10:10 The covenant of which Christ is mediator

        9:1-10 The first covenant as copy and anticipation

        9:11-14 The second covenant as accomplishment

        9:15-22 The inaugural mediation of the second covenant

        9:23-28 The eternal, heavenly, and final character of Christ's ministry (divine drama)

        10:1-10 The bodily offering that accomplished God's will (human drama)

    10:11-18 Conclusion: The better ministry

*10:19-25 Transition, frame with 4:14-16

10:26—12:29 Exhortations toward faith and progress

    10:19-31 Exhortation to faith and warning against apostasy (reusing 10:19-25)

        10:19-25 There is now forgiveness (10:18), so approach!

        10:26-31 There is no other or further offering for sin (10:18), so do not refuse the one given!

    10:32—12:3 Enduring in the great contest of faith in the promise

        10:32-39 A call to endure based on their earlier history and the promise of Habakkuk and Isaiah

        11:1-40 Examples of enduring faith from Israel's history

            11:1-2 Opening thesis: What faith does.

            11:3-7 Faith and the biblical story before the patriarchs (Gen 1-11).

                11:3 Faith and the word of creation.

                11:4 Abel's faith through which he was attested to be righteous.

- 11:5-6 Enoch's faith by which he pleased God and because of which he did not see death.
- 11:7 Noah's faith by which he became an heir of righteousness.
- 11:8-22 The patriarchs (Gen 12–50).
- 11:23-31 Moses, the exodus, and the conquest (Exodus – Joshua).
- 11:32-38 Faith in the remaining history of the old covenant (Judges and following).
- 11:39-40 Closing summary.

12:1-3 A call to endure based on the example of Jesus

12:4-17 Enduring as the genuine children of the covenantal Father

- 12:4-11 Developing the image: Undergoing hardship as authentic children of the covenantal Father
- 12:12-17 Applying the image: Live as strong-bodied, stout-hearted children of the covenant, secure in your place, pursuing its life, taking care of the family, and cherishing your birthright

12:18-29 The grand finale: closing vision of the promised inheritance, the peril of refusing the promiser, and a final warning/exhortation

- 12:18-24 The reason why they must endure in the great contest and as genuine children of the covenant
  - 12:18-21 Negatively: The mountain that pointed to the goal (old covenant and present age)
  - 12:22-24 Positively: The mountain that is the goal (new covenant and age to come)
- 12:25-29 Final warning and exhortation
  - 12:25-27 Warning: Listen to the divine word for it has inaugurated the final judgment
  - 12:28-29 Exhortation: Worship God suitably in obedience to the word spoken in the Son

13:1-17 Peroration

13:1–6  Specific applications on conventional topics

13:7–17  Restatement of the call to perseverance in connection with an endorsement of the church's leaders

   13:7  Recall the message of the former leaders

   13:8  Recall who Jesus Christ is

   13:9–14  Follow Jesus outside the gates

   13:15–16  Render worship corresponding to faith

   13:17  Submit to your leaders who share in your pilgrimage with special responsibilities

13:18–25  Closing

For the purposes of exposition, in this commentary the text has been divided into thirty-seven units.[6] A few of these units group or divide within the preceding outline.

## Looking Behind the Text: The Original Setting

Questions of who, where, when, and why are tangled together. The name of the human author is unknown. Origen's oft-repeated comment, "who wrote the epistle, in truth God knows" (Eusebius, *Hist. eccl.* 6.25.11–13), probably refers to the *pen* rather than the *voice* of the letter, but it has served as a convenient bottom line for many. For this reason there cannot be certainty that Paul did not write the whole of the book or possibly the final verses, but there are strong arguments against such theories. That the writer was a male remains probable, partly in the light of the grammar of 11:32, though again certainty is not possible. The mere listing of other possible names (e.g., Apollos, Barnabas, Luke, Clement) supplies no reliable basis for further interpretive inferences. What we know of the author is what we gather from what he wrote. He was a highly educated, literate, eloquent person, theologically mature, pastorally hearted. He had a history with this church, but we cannot be sure he had been numbered among its "leaders." More on his background anon.

The earliest manuscript of Hebrews in our possession, P$^{46}$ (c. AD 200), carries the heading, "to the Hebrews," a theory on the audience that must already have been established in some circles (cf. Eusebius, *Hist. eccl.* 6.14).

---

6. This more-or-less arbitrary number of expositional units stems from the form of the series for which the commentary was originally composed.

Allied with this was the assumption that this text had been addressed to believers in Judea. Both of these associations seem to have been grounded in inference rather than reliable traditions. There is no conclusive evidence or argument against a Judean destination, but 1) the phrase "those who come from Italy" in 13:24 can imply that Italians are sending greetings back to their homeland, 2) there are strong parallels with 1 Peter, which is another epistle associated with Rome, 3) the earliest evidence of Hebrews' thought is *1 Clement* which was written from Rome in the late first or early second century, and 4) the general circumstances and other details comport with a Roman (or Italian) destination.[7] That the audience was in Italy and probably Rome is our own assumption but it can be only speculation. The church may have been in Asia Minor, Syria, Judea, Egypt, or elsewhere. More on their background anon.

If, for the sake of argument, it was written to Jewish believers in Judea (or elsewhere, for that matter) tempted to return to non-Christian Jewish temple worship (whether directly or indirectly via the synagogue) then it would naturally stem from some time before AD 70 when the Romans destroyed the temple. But Hebrews' argument revolves on Moses's tabernacle and never mentions the temple. It is also more forward looking than backward looking in this sense: If one used the analogy of two married couples, one of which suffered from a desire of one of the members to return to his parents' home, the other of which suffered from a simple failure of one of the members to have embraced married life as fully as he should have done, Hebrews sounds more like the latter. Its message is less like, "Do not go back home," than it is like, "Move forward!" Such a message could be addressed to the church of any time or place. The argument's strong rootedness in the OT does evidence a readership already fully invested in those Scriptures and, at least in principle, in the sanctuary-centered life of Israel, but the preacher's theology of divine speech would have required the expositional strategy he follows for Gentile as well as Jewish Christians. Moreover, particular texts (2:3; 5:11–14; 13:7) suggest a later rather than earlier date, as does the way in which the letter's teachings seem to be building on a theologically developed confession. The church, we theorize, was probably of mixed ethnic character, particularly if we are right in locating it in Italy or anywhere else outside of Judea, and if we are right in thinking that the letter was sent at least as late as the early 60s.[8] The invisibility of the Gentiles is part of the larger absorption of the audience into the "heavenly" story of the promise. We may observe that many a Gentile congregation has subsequently believed

---

7. Koester, *Hebrews*, 48–50.
8. See Laansma, "Hebrews and the Mission," 328–34.

itself to be directly addressed by this text; the substance of its message has proved meaningful to a Gentile readership. It would be strange if the preacher missed the implications for a decentralized mission that were built into his own argument. The theory that it was written to believers in Rome (or environs) after the experiences of Claudius' temporary expulsion of the Jews (AD 49; cf. 10:32–34; Acts 18:2) but before Nero's deadlier persecutions (AD 64–68; 12:4) had taken hold has a satisfying fit. Nothing, however, finally excludes the possibility that the letter was written after the destruction of the temple, albeit prior to the composition of 1 Clement and Timothy's death (unknown, but likely within the first century).

The lack of precision on such things is a problem that becomes amplified when it is a matter of finely-tuned historical theories, but is a significantly exaggerated problem in other ways. The historical glass is more than half full. There is for us no doubt that the letter emanates from the same period as the rest of the NT writings, that it represents a witness at one with that of the apostles, and that, even if it is not from Paul's hand, it belongs to the Spirit's own witness among the other canonical writings.

For the rest, space allows only the stating of our conclusions which will be operative for our own exposition: For all its uniqueness, Hebrews shares particular parallels with the writings of Luke (especially Acts, and particularly Acts 7), Peter (1 Peter), Paul, and John. Its teaching is deeply rooted in the apostolic tradition, which it is faithfully developing. The Timothy mentioned in 13:23 can be taken as Paul's associate, evidencing a concrete link with Paul's mission and gospel. Its message is centered on strengthening the core of fellowship in perseverance but it everywhere breathes the theology of a church caught up in mission. It is a church that is the result of mission and its theology is the theology of an inclusive, outward-moving mission. Signs of inner Jew-Gentile tensions over matters of law are non-existent; all believers are together the seed of Abraham (2:16) striving as one people toward the goal.

The beginnings of the church reached to the period relatively soon after the gospel events (2:3) but some time must have since passed (5:11–14; 10:32; 13:7). The earliest history of the church was characterized by a robust life of faith that met with and endured public persecution and that upheld the life of fellowship. Their unbelieving society had attempted to shame them back into conformity; they had suffered loss of property and some had been imprisoned. It is possible that there had been a season of relative calm and that storm clouds now loomed. Whether or not that is the case, there had been a waning of faith among at least some of the church's members. The specific charges lodged are that some had begun to forsake the Christian assemblies (10:25), that the church as a whole had not matured as it should have done given the time (5:11–14), and that they have forgotten how God addresses them as his children (12:5). Beyond this we note passive (e.g., drifting [2:1]), active (e.g., rebellion), and external (persecution) aspects of the problem[9] that are vague enough to accommodate a range of hypotheses. On the one hand there is the failure to persevere in the "approach" to the divine throne with a confidence that is based on Christ's atonement, with an understanding of the way of salvation, and with a sense of urgency in keeping with the historical moment (inhabiting what is unseen). On the other hand there is a failure to persevere in the life of bodily fellowship and in their public witness (the visible). Hebrews calls them to faithfulness in both spheres but the greater emphasis falls on the former, suggesting that it—the confidence to approach through Christ in the understanding of God's history—is the real epicenter of their problems. Whether or not this is how the readers would have described their situation, this will have been the preacher's diagnosis.

## Looking in Front of the Text: Hebrews' Reception (Canonicity)[10]

Questions of canonicity are by their nature never questions of historical judgments only but nor can our historical judgments about this text go unaffected by our conclusions on canonicity; this holds as much for those who reject Hebrews' place in the canon or reject the very category of canonicity, as it does for those who affirm these. We therefore pause to enter its consideration here in the midst of our introductory historical and literary comments.

There was no immediate and direct line to acceptance for Hebrews as there was for other parts of the NT. The Western and Eastern branches of the church in the first three centuries handled it differently. In the West, Pauline authorship was doubted or rejected and the letter's strong wording of 6:4–6, among other things, sat awkwardly with that tradition's more hopeful views of the restoration of lapsed Christians to fellowship. Hebrews' authority was accordingly placed in doubt, though it was read and respected. In the East, Pauline authorship was more widely accepted and the letter's theology

---

9. Ellingworth, *Epistle to the Hebrews*, 78–80.

10. The canonization of Hebrews is treated in all good commentaries and elsewhere. Koester, *Hebrews*, 19–63, is particularly helpful and expands considerably on our summary of Hebrews' place not only in the canon but the church's life and thought through the ages.

resonated with the philosophical and mystical bent of their thought and practices.

Eventually Hebrews found a constructive place in the church's christological controversies and its teaching on repentance came to be interpreted in ways less problematic for the practices of church discipline. When Jerome (d. AD 420) and Augustine (d. AD 430) leaned toward Pauline authorship—more out of respect for the Eastern church's tradition than the evidence of the text itself—the recognition of Hebrews proceeded on a steadier track toward broad acceptance. The canonical lists of the fourth and fifth centuries affirmed it as such, though it eventually settled into place at the very end of the Pauline collection, on its margins, as it were. Questions of authorship were renewed at the time of the Reformation, with more or less affect on the question of authority. In the modern period Pauline authorship has been widely (not universally) rejected, including among many who fully affirm its canonical character.

One could say in retrospect that Hebrews declared its own authority and its place in the Christian canon, possessing the (finally) irrepressible voice of apostolicity. Direct apostolic authorship has never been a requirement for inclusion (cf. Luke–Acts), and it is to be expected that authentic witnesses will jar us with their unique perspectives as much as they will affirm one another in the unity of their convictions. The church stands under the Scriptures, not over them—though the Scriptures indubitably came through the church by way of authorship and recognition. By analogy, the Lord himself came through human parentage and is acclaimed (or not) as Lord in the world though he is its Lord. On such scores as apply, Hebrews has passed the test and must therefore be read for what it is, inspired, canonical divine speech.

## Looking Through the Text: The Preacher's Strategy

As already indicated the preacher's strategy is to translate the readers' lives into the heavenly drama of the Son's salvation. This is the real context by which to make sense of their social-psychological-physical lives, to be sure without any reduction to the reality and importance of the latter.

The sermon is a soundly-reasoned argument with themes that give it a distinct profile. Its coherence, however, finally consists not in syllogistic argumentation nor in abstract (e.g., the superiority of Christ) or specific themes (priesthood, covenant, divine speech, perseverance, etc.) but in the *history* of God's covenantal speech which attained its goal and revealed its center in the *Son*. The Son is the one in *and as* whom God speaks his world-creating, -governing, and -cleansing word, within which world we are created participants. As the Father of the Son who is Jesus his newly spoken word is one with all his words. Or rather, all his words are now found to have been oriented on the Son, to whom they witnessed; they were expressive of the Son. The flip side of that claim is that the Son is known in those earlier words, and thus as priest and offering according to the shadows and copies of Moses. This is not merely a convenient set of categories for a Jewish readership but the divinely created light in which the Son's person and work are known.

That history not only enables us to see the Son but with him ourselves and his salvation in our own time. This is the time in which the Son's salvation is given in the word of promise—gospel—while the already-enthroned Son waits for his enemies to be made a footstool for his feet. That image of the enthroned-but-waiting Son accounts for the ongoing resistance to his rule (persecution, temptation), the provision for the present, and the certainty of hope. The proclaimed word of forgiveness, as a word of promise, must be received in faith, which means a faith that falls into step with this history and that perseveres in this to the end. That way of faith is none other than the way of the Son's learning of obedience through his suffering, again illuminated from the history of Israel's pilgrimage as God's covenantal children. In all of this, Hebrews is a retelling of the entire history of creation and its salvation, prepared and anticipated in the old covenant history, accomplished in the now-inaugurated new covenant, verging on its great dénouement.

The thread that unites this story is the one already supplied by the Scriptures, namely, the promise of God to Abraham that he would inherit the world (Rom 4:13) and that all nations would be blessed through him. Hebrews affirms nothing of the cosmos or its history that is not known from and by this history; it pretends to no metaphysical commitments that do not emerge from this history. It is interested in the literal fulfillment of that historical promise. The promise, it is understood, concerns the entrance into the inheritance, which is the world fully consumed by the holiness of God, God's own resting place. This is the original intention for the world; the association of that resting place with the creation sabbath has this intention. That promise was elaborated in the covenant established with Abraham's seed through Moses, a covenant that dramatically enacted the (at that point still-blocked) entrance into the holy space of God's presence. The challenge posed to the promise was the unfittingness of the seed to make that entrance, defiled as it was by sin and under the sentence of death. The covenant, as the bond of willing parties, was accordingly a failure because of Israel but, because God is faithful, it will not fail. The history of failure was enacted in the shadows and copies of Israel's history. The act of salvation was not an act of mere power imposed on creation, but the free choice of the Son to receive the body prepared for him—created existence is not foisted on humankind, but freely chosen by our first member—sharing fully in the blood and flesh seed of Abraham and as a man doing God's will to the uttermost. Abraham's seed kept covenant. By his self-offering his brothers and sisters are cleansed of their defilement. Because of his suffering he is crowned with glory and honor. As the God-man fitted for this exaltation he has entered the Most Holy Place of God's presence and is seated on the divine throne where he waits for all things to be placed under his feet and where he always lives to intercede for those who draw near to God through him. Thus the promise of Psalm 8 concerning the created status of humanity is fulfilled. What remains is the doing away with all that is not of the holiness of God, the great "shaking" of which Haggai spoke (12:25–29).

We can focus this history further: The story of Israel is not merely one that leads up to the Son; it is the Son's own history in shadows and patterns. Even more basically we must say that real history is the history of the Son, and from it we understand Israel's history. If that seems too abstract and therefore unlikely we should remind ourselves of the comparison of the tabernacles—the true tabernacle preceded Moses's (8:5), casting its shadow down from heaven and back from the Son, and its history overarched the whole of time (9:12, 14, 26)—and then repeat that the rest of the cosmos is understood from this. The universe itself was made "through" the Son and he is the heir of all things; he bears all things by his own powerful word.[11] This applies not only to the history that preceded Jesus but the history that follows, which is why the post-resurrection church correctly finds itself inside the gospel narratives of Jesus' life—not just in the sense that we benefit from those events but that, for instance, we are in the boat with the other disciples undergoing what they did in a storm on the Sea of Galilee or that the raising of Lazarus is a manifestation of the general resurrection. Hebrews accordingly directs its readers to find their story in either Jesus' own (2:5–16; 12:1–3; not to mention 9:15) or in Israel's (e.g., 3:7—4:11). These are really one and the same, but their center is always Jesus.

Israel's story is invoked by the preacher both in particular allusions (OT quotations) and sweeping gestures, both in its telling moments and in its whole arc. In the history of Israel we are in the lives of the Patriarchs, in the exodus, at Sinai, in the wilderness, on the borders of the land, occupying

---

11. Language like this in 1:2–3 cannot be tossed to the side as an outlier sentiment nor treated as a literary code for some other idea entirely, for instance, that Jesus is being thought of as wisdom personified.

the land, and at the Most Holy Place. Two demonstrations of this can be mentioned as illustrative: The exhortation of 3:7—4:11 based on Ps 95:7–11 is unmistakably set against the story of Israel's apostasy when they stood at the border of the land and refused to enter (Num 13–14). More fittingly we should say that the churchly readers are to find themselves with Israel in Deuteronomy now looking back on that earlier apostasy (Deut 1:9–46). The generation that rebelled at Kadesh had died, their children now stood again at the border, and they were being commanded to live in obedience. Moses reminds them that they have not yet "come to the rest and to the inheritance that the LORD your God is giving you." (Deut 12:9). When they do arrive the Lord promises that he will give them rest from their enemies and choose a place for his Name where they will bring their offerings (12:10–11). This history carries forward to David in 2 Sam 7:1–29 and on into the son of David, Solomon (1 Kgs 5:3; 8:56; see further on Heb 3:7—4:11 and 12:18–29). It is into this history that Ps 95:7–11 fits, but now, in the context of Hebrews, it is recognized that the true history being enacted was that of *the* Son who is the pioneer for his fellow seed (Heb 2:10) and that the resting place was to be the whole world made God's Most Holy Place. The promise remains (Heb 4:1, 6) and enduring faith that does not replicate Israel's rebellion is the need of the hour. But how can they, unholy, enter God's holy presence? That is what the long exposition of 4:14—10:25 will unfold.

Again, the exhortation of Heb 12:4–11 based on Prov 3:11–12 is finally to be set against the sweep of Israel's experience of God's disciplinary measures by which she would be purged of her sin and made fit to inherit what had been promised, especially as this is seen in the great prophecies of Isaiah and Jeremiah. The frame of reference is not that of a Jewish or Greco-Roman household as such, as if merely to put an encouraging spin on the experience of hardship. The point is to assure these Christian men and women of faith that they are the genuine children of God's household, Abraham's seed, the people of Israel and of Judah with whom God has established his new covenant (Heb 8:7–13), and that just for this reason they find themselves on the difficult Way of God (Heb 12:12–13). The need is to persevere in obedience, just as their elder brother did (Heb 5:7–10), and not to forfeit their covenantal birthright as did Esau. For they are come to Mount Zion itself (12:22) and nothing but the conclusion remains (12:25–29).

Hebrews is the great retelling of Israel's entire story now successfully summed up and concluded in the career of the Son, in whose footsteps we walk with the support of our enthroned, empathetic high priest and on the basis of the covenant concluded in his blood once for all. The path before us is, however, God's Way that must be travelled to the end or everything is forfeited.

By locating us so thoroughly in heaven's drama is Hebrews so heavenly minded as to be of no earthly good? It has certainly not received its due from earthly-minded historians of early Christianity frustrated by its indifference to their project. It has admittedly appealed to the philosophically-minded speculators of theology. There is, however, every reason to expect that its original readers grasped its point for their lives on their Roman streets. Its call to "go . . . outside" (13:13) had nothing to do with escapism but would take them right into the hurly burly of their cities. We may suspect that those of its readers through the centuries who have found strong encouragement in its teaching have been of the same ilk. No doubt they have found here, too, strong meat in the way this gospel robs the usurping powers of the shrine and basilica of their authority by ushering the person of faith straight into God's presence on the power of Jesus' atonement alone, by identifying their brother Jesus as the sole mediator in this matter, and by locating their citizenship foursquare in the promised inheritance. Truly the one who had the power of death was broken, and with that all the instruments by which he ruled their lives are made useless.

## The Preacher and the Philosopher

As we continue to look into and through Hebrews' vision, it is helpful to observe what could be considered the mode of thought represented in Hebrews. What is the relation of Hebrews' author to his cognitive environment? In what ways does this thinker share in the thought patterns of his own context? A comprehensive treatment of such questions would take us on book-length detours, so we will limit ourselves to a particular parallel that has exercised a strong influence on interpreters.

Partly because of the uncertainty over author, readers, location, and timing, the question of how Hebrews relates to its environment's thought worlds has garnered much attention. Such questions have always mattered, but moderns have a peculiar interest in such things. In part, however, Hebrews' contents thrust the question upon us. Its language carries numerous parallels with (among other texts) the first-century Alexandrian Jew, Philo (c. 20 BC–AD 50), who wedded his Jewish traditions with Plato's thought and read the OT in an allegorical fashion. For him, this involved among other things a strong metaphysical dualism that correlated the "heavenly" with the eternal, stable, unchanging realm of ideas, and the "earthly" with what is inferior, secondary, shadowy, and transient. A range of theories posit some sort of connection between Hebrews and the pattern of thought represented in Philo and related thinkers, while a range of alternative theories contend against anything more than parallels of expression that substantially differ in meaning. The view of this commentary is closer to the latter end. Covenantal, apocalyptic, historical patterns bound to christological convictions are what are expressed in Hebrews through wording that sometimes reminds of the Alexandrian's writings (e.g., 8:5; 9:9–10, 23–24; 10:1; 11:3, 8–16; 12:27). Hebrews' conceptions themselves are at bottom one with Paul, Peter, and Revelation, though of course the teachings and emphases are distinctive. Our commentary will explain further what this means.

One important part of this conversation relates to how Hebrews interprets the OT. Is he reading "allegorically"?[12]

There is a range of ways of reading "allegorically" and not all are objectionable (admitting that "objectionable" reflects the standpoint generally represented in this introduction and commentary). The more objectionable form dissolves both history and literature in a strong ideological mixture, a form not absent in Philo. Isolated events, persons, and phrases become symbols in their own right so that alien thought structures can be "discovered" in the "code," as if they had always been there. For this approach, if a divine, all-knowing voice is behind the text, all the better.

By way of illustration, Philo approvingly describes the reading approach of a group known as the Therapeutae:

> And these explanations of the sacred scriptures are delivered by mystic expressions in allegories, for the whole of the law appears to these men to resemble a living animal, and its express commandments seem to be the body, and the invisible meaning concealed under and lying beneath the plain words resembles the soul, in which the rational soul begins most excellently to contemplate what belongs to itself, as in a mirror, beholding in these very words the exceeding beauty of the sentiments, and unfolding and explaining the symbols, and bringing the secret meaning naked to the light to all who are able by the light of a slight intimation to perceive what is unseen by what is visible. (Philo, *Contempl.*, 78 [Colson, LCL])

When, over the church's history, strains of this reading strategy pushed their way from the periphery to the center there was eventually a reaction, particularly among the Reformers and their heirs. In retrospect we would say that the gospel itself would not tolerate that type of allegorical reading because that strategy did not agree with the nature of the Scriptures, not merely that there had been underlying philosophical shifts reshaping the

---

12. One helpful discussion is that of Svendsen, *Allegory Transformed*. His exegesis of Hebrews itself is not a strong part of his argument, in my judgment.

interpretive dispositions of the Reformers. Yet, even since that time at least pockets of the church have preserved the sounder instincts that tend toward the "allegorical" and that explain why it developed and held sway as long as it did. There was a baby in the bath water.

The preacher of Hebrews was no allegorist in the objectional manner just described, as was Philo. Yet a challenge to saying this consists in that the objectional reading strategy just described bears a resemblance to something different and necessary, not unlike the resemblance of Pharaoh's magicians to Moses. In part, the difference goes to truth claims. Has God in fact spoken in the Son who is Jesus or not? Is Jesus properly addressed as God or not? Is this in fact the same God who spoke to Abraham and through Moses, and is he faithful and true? For the larger part, Hebrews takes such questions as answered, given its audience and the situation. But when such questions are answered they carry with them convictions—assumed more than expressed—of the nature of God's speech through all history. Among other things, the gospel's answers to such questions require us to take history *and history's narrative* with full seriousness. This is not because there is a pre-conceived theory of history or of literature and such. No, the cause of this stems from the fact and nature of the incarnation, the fact and nature of the Son's own history. In short, we learn from the incarnational form of his self-revelation how God has spoken and submit all our reading and interpretation to that knowledge, which is then necessarily mindful of literature (not merely words) and history in its seamless, organic whole from beginning to end. But for the very same reason it recognizes that the whole of that history and its literature depends on its being bound up with the Son, who is its origin, who bears it along and cleanses it, and who is heir of all things. These tendencies—respecting history, narrative, literature, on the one hand, and reading christo*centrically* (not merely christotelically), on the other—are not in competition but are mutually dependent. If history is not the history of Christ then it has lost its only possible center (because he is the actual center) and all flies apart. Only individual scholars with their personal theories can posit coherence, but their theories are merely opinion and are rightly received as such. But when the text of canonical speech is read "christocentrically" we are *all the more* committed to reading it in the light of history and literature and indeed all that properly belongs to the human experience.

It is in this tension, rightly balanced and preserved, that Hebrews' argument works from beginning to end, giving us a touchstone for all proper reading of the Scriptures. There are a variety of ways in which particulars of Hebrews' exposition will come close to or even touch Philo (at least in externals), just as will be the case with other Jewish voices of antiquity that are equally absorbed with the Scriptures. But the differences are far more important and they are completely controlling.

In short, and with an eye on the wider range of first century parallels that have been proposed as the "key" for Hebrews' thought, we affirm that Hebrews, as canonical, divine speech, is not a patchwork of ideas drawn from diverse sources and tossed out for consideration, as if in the hope that some useful insight can be salvaged for the larger human enterprise of understanding. Rather, as revelatory speech, it moves with total certainty from its beginning to end in infallible exposition of the truth. Our receptions of Hebrews' vision will always be imperfect, but we may be confident that it not only gives us a reliable vision but illuminates the path to right understanding.[13]

## Meeting Jesus Again

From that mode of thought we can turn our attention to that to which Hebrews' witness chiefly points: the Son.

The distinction between translating for someone and putting words in their mouth blurs, but we may hazard that world leaders who have personal translators working for them in a sensitive negotiation assume that there is a difference. With that rough comparison in mind we may say that our task as a commentator is to let the writer of Hebrews be the theologian in the room; our role is to translate. The teaching of the letter therefore follows in our commentary. It might nevertheless be of some use to the reader to get a broad view of this commentary's conclusions on Hebrews' vision of Christ. If at any point I misrepresent and steer the reader wrong, we live in hope that the Word will make himself heard in spite of and even against me.

It must first be said: Hebrews is a sermon exhorting the members of a house church to persevere in a faith that corresponds to the word of forgiveness and cleansing that God has spoken in the Son. That salvation, as both God's word and deed, is contained in Jesus Christ—all that is true of, in, and through him. Everything depends, then, on knowing him. At its broadest (not restricted to Hebrews), he is finally known by the things said about him, by the things done and given through him, by what he says and does, and by the names and titles he bears—all within the context of the history

---

13. Nothing said here or elsewhere in this commentary takes a dim view of the value of historical investigation or excuses shoddy work in that regard; disregarding such work would represent a shallow view of what canonical speech is. The exposition to come will draw heavily on the spade work of historians, albeit in ad hoc fashion. Yet in doing so we must receive Hebrews for what it is: divine-human speech.

of God's word and deed, and only when the Son himself shows us the Father and makes him known in the Spirit as the believing community proceeds in obedience. God reveals himself through himself.

Accordingly, the knowledge of Christ—or christology—is inseparable from participation in his benefits. It cannot be pursued without loss if our interest is only in building a profile of his person. This applies to all aspects of the knowledge of him, including the study of the particular names and titles that are used of him.

Thus, the particular names and titles given him are not things that can be understood in isolation from the rest of what must be the case if we are to know this one. But if this is understood and maintained, there is real gain in considering these names and titles (henceforth simplified to "names").

The five routine names used in Hebrews are Son, Jesus, Christ, Lord, and priest. Mediator follows as a close sixth (8:6; 9:15; 12:24; cf. Guarantee in 7:22).[14] Through Ps 45 he is addressed as God (1:8–9). Also mentioned are apostle, shepherd, and, by implication, king (e.g., 7:1–2; cf. 1:3, 8–9, 13; 12:27); by more remote implication, prophet (1:1–2; 2:3; but after 1:1–2 the prophetic identity is the water in which the argument swims). Note also "son of man" in 2:5–9, though whether the titular sense is intended is properly questioned. Perhaps one could include here also forerunner, pioneer, perfecter, minister, heir, though these are more like ad hoc ways of expressing what he does or is. He is of course not only priest but offering, but Hebrews nowhere designates him as the Lamb of God, let alone a bull, calf, or goat. Despite the fact that he is portrayed as the speech of God, not even in 4:12–13 is he called the Word (Logos) as in John's Gospel.

*Son*: Being the assumed identity even where he is not named as such (e.g., 2:5–18), this name seems to capture the identity and drama at their farthest reaches: vertically (the descent, ascent, heavenly-earthly), horizontally (eternity past to future as well as the narrower drama of the descent and ascent; typologically it aligns with patterns and expectations of Israel), theologically (indicating relation to God, identity in distinction; his sharing in divine authority and power), and anthropologically (sharing in blood and flesh with his siblings, the seed of Abraham; the Davidic king; being tempted; representing, etc.). It is aligned both in antecedent expectations and in Hebrews with both royal and priestly identities and roles. As a way of knowing Jesus, "Son" is not reducible to particular Jewish or Greco-Roman notions but has been filled out by Jesus' presence in history and in Scripture

---

14. I owe thanks to Daniel Treier. Through personal conversations about his work on Christ as *mediator* (forthcoming), my rethinking of that category and its relationship to the other names and titles was stimulated.

as the church has come to grips with and developed its confession prior to the composing of the sermon that is Hebrews.

*Jesus*: Being the name by which he was known in "the days of his flesh," it seems to refer particularly to him as the concrete figure of his past history who is now raised and crowned with glory and honor. He is the man who lived, did God's will, suffered, tasted death for all, and was raised and exalted.

*Christ*: This seems to connote the one anticipated by Israel (messiah), witnessed to in her prophets (esp. Moses), who would achieve her hopes and, as such, serve as God's appointed priest-king. It is not clear that these connotations have so eroded that the term is merely a personal designation, though it is equally unclear whether those connotations are fully activated in every use of the word. There might be echoes of this title's embeddedness in the gospel narratives (5:5; 6:1; cf. 11:26).

*Lord*: Admittedly this is not used frequently but it seems to connote the one confessed with the church, the pre-resurrection Jesus from the viewpoint of his resurrection (2:3; 7:14; 13:20); though see 12:14 and possibly some of the other uses of the word where it could be taken as referring to God as such or to the Lord Jesus. The tradition has already identified this title with the Lord (YHWH) of the OT Scriptures (e.g., 1:10).

Our conviction that there exists some degree of interchangeability in the usage of these names is due to this: If we attempt to find a strictly consistent strategy in the employment of these names and to discern a coded message thereby in particular passages, it is hard to resist the conclusion that we are artificially clamping a theory down on the text. No doubt this is due to the ultimate coalescing of all that the separate names can signify in the single, unified figure and his history, and thus the mutual influence that the separate names have already had on each other even before this sermon was composed. There were never strict lines of difference and any lines are further blurred when the names are more governed by their subject than he by them. It is an error to think of these "identities" as "natures" that must have their own version of the hypostatic union; none of these terms aligns just so with the later debates that gave us the creeds.[15] We must also consider the sermon genre, which relies on freedom of expression in achieving rhetorical

---

15. Even so, it is interesting that the writer can say that is is *Jesus* who was made lower than the angels (2:9; cf. Phil 2:5), identifying the one known as blood and flesh with the *Son* in his personal movement from pre-incarnation to incarnation. This, of course, does not need to contradict the doctrine of the "enhypostasis" of Christ, namely, the idea that the human person Jesus had subsistence only in union with the Logos. Hebrews affirms personal unity and continuity in the movement from pre-incarnate to incarnate existence but is not otherwise observing the later technical distinctions in its language.

ends. Again, the entire problem of title-christologies—reducing Christ to the sum of what the individual names and titles are taken to mean—should not be given new life. The titles are situated in a drama that brings its own elements to the mix, as was said above and as the opening series of OT citations in 1:5–13 illustrates.

The one who is *priest* is the one who is Son, Jesus, Christ, and Lord, so that the associations that attach to the latter are in some sense transferable to and activated in that priestly identity and role. At the same time, the identity of "priest" is not an empty cipher but one filled with its own history and content through the order of Melchizedek and Aaron's shadow as well as the givenness of Jesus, with the result that his identity as priest has already shaped the conceptualization of him as Son, Jesus, Christ, and Lord. Hebrews is not merely homogenizing all these categories but it isn't laboring to keep them distinct either. As priest—strictly the royal priest who is and acts as the word of God—he has left heaven for earth where he participates fully in the humanity and human situation of the seed of Abraham; inaugurates the new covenant through his self-offering; qualifies the people for its benefits; unlocks and releases those benefits for them; from the divine throne represents, supports, and supplies his people with these blessings for their salvation; and establishes that covenant as the certain, imminent, universal rule of God. As to when he is appointed as priest, there are strong indications that it correlated with his accomplished offering, perhaps specifically his resurrected entrance to God's presence. Yet the latter is continuous with his incarnation (10:5–10) and life of obedience (5:1–10; 10:5–10), and at places his death as such seems to be the key priestly act.[16] It is forced to correlate stages before and after his heavenly Session with Aaronic and Melchizedekian patterns. That he is *high* priest arises not directly from a Scriptural pronouncement—Ps 110:4 does not say *high priest*—but from his uniqueness (he is alone in his order), eternality, and role (his work correlates with the Day of Atonement). For further on his priestly appointment, identity, and role, see 4:14—5:10 and 7:1–28.

This leaves *mediator* (8:6; 9:15; 12:24; cf. Gal 3:19–20; 1 Tim 2:5–6), which overlaps with his role as the guarantee of the better covenant (7:22).[17] In particular the term mediator seems to be used of his priestly role in the inauguration of the new covenant after the pattern of Moses (9:15–22, which 8:6 anticipates and 12:24 reprises), but even in 9:15–22 this is one

---

16. If we were inclined to press points, we could insist that his priestly role also had a termination, namely, when he sat (10:12–13), though this does not comport with other statements (e.g., 4:14–16; 10:19–25).

17. It may be that the verb *mesiteuō* in 6:17 is fully intended in this sense; see Griffiths, *Hebrews and Divine Speech*, 111–14.

fabric with his self-offering as the event to which the Day of Atonement and other sacrifices witnessed and also with his on-going mediation (7:25). Moreover, insofar as 8:6 serves as a kind of reverse outline for the whole of 8:7—10:18, the words "the covenant he mediates is better" are a stand in for the whole of 9:1—10:10. There are reasons to think that the identity of "mediator" was a loaded one, having received some shaping in the church's confession (cf. 1 Tim 2:5–6) and indicating the Son's qualification as both divine and human in the work of revealing God and achieving atonement as reconciliation. The traditional concept of a mediator could have shaped the way in which Christ as priest was to be presented in broad terms, though the preacher chose to make limited explicit use of the word and to concentrate its force on the covenant inauguration—which, again, is of one fabric with the rest of what is involved in Christ's self-offering.

To reiterate the point about the way in which the history of the shadows and patterns and the history of Jesus have to be taken into account: In Israel's history there was a drawn out sequence of exodus, wanderings, Sinai, preparations for the tabernacle, inauguration through Moses, implementation through Aaron with the Day of Atonement at the center. In Jesus' history all this happens in a stroke and in a way that resists assigning discrete effects to separate stages of his work. Therefore the true Day of Atonement is achieved in Christ by the very same self-offering that inaugurates the covenant history within which (by the logic of the patterns) the Day of Atonement would be observed. That he is *mediator* is expressly stated in Hebrews to highlight his role as inaugurator, the one who brings all these things into effect, but this is said only with the understanding that the inaugurating sacrifice is also the cleansing sacrifice that qualifies the people for entrance. Obviously—and this is contextually warranted—he is mediator in the latter sense also.

It can be asked why Hebrews does not content itself with the already-established idea of Christ as an offering but, uniquely, goes on to name Jesus as our high priest. No doubt an expositional mindset encountering Ps 110:4 is part of the answer, but it is not likely the image would have been pursued beyond an intuition unless it proved fruitful on many levels and also comported with the person and work of the Son as already confessed. The idea of priestly representation and intercession is potent in itself, but it also brings in its wake the much larger treatment of the systems and the covenants within the history of God and his word, culminating in the announced gospel.

As for the question of deity and humanity as such, neither can be taken for granted. Moderns may take humanity as a starting point and debate whether deity is applicable, but in the history of christology it has frequently been the other way around. In Hebrews we can note the way in which the Son can be addressed as God outright (1:8) and without so much as pausing for reaction. We can then note the rhetorical effort to assert full humanity and we might wonder if the deity of the Son was a given and his full humanity was in question and in need of reinforcement. This latter seems closer to the mark if either of these identities was needing buttressing, but it is more likely that neither was really a bone of contention as such. What was needed was a deepening of both emphases—along with other aspects of their confession—in the interest of the teaching about the great salvation.

But moderns do in fact balk at this point of deity for a variety of reasons so it is worth noting the ways in which Hebrews expresses this. Firstly, it must be said that we do not subscribe to the absurd theory that the writer could not have thought a thought unless it can be documented elsewhere in his world. That he did not have the capacity to think coherently, to foresee what he was going to say or remember what he had already said, or that he did not understand the implications of his words are all theories that are in need of demonstration. That said, Hebrews' affirmation of the Son's deity is there in the text by the ascription of status and roles that were unmistakably those of deity in antiquity (positioned above the angels; eternity; creator).[18] It is there in the angelic worship accorded him. It is there through the employment of language and traditions that apostolic teachings had already developed to confess this identity (wisdom; descent-ascent of Phil 2:6–11; pre-incarnation existence and incarnation; sinlessness; Ps 110:1; Ps 2:7). It is there through particular analogies that cast the Son in God's role (3:4; possibly 9:16–17). It is there in calling him God outright (1:8) and applying OT texts about God or YHWH to the Son (1:6–12). It is there by placing him alongside God and the Spirit in the lead roles of salvation. It is there by the divine, eternal, complete, world-ending effects that are claimed for his salvation. It is there by the very logic of his priestly and mediatorial role. It is there by the fact that the items we just listed are not present like fragments clumsily appropriated but uncomprehended. They are harmoniously present within a coherent story. Efforts to resist this conclusion must necessarily and always do resort to a divide-and-conquer strategy. Even though it leaves the hard work for the later ecumenical efforts of the church to sort out, it must be said: Hebrews witnesses to Jesus' divine identity in distinction from the Father. As we have already said, this perspective on the Son who is Jesus is so firm and full that we are caused to marvel at the equally strong assertions of his full humanity. But human he is.

---

18. Bauckham, "Divinity in Hebrews," 15–36.

As for his deity and humanity in his activity, there has always been a tradition of assigning certain roles or activities to either his deity or his humanity. It is not to pass judgment against all such readings to observe that Hebrews itself is more inclined to assign the Son's work to his full identity: the Son's work is carried out as the Son—as God-man—from his incarnation (an act of obedience in his role as our representative, an act that is uniquely his prerogative as the one who can chose to accept his body) to his exaltation (taking a place which properly belongs to God, not merely an exalted human; but doing so as one of us). The same must be said of the atoning work that spans these points. Likewise, his life won through resurrection is somehow improperly separated from (even if it might be distinguished from) his eternality by nature. The comparison with Melchizedek that launches 7:1–28 characterizes him as "without father or mother or genealogy, having neither beginning of days nor end of life" suggesting that the "indestructible [endless] life" of 7:16 is somehow owing to something intrinsically indestructible as much as it is to what is shown to be and won as indestructible in the resurrection (cf. John 10:18).

In the Son both God and the chosen seed of Abraham keep covenant, as was fitting and necessary. In him, and as the Son, God takes responsibility for his creation and works salvation, as he alone was able (Isa 59:16; 63:5). He does so as the one who created all things for himself, acting in faithfulness to his handiwork and with transcendent power. He does so as the one whose saving work is his speech and whose speech is the act of salvation, communicated by the Spirit in the word of the gospel. He does so by giving us himself, who alone is life. Yet he does so as one of us, so that by sharing in him, the heir of all things, we receive the promised inheritance.

## Jesus and the Old Testament Witness

In the course of our exposition we will be led to account for Hebrews' appropriations of the OT Scriptures and the challenges these pose for modern sensibilities. At present we wish only to take up the thread we let drop above and suggest a broad way of thinking about what is happening for what it is worth.

In modern fiction it is not uncommon to notice what could be called fragmentary "images of Christ" scattered among the characters of a story or even in the plot line as such.[19] The device is all the more compelling when the image of Christ is assigned to a character so completely *unlike* Christ. One thinks of Edward Wallant's *The Children at the Gate* or the whiskey

---

19. I owe personal thanks to Rosalie de Rosset for help with this idea.

priest in Graham Greene's *The Power and the Glory*, though the possible illustrations are many. Again, we will take recourse to the different image of light shown through a dispersive prism. The one, integrated light is dispersed into its several colors. Or again, we may think of an abstract painting of a woman. The painting has an historical individual as its subject yet the image is of such a character that the human subject could not be guessed unless she revealed herself to us in person. All her features are present but rearranged and distorted in other ways such that she is truly the one present, she and no other, but unrecognizable without direct knowledge of her in person. In fact, the abstract image can be said to reveal her essence more truly than a realistic image could give us.

Each of these analogies—images of Christ, a prism, abstract art—provide ways of appreciating how Christ is present in the OT shadows and copies for Hebrews. His one, integrated atoning act is represented in the rites of the OT that are radically diverse in character and that may even be chronologically distinct. His image is scattered among personalities so unlike each other and so unlike him as to be untraceable, and yet the correlations represent the OT divine-human authorial intention. Christ's profile and that of his work is indubitably (as a matter of truth) that of the OT witness and yet unrecognizable in that portrayal until he steps into view as himself. All along the OT witness was signaling its incompleteness and its prophetic character while God's speaking awaited its self-expression in the appearance of the Son who is himself the radiance of God's glory,[20] but all along it was speaking of this one and no other.

It will not do to expect easy correspondence. Where we find the most compelling foreshadowing we find the most striking dissimilarities. He is not so much answerable to the patterns as they to him, and yet he commands us to see him in them and it is clear that we cannot see him in himself without them. They are the clothing of his glory, the revelation of his person and work.

It is not our work in what follows to unlock the interpretive secrets behind this exposition but we will hazard its source, which is none other than the "christological big bang" of Jesus' own presence in which he embodied those Scriptures, enacted them in his obedience, taught his disciples, received his Father's vocal witness from the skies, and, not least, opened the Scriptures themselves (and his disciples' minds) in the days separating his resurrection and his ascension. Subsequently he poured out his Spirit through which this understanding unfolded in the obedient life of the church. The birth of the new creation brought all this to existence. Patterns

---

20. Caird, "Exegetical Method of Hebrews," 44–51.

of interpretive reasoning are evident in the samples of this reading that we have in the apostolic writings of the NT though the hints are never so full as to enable us to reduce this way of reading to a set of strictly rational rules of a method.[21] We must read as did the apostles but then this will mean that we must carry on as they did in the same Spirit, participating in the same obedience of the Son's own mission. The question of hermeneutics (roughly, theory of interpretation) is nested inside of the larger movement of obedience in the Spirit. Hebrews is not a handbook of Christian hermeneutics but it is an authoritative guide to how the OT Scriptures must be read and how Christ must be known.

It is not that the modernist demand to reduce all things to reason—defining "reason" in a somewhat limited way—is a wrong approach as such, and it is one that must be respected in any earnest attempt to translate the gospel in compelling ways for a modernist (and "post-modernist") audience. It is rather to say that what is actually happening in the gospel cannot finally be reduced to those particular tests of "reason" (of the modernistic type) and the insistence on doing so will distort our perceptions. It is not the purpose of this commentary to explore this question in its own right, but we cannot avoid acknowledging it in this general fashion if we are to read Hebrews sympathetically and properly.

## Jesus and the Heavenly Tabernacle

At more than one point (e.g., 4:14–16) we will register the view that the pattern shown Moses was none other than the Son and that the copies and shadows corresponded to him and his work more than to heavenly architecture and furniture. This requires at least a brief justification and explanation.

There are ways of *affirming* a given writer's beliefs about heavenly objects—however they may be imagined ontologically—that can share in the same modernist assumptions about things and language as do *denials* of those beliefs. To illustrate: a modernist, scientific mindset might find it more agreeable to imagine that Hebrews intended the language about the heavenly tabernacle as "figurative" rather than "literal." We might insist in opposition that this is anachronistic. What is agreeable to us is irrelevant; the ancients "would have" (naturally, we suppose) taken the language "literally,"

---

21. The study of apostolic interpretive methods and principles has been fruitful, even if theorists have reached differing and even incompatible conclusions. For a cross-section of some of the theories, Beale, *The Right Doctrine*, is still useful. An analogy from the modern music industry is instructive in thinking on the almost limitless number of paths a text and its ideas could take from its origin through its stages of appropriation (McCabe, "Inspiration.").

for which parallels can be marshaled. And yet upon inspection it may turn out that the latter view is guilty of assuming that only what is *not* "modern" (meaning, some belief held by modern people) can be "ancient," which is a back door sort of way of imposing modernism on antiquity. It may in fact be equally mistaken to assert that a particular ancient thinker either *did* or did *not* believe that things "were" (or "are") as imagery like that of Hebrews presented them. Self-consciously, these were symbolically freighted ways of talking about what exists in the most serious of ways, ways that were normatively determinative for right and wise conduct within empirical history.

Yet it stands to reason that then as now—think of the differences of views even among modern Christians!—individuals may have intended such language as that of Hebrews more or less symbolically, more or less "literally." One may wonder if all Israelites at the time grasped Solomon's expansive view of God's relationship to heaven and earth (1 Kgs 8:27), a view that seemed both to affirm that God was uniquely present in the Most Holy Place of the newly built temple and yet was unlimited by that space. Putting before an ancient (or many a twenty-first-century person invested in a "mythological" conception of the universe) a model of the physical structure of the universe (heliocentric and so forth) may have precipitated either a cheerful shrug (acknowledging the truth and value of both perspectives), violent opposition, or a crisis of faith.

Taking these preliminary remarks further would draw us too far afield, requiring us to take on board anthropological, linguistic, exegetical, theological, and other perspectives. Rather we will merely indicate the considerations that draw us toward the view that Hebrews' intention was that what Moses "saw," to which his copies and shadows corresponded, was the Son and his work as enacted in the accepted gospel (which does not mean a fully understood or articulated gospel), while these same copies and shadows form for us what can be described as linguistic-visual "basic particulars" for seeing the Son, images past which we cannot get as if trying to get to our sort of empirically grounded description.

The following considerations are not ranked in order of importance, nor are they exhaustive. Our exposition will register a number of comments along these lines, albeit in passing and without attempting to gather then into one formulation.

Firstly, for the sake of comparison, one could think of the geography and map of Tolkien's Middle Earth. As one reads the history of *The Lord of the Rings* it is clear that we are to think of that map as real and consistent; it is the physical setting of the story without which the plot would be shapeless. Or again, the geography and map of Palestine behind the canonical Gospels works the same way. If in either case that physical given were to be strangely and unpredictably morphing into other shapes as the story progressed, the whole narrative would take on a transformed sense. And yet the latter is closer to what we encounter in Hebrews, in which, as our reading will observe, the heavenly world of the drama morphs and bends according to the point being made. Is there a heavenly curtain? Does it stay in place (temporarily? forever?)? Are there divisions of the heavenly tabernacle between a holy place and most holy place, with two curtains? Is there an ark, and are the other items of Moses's tabernacle present and functioning in heavenly one-to-one correspondences? Why are some features and rites seemingly missing? Is the liturgical movement vertical or horizontal?[22] The questions multiply. The point can be overdrawn, but the impression remains: The cultic geo-architectural background is not stable in the way that Tolkien's or the Gospels' maps are. We can imagine that the writer of Hebrews was simply not in control of his conception, or perhaps was deceptive, thinking that the readers would not notice. We can also persevere in the conviction that we have failed to make good sense out of Hebrews' language, which does in fact yield a consistent picture of a definite map and architecture. But we can also conclude that the controlling reality is not geography and architecture but the Son himself and his work.

Secondly, as G. B. Caird rightly observed about apocalyptic broadly, "When an author writes a book consisting wholly or mainly of symbols, there is a prima facie case for not supposing him to be a literalist; and the case holds even if he should prove to be a slavish imitator using conventional imagery and with little imagination of his own. But this generalization does not decisively settle the more particular question whether the apocalypticists intended their eschatology to be taken literally. That can be determined only by reading the books."[23] Given that each writer and writing must be taken one-by-one, when Hebrews is laced through with the symbolism of apocalyptic there is "*prima facie case* for not supposing him to be a literalist" respecting heavenly structures, external to the person of God and necessarily instrumental to the accomplishment of atonement, structures within which—as something containing the Son, rather than contained by the Son—the Son moves.

Thirdly, there is a strong implication that what was "upper" and "prior"—the heavenly pattern shown Moses (8:5)—was identical with what was at that point yet future, that is, what was found to be the case in the Son (9:11; 10:1).

---

22. E.g., Ellingworth, "Universe in Hebrews," 337–50.
23. Caird, *Language and Imagery*, 262.

Fourthly, it is probably deficient to think that in Hebrews' intention what was shown Moses was merely physical infrastructure, the structures, accoutrement, and paraphernalia with and within which the priestly liturgy would be enacted—as if a building waiting to be used, vestments laid out and waiting to be donned. There is good reason to suppose that the heavenly pattern included the drama enacted therein (8:1-6; 9:1-10). Yet when we pay attention to the correspondences drawn between Jesus and the Mosaic *rites*, there is a tremendous freedom of both selection and conflation—not to mention that Jesus *himself* is the offering and the priest. The controlling center, the stable reality, is the Son and his work.

Fifthly, the *effects* of the Son's atonement are cast back over history, suggesting strongly that for Hebrews the atonement itself, though once for all at the end of the ages (9:26; cf. 4:3), was ever present.[24]

Sixthly, if we dig down into Heb 3:1-6 and its use of the OT there is a convincing argument to be made that what Moses saw (Exod 33-34) was none other than the Son.[25] In 11:26 Moses reckoned specifically on the reproach of Christ, hinting at the content of his vision.

Seventhly, on Hebrews' terms, considered broadly, it is backwards to think of the Mosaic structures and rites as the "literal" and the realities of the Son as "spiritual-figurative." The Mosaic structures and rites are copies, shadows, parables that witness to the actual.

Eighthly, if we undertake to interpret the respective passages of Hebrews as if they are oriented on the Son, his salvation, and his people, allowing the cultic imagery to bend and adapt as the case requires, there is a satisfying result in both the parts and the whole. If, however, someone objects that here or there the writer patently contrasts "earthly" and "heavenly" and assigns events to this or that realm, or to this or that point on the timeline, and if we then try to draw a single picture or a single timeline, the disagreements multiply. If we on our side are asked to explain these we can only respond that we are being asked to account for problems that arise through the denial of our premises.

Ninthly, the idea that God and the Son are *themselves* the temple of God was certainly in the apostolic air (Matt 12:6; John 2:21; Rev 21:22).[26] The referent and meaning of the word "temple" in such a context is "Christ."

---

24. Depending on how Rev 13:8 is translated (contrast NIV and ESV) the idea might be more directly expressed there. Cf. 1 Cor 10:1-4; Rom 3:25-26.

25. D'Angelo, *Moses in Hebrews*, 95-199, 248-49, 254-55, 259-63. Attridge seems to be making a related argument in "Antithesis," 1-9; cf. Attridge, "Response," 208.

26. In Revelation, this statement follows several definite, realistically descriptive assertions about the heavenly temple (*naos*): 7:15; 11:1, 2, 19; 14:15, 17; 15:5, 6, 8; 16:1, 17.

Likewise, we are not surprised that the extended description of Ezekiel's temple would be prefaced with these words: "I will not hide my face anymore from them, when I pour out my Spirit upon the house of Israel, declares the Lord GOD." (39:29); and that it closes with these words: "the name of the city from that time on shall be, The LORD Is There" (48:35). The implication seems to me to be that *Israel* is the dwelling place, the temple; this would seem to be how Revelation took it.[27] The church as the temple is commonplace in the NT. The point is not that Hebrews' conception is identical to these, but that one cannot assume that an "ancient mindset" would automatically or naturally lead to "literalistic" interpretations of the language.

Lastly, theologians have for excellent reasons been driven *precisely by Scripture* inexorably to the conclusion that there is no revelation or atonement *external* to the person of the Son and that there is no way to separate the speech and the work of God.[28] The Son *is* the revelation of God and he *is* salvation.

> In Christ, what God communicates to man is not something, but his very self. This is distinct from all other acts of God. This is God's unique act, his reality-in-the-act, and apart from this act there is no God at all. In the act of creation, God does not communicate himself, but creates a reality wholly distinct from himself, but here in Jesus Christ God acts in such a way that he is himself in his act, and what he acts he is, and what he is he acts.... This unity of person and word, and person and work, and therefore of word and work, means that we cannot in any sense think of the work of revelation and reconciliation as a kind of transaction objective to Christ, or simply as an act done by Christ. It is above all the person of Christ revealing so that revelation cannot be separated off from his person. Similarly, it is the person of Christ atoning, so that atonement cannot be divided from Christ's person.... The atonement is his person in action, not the action by itself.[29]

There is no reason or need to think that all this was present to the mind of this writer, but it is arguably consistent with the direction of his gaze. He was attempting to communicate the person of Christ. The coherence of his imagery, therefore, does not consist in his exegetical methods or the images as such but in the person of the Son to whom the images coherently

---

27. Beale, *Revelation*, 1061–62.
28. See for example, Torrance, *Incarnation*, 37, 107–9, 184, and Torrance, *Atonement*, 93–94, 124–25, 148–53.
29. Torrance, *Incarnation*, 108.

witnessed. As already indicated, this does not entail the conclusion that he then thought of this heavenly tabernacle language as *merely* figurative, in the sense that moderns might intend that. In any event, it is due to such considerations, among others, that we will assert that for Hebrews the pattern shown Moses according to which he constructed the copies and shadows was the Son and his salvation as such.[30]

## The Great Salvation

Inseparable from the Son is his great salvation.

The palette of salvation in Hebrews is predominantly priestly, sacrificial, and covenantal. This is no straightjacket, however, for the driving interest is to witness to "such a great salvation" in pastorally restorative and encouraging ways. The portrayal is not cultic monochrome. The *kingly* subjugation of Christ's enemies is an elephant in the room, for instance. Nautical, athletic, agricultural, pedagogical, domestic, legal, economic, martial, and other imagery is laced through. Likewise, if we concentrate on the sacrificial language we will observe that though the Day of Atonement looms large it is not allowed to be systematically controlling. That prerogative belongs to the event of the Son's offering itself, to which the *entire, integrated* Mosaic cultus witnessed.[31] The Day of Atonement merely signifies the goal of the entire journey of the promise: entrance, once and for all, into the immediate presence of God.

For the moment it is necessary to bring together just some of the more common cultic ideas, leaving further touches to the exposition to come.

---

30. In case it needs to be said, we are attempting to understand how Hebrews is intending, for the purposes of this word of exhortation, the language of the heavenly pattern shown Moses and the heavenly tabernacle pitched by God. We are not implying that the world to come does not consist of bodies (1 Cor 15) and (re)created environment, which (based on the resurrection body of the Lord) involves definite forms. Still less are we forgetting that as human the Son existed as finite body, with all this entails. Post-resurrection he continues to exist as body—indeed as flesh and bone (Luke 24:39), capable of consuming this worldly fish—yet with what limits we do not know (Luke 24:31, 36; John 20:26; 1 Cor 15:35–58). The Scriptural imagination makes beggars of ours (Ezek 10:17). Nor have we forgotten the eye-witness-based accounts of the ascension as a vertical movement (Luke 24:51; Acts 1:9–11); that very narrative should occasion more probing reflection on space and spheres.

31. We will have occasion to observe that the idea of, for instance, a *substitutionary* offering is operative at points, even though the sacrificial imagery on its own would not seem to involve or require that idea. The larger reality of Christ's salvation exerts a pressure on the images—new wine in old wine skins—and Hebrews has no final interest in suppressing this, unless perhaps there is merely the need to keep the rhetoric effectively focused for pastoral ends.

This will be a little dense, but for those of us not raised in the Jewish ritualistic heritage of the first century a piecemeal discussion of these things as they arise in the text would leave something to be desired. At the least we can provide a reference point from which to take bearings as we wade into the exposition.

Koester nicely summarizes some of it, as a place to start:

> *Purification* [= cleansing] means purging away uncleanness, *sanctification* [= consecration, making holy] means making something fit to be brought into the presence of God, and *atonement* [= 2:17] involves reconciling God and human beings. *Completion* [= perfection] is a complex idea that deals with the accomplishment of God's designs for people, culminating with everlasting life in God's presence. The human response is found in *faith*.[32]

On *blood*, see 9:1–10. The word *atonement*, when it translates *hilaskomai* (2:17) and its cognates, characterizes Christ's offering as propitiatory (appeasing a wrathful god), expiatory (removing or making amends for what offends), or both. In broader theological usage it can encompass the whole of at-one-ment, reconciliation, with respect either to the means of accomplishing this or the results or both.

Within the shadows and copies of the Mosaic tabernacle and its system there were gradations of holiness from the Most Holy Place, to the Holy Place, and so forth out to the whole camp/land of Israel. The people could be cleansed of ritual and moral impurity but were not consecrated as were the priests and the high priest. These categories collapse in Hebrews, however, since this great salvation brings the whole people (cf. 13:12) directly to the Most Holy Place of God's presence, first (now) in the person of their brother and high priest, and ultimately in their collective entrance—all in an achievement of a total/actual/eternal salvation that is at once "already" and "not yet." When the Greek words for *salvation* itself are used (1:14; 2:3, 10; 5:7, 9; 6:9; 7:25; 9:28; 11:7), the salvation is characteristically future (e.g., 1:14, 6:9; 9:28) but it can describe the entirety of present and future (e.g., 2:3, 10) or refer to the ongoing event (7:25). Though in 5:7 the word *save* seems to refer to the resurrection and some other texts could be read with that focus (= "salvation from death in bodily resurrection") it does not seem so limited in every occurrence. Without making the words for perfection, sanctification, cleansing, forgiveness, redemption, and salvation synonymous they can used in overlapping ways, as they are in 9:1–28. They are

---

32. Koester, *Hebrews*, 119.

heaped up as if radiating the glory of the singular masterstroke of the Son's person and work.

Along with "cleansing," "perfection" is one of Hebrews' favorite categories. Perfection "signifies fullness and completeness for whatever a person or thing is meant to be and do, often as a result of training and practice."[33] The terminology has strong associations with consecration of the priests in the OT, though Hebrews fashions its own usage. Christ is "perfected" (2:10; 5:9; 7:28) and is the "perfector" of faith (12:2) and of believers (10:14). The beneficiaries of a covenantal arrangement can also be said to have been or not been "perfected" (7:11, 19; 9:9; 10:1, 14; 11:40; 12:23). Some texts bring it into close relationship with the language of sanctification and cleansing (2:10–11; 9:9–10 followed by vv. 11–14; 10:1–2; 12:23–24), though there is a clear distinction in that Christ is not himself in need of sanctification[34] (2:11; 7:26–27; 10:10, 14) though he is "perfected." Ultimately perfection is everything involved in effecting arrival at the goal of creation's and salvation's history. It is the vocational qualifying of the Son as high priest who shares fully in the humanity of his siblings, obeys perfectly, offers himself, is raised,[35] is enthroned, and intercedes for his people. It is the application of his priestly work to his brothers and sisters who are bound to him and

---

33. Marshall, "Soteriology in Hebrews," 261.

34. This contrasts with the way that John uses the language of sanctification (e.g., John 10:36; 17:19).

35. Heb 7:28 forms an inclusion with 5:1–10; 5:9, in turn, picks up the thread from 2:10 where the idea is that the Son was perfected "through suffering." The emphasis of "perfecting" seems to fall on the *sufferings* that made him a merciful, faithful, empathetic priest. Along the way to 7:28, however, more of the Son's story has been rehearsed or hinted at, all of which is indicated in 7:26–28. This would include dealing with the problem of corruptibility through resurrection, a problem highlighted in Moses by the laws of ritual impurity, since these latter arguably address the problem of human mortality and corruptibility as unfit for God's presence; cf. Moffitt, *Atonement and the Resurrection*. I do not find Moffitt's idea of "the logic of resurrection" to be as fully controlling as it is in his argument (his exegesis of Hebrews seems to me forced at points, as if attempting to make Hebrews say what other Jewish texts say more clearly), but I strongly agree that it is ingredient in Hebrews' larger mix of atonement theology and Moffitt's work deserves very close, sympathetic attention. The atonement, as a reality, has more dimensions than any one human perspective can convey. Hebrews has its own emphases but has no interest in limiting its vision to these, which would amount to limiting the atonement itself. As a result, we find hints and gestures to other and deeper features of the atonement also at work and also necessary for this vision of Christ as priest and sacrifice. Among other things, Moffitt helps us hold together ideas of ritual and moral impurity as these were operative within the single fabric of Israel's cultic system *and* Jesus' effectual work. This is a much more satisfying account than those that suggest, for instance, that Hebrews treats ritual impurity as merely part of the shadowy symbolism of the Mosaic system while moral impurity is the real concern addressed in the atonement of Christ.

each other in the new covenant he inaugurated. It is a matter of qualifying them to approach the holy God's throne and eventually enter where Jesus has gone ahead of them. It is the promised approach through Christ to God. Rather than speaking of the "fulfillment" of the OT Hebrews prefers to show how the imperfect anticipated that which alone brings us to the goal, the perfect (cf. 1:1–4).[36]

As savior (a descriptor not actually used in Hebrews, so that it might serve here as a generic term), the Son works *with* us and *for* us. He is example and provision, and these roles overlap. *With* us and for us he is "perfected" and "saved," but in Hebrews' cultic logic he could not be the cause of our salvation if he were in need of cleansing, sanctifying, and forgiveness (7:26–28; cf. 4:15; 9:14). These latter are what he does *for* us, so that when the words "perfecting/perfection" and "saving/salvation" are then applied to us they cover both what he did with us and for us, including the cleansing, etc.

To look at it through the lens of Hebrews' text, Heb 2:5–18 breathes enough of the above terminology through the church's existing confession to tell the whole story in brief, hinting at what is to come in the exposition. In the discussion of Christ as priest (5:1–10; 7:1–28) the imagery contracts to perfection and salvation, focusing the basic question of whether the goal of the promise is attained or not. We need a priest who will bring us there, and with that comes a change of law, a new covenant. In 8:1—10:18, then, the exposition plunges fully into the sacrificial realm; in 9:1–28, in particular, most of the key terminology clusters (cleansing/purification, sanctification/consecration, perfecting/completing, forgiveness/liberation, salvation, redemption).

The result for the beneficiaries of this work is that they are qualified to do what only the Aaronic priests could do, approach the divine throne through Jesus and ultimately to enter where he has gone. This is indeed a priestly prerogative, but Hebrews nowhere calls us priests, reserving that role for our brother and high priest. We are the holy ones (3:1; 6:10; 13:24), the entire people of God dwelling forever in the house of the Lord.

## Salvation as Gift

John Barclay has recently subjected the idea of "the gift"—broadly in anthropological, biblical, and theological contexts—to fresh investigation and

---

36. For a full discussion, see Peterson, *Hebrews and Perfection*; Attridge, *Hebrews*, 83-87.

clarification.[37] His work provides a valuable filter through which to clarify important aspects of Hebrews as we continue to contemplate its vision of salvation.

The word *grace* (*charis*) is not alone in touching this idea of "the gift" but it is a potent term in this connection, both in the wider Greek speaking world and the NT. This word itself is not given thematic attention in Hebrews (God's grace: 2:9; 4:16 [2x]; 10:29; 12:15; 13:9, 25; cf. 6:4 and the "heavenly gift"; our responsive "grace"/thanks: 12:28), though its use favors the inference that the preacher's idea of grace is christologically conditioned in ways that are indebted to other NT traditions.

In Hebrews, so far as word use, *grace* is singularly characteristic of the gospel such that being excluded from grace (12:15) or insulting the Spirit of grace (10:29) is equivalent to loss of salvation. In 13:9 it is again a token for the whole gospel as a source of strengthening/confirmation that contrasts with "foods." In the latter there is an echo of Esau's fall from grace for the sake of food (12:15), hinting at the larger linkage of grace and the preached *word* that promised the inheritance. The first use of the word *grace* (2:9) characterizes the means by which Jesus tasted death in behalf of all, that is, *by the grace of God*. It could there be referring to the goodwill shown Jesus in response to his prayers (5:7–10; i.e., he was resurrected and enthroned so that his death could be the atonement it is) and/or the fitting way in which God perfected Jesus through those sufferings as the leader of the salvation of his brothers and sisters (2:10–18). In 4:16 it is a general descriptor of the divine throne on which our high priest sits and it is coupled with the closely related term *mercy* as what is to be expected from God; together mercy and grace encapsulate the character of the empathetic help supplied through our high priest.

Barclay argues that "grace" can be "perfected" (perfected = draw an idea out to its extreme in some way; this use of the word "perfect" has nothing to do with Hebrews' use of that word) in at least six ways: superabundance, singularity, priority, incongruity, efficacy, and non-circularity. Any given writer may "perfect" the idea in one or more of these ways. At the level of everyday language use, no one way of "perfecting" the idea could make a privileged claim on the word; these were not better or worse ideas but merely different, and the different ideas could make use of the same vocabulary. Obviously things are altered when the idea is developed in a particular way within a coherent and particular version of the gospel, such as in Paul's usage. Paul's definition of terminology may not be determinative

---

37. Barclay, *Gift*.

for Hebrews at the level of word usage, but there are canonical-theological dynamics that must be accounted for as these witnesses are taken together.

For Hebrews, thinking both of word use and wider context, the gift partakes of:

*Superabundance*: The gift is once-for-all. The wide range of Christ's benefits as priest and offering are sufficient, eternal, complete, perpetual. Nothing good exists outside of the promised inheritance.

*Efficacy*: The gift qualifies worshippers for the approach to the presence of God in contrast with the Mosaic system, though it can be insulted and fallen short of. The efficacy of grace is objectively total and accomplished but awaiting and dependent on faith's appropriation in the present; we have a cleansed conscience, but must take that to heart in faith.

*Incongruity*: According to this "perfection," a gift is distributed without regard to merit.[38] Firstly, incongruity is implied in Hebrews in that this gift in all its facets is "for all," the "many," or "the people" (beyond the priestly class); some of the names of 11:1–40 highlight this.[39] Again, see Heb 9:15. There is no indication of a gradation of need, even if someone happened to be Judaism's current high priest; all seem to stand equally in need of Christ's benefits, equally without merit, indeed, equally meriting death. Secondly, beyond this general statement it is necessary to make some distinctions: Insofar as the faith of the Son is the faith of our human brother,[40] the gift of salvation granted to him and his being crowned with glory and honor are entirely *congruous* with his merits (2:5–9; 4:15; 5:7–10; 7:27; 12:1–3). As

---

38. In the wider world of Greco-Roman antiquity, it was natural to reserve gifts for those who merited them; there was nothing inherently contradictory between a "grace" (gift), so understood, and merit. Giving the gift without discrimination cheapened the gift itself. If it was in fact a matter of giving the gift without regard to merit, Barclay would characterize the conception as perfected in terms of "incongruity." One question to be put to Paul, for example, would be whether the grace of salvation in his gospel was "incongruous" only in that it extended to Gentiles, or that Jews and Gentiles were equally without merit, equally deserving of divine wrath but equally offered divine grace, or some other scheme.

39. Further refinements: firstly, in contrast to Paul, there is no explicit attention to the Jew-Gentile issue. Secondly, Luther's strong idea of the Christian life as a permanent state of incongruity (Barclay, *Gift*, 116) finds partial echoes, at least, in the need of a daily approach to the divine throne and Christ's ongoing intercession. Thirdly, it is unclear if the gracious act of God is incongruous with the creature as such (before sin), or only with the creature as it has become defiled. Certainly it is with the latter. The former is beyond the horizon of what is said, though it might be hinted at in some sense by the correlation of this creation with the old covenant and by the language of Psalm 8 (Heb 2:5–9).

40. In Hebrews it will not be possible to think of Christ's faith as an "apocalyptic" work *of God*, as if *not* a human response; it is indubitably a response of a human, Abraham's seed, albeit a distinctive human, the Son of God who is also called God and Lord.

for his brothers and sisters, salvation is incongruous now, but it anticipates a removal of all that can be shaken and of spirits made perfect so that in the unshakable kingdom there will be congruity between the gift of participation and the state of its recipients—and yet it remains eternally the effect of incongruous grace, and eternally depends on the faithfulness of the one who intercedes (7:25), so in some senses incongruity is eternal. Between baptism and Christ's second appearance the situation is complex, leaving much unspecified: a once-for-all cleansing and forgiveness that is applied unilaterally; an ongoing intercessory and atoning representation; a disciplinary process leading to incremental progress in lived-righteousness, roughly coordinated with the language of perfection and sanctification; a final state of having-been-perfected. Rather than thinking of the life of faith as a preamble that leads organically to the state of complete perfection following resurrection, we probably do better to think of the future resurrection as the true beginning point that is partially, falteringly expressed already now from baptism to either death or Christ's second appearance; we do not build toward it but rather live from it. Thirdly, did God choose Abraham and Israel because of some merit in them, or, again, due to a hidden scheme built into the very fabric of creation that distinguished between human creatures? Nothing indicates as much. Presumably their reception of the promise was for the sake of the seed, whose merit alone is highlighted. The promise and its gift came to the Fathers incongruously; the gift came because God willed it (10:1–10).

*Priority*: The initiative falls entirely on God's side with faith as the response. There is, however, no hint of a special, individualized call or hidden election, much less a reprobation (see on 9:15).

Both *singularity* and *non-circularity* do not describe Hebrews' idea of grace, since with God's approaching holy presence the threat of punishment is strong for those who are "enemies" (against singularity, which would insist that God is *only* loving, merciful, and so forth, tending toward universal salvation) and a return both of faith/obedience and gratitude/praise is expected from those to whom the gift is granted (against non-circularity, which would insist that *nothing* is expected in return for a gift). Further, God "rewards" the faith that is itself the response to the initial gift (6:9–10; 10:35; 11:6, 26), which is a natural reflection of gift giving as a social bond.

Does faith then cooperate with grace in the sense that an infusion of initial grace enables a human work of obedience upon which further grace is conditioned, and so on? In 10:35; 11:6, 26; and related texts the "reward" is clearly the final reception of the promised inheritance; an ongoing, cyclical pattern of reciprocity is not operative in those contexts.[41] A cooperative idea might be implied in 6:9–10, however, though we finally doubt that such a logic is at work. The vantage point of God's remembrance or forgetfulness in that context is the final judgment (relating to the things that belong to ultimate salvation in 6:9). The threat for the readers is that of forfeiting what is already "there" in their record of obedience, what is already sharing in the atonement and its benefits—the existing track record of faith, which is the "substance" of things hoped for (11:1) and a share in Christ (3:14)—and so what is potentially approved by God (compare 10:35). The need is of perseverance to the end (6:11) so that the promise will actually be inherited (6:12).

Salvation in this context is cast as a reward but only as the reward of faith's reception of the absolutely prior, unprompted, unearned, love-motivated (6:9; 12:6) heavenly gift, a reception that is entirely active in conforming its life to the promise in ways that are for the time being costly. This idea of a reciprocal exchange utilizing the idea of a reward thus partakes of more than one idea:

1. In everyday practice of the Greco-Roman world, gift giving played a cultural role in establishing, deepening, and maintaining social bonds. By conceptualizing the divine gift as expecting a return of faith-obedience and praise, which is, in turn, rewarded, Hebrews is not violating a Lutheran-styled rule of "pure grace," but merely utilizing the cultural idea of reciprocal gift giving as a function of friendship. The parallel is limited to the positive point about healthy reciprocity in a loving relationship. In the end, for Hebrews the future divine "reward" is the gift already given, which is eternal and once-for-all, already perfected, in which the believer already participates (6:4–6)—indeed, it is that which makes possible the proper response of the human creature (8:7–13). It is not made, achieved, or won by the believer, but entered.

2. The baptized enjoy real participation in the benefits of salvation, whether or not they persevere or forfeit all. The baptized (= the people of God in a local gathering) are said to have been enlightened, to have tasted the heavenly gift, etc. (6:4–6). Their participation in salvation was real, not merely theoretical and imagined. It is of a piece with this that their past of *obedience* is thought of as belonging to the fabric of that gift; this past life belongs to salvation; it is the *future* salvation "falteringly" expressed already, and so a fruit of the *gift* (see above).

---

41. In these texts, the "reward" is not "payment for labor" or "earned wages" but the freely-given, uncoerced return to suitable recipients; cf. Barclay, *Gift*, 197, 316, 485.

Yet, just as the gifts of 6:4–5 could be forfeited, so also the past life of obedience.

3. Faith has the character of staking everything, including one's present economic and social welfare, on the promise, and thus on the yet-future inheritance (it is the "treasure" in heaven). Hebrews styles salvation as a reward in keeping with the competition between present and future gain, present prosperity and a future inheritance. It is part of the effort to draw their attention to the city to come, and to put all their eggs in that basket. The overall framework of salvation—not least the fact that God unilaterally struck the decisive blow once-for-all in the offering of the Son, without reference to any prior cause than his goodwill—excludes the possibility of interpreting the "reward" as achieved anywhere else than in the Son's work "by the grace of God," and then derivatively in the faith that participates in the Son's salvation. The Son is the "heir of all things," and he shares his inheritance with the children given to him.

It remains evident from the logic of 5:11—6:12 (cf. 10:26–31; 12:15–17) that while the grace of God is prior and perennially unconditioned, and while it is efficacious in cleansing the conscience and qualifying for the approach to God through Jesus, it is not efficacious in the sense that it causes all of the "ground" on which it showers to produce the intended harvest. When the ground proves to be unfruitful—the mystery of sin!—that ground is rejected and burned. This does not involve the entailment that the ground that does bear fruit is "deserving" of grace, however. Such ground simply continues to receive the incongruous, prior, effectual, superabundant grace. Consequently, it simply does what comes natural: it produces good plants. It belongs to the power of God in creation and salvation that it, the creature, does produce—the creature is the subject of the verb "produce"—but only because and as created in Christ.[42]

---

42. To be living in the Spirit as opposed to "flesh" is not to be made a passive body animated by an alien force, but to be alive in the only way creation can be truly alive. To be without the Spirit of God is to be dead, thus powerless. To have the Spirit is to be fully human, to be fully a creaturely agent, and thus wholly responsible and free for *creaturely* obedience. The word "independent" can be problematic, but something like it seems important in keeping with the general doctrine of creation as not-God. The corollary of God's radical otherness is creation's separate existence, not as without dependence but as possessing, by and within the divine endowment, by and within the power of the divine gift, the status of its own existence. Ingredient in this for humans (whatever is said of the rest of creation) is their distinct existence as whole persons, and thus fully *volitional* existence.

## Salvation as Covenant

For Hebrews, the clock of history is measured less by planetary movements than events of divine speech, with the underlying continuity provided by the promise and sequential change provided by the covenants that give the promise expression. This is not a matter of glossing "real" history with theological interpretation, as in the dominant conception of modern culture's outlook. For Hebrews, covenant precedes cosmology; as goes the tabernacle, so goes the world. The word of God always leads, being that by which all things where *made* and that by which they are *borne up and along* to their goal. And that word is finally spoken not only in but *as* the Son, the heir of all things, through whom the universe was created.[43]

Along with Ps 110:4, taking pride of place among the divine utterances is the prophecy of the new covenant in Jer 31. Well before it is quoted in Heb 8:7–13 it looms behind the language of Hebrews (see on 2:10–18; 7:12, 22). Not only does this text serve to signal how God's earlier speech announced the true nature and limits of the Mosaic covenant from within that earlier history, but it established the hope that the very idea of a covenant that is securely grounded, authentically realized *by both parties*, and permanent in effect was not merely a dream. When God determined to establish his eternal covenant, it would not be by sheer divine fiat, imposed from above. It would not be a sham or charade, boasting harmonious relations while one side lived in open rebellion. The human partner would keep the covenant fully and perfectly, showing itself to be fully worthy of the favor of its Lord. This the Son-who-is-Jesus did, when he chose the will of his Father in the act of accepting a human body for the sake of making it an offering and redeeming his fellow children; this he did when he learned obedience through suffering, never sinning; and *on account of* the suffering of death he was crowned with glory and honor. In that very movement of obedience he cleared the ground for the children of promise who had been given to him, the seed of Abraham. His obedience took the form of an offering that was at once the inaugurating sacrifice of the covenant and the great Day of Atonement. By dint of this there was total remission, redemption, cleansing, and atonement. Not only was the slate clean, but a new beginning was inaugurated that gave them a share in the Son and his Spirit of obedience. The law was now written on their hearts.

It is this—fully accomplished once-and-for-all—that constitutes the beginning from which the future unshakeable kingdom proceeds, but it is this same beginning that already now finds expression in the faith-obedience

---

43. See Laansma, "Living and Active Word."

that falteringly, stutteringly, but resolutely plots its course on the line of that promise.

This history is the story that occupies Hebrews and it is no accident that on the heels of the Son's obedience (10:1–10) it is that prophecy of the new covenant that is recalled once again by way of closing the central exposition of 5:1—10:18.[44] From that point on (10:19—12:29), the sermon revolves on the faith-obedience that is the emblem of the members of this covenant, and it is not in passing that the opening words of that last section characterize the Son's salvation as the new and living *way* (10:20). This *way* is not merely one of a vertical "going up" to approach God in worship, but a "going out" to bear Christ's shame (13:13), and a "going on" to the city that is coming, Mount Zion.

## The Wrinkles in the Plot

In order to deepen the story in which Hebrews participates but to do so in brief compass, it is necessary to borrow language from elsewhere in our theological lexicon. The risk is that we flatten out the telling and even prompt misunderstanding where Hebrews either does not use a particular image (e.g., "new creation") or uses similar language in distinctive fashion. But if interpreters appeal to the larger pattern of thought within Philo or the Qumran community to read between the lines of Hebrews, it seems warranted to do so by appealing to the larger patterns of apostolic thought in which Hebrews so manifestly participates. Our conviction—with the caveats just noted—is that these distinct apostolic witnesses do in truth focus one gospel, one reality.[45] At the very least, the following will put our cards on the table, indicating how the following commentary understands these things.

Viewed from one angle, Israel, the Jewish nation, is (always, only by gracious act of God) a people that is "near" in contrast to the Gentiles who are "far"; the advantage of the Jew is "much in every way"; Israel represents the native olive tree in a way that is not true of the Gentile, who is a wild olive branch that must be grafted in "against nature." It would seem that the people of promise, the seed of Abraham in the Jewish people, somehow shared in the incarnation of the Seed, at least by derivation. The Jew is never this by nature or possession, but by virtue of the promise given to this people, the promise formalized in the covenant and all its attendant blessings, the promise always and only received in faith. But the Jew is this. Yet from

---

44. This is seen clearly by Lindars, *Theology of Hebrews*, 98–102.
45. See the title and argument of Marshall, *New Testament Theology*.

another angle, Israel is as far from God as the Gentile. There is no distinction. For both, the way can only be as radical as death and resurrection. The Jew, no less than the Gentile, must be adopted if they are to become genuine children of this family; the Jew, during the time under law, is no different than a slave. All are equally in need of cleansing, forgiveness, perfecting.

It is also true that the history of Israel is not only her history, but the history of humanity. Abraham was chosen not for the sake of the salvation of the Jews, but the salvation of all people. The God who chose Abraham was and is the God of all peoples, the creator of heaven and earth. We then take to heart how Canaan and the temple were a new Eden, as it were, a new beginning to the story of the world. But whereas Adam's story ended in judgment and death, Israel's would end in life from death—via judgment, that brought the old story to an end, to its intended outcome—and thus would bring the new story to birth, unlocking what was promised Abraham for his seed, a seed comprised of Israel and all nations. It is, then, the hope of Gentiles to be grafted into Israel's history, which necessarily means into the history of Israel and the promise given to her forefather, Abraham. In Hebrews, then, all of Christ's brothers and sisters are the seed of Abraham.

Yet again, the history of the world is divided into the history before and after Jesus Christ. Before is the time of Moses and his covenant. After is the time of Jesus and his covenant, which has made Moses's covenant old. But then we see that this new covenant is nothing less than the new creation, dividing this age from the age to come. We see further that this new creation (with its covenant) was already in effect from the foundation of the world, which is why faith was possible from Abel on, why it is said that Christ would have to be offered many times *from the foundation of the world*, why forgiveness for OT believers was possible through sacrifices that could not take away sin, why the word spoken through Moses can be described as "gospel," and how it is that Moses's tabernacle was to be fashioned according to what already existed whole in heaven. And we see also that the old creation (with its covenant) is still ongoing, contemporaneous with the inauguration of the new, until the great removal. The "overlap" of the ages is something that was true in one way before Christ and in another way after Christ, but there was always an overlap. In order to show the continuity of God's speech of past and present, the presence of faith in the one promise across history, and the culmination of all things in the Son—the culmination that defines the present moment with its possibility and its urgency—Hebrews dwells more fully on the overlap that *preceded* Christ than most other NT writers, even as it draws more sharply the line that separates and distinguishes the new covenant/age from the old. At the same time, Hebrews develops in its own fashion the overlap that follows

Christ as a continuation of the time of the promise within the conditions of the old age even after the promised new covenant (with the world to come; 2:5) has already been instituted as a world-invading reality (3:14; 6:4–6; 11:1). More on this as we read Hebrews itself.

It is within this dynamic that the law of Moses (Torah) has its history. The Torah before Christ was part of the chrysalis of the gospel. Detached from Christ in his death and resurrection, it is no longer alive but lifeless matter, the shell from which the new organism emerged. Paradoxically—for here all analogy breaks down in light of the active presence and application of the gospel before Christ and the continuation of the present already-judged age after him—that same Torah remains organically related to Christ as long as the present age continues, and so remains in that sense—as rightly related to Christ—a part of the living gospel. Turning back to it as if it was something in itself, is to find that it is merely a dead casing, worthless. To disown and renounce it for what it was and what it continues to be, a witness to Christ, the gospel in the idiom of shadows, is to disown and renounce Christ.

## The Hope of Salvation

We begin to close this introduction by returning to Hebrews' vision of the goal of salvation, that toward which we are summoned to move.

The reader of an English translation of Hebrews, if not also the reader of the Greek text, might be excused for missing the character of salvation as a *place* in Hebrews until as late as 11:10. From that point on it is obvious, leading up to 12:22–24 and 13:14. Yet all along it has been a question of approaching or entering into a place, the Most Holy Place of God's throne, and in 2:5 we discover that it is the coming *world* about which the preacher has been speaking ever since the sermon's beginning. It is in this sense that we should understand 3:7—4:11 as well, as a matter of God's resting *place*; likewise the inheritance (1:2, 14; cf. Deut 12:9).

Hebrews' vision of a secure home and household is a compelling one. Our cities are not built to last. That the readers had suffered significant social and economic hardship is clear (10:32–39) and this dimension of a life of faith is highlighted (11:24–26, 35b–38). If we diminish what could be called the merely human aspect of this—that which would be experienced by all peoples regardless of their belief systems—we have departed from Hebrews' and the gospel's outlook.[46] The loss of one's "world" can be the

---

46. The role of honor and shame as well as patron and client relations in the Greco-Roman world as these relate to the situation of the readers is amplified (helpfully, but

experience of any individual, family, or other social group in any otherwise stable political state, though the horrors of a collapsing civilization are the stuff of apocalyptic nightmares.[47]

If, however, we fail to recognize that all of this spatial imagery coalesces against the backdrop of Israel's inheritance of the land, her resting place, with the Most Holy Place of the temple as its center, we have failed to appreciate Hebrews' entire vision of salvation. It is not a city as such that forms this vision, but the Jerusalem that is above, the Mount that is before us. This city has a name. Rome was the greater city by any human standard, and was probably the city that loomed largest in the social existence of the original readers, but in the perspective of the history of God's speech Rome was no equal of Jerusalem. Moreover, this city on which hope centers does have a history. Just as the Son is known from the shadows and copies constructed according to God's command, so this city. This understanding draws us into the broader, integrated drama of Israel's pilgrimage as we see that in the Pentateuch and then reenacted in the prophets. Again, to find one's identity in relation to a city requires that we know something of that city's ethos, and in the case of this city this is what was revealed through the covenant that centered in the life of the sanctuary. This aspect of Hebrews is more implicit than explicit but it is everywhere the air we are breathing in its exhortations. To draw near to the divine throne is to participate in the full compass of covenantal life inscribed in the laws for Israel—as these carry over in the righteousness realized in the new covenant. Hebrews' vision is finally that of the fullness of the covenantal life with God and neighbor that was presented in the shadows and copies of Israel's history. What lies before us, and what is to shape our lives even now, is our citizenship in that city. As such, we do not retreat from but actively inhabit the cities of this age whether or not they will have us.

## Encountering the Holy

That place of salvation is the place of the *holy* God of Israel.

One of the off-putting features of Hebrews for moderns is the controlling language of holiness, cleansing, and the like. If any aspect of its vision belongs to the scientifically debunked thought of antiquity's mythological

---

to the point of overstatement) in the work of deSilva, *Perseverance in Gratitude* and deSilva, *Despising Shame*.

47. Examples of the latter are easily drawn from the OT and the literature of other societies. For one vivid narration of Rome's collapse, see Manchester, *A World Lit Only by Fire*, 3–5.

world it is this. However backwards the rest of the New Testament writings remain, they at least seem to represent a step forward for humanity's emergence from myth's hold on the mind. For many, Hebrews can itself be interpreted as a welcome translation of all of this quasi-magical blood-spilling ritual into the more palatable ideas of human interiority and moral formation.

Yet only by isolating certain of Hebrews' comments can the latter conclusion be sustained. Body and blood sacrifice is not rejected but brought to its goal in the blood, flesh, bodily sacrifice of Jesus. The approach to God is not made without a sacrifice ritual. It is made through the once-for-all offering of the body of the Son. Blood is a symbol but only with reference to the material, physical blood of the Son. When this is seen even the word 'symbol' becomes inadequate if it masks the reality that all language, including scientific language, is symbolic and that in Jesus' blood, which means in his whole person, we have to do with the living and active presence and power of God. The language of symbolism is getting at the way of understanding this reality and its effects by associating it with the copies and shadows ordained by God himself.

Our intent in saying these things is limited to asserting that Hebrews is not giving us conceptual categories that must be "de-mythologized" so as to connect them to reality as moderns conceive it by their scientific standards of knowing. If we do that we have only projected our world onto Hebrews' or screened out what is essential to our loss. Instead Hebrews compels us to recognize the reality that creation exists in the presence of the holy God, that history is a matter of his covenants, and that the encounter with God's holiness—the cultic—is simply a fact of human existence as well as its destiny. Where this is not acknowledged it is no less true but only suppressed and distorted. If we think otherwise we are not receiving Hebrews' witness but arguing with it. Our efforts of understanding, translation, and explanation must work with and for that witness. Hebrews' vision of covenant and sacrifice is the one most needed by moderns. It is a vision to be inhabited.

## The Summons

We have said that the call of Hebrews is less, "Do not turn back!" than it is, "Move forward!" "Let us approach!" Disobedience here, it must be understood, is the characteristic failing of the human creature. Whether through sloth, indifference, ignorance, desire for the harlot Babylon, fear, guilt, pride, or enmity the characteristic failing is that of Adam hiding, the Israelite not seeking the Lord, David sending the ark off to Obed-Edom. It had been Israel's, and thus humanity's downfall. Turning to the Lord is the first act of obedience, from which all else follows and all else is possible. Hebrews concentrates all its effort on stirring us to do this one thing, not out of disinterest in the larger life of righteousness that characterizes full covenantal life (Heb 5:11–14; 6:7; 12:4–17; 13:1–17) but precisely because the rest is contained in it.

In truth, drawing near, through Christ, is not a burden (1 John 5:3; Matt 11:28–30). There is no greater good or beauty to be desired than the Lord (Exod 15:11; Pss 27:4; 34:8; 50:2; 89:8). With him there is perfect satisfaction (Pss 103:5; 107:9). Yet we recoil, wander, and flee due to our own falsity and defilement. The Scriptures witness to our inability to stand in the presence of the holy God apart from Christ and the terror of its threat when it appears (Exod 19:12–13, 20–24; 20:18–21; 33:20; Isa 6:5; Luke 5:8; Heb 10:31; 12:29). And it was for our preservation and salvation that his holy grace kept us at a distance while showing us the way to dwelling with him (Heb 9:6–10)—the way of the word of promise, first spoken to Abraham and then kept in his seed, the way that *is* the Son in and as whom God speaks.

Hebrews, in fact, is finally about the ways and the way of God, the very themes that had carried through God's speech in the prophets (Isa 11:16; 35:8; 40:3; 57:14; 62:10; Jer 6:16; 21:8; 31:21; 50:5). Have we known his ways (Heb 3:10)? Will we travel his way (Heb 12:1, 12–13)? Will we avail ourselves of the new and living way (Heb 9:8; 10:20)?

*Since then we have a great high priest who has passed through the heavens, Jesus, the Son of God, let us hold fast our confession. Let us then with confidence draw near to the throne of grace, that we may receive mercy and find grace to help in time of need.*

*Therefore, brothers, since we have confidence to enter the holy places by the blood of Jesus, by the new and living way that he opened for us through the curtain, that is, through his flesh, and since we have a great priest over the house of God, let us draw near with a true heart in full assurance of faith, with our hearts sprinkled clean from an evil conscience and our bodies washed with pure water. Let us hold fast the confession of our hope without wavering, for he who promised is faithful.*

"Today" he has spoken (3:1–19). The promise remains (4:1–11). It is simple unbelief, disobedience, faithlessness not to hold fast to the word and obey the command. There are no excuses, least of all our weakness. There is also some urgency.

*Christ, having been offered once to bear the sins of many, will appear a second time, not to deal with sin but to save those who are eagerly waiting for him.*

That day is drawing near (10:25), which means that God no longer keeps us at a distance but in his holiness approaches, and escape is impossible.

*Yet a little while, and the coming one will come and will not delay.*

Heaven is reclaiming earth. He comes in his gracious act of atonement in the Son, so that the very thought of escape is the height of irrationality. Yet sin's fear and enmity run deep. Faith alone, looking into the face of this approaching holiness, makes bold to approach in obedience. But he comes either way in his holy love. In his *holy* love.

*See that you do not refuse him who is speaking. "Yet once more I will shake not only the earth but also the heavens." This phrase, "Yet once more," indicates the removal of things that are shaken—that is, things that have been made—in order that the things that cannot be shaken may remain. Therefore let us be grateful for receiving a kingdom that cannot be shaken, and thus let us offer to God acceptable worship, with reverence and awe, for our God is a consuming fire.*

# The Letter to the Hebrews

## 1:1–4

*"Whoever has seen me has
seen the Father."*

### Context

Hebrews was sent as a *letter* to a house church by a person who shared a history with this church and who hoped to visit it soon (see 13:18–25). Even so, it is a literary *sermon* and begins as such. The opening lines command the floor and bend the mind to the fact that God has *spoken* in and as the Son. When all is said, it is to this same emphasis of divine speech that the sermon will return at its end (12:25–29). If we have read ahead, we will know that there are waiting for us some bracing exhortations to listen to what God has said, the force of which have been felt fairly immediately by churches through the centuries. But there are also some densely woven theological statements and expositions whose meaning and relevance are less obvious. These opening verses, their formal and theological beauty notwithstanding, might fit in the latter category. They dazzle us but we do not yet see their implications for life. But then if we had gone straight to the "So what?" of the closing chapters we would have been asking, "How do we know that God has in fact spoken again, since the prophets have fallen silent and the glory forsook the temple? Who is this Son in whom God speaks? What is this 'great salvation'? By what authority are these claims about the new covenant made? How do we know they are true and worthy of our very lives? How does this gospel square with the reality that our situations have not improved but in some ways worsened? If this is the God of Abraham who speaks, how can this speech be reconciled with what he said earlier? Is he a faithful God?" Without answering these questions all those great exhortations would be floating in thin air. The writer therefore begins by dwelling on the answers to these questions in ways that anticipate, reprise, and grow. These opening lines of poetic prose give us *the Son* in and as whom God has spoken. In these four verses there is both less than what will be developed in the rest of the sermon and more. Both in these verses and in what follows the preacher will be making use of a good deal of what the church already confesses, some of which he will only hint at or mention, some of which he will review more fully, and all of which forms the core of convictions from which every line of his exposition follows—for those with eyes and ears. The whole exposition to come is latent in what they have already confessed. It is a matter of calling their attention to this, for the sake of both understanding and obedience. As will eventually become clear to later readers such as ourselves, it is a marked degree of inattentiveness that has led to a weakened church. The beginnings of apostasy are already noticeable. As involved as the argument will become, every word of this sermon is in fact a loving, rhetorical struggle for the life of this church, beginning with this powerful statement of the fact that God has spoken in these last days in and as the Son who sits on the divine throne at the right hand of his Father. And this Son has cleansed his people of their sins. Beginning of the end of story.

A sketch of the Greek sentence structure of vv. 1–3 indicates how to understand its logic:

> *having spoken* through the prophets
>
> God spoke in the Son
>
> > *whom* he appointed
> >
> > through *whom* he made
> >
> > *who*
> >
> > > *being* the radiance
> > >
> > > *bearing* all things
> > >
> > > *having* cleansed
> >
> > sat

## Background

The audience was a church that had received the gospel second hand (2:3) but still stood within decades of the turn of the ages from first to new covenant. As such we can almost hear the question of John 9:29 lurking, including the deeper strains that John's context gives it: "We know that God has spoken to Moses, but as for this man, we do not know where he comes from." The answer to this challenge will be load bearing for everything to come in our sermon. We must bear in mind that Hebrews is concerned exclusively with the Son *who is Jesus*, though the name Jesus will be withheld until 2:9. But, in common with the rest of the church, these believers already confessed Jesus *as the Son*, and so the writer cashes in that confession for maximum effect in this opening salvo of 1:1–4. The gospel tradition—beginning from Jesus' own life and teaching—had already developed ways of understanding and expressing (not inventing!) who it was that had come to them and then gone to take his place on the throne, accomplishing their salvation (10:5–18). One particularly potent and fitting mode of doing this was via the personified figure of divine wisdom (e.g., Job 28; Prov 1, 8, 9; Wis 6:12—11:1; Sir 6, 24, 51; *1 Bar* 3:9—4:4); see especially Heb 1:3. Elsewhere in the NT, note, e.g., Col 1:15–20; Phil 2:6–11; 1 Cor 1:30; Matt 11:25–30. Hebrews makes bold to identify Jesus as God outright (e.g., 1:8) and will apply to him language that is in the OT applied to YHWH (e.g., 1:10), so this use of wisdom is not a limiting one but rather part of the way in which the diverse forms of OT speech (1:1) witnessed in advance to the one in *and as* whom God speaks.

> "For wisdom is more mobile than any motion; because of her pureness she pervades and penetrates all things. For she is a breath of the power of God, and a pure emanation of the glory of the Almighty; therefore nothing defiled gains entrance into her. For she is a reflection of eternal light, a spotless mirror of the working of God, and an image of his goodness. Though she is but one, she can do all things, and while remaining in herself, she renews all things; in every generation she passes into holy souls and makes them friends of God, and prophets." (Wis 7:24–27 NRSV)

## Comments on Wording

1:2 *he has spoken to us by his Son*. The teaching of Jesus (e.g., Matt 5–7) is assumed (e.g., Heb 2:3) but not reported in Hebrews. Where the Son speaks in Hebrews it is in the words of the OT (2:12–13; 10:5–7). Chiefly, however, it is what Jesus *did* as breathed through the OT and the gospel that constitutes this act of speech. Ultimately, it has to be said that God speaks by *and as* the Son.

*appointed the heir of all things, through whom also he created the world*. This is a twist on their confession (e.g., 1 Cor 8:6; Col 1:15–16; Rev 22:13; cf. Rom 11:36; Heb 2:10) that echoes Ps 2:8. For the Son's role as creator, see 1:10; 3:3–4; see also the introduction to this commentary for the wider interplay between creation and salvation history. Only he who made all things can save and remake all things, and being the faithful God he is he does so. The Son having condescended to share fully in the blood and flesh of his brothers and sisters, his identity as the one who is the goal of creation (Col 1:15–16) becomes the child (seed) who inherits the promise on our behalf.

1:3 *radiance of the glory of God and the exact imprint of his nature.* Language first devised for personified wisdom is used to express who the Son is; the reference to *glory* is also reminiscent of Exod 33–34.

*upholds the universe by the word of his power.* Continuing with wisdom language, Hebrews expresses that it is the Son's own word that upholds creation and carries it to its goal. The cosmos has no other history. For the Son's priest-king rule, see, e.g., Ps 110:1; Ps 45 (Heb 1:8–9); Ps 8 (Heb 2:5–9). The "upholding" (bearing) of all things includes the Son's atoning work, and the divine "word" includes the Scriptures taken up by the Son (e.g., 2:5–9).

*making purification for sins.* The one who sits on the divine throne (Ps 110:1) is a priest forever (110:4). This anticipates 10:11–15.

*sat down at the right hand of the Majesty.* This direct allusion to Ps 110:1 announces a key text for the rest of the sermon. The force of the image is that the Son shares the divine throne itself; cf. Rev 3:21; 7:17; 22:3; Matt 28:18.

1:4 *superior to angels.* Angels are brought into the sermon firstly because Ps 8 was linked to Ps 110:1 in the confession (e.g., 1 Cor 15:27; Eph 1:20–23; Phil 3:21; 1 Pet 3:22), and the sermon is headed for that psalm in Heb 2:5–9. See also on 1:5–14 and 2:1–4.

*the name he has inherited.* The name could be the Tetragrammaton, YHWH (Exod 3:13–15; cf. Phil 2:9–11), but the stronger indication is that it is the name of *Son.*

## Comments on Theological Themes

Regarding God's past speech in the prophets, for Hebrews' readers the "old is true" and this is the one God's speech. It is therefore honored and authorized as a limited shadow, pattern, and witness to the Son. Nothing more than that, but it is that. Nor can this be said of any other human speech. As such the OT shares in all that is true in the Son. In the Son alone it finds its coherence. Conversely, any account of the Son must do justice to this divinely spoken self-witness. Again, to reject the Son is to reject that former word and so to reject God himself. These convictions give rise to the entire exposition to come.

The world's time is marked supremely by the key moments of God's speaking. Because God spoke in the Son, *these last days* are the beginning of the end. The world continues as it has, as if nothing happened to the outward gaze. But the key change that brings an end to this world and the beginning of the next (2:5) has already occurred and its change is already at work (6:4–6). This is what faith makes real in the present (11:1–2).

Verse 2b entails that the world itself is bound up with God's promise to Abraham of an inheritance. The promise is fulfilled in the Son, the proper *heir*, who took the blood and flesh of the seed of Abraham (2:5–16). As will become clear, the covenantal family of God is finally that community that responds in faith to the end.

Using the language of *radiance* and *exact imprint*, the Son's relationship to God—both identity and distinction—is expressed with the emphasis on the truth that he is the way in which God is seen and known (John 14:9; cf. 1 John 2:23). Jesus was and is God's speech as God in human flesh. It is *here* that God is seen and heard; it is here that he is *seen and heard* (e.g., Matt 11:27; John 1:18; 6:46; 8:19; 10:30; 20:28–29; 1 John 1:1–4; 5:20–21).

The story-in-miniature in 1:3b–4 anticipates among other texts 2:5–16 where it will be clear that the Son assumes responsibility for the history of humanity. This cannot be understood as mere trail-blazing for others to follow, even if that imagery is also employed in Hebrews. It is not that he does this and then believers also do this, but that his history is made theirs; only then and as such is it re-presented in their pilgrimage, as it must be.

Whether the appointment of the Son as heir was pre-creational or at the point of his exaltation is not determined by this passage. Yet we should understand that he is eternally God's Son before the exaltation *and* he inherits the name of Son upon his exaltation. As Son among "the children" given him (2:12–13), he inherits this name for the seed to whom the promise was given (2:16).

## Teaching Hebrews 1:1–4

1. Scripture, revelation, and canon. Verses 1–4 comprise what was known as the *exordium*—that part of the discourse that both introduced the subject matter of the whole and prepared the listeners to receive it in the proper frame of mind. It did not need to be a kind of précis, as if the writer was compelled to tick off every key theme to come, but it would be poorly constructed if it did not orient our minds along the right lines. It is therefore crucial to notice that the entire discourse to come—for all its ritual drama—is about God *speaking* in these last days in the Son. Like a stone twice skipped across a pond, this theme will round out the opening movement (4:12–13) and the sermon itself

(12:25-29) prior to its peroration of 13:1-17. Salvation greets us in the form of the inscripturated promise proclaimed through the Jesus Christ and Jesus Christ proclaimed through the inscripturated promise. It is for this reason, chiefly, that the sermon brings Christ and salvation into such a complete integration with God's earlier speech. The sole and sufficient response to this word is faith as a life of obedience to the end (10:19—12:17). Contained in this is the proper understanding of the relationship of the OT and the NT, as the exposition to come will instantiate and illustrate.

2. Christology. Bound up with the foregoing in ways that rise to the level of John's Gospel, the Son himself is supremely the revelation of God—because as God (in identity and distinction) he received the body prepared for him (10:5-10) and shared in the blood and flesh of Abraham's seed (2:10-16). His personal pre-existence is assumed as is the sharing in blood and flesh (2:14) and bodily resurrection (13:20). The emphasis here in the exordium falls on his cleansing and exaltation/enthronement as the moments to receive the most attention in the sermon and as the basis for the exhortations (e.g., 4:14-16; 10:19-25). If he is not who he is claimed to be here, nothing follows. As goes christology, so goes the rest of our faith.

3. Salvation. Bound up with both of the foregoing, we can see that God acts savingly in his speech, and speaks in his saving action. God's speaking and acting are two sides of one thing, in keeping with Jesus' claim to be the way, the truth, the life (John 14:6; 11:25). For Hebrews salvation will be a matter of cleansing (1:3) so that the promise of entering into God's holy presence is fulfilled. This was the inheritance promised Abraham, and it is the story back of all of Hebrews. As the same promise it is the pronouncement of forgiveness (10:11-18) in the new covenant effected in Jesus' blood. The history of the entire cosmos, from its creation to its end, is determined by this history of the promise and the Son. The word spoken in the Son addresses all humanity so that, objectively speaking, all are responsible for it. Thus the urgency of this "word of exhortation" (13:22) and the urgency of the mission to all nations that is everywhere assumed in Hebrews.

4. Preaching. The exordium is at once "sermon, creed, confession, hymn, praise, acclamation, exposition, argument, and celebration."[1] It is one of the most artistically formed sentences in Scripture, setting a high

---

1. Thiselton, "Hebrews," 1454. He characterizes this as a multilayered model of preaching, teaching, and praise that sprang from scriptural learning, sensitivity to the audience, and meticulous preparation.

bar for our attempts to communicate the gospel in fitting and pastorally effective ways. Art that serves the gospel is only good.

# 1:5–14

*"You will see heaven opened, and the angels of God ascending and descending on the Son of Man."*

## Context

THE EXORDIUM (1:1–4) HAS set the tone and the agenda for the sermon. It also introduced the leading foil—angels—which will be used to set in relief who the Son is, the one in and as whom God has spoken his word of cleansing (1:5–14). When this theme continues after a brief exhortation (2:1–4) it will develop the Son's career (2:5–18). The preacher liked to bundle associations and arguments so there is no one reason why angels are brought into the mix but two reasons are immediately evident and a third can be inferred. Firstly, Ps 8 was routinely joined to Ps 110 in early preaching (see on 1:1–4) and the writer is headed toward Ps 8's exposition in 2:5–9. The Son's place on the divine throne over the angels is exploited as a way of contemplating who the Son really is and how the promise reaches its conclusion in him; this of course is done through the Scriptures because of the theme of God's speaking. Secondly, as is noted in 2:2, the angels were to have played a role in the giving of the first covenant that has now given way to the new covenant. As a sign of divine authorization the angels mark the great weight of the first covenant, and so the even greater weight of the new covenant. Thirdly, with God as creator, history always proceeds from heaven to earth. This contemplation of angels has a literary effect not unlike that of Rev 4–5. We are brought into the heavenly throne room where the work of God originates so as to move from there to earth where the Son joins his people and becomes their high priest.

As for the arrangement of the seven citations, which tease out 1:1–4: The first (Ps 2:7) and last (Ps 110:1) are prominent elsewhere in the NT and would have formed cornerstones of their confession. The mid-point passage (Ps 104:4) is reprised in v. 14. Again, in the first two God addresses him as Son, while in the third the angels are to worship him. The fourth indicates the created and thus limited nature of the angels as servants, while the fifth and sixth declare the Son's eternity as king and creator. The seventh, complementing the first (compare 5:5–6), is a key text for the whole sermon, and indicates where 1:3 was going. Finally, v. 14 provides a closing flourish that uses the middle citation to return to the theme of the inheritance promised in the divine speech (1:2). This will form the segue into both the exhortation (2:1–4) and the next stage of the argument (2:5–18).

In the main, the imagined setting for all seven citations is the post-resurrection enthronement of the Son, but the writer does not labor here or elsewhere (e.g., 7:16) to keep that distinct from the Son's eternity (e.g., 1:10–12). Son he was, and Son he became. In 1:5–14 the portrayal is of the risen, enthroned Son, yes. But more than that, he is the one who was already Son, who received the body prepared for him, who obeyed and was crowned. He is the Son of God—God, Creator—and the seed of Abraham—man—who inherits the glory that Adam forfeited. Heb 1:5–14 is the praise of the one who is Son not merely in one moment or aspect, but the Son who is Jesus and who can be addressed as God and Lord.

## Background

Throughout his sermon the writer will make use of the Greek version of the OT, the Septuagint (LXX). The translation of the Pentateuch occurred in the third century BC and the rest of the OT trickled out over the following century or so. It was never a single translation to begin with, therefore, and the many copies would have added differing readings. Whatever books were to hand would have existed in scroll form; much of of it would have been committed to memory and cited as such. The extent to which there was a definite canon of Scripture before AD 70 is debated. All of Hebrews' citations are from the books included in the Protestant canon, but there are also echoes and allusions to other writings such as Wisdom of Solomon (see 1:1–4) and the history of the Maccabees (see on 11:32–40). Hebrews has no qualms accepting the Greek version directly as God's speech, consistent with the likelihood that 2 Tim 3:16 includes in its scope the LXX. Though there is no evidence that the writer of Hebrews knew the Hebrew language and though Hebrews' argument can make use of the LXX's distinctive wording (e.g., 1:6–7; 10:5–8), we take for granted that Hebrews' interpretations have been informed by many influences including (possibly) other interpreters directly engaged with both Hebrew texts and alternative wordings of LXX scrolls. Like other early Christian interpreters of the OT the writer of Hebrews shares the *formal* principles that would have been utilized by most ancient interpreters. Just for that reason, the very different interpretive conclusions they drew compared to their Jewish neighbors must be indebted to their *material* principles, that is, for instance, their convictions about who Jesus Christ is and the reality that he was the subject matter of the OT; again, their convictions that the Spirit was involved in their reading (e.g., 3:7) and that their reading practices were to be shaped by obedience (see 5:11–14). It was in fact just such convictions that were indicated in 1:1–4 and that are now cashed in. Using the words of the Scriptures God speaks directly of and to the Son or about the angels in their relationship to the Son.

There is no basis for thinking that 1:5–14 is correcting deviant speculation about angels and the Son, nor is it encouraging mystical participation in angelic liturgies. The argument of 1:5–14 is satisfactorily explained by the rationales noted above. The preacher is turning our attention to the *Son*. The exalted status of angels is assumed as well as their prominence in revelatory (especially apocalyptic) texts. Beyond their relationship to the Son and his salvation, however, little is said of the angels that could not otherwise be read off the surface of the OT as cited.

Not all of the passages cited in 1:5–14 had been a part of Jewish messianic hopes. Their use here is for in-house consumption, as it were, not to prove that Jesus is messiah or even that he is God, but to extol him as the one in and as whom God speaks and works salvation.

## Comments on Wording

*1:5 You are my Son, today I have begotten you.* No angel is addressed as son like this. Ps 2:7 was a well-established text in Christian traditions. Its chief point for Hebrews is the declaration of Sonship, though the *today* may refer to the resurrection where he was revealed as the Son he was (cf. Rom 1:4). As originally written it described a human figure in terms of his representation of God before the people, but as applied to Jesus it indicated who he is by nature. There can be no exegetical bridge to this latter meaning. It is firstly a claim about what is simply true and goes back to Jesus' claims through his words and actions, God's pronouncements in word and deed (Mark 1:11; 9:7; 15:39), and the Spirit's witness. The original application of the psalm to a Davidic king such as Solomon is not canceled but it is being treated as among the shadows and patterns that witnessed to the Son (8:5).

1:6 *when he brings the firstborn into the world, he says, "Let all God's angels worship him."* This is in reference to the heavenly world of his enthronement (2:5) though the Greek wording lends indefiniteness as to timing and so probably has in mind a certain achievement that is in process of completion. The emphasis is on what is *true* with respect to the angels and the Son. The citation is from the LXX of Deut 32:43 (cf. LXX Ps 97:7); in the original context the one worshipped is God. The Son's deity is both assumed and expressed in this worship,[1] and the Son's humanity is celebrated in anticipation of 2:5–9.

1:7 *He makes his angels winds, and his ministers a flame of fire.* Compare Ps 104:4; Hebrews is relying on the wording of the LXX. The preacher is not exploiting an idiosyncratic translation or stressing the specifically non-corporeal nature of angels but rather indicates non-controversially the *created* and thus *limited* nature of the angels as *servants* by way of contrast with the Son's *eternity* as *king* and *creator*. In Hebrews' context the upshot will center on the universally authoritative and unchanging *word* that God has spoken in the Son in contrast with the provisional and not-yet-perfect word spoken through angels (2:1–4); the law serves (witnesses to) the Son. As such they are ministering spirits in subjection to the Son and are sent to serve the seed of Abraham, who will inherit salvation with the Son (1:14; 2:5–9).

1:8 *Your throne, O God, is forever and ever.* Ps 45:6–7. The Son is addressed as God outright (cf. John 1:1; 20:28; 1 John 5:20; possibly Rom 9:5; 2 Thess 1:12; Titus 2:13; 2 Pet 1:1), but there is consistently identity with distinction. From the perspective of Hebrews, that this address is in the form of a citation from Scripture makes it all the stronger since it is God's own witness. Hebrews never calls him King but it is entailed (e.g., 7:1–2; cf. 1:3, 8–9, 13; 12:27). He is the priest-king-prophet.

1:10 *You, Lord, laid the foundation of the earth in the beginning.* Ps 102:25–27; cf. Heb 1:2. In the original context the *Lord* is YHWH so this application is as potent as 1:8.

1:13 *Sit at my right hand until I make your enemies a footstool for your feet.* Ps 110:1 is one of the most utilized OT passages in the NT (at least 22x) and was alluded to in 1:3. Cf. Matt 22:41–46. Hebrews will contemplate it from almost every angle: The very act of speaking, the address of Father to Son, the act of sitting, where he sits, the promise of complete subjugation and the delay until it is accomplished.

---

1. There were Jewish legends of a refusal of the angels to worship Adam in the Garden. Hebrews shows no acknowledgement of this, however, making it speculative to propose that the worship of the risen Son (a new Adam) is *intended* specifically as a response to that legend.

1:14 *ministering spirits sent out to serve for the sake of those who are to inherit salvation.* Cf. 13:2. The angels are the Son's entourage whose only role is to serve in his train and at God's command. Since his is a saving-doxological movement on behalf of his brothers and sisters the angels have no other role and never have. This is their proper honor. This has implications, too, for the word delivered through them (2:2). The inheritance of the Son (1:2) is here shared with his brothers and sisters, which accounts for their status relative to the angels (2:5–16; cf. Gal 3:16, 29). Therefore, all that was said of the Son and his rule constitutes the kingdom being granted believers as their inheritance (12:27).

## Comments on Theological Themes

Clearly the early Christian interpreters of the OT operated in ways that make moderns uncomfortable, raising questions of whether we must or can "do what they did" in our exegesis. We recall, then, the observation that it was their core theological commitments and practices—what we called *material* principles—that were the real key to their readings, and these of course are authoritative for us. They are really just the key commitments and practices of the gospel itself. There is a relationship between material and *formal* principles, the latter being what we moderns usually think of first when we think of rules of exegesis. For instance, the gospel discourages readings that do not respect the literary and historical aspects of God's revelation. But the gospel's material principles finally allow room for a limited range of formal principles, which explains the relative stability of the church's reading down through the many centuries in spite of the variations in formal approaches. What is required is neither a simple *replication* of what Jesus and the apostles did nor a simple *replacement* of their exegetical methods with our modern ones. What is required, rather, is the faithful *translation* of what they did into our cultural setting for the sake of effective proclamation and mission.

There are deeper riches contained in these divine testimonies to the Son and his salvation to which we should at least gesture. It is not hard to imagine how these things would have encouraged an audience struggling with hardship and losing hope: Ps 2 portrays the futility of the nations' rage against God and his Anointed One. His King is installed, his own Son, whose inheritance is the nations and the ends of the earth his possession; he rules them with an iron rod. Second Samuel 7:14 (1 Chr 17:13) promises God's people a secure place and freedom from the menace of enemies, that is, a resting place; God will provide David a house and a Son, who will build

God's temple and whose kingdom will endure. Jesus is that Son, in whom God's promise is fulfilled. Deut 32 and related passages celebrate the vindication of God and his atonement. Ps 104 depicts God coming in his glory to save and provide, attended in his glory by ministering angels who do his bidding. The angels are a sign of his glory, but the Son is the radiance itself. Ps 45 praises God the enthroned Son, for righteousness will be the scepter of his kingdom; he loves righteousness and hates wickedness. His identity as high priest will be the dominant one in what follows, but according to Ps 110 he is the Priest as the King seated at the right hand of God, an identity that is ever relevant to the whole of Hebrews. The Son reigns. Psalm 102 is a psalm for the afflicted one who is reminded that God the Son is Creator, the one who will bring all things to their conclusion but who himself is unchanging—whose saving word and work is therefore permanent. The Son's glory is not an abstract glory but the glory of his saving movement (2:9). In this, the angels have no independent existence, will, or role but embody and signify the will of God done perfectly in heaven (Matt 6:10) and moving to earth that it might also be done there, the will that is entirely that of his love.

## Teaching Hebrews 1:5–14

1. Scripture, translation, interpretation, canon. All of the things just listed are at stake in the way that Hebrews opens its argument by a series of citations from the OT Scriptures. What Scripture is, where and how its meaning is to be found, the possibility and necessity of its translation-in-mission (translation is not a problem to be solved but a possibility and command to be obeyed), and its scope are finally all clarified with the revelation of the one who is the radiance of God's glory.

2. Christology. These verses elaborate what is said of the Son in 1:1–4 by deepening and broadening them through God's own witness in the Scriptures. We are sons and daughters by grace, but he is Son by nature. He is the heir of all things, and we inherit salvation because he condescended to share our blood and flesh and bring God's creative word to its intended goal. Son he was, and Son he became. Savior he was, and savior he was revealed to be in his resurrection and exaltation to the right hand of God—as he is praised through these Scriptures. The truth that he is the one in and as whom God speaks has many facets but it includes this, that in uttering the OT Scriptures it was the Son whom God intended as their subject matter and in these last days he makes this explicit. These Scriptures are not merely applied to

the Son as if at a stretch but rather he is their most basic and original meaning. The entire sermon to come is founded on this truth.

3. Salvation. The truth that the Son is God *for* us (as also humanity for God) is more assumed than emphasized in 1:1–13 but it is very much the theme and it breaks through in v. 14 in preparation for the warning of 2:1–4 and the further exposition of 2:5–18. So much is this true that when we arrive at 2:5 the preacher will observe that it is the world to come about which he has been speaking all along. As noted above there is much to harvest from these citations about this "great salvation" (2:3).

4. Angels. Heb 1:5—2:16 might be the premier biblical text on angels, where they are not merely present and active but brought into contemplation. Yet when this occurs we find that their entire meaning as creatures centers on the Son and his salvation. If attention is given them, if it is to honor them, it must follow their gaze to the Son on the divine throne and then follow the Son to the world and his fellow children. Their status over humanity was a sign of the disordering of creation (2:5–9), so that although their role in the giving of Moses's law was a sign of its greatness (2:2) it was also a sign of its temporary and provisional role as a witness to the Son (3:5; 5:5; 10:1). He descended below the angels (placed himself under the law) to the point of death on a cross (Phil 2:6–11), tasting death for everyone (Heb 2:9). He was then crowned with glory and honor with all things, angels included, under his feet. In this way, the promise for humanity latent in Ps 8 was fulfilled.

# 2:1–4

*"The one who rejects me and does not
receive my words has a judge."*

## Context

THE FIRST IN A series of exhortations, 2:1–4 does several things. It allows the audience to settle back into their seats after that remarkable beginning to the sermon while at the same time it bracingly summons them to greater attentiveness. It begins to make explicit what this teaching must mean for life even as it adds to the teaching. Again, if we take 1:5—2:18 as a single thread of thought, then 2:1–4 does much the same thing that 5:11—6:20 is going to do: The sermon will begin a topic (in the later passage it will be an exposition of Ps 110:4), pause for a warning, and then continue with the same theme but on a different plane. In both cases what is said before the warning lays a foundation for what is to be said after.

It is well that the student of this letter glance ahead to the coming warnings (5:11—6:12 and those within 10:19—12:29) to gauge the seriousness of the situation of the readers and the urgency of the preacher's concerns. In that light the relative gentleness of this first warning can be appreciated while its restrained power is also heard. It is evident that this is a pastor. He is not out to make a point. He is out to win the lives of people he loves, and he wishes not to lose their attention but rather to gain it.

The internal argument of 2:1–4 is made up of two Greek sentences: Firstly, we have the exhortation proper (v. 1), which is not a command but an assertion of what is necessary. Secondly, this is given support (vv. 2–4) by another artfully rounded sentence such as was used in 1:1–4 (called a *period*). This simple structure involves, however, a number of rationales for the exhortation: It begins with *therefore*, alluding back to all that precedes. It gives a result to be avoided (*so that we do not drift*) as well as a basis (*for since the message . . .* ). Finally, vv. 5–18 supplies a further basis when it begins with *for* (= ESV's *Now*).

Therefore we must pay attention

> so that we do not drift

For (if the message spoken was firm) how will we escape

> neglecting such a great salvation
>> which (having been first spoken through the Lord) was confirmed by those who heard
>>> God himself testifying

## Background

Firstly, beginning here we notice that the writer's strategy is less one of translating the gospel into the story of their Italian lives than of translating their lives into the story of the Abrahamic promise. This strategy—so effective rhetorically and theologically—is in part why it is difficult for us to reconstruct their situation. For our reconstruction see the introduction to the commentary.

Secondly, most twenty-first-century readers of this commentary will not doubt that God spoke and founded the new covenant in Jesus, but evidence for that historical event will have been lacking for the original readers who are coping with the costs of faith. As if anticipating the new covenant text itself (8:7–13) the writer uses the language of legal confirmation and witnesses at this point, establishing the reliability of the word proclaimed to them. God *has* spoken and the new covenant *has* been confirmed. The need for the writer to do this is a matter of this church's history. The institution of the new covenant itself is an historical event of the first magnitude.

Thirdly, it is evident that this church has heard at least some of the story of Jesus' life such as we have it in the Gospels (e.g., 2:3, 8–9, 14–18; 5:7–8; 6:1, 6; 7:13–14; 12:1–3; 13:12). He wishes for them to hold this history before their eyes along with the Scriptural witnesses.

Fourthly, we must speculate to some extent on the origin of the tradition that the law was mediated through angels (2:2). The original accounts of the Pentateuch made no mention of angelic mediation though Ps 68:17 hints at angels attending God as he ascends from Sinai to the temple mount in Jerusalem. Reference can also be made to Deut 33:2; the Hebrew is ambiguous but the LXX's rendering made the presence of angels explicit. Jewish traditions, however, took angelic involvement in the giving of the law for granted (e.g., *Jub.* 1:27; 2:1, 26; 5:1-2; Josephus, *A.J.* 15.5.3 [possibly]; CD 5:18), as did Paul (Gal 3:19)[1] and Stephen (Acts 7:38, 53; cf. Herm. *Sim.* 8.3.3). It is possible that allusions such as that to the angel of the Lord at the burning bush (Exod 3:2) and the angel God sent before the people (Exod 14:19; 23:20-33; 32:34; 33:2; Num 20:16) were partially in mind, insofar as they make explicit the presence of angels in the history of the exodus within which the law was given. It might be that the cosmic phenomena surrounding the giving of the law on Mount Sinai were later associated with the "angels of the elements."[2]

## Comments on Wording

*2:1 pay much closer attention to what we have heard.* "Attentiveness" involves both growing understanding (cognitive aspects) and embodied, social involvement (behavioral aspects), just as "faith" will be interchangeable with obedience (e.g., 3:16-19); see 5:11-14. What the preacher will be teaching is latent in what they have already heard and confessed so that they are to be faulted for not having discovered these things. There is no benign inattentiveness.

*drift away.* The nautical image can have the sense of drifting away from a mooring or by one's intended anchorage. Even passive neglect in the face of clear warnings amounts to positive rejection; later passages will mention more active rebellion (3:7-11; 6:6; 10:26-31), either as a general possibility or as realized by at least some. Here and elsewhere the writer envisages just two possibilities: a process of growth or one of apostasy.

*2:2 the message declared by angels proved to be reliable.* See above for the tradition, and see on 1:5-14 for what this signals about the relationship of the covenants that were both spoken by God.[3]

*every transgression or disobedience received a just retribution* (cf. 10:28). These punishments themselves belonged to the shadows and patterns of the

---

1. Bruce, *Galatians*, 176-78, doubts that any of the proposed parallels prior to Galatians amount to Paul's claim that the angels *administered* the law.

2. Betz, *Galatians*, 169, citing LXX Pss 102:20; 103:4; *Jub.* 2:2; *1 En.* 60:1-2. Within Ps 68 note vv. 7-9, 32-35.

3. Given the angels' witness to the old covenant as heaven's speech we might hazard that their presence at the birth of Jesus was in its own way the law's worship and service of the Son. In Heb 1:14 their continuing service of the heirs is for the advance of this same story. For us to fail to do the same—work for that advance—would be to fall out of step with their witness and that of Moses.

drama of the Son's salvation (8:5), indicating the ultimate consequences of the speech of God in the Son (see on 12:25–29).

2:3 *how shall we escape if we neglect such a great salvation?* The *greatness* of it, that it is *salvation*, and its *inescapability* are all indicated in 1:1–14, but it is the exposition to come that will fill all of these out. After that is completed another version of this warning is given in 12:25–29, which see. The term for *ignore, neglect* could be a softened characterization of what was in fact their more open affront but it is more likely a rhetorically understated way of getting at the immense danger of even neglect. It might be objected that the idea of just recompense, which was just invoked in v. 2, would require a penalty no greater than divine "neglect." This would misunderstand both the seriousness of despising the blood of the covenant (10:29) and the seriousness of divine neglect.

*was attested to us by those who heard.* The term for *attested* is a cognate of the term used for *binding* in v. 2; they both have legal connotations. The gospel of the new covenant—effected by Christ's offering (9:1–28)—was duly confirmed by the apostolic witness (cf. 1 Cor 1:6; 11:23; 15:3; Phil 1:7), with God himself bearing witness (Rom 15:19; 1 Cor 1:4–7; 2 Cor 12:12; Gal 3:1–2; cf. Acts 3:1–10; 14:3–11).

2:4 *by signs and wonders and various miracles and by gifts of the Holy Spirit distributed according to his will.* Some of this may have been reported to the church via the tradition but some will have been their first hand experience (6:4–5). The writer does not encourage confidence in miracles but in the divine word attested by them with its command to approach the divine throne in the boldness of faith, which is faith in the divine pronouncement of forgiveness. For the Holy Spirit, see 3:7; 6:4–5; 9:8, 14; 10:15, 29.

## Comments on Theological Themes

The coming argument will clarify the preacher's assumptions, so that without glancing ahead we can run the risk of imposing alien categories on what he expresses somewhat generally at this point. We will need to unfold this with Hebrews itself, but a sketch is necessary here. One of the cords that runs through Hebrews and holds it together is the promise of (covenant with) God to Abraham, which finally is that he would inherit the world (Rom 4:13) and that all nations would be blessed through him. Over the subsequent history of that promise it was clarified that this covenant concerned God purposes for creation from its foundation (e.g., Ps 8:4–6; Heb 2:5–9; 4:3–4); it was for the purpose expressed in this promise that God had created the world, so that the promise is in reality the inner secret of the very cosmos. One must say that the covenant is the internal basis of creation, and creation the external basis of the covenant. The full vision of what was promised was indicated in Moses and the prophets (particularly Jeremiah 31) but finally revealed in the Son, namely, entrance into God's resting place, the holy city of God, the sacred presence of God himself (Heb 3:7—4:11; 11:8–16; 12:22–24; 13:14). From this vantage point Hebrews clarifies how the OT indicated precisely this. The tabernacle of Moses (and the entire covenant that revolved on it) was a provisional stage in the journey of the promise. As a copy and shadow constructed after the heavenly original shown him (8:5) it symbolized 1) what was in store, namely, entrance of the people and all creation with them into God's holy presence, and, 2) how it would be achieved, namely, priestly mediation and cleansing, sanctifying sacrifice. Within its system its sacrifices accomplished nothing and everything. *Nothing* in themselves, not even partial forgiveness, in that the blood of animals cannot take away sins (10:4, 11). *Everything*, and thus full forgiveness, as a shadow of Christ enacted in faith. The very structure of its system attested that it did not "bring perfection" and that "the way into the holy places is not yet opened" (7:11–18; 9:8–10). Yet it remains that it was God's own chosen way of disclosing how the promise must be understood.

We must let Hebrews tell the rest of this story, but this is enough to say this: It is into the history of *this* promise that Jesus stepped—he took on the blood and flesh of the seed of Abraham (Heb 2:10–16) who had broken his covenant (Deut 11 and 27–28) and shown the impossibility of its realization. He did this so as to bring *this* promise to its goal and unlock its blessings for all nations and the world as such. *This* is the *great salvation* (2:3), since he died as a ransom to set those who are called free from the sins committed under the first covenant so that they may receive the promised inheritance (9:15). It is of course an entailment that this great salvation has to do with deserved *punishment* (recompense) and ultimately with a deserved punishment of *death*, which is met in the Son's death (2:1–16; 9:15; 9:12—10:10, 26–31).

## Teaching Hebrews 2:1–4

1. Some parts of Hebrews virtually preach themselves. The role of the commentator is limited to nudging things down the text's own channels. What was said under Context and Comments on Theological Themes is key for this purpose. Lest in our own preaching, however, we think that application should be "left to the Spirit" we note that

our preacher does both teaching and application. His doctrine and application are really the two legs of a single stride forward, just as cognitive understanding and obedience of life are the two legs of faithful reception that are necessary for progress of any sort. By this same token we note that Hebrews' exhortations are merely different versions of its expositions, and vice versa. This means that its story of priesthood and sacrifice is not merely a convenient way to communicate the gospel to ancient Jews, but a necessary way for it to be received by all. What Hebrews makes clearer than perhaps any NT writing is that the gospel *is* Christ in the OT and the OT in Christ. It will only occasion the "drift" against which he warns if this is not embraced as fully as this sermon requires of all believers no matter what their ethnic and religious background.

2. Christology. The Lord is mentioned only once here, but as the opening *therefore* tells us, not to mention the logic of the entire sermon, it is a matter of paying the most careful attention to *him*, for he is *Lord*.

3. Salvation. The *great salvation* is the greatest of goods: Life from death! The joy-filled celebration of arrival at the city of God, delighting in the knowledge that God's face is—finally, fully—shining on us (Num 6:24–26; Heb 12:22–24). Life as it was meant to be, and *will* be forever. It can, however, be refused and because all good, and truth, and beauty are concentrated there, there is none of this life outside of it. To refuse it is death in the darkest, most hopeless reaches of abandonment.[4] Creation's hour has struck, the way of life or death is before us (Deut 30:11–20), and there is no escape. From Moses we learn that and how this is so (2:2). From the way in which God has spoken we must admit that it has been indubitably confirmed (2:3–4).

4. Perseverance. A key element of salvation for Hebrews is introduced in 2:1, the need for perseverance. Like some other NT writers, Hebrews portrays salvation as primarily a future destination for the people of God who are on pilgrimage toward it. Faith, in this perspective, is a matter of a *life* of faith, and faith is a matter of *obedience* to the divine command that is involved in the promise. Faith is therefore not a past, one-off decision, but a mode of living on the way, and if one abandons the path, one does not arrive at the goal. To be sure, God's act is prior, it is sufficient, it is irreversible, and it is *grace*. Faith is not the achievement of salvation but the *response* to it. But. Without faith it is

---

4. By way of partial analogy, see the drama of Gen 27:37 (cf. Heb 12:14–17). The exclusivity and finality of the situation are absolute in the word now spoken in the Son.

impossible to please God (11:6). There is much to learn about this, but for the moment it is enough to hear the exhortation *lest we drift away*.

5. The Holy Spirit. Though Hebrews does not feature the Spirit on the scale of Acts and 1 Corinthians the Spirit's presence in the community and role in the history of salvation is vital. At this point the gifts of the Spirit are mentioned in language that relates to the distributions of Israel's inheritance (Josh 11:23); we are recipients of the true inheritance. One could also say that in 2:1–4 we find not so much Trinitarian theology as its assumption in the salvific co-acting of God (Father), Lord (Son), and Holy Spirit.

# 2:5–9

*"All authority in heaven and on earth has been given to me."*

## Context

HAVING ANTICIPATED Ps 8 ever since 1:4, and having praised the Son relative to the angels in 1:5–14, when the preacher now says, *made lower than the angels, . . . crowned with glory and honor*, our imaginations are primed—both for the meaning of his condescension and his exaltation. We have also been prepared to see that 1:1—2:18 concerns the word of salvation spoken by God (1:1–4): Firstly, the one in and as whom God *speaks* (1:5–14), and now what he has *said* in and as the Son (2:5–18). When the argument advances a further step it will concentrate on the *response of faith* (3:1—4:11) before reprising the theme of God's word (4:12–13).

We have been telling the background story of the promise in the preceding units and "we do not have time to" repeat or "discuss these things in detail now." The preacher is translating their lives into the story of that promise, having determined that the problem of flagging faith will be most effectively met by getting them to see their time for what it is "in these last days," a time during which *we do not yet see everything in subjection to him* but we *do* see Jesus crowned with glory and honor as a sympathetic high priest.

Considering 2:5–18 as a whole we can summarize it in part like so: Since the promise of salvation was delivered to the seed of Abraham it was fitting and necessary that the Son would become like them in every way so as to make their entrance possible and help them to the goal. Putting it like this tends to the conclusion that although the once-for-all sacrifice is an element, the leading focus *for the moment* is on the sympathetic help for the way that the travelers may hope to gain from their Elder Brother. Both the once-for-all-ness and the on-going help are essential, but as the preacher tends to do in the framing sections of 1:1—4:16 and 10:19—12:29 he places emphasis on the ongoing *journey*, the provision and outlook by which they can cope with its hardships, and the certainty of the inheritance won for them.

## Background

Psalm 8 is not known to have been a messianic text among the Jews but it was an important one for the early Christians, particularly in relation to Ps 110:1. Just as he will do with Ps 110, the preacher will now harvest a bit more from Ps 8 than was usually done. Looking at the psalm itself, from the perspective of the knowledge of God's name humankind's place in the world is contemplated. Viewing humanity alone against the backdrop of the cosmos it would seem too small for God's attention. Yet the God of Israel has assigned us an exalted place, just a little lower than the angels (or, as otherwise interpreted, than God) and crowned us with glory and honor. He has made us rulers over his works and put everything under our feet (Ps 8:3–6). The psalm's lines involve parallelism: Being made a little lower than the angels[1] and being crowned with glory are saying the same thing, both lines underscoring the *exalted* place of humans in the world as God has revealed it.

What we have in Hebrews is not so much an exegesis of this psalm as the results of an exegesis, results that freely recast its contents so that it says more directly what it was always saying—since in truth it was speaking of the Son who is Jesus. Even on its own terms the psalm sits a little uncomfortably with things as they stand, where humanity's place with all things (even intending "all things" with the psalm's more limited scope) under its feet is not perfectly obvious. Yet just as the revelation of God's name to Israel had corrected a false inference of humanity's insignificance, so now the revelation of the Son's name has shown how far humanity has always been from the glory of which this psalm truly speaks and how impossible its entrance into that glory would be (see on 2:1–4). As such, in its own way the psalm expresses the promise of God for humanity that has stood in tension with the situation on the ground ever since the foundation of

1. The LXX translates with *angels*, from which Hebrews proceeds. It is impossible to know if the preacher was aware of the alternative interpretation of the Hebrew text, though we are free to hazard that if he did he would have seen even greater coherence between it and the sense of the tradition as we find it in Phil 2:6–11. In any event, he proceeds from the given wording, which is also in keeping with what we find elsewhere (Eph 1:20–22; 1 Pet 3:22). Granted his assumption, his reading is theologically sound.

the world while it awaited the realization accomplished in and by the representative Man. The story that the psalm actually awaited was that of the Son's descent below the angels—that is, his sharing in the blood and flesh of the seed of Abraham, the heirs of the promise—his tasting of death for all, and then his exaltation to be crowned with glory and honor. This brings the vision of the psalm to its intended goal through the obedient Man, and it unlocks the blessings promised through Abraham. In 2:5–9 it is that descent and ascent, which was a common part of the church's confession (e.g., Phil 2:6–11), that will be highlighted in terms of past, present, and future. Following this, 2:10–18 will dwell more thoroughly on what it meant for him to descend "below the angels."

Hebrews is a sermon, not an academic journal article, and therefore does not hesitate to cut to the chase. In "quoting" the psalm it omits a line ("You have given him dominion over the works of your hands"), ignores the poetic parallelism, and converts the remaining lines into a chronological telling of the Son's story: Instead of taking *you have made him*[2] *a little lower than the heavenly beings* as a measure of humanity's *exalted state*, it is referring to the Son's *humiliation*. The next lines then refer to his exaltation (*crowned*) and eventual perfected dominion (*all things under his feet*). Following this "citation" Hebrews extends the interpretation.

## Comments on Wording

2:5 *the world to come, of which we are speaking*. The reference is back to the inheritance of the Son (1:2) as celebrated in 1:5–14 and the great salvation of 2:3; see 12:18–29. The provisionality of Moses's law and that of angelic authority relative to humanity were bound together in history. The Son's exaltation carries his family with him to the fullness of their human glory and the true completion of God's purposes according to the promise to Abraham. See 1:1–14 and 2:1–4.[3]

2:6–8a See above. The Greek pronouns are all singular, but carry the dual reference to humanity and their representative (one thinks of the ambiguous images of rabbit/duck, old woman/young woman or Rubin's

---

2. The NIV translates with "them" to gain a gender neutral translation, which we agree is justified by the fact that Hebrews seems to intend a dual reference to humanity *and* the Son who is their representative. In our view, however, the recasting of the psalm is conclusive evidence that the intention at this point is to allude especially to the Son and so we are focusing that reference in our interpretation.

3. It is speculative but possible that angels, associated with the law, symbolize the barring of the way to paradise, just as the law barred entrance to God's presence. The Son enters, the angels submit, and Ps 8 is fulfilled.

vase). The chief actor is the Son as representative and leader (v. 10), as explained above.

2:8b *At present, we do not yet see everything in subjection to him*. In this first part of the exposition the dual reference is retained but shifts emphasis to humanity (most pointedly, those joined with the Son as his brothers and sisters) as a reflection of the reality that God has *not yet* brought all the Son's enemies under his feet as Ps 110:1 promised (1:13; cf. 1 Cor 15:20–28).[4] The preacher desires his audience to see the drama at its full sweep, within which the present appearance of weakness—the cause of their present disillusionment—is understood as a divinely ordained season between the first and second appearances (cf. 9:28).

2:9 *but we see him . . . namely Jesus*. The first appearance of this name is emphatic. The Jesus known from his history *is* the Son whom they confess. He lowered himself (Phil 2:6–11) to lead his family to their promised inheritance (Heb 2:10).

*crowned with glory and honor because of the suffering of death, so that by the grace of God he might taste death for everyone*. The obedient Man foreseen when God made his promise to Abraham did God's saving will perfectly and was exalted to the divine throne. Note that the purpose—*tasting death for everyone*—required both the *being made lower* (humiliation) and the *being crowned* (exaltation), for without the resurrection and exaltation how could his work be "for" anyone? For the fuller telling, see 2:10–18 and especially 10:5–18. That he *tasted* death is a quiet but triumphant observation that he defeated it; it did not hold him (2:14–15; 13:20). It is equally a declaration that he, supremely and solely, underwent death in its most complete form. As in 2:1–4, the assumption is that he fulfilled a sentence of death that properly belonged to his family in their rebellion against God's covenant. For *grace*, see the introduction to this commentary.

## Comments on Theological Themes

The angels' relationship to the law (2:2) lends symbolism to the Son's being made lower to them for a time. It reminds of Paul's characterization of the Son as one born of a woman, "born under the law, to redeem those who were under the law, that we might receive adoption as sons."

The Son's descent represents an act of (human) obedience that transcends and envelops his brothers and sisters. It is of a piece with the suffering of death on account of which he is crowned and enthroned, which

---

4. Death is probably not the only enemy in view, but will be included among the enemies overcome in the Son's resurrection (2:14–15; cf. 1 Cor 15:26).

also fits him to be the leader of their salvation as a merciful and faithful high priest. That his descent was that of the eternal (1:1–4, 10–12; 7:1–3; 13:8) Son prepares for the claim that his work is effective once-for-all. For Hebrews, the humanity of the Son is implicated in the entire history of the divine Son's obedience, beginning with the incarnation itself (10:1–10), and also in its effects, including his place on the divine throne as God.

The Son's exaltation to the divine throne " with angels, authorities, and powers having been subjected to him" (1 Pet 3:22) is his place by nature, as the one who is worshipped as God, and it is his by the merits of his obedience, because of which he was raised and crowned. That he sits there as a human belongs to the mystery of the incarnation. The share of his family with him in this rule is theirs by grace, so that their final status over the angels is not a mark of theosis (divinization)—not, at least, in the absolute sense of theosis—but of a reordering of creation according to the pleasure of the Creator.

Capitalizing the word Man in reference to Jesus, as we have occasionally done, is dangerous. Where we do capitalize it, this is meant to convey that as one of us he is unique (7:26–28) and solely our representative, but not that he is somehow other than or less than fully our blood and flesh brother or that his condescension somehow stopped short of its perfection. As one of us he looked up to heaven and as one of us and for us he was enthroned.

These verses also speak to the doctrine of the human creature (theological anthropology). The human creature is a wonder, mysterious, an object of endless fascination, both individually and in society. One could meditate on humanity's exploits of exploration, athletics, battle; its creativity and invention; its courage, tenacity, adaptability, industry; its sheer variety and more. Yet, within an ever expanding cosmos, humanity is so small and fragile; the loss of the entire species would seem to have no greater effect on the cosmos than the loss of the insect you may have killed today. The psalmist considers all of this not from the viewpoints of physics and humanism, however, but the inexplicable (apart from grace) faithfulness of the creator God who chose Abraham that all nations might be blessed in him; the glory of humanity is not innate but bestowed by the covenant Lord, YHWH. What is new with the revelation of the Son is the discovery that this

> "Everyone must have two pockets, so that he can reach into the one or the other, according to his needs. In his right pocket are to be the words: 'For my sake was the world created,' and in his left: 'I am earth and ashes'" (Rabbi Bunam of Pzhysha [Buber, *Later Masters*, 249–50]). Jesus alone could say this properly. The rest because he shares this with them.

bestowal would be realized first in the man Jesus, and then those who share in him.

## Teaching Hebrews 2:5–9

1. Christology. The one who was Son eternally with God and who lowered himself below the angels—that is, left his rightful place and entered the sphere of creation, becoming himself a creature—is the one whom we see as Jesus, the same Jesus who, as a man, we see as now resurrected and exalted to the divine throne, waiting for his enemies to be brought into subjection to him by his Father. He is so perfectly one with us that his identity can be fused with the language of Ps 8. As a result we can see how its promise for humanity is brought to its realization only in the Son's history of salvation. As a man who is our representative Man he did God's will perfectly (10:5–10). Because of this he was raised from the dead and crowned as king over creation, bringing about our appointed end. In so doing, by God's grace he exhausted death for all. Objectively speaking, there is nothing that remains to be done except respond with the obedience of faith, as this will be elaborated in coming units.

2. Salvation. The promise of Psalm 8, which was penned in (and from within) the later history of Israel, is not a more basic and a broader vision than that of the Abrahamic promise, but is precisely a further elaboration of what was promised to Abraham. The promise is the inner secret of the cosmos. Thus, the preacher still has in mind what he said in 2:2 and will expound in the chapters to come concerning how this promise was revealed and carried forward in Moses. The promise to Abraham that he would inherit the world and that all nations would be blessed through him was revealed in the Son to be bound up with God's purposes from the foundation of the world leading to the goal of unhindered, perfect entrance into his own holy presence; this is the world to come, the abiding city. Psalm 8, as another of the testimonies of God's speech in the prophets (1:1) that has now been spoken in and as the Son (1:2), enables us to see how the Son who is Jesus brought that promised history to its goal. In so doing, by exalting the Son over the angels through whom the word of Moses was spoken (2:2) this exposition quietly alludes to the change of law that will be explained later (7:11–18; 8:7–13; 10:1–10). Again, the ambiguous history that we experience on the ground (all things *not yet* subject to "him") is accounted for so that we may have confidence (2:8–9). Indeed, our

confession shows that the present hardships are not anomalous at all. This exposition shows further that no matter how unclear our present circumstances, we know the course of history by which they are determined and to what end they tend. Lastly, from all that is said in these lines we see that this salvation *could* not have come about otherwise, and thus the totality of *grace*.

3. It is to be understood that Jesus' descent left none of his brothers and sisters beneath him (Phil 2:7–8; cf. Heb 10:34; 11:35–38; 12:1–3; 13:3). The prospect of death alone—without family, friend, reputation, or legacy—oppresses the human soul; it is one of the cruel instruments of the one who has the power of death (2:14–15). But in remembering the Son of Man God has promised that he remembers these too, nullifying the world's judgments.

4. Humanity (anthropology) and sin. Not only is the Son the full revelation of God, but Jesus is the full revelation of humanity. In the sequence of history and the canon, Gen 1–2 precedes Abraham and both precede

> We have emphasized the situation of the readers' suffering. But why? Because it is the elephant in the room, including in 2:5–9. It is the presenting problem, the "visible" to which the writer opposes the "invisible"—and because we are no different. In teaching these things we must never adopt or encourage an escapist attitude toward the problem of this world's pain. In the final volume of Rick Atkinson's magisterial trilogy of World War II, which takes us on the difficult journey through the evils of that war, he mentions a small notebook left by twenty-nine-year-old Lieutenant Hershel G. Norton of Aurora, Illinois:
>
>> Shot in the right leg and hip during a fire fight with the Japanese in New Guinea, Horton had dragged himself into a grass shanty and, over the several days that it took him to die, he had scribbled a final letter in the notebook. "My dear, sweet father, mother, and sister," he wrote. "I lay here in this terrible place, wondering not why God has forsaken me, but rather why He is making me suffer." (Atkinson, *Guns at Last Light*, 640)
>
> Neither the Scriptures in general nor Heb 2:5–9 in particular avoid this question or in the least deny its depths. In keeping with the previous point, however, they illuminate it from nowhere else than the Son of God in whose person God took full responsibility for evil and death and took them wholly into himself for us. It is from this vantage point that we can develop a "theology of suffering" which avoids both the Scylla of calling evil good and ascribing it to God and the Charybdis of minimizing or ignoring its existence.

Jesus, but once Jesus appears we find the center of all God's revelation of both himself and his work. Jesus is the Alpha and Omega, the heir of all things through whom God made the world. However true it may be to say that humanity possesses glory by dint of its created nature, it is ultimately and priorly true that it is given in the grace that came through the Son. Here first humanity is achieved and shared, though it can be refused. Hebrews does not openly dwell on the "fall" of humanity but it does hint at it through the disorder that is out of keeping with the vision of Ps 8, and in other ways it echoes Gen 3 (2:14; 5:14; 6:8; 9:27). Because the history of the promise to Abraham is the inner secret of the cosmos, Hebrews places greater emphasis on the failure of that history (Israel's), its consequence of death, and the Son's death as the means by which the promise is achieved (9:15).

5. Ecology. Psalm 8 is a classic statement of the dominion of humanity over the other works of God's hands, but it must be recognized how this dominion comes—by grace and not by any prior right or achievement—and that coming in the grace of the Son any dominion is in subjection to and imitation of the Son's benevolent, just, loving, self-offering journey and manner which were for the life and flourishing of all of his works. Hebrews shares neither the modern notion of a "return to nature" nor that of a conquest of or escape from nature. In Hebrews, a particular man, Jesus, chooses neither with nor against nature but with God and thus for nature—this nature, which it will not abandon or forsake at any cost—and for his brothers and sisters, which means against all that is against God.

## 2:10–18

*"I have compassion on the crowd."*

### Context

THE SON BECAME A man belonging to the seed of Abraham, and he did so in such a way that the promise would be brought to its goal, its benefits unlocked for the other children, and he could lead them to their promised inheritance.

The preceding units (1:5–14; 2:1–4, 5–9) have all accounted for the role of angels in the argument thus far, which was chiefly due to their presence in the LXX of a classic text, Ps 8, but also because of their prominence in revelatory texts and salvation history. It is not angels that were in focus—which indeed would betray their own purpose—but the Son and his salvation in the history of God's speech. That telling of the story of Ps 8 in 2:5–9 by itself flooded light on this great salvation, but in preparing the ground for an exposition of the priestly work of the Son (2:17–18; 10:14–25) there is more to develop. It was said that Jesus was made lower than the angels and suffered death—because of which he was crowned with glory and honor, that is, with the authority and power to bestow his benefits. It is this story that 2:10–18 will contemplate further, culminating in the formal announcement of what will be the great theme to come, namely, the Son as high priest and sacrifice (vv. 17–18). The history to which the angels have witnessed must be understood. When that is done they will make a final appearance (2:16) until we meet them again in the coming city (12:22–24), if we do not encounter them en route in the form of strangers (13:2).

The general thought is as follows:

It was fitting that God should make the pioneer of their salvation perfect through what he suffered.

> [For they] are of the same family
>> So Jesus is not ashamed to call them
>> brothers and sisters.

> [Therefore] he shared in their humanity
>> so that he might break the power of him
>> who holds the power of death
>>
>> and free those who were held in slavery
>> by their fear of death.

> For surely it is not angels he helps but Abraham's descendants.

For this reason he had to be made like them

> in order that he might become a merciful
> and faithful high priest
>
> and that he might make atonement for the
> sins of the people.

> [For] because he suffered he is able to help those
> who are being tempted.

From the viewpoint of God's speech enacted in the Son's obedience: he made the Son lower than the angels and then crowned him, so that by his grace the Son might taste death for everyone (2:5–9). He did this *fittingly*, perfecting him through suffering that he might become a merciful and faithful high priest and make atonement (2:10–18). From the viewpoint of what the Son did in obedience: by what he did *with and for his brothers and sisters*, he opened the way and blazed the trail. By how he did it, *he showed them the way* they must go. By virtue of his history, he is able to *support* them. The inheritance promised to Abraham in its newly revealed fullness has been obtained and what remains for faith is to embrace that realization as both provision and pattern.

## Background

For readers distant from the world of covenant and sacrifice the mention of Abraham in v. 16 and of priesthood and offering in vv. 17–18 might seem abrupt. The storyline on which these plot has, however, been the controlling one from the beginning (see the earlier units). What was promised through Abraham was for the sake of all nations. Salvation is from the Jews. It was revealed by stages through Israel's history, as were also the obstacles of sin, uncleanness, and finally death itself. Not least, this occurred through Moses's law, which attested its own provisionality as a witness to Christ, but which also revealed both the goal and the way to it. At points, especially in Jer 31, the true atonement-to-come was more openly anticipated in the shape of a new covenant. This was accomplished by the Son, Jesus, as outlined in 2:5–9. It is in this way that God has spoken in these last days.

If that whole drama with its script, scenes, and actors is held behind the text we see the unifying logic of Abraham, covenantal family, angels, death, perfection, sanctification (which is to *make holy*), priesthood, and atonement. One of these elements that is introduced here—perfection—is a constant through Hebrews. For that idea along with *salvation*, and *sanctification* (make holy), see the introduction to this commentary.

## Comments on Wording

2:10 *for whom and by whom all things exist.* Note the parallel with the Son (1:2–3), through and as whom God accomplishes his purposes for creation as indicated in Psalm 8 according to the promise he had made to Abraham. See the introduction to this commentary for the wider interplay between creation and salvation history.

*in bringing many sons to glory.* The Greek can group both sexes as "sons," making their bond with the Son conceptually strong, and anticipating their treatment as children in 12:4–13. It is a matter of "leading" them, which recalls God's leading of Israel his son out of Egypt (8:9), or after the exile back to the land, or more broadly on Israel's way to his goal as this runs through the whole of Isaiah. In 13:20 the Son as Shepherd is led up out of the dead. Their destination is the inheritance (1:2, 14) conceived as a share in the Son's kingdom of glory (2:9; 12:28).

*fitting that he . . . should make the founder of their salvation perfect through suffering.* See above; cf. 7:26–28. The covenant of God and his people would be no fiction imposed by fiat from above, but would be realized through both parties keeping covenant—although this was shown to be impossible. Yet God would bring it about fittingly, for his own glory and our salvation. The one of us who would keep covenant was the Son, Jesus, who obeyed God's will in the taking of a body and offering it for his brothers and sisters (10:5–10), so that the covenant would be inaugurated, they would be cleansed, and the family would receive the inheritance (9:1–28). In this act of obedience he was qualified as the offering and as the sympathetic priest who would intercede for them. The word for *founder* recurs in 12:2; it can have the sense of a *leader, pioneer,* or *instigator*. It certainly is used for the way he opened and led the way; it might be used with a view to his defeat of the devil (v. 14). Cf. 6:20.

2:11 *all have one source*. That is, Jesus and his siblings were "out of one," which probably alludes to Abraham (2:16; 11:12; cf. Gal 3:16). It is this idea with which vv. 11–14 continues with a view to v. 16. It can be taken as an allusion to God's family ("one" = God) without disruption to the general interpretation we are advocating; the vagueness of the wording may intentionally encompass both Abraham and God.

*he is not ashamed.* That is, he (Jesus is not named here; the NIV repeats the use of his name from v. 9) is not ashamed of his humiliation in which he not only shares in their weakness but takes responsibility for their faithless history (9:15), nor will he be deterred by the shame of the cross (12:2). He brings about a family of faith of whom God is not ashamed to be called their God (11:16). Cf. Luke 9:26; Matt 10:32–33.

2:12 *saying, "I will tell of your name,"* etc. Ps 22 is not known to have been a messianic psalm, but it was voiced by Jesus from the cross and applied to the scorn he endured (Matt 27:43, 46; cf. John 19:24; 1 Tim 4:17; 1 Pet 5:8). Its whole context speaks to the full identification of the Son with his people, the descendants of Jacob and Israel (Ps 22:23). As their priest he gave voice to their affliction, was heard (Heb 5:7–10), and the result extends to "all the ends of the earth" (Ps 22:27–31).

2:13 *I will put my trust in him. . . . Behold, I and the children God has given me.* Cf. 5:1–10. Isa 8:17–18 (cf. 2 Sam 22:3) was not heavily cited in Judaism, but the context was important for the NT (Matt 1:23; 4:15; 13:14; Acts 28:26; Rom 9:33; 1 Pet 2:8; 3:14–15; Rev 4:8).[1] The first citation indicates his solidarity with his siblings, the second his relationship-in-distinction. The context of Isaiah, like that of Ps 22, is one of public opposition to the prophet, which would resonate with Hebrews' readers. Again, the Son here expresses solidarity with Israel and so brings God's purposes for Israel to their goal.

2:14 *destroy the one who has the power of death, that is, the devil.* 1 Cor 15:54–57; 2 Tim 1:10; Rev 12:10; 1 John 3:8; cf. Wis 1:13–14; 2:23–24; Matt 12:29; 16:18. The resurrection and exaltation are assumed and necessary but the explicit emphasis falls on his death as a sign of what grips the descendants of Abraham and of the sanctifying, atoning, freeing act that wins through for them to the inheritance. It is not merely pain and the challenge

---

1. Guthrie, "Hebrews," 949–50.

to the life-instinct that hold such terror, but death *in sin* and sin's history (1 Cor 15:56; cf. Heb 9:15). He broke the devil's bodily hold, but even more basically he broke his power and authority. The victory over the devil does not stop there, however, but includes the sympathetic help this high priest offers those still menaced by that foe (2:17-18).

2:16 See above; also Isa 41:8-10. In the first instance the *offspring of Abraham* refers to Abraham's descendants, Israel, in keeping with the humanity-in-history that Jesus shares and the story he completes. It is everywhere the assumption of Hebrews, however, that all those of faith are incorporated and it is most improbable that Gentiles are not also in view. Paul reasoned this out in his own way (e.g., Rom 9:6-9; Gal 3:15-29; Eph 2:11-22; 3:6); cf. Isa 19:23-25; 49:6; Ps 87; Matt 3:9.

2:17 *he had to be made like his brothers in every respect.* That is, like *his brothers (and sisters)*, the same group as 2:12, which in 2:16 have been pointedly called the *offspring of Abraham*. He did not become an abstract human, but identified with a particular history (7:14; cf. Matt 1:1-17; Rom 1:3; 9:5; Gal 4:4), so as to bring that history to its conclusion for all nations. *In every way* is qualified by 4:15; 7:26-27. The contextual emphasis that Christ had to be one with those he redeemed so as to provide an atoning sacrifice (himself; 7:27; 9:11-14, 25; 10:10) is consistent with a substitutionary idea, though this is not asserted as such in Hebrews.

*merciful and faithful high priest.* For *faithful*, see 3:1-6. For *merciful*, cf. 4:14—5:10. On *high priest*, see the introduction to the commentary and on 4:14—5:10.

*make propitiation for the sins of the people.* This atonement (*hilaskomai*, only here; cf. 8:12; 9:5) can be understood as propitiatory (cause the deity to be favorably disposed), expiatory (remove the offense to the deity), or conceivably both; the use here with a direct object favors the expiatory idea (cf. 13:12), though the larger context expands this in ways that are closer to propitiation. Verses 17-18 seem to have in mind both his once-for-all offering and his ongoing intercession.

2:18 *he is able to help those who are being tempted.* Cf. 4:14—5:10; 10:5-10; 12:1-3; 13:12. The central section of 5:1—10:18 tends to concentrate on the once-for-all offering while the framing units (1:1—4:16 and 10:19—12:29) emphasize the ongoing provision of his heavenly session and the children's continuing need to appropriate this salvation and practice their faith. This is a matter of emphasis only, however, and there are exceptions in both the frame and the central section.

## Comments on Theological Themes

As the Son takes the OT Scriptures on his lips in response to the Father's address to him (e.g., 1:5, 8–10), and with the Spirit also speaking (3:7; 10:15), we are allowed to hear the Trinity in concert.[2] Eventually the family joins in (13:6). What Jesus says here indicates *that* he fully identifies with us, but also *how he intercedes* for us in that identification, and how he is an *example* for what it means to be obedient children. By the same token we are permitted a glimpse of what it means concretely for the Son to "bear all things by his powerful word," as he actively enters into the history of that word, takes it upon himself, even on his lips, and brings it to its goal (1:3).

Does humanity need to be delivered from God's hands (10:31) or the devil's (2:14–16)? Answering can lead either to doubting Hebrews' logic or more deeply into the atonement. It is not hard to imagine that the OT pattern of *God's* deliverance of Israel to Assyria and Babylon from which then *God* delivers her is only the visible tip of the iceberg that is the true and full drama intended by Hebrews. As such, there is no basis for suggesting that the allusion to the defeat of the devil in 2:14–15 is merely another traditional image appropriated without concern for how these traditions cohere. It is a sign, rather, of the true depths of the disaster Israel had brought on herself (9:15)—depths that came fully to light only in the event of the salvation. It was for this that we needed the high priest we have.

If indeed we take the need of release from the devil's hold as a somewhat direct indication of the plight, and therefore of the depth to which the Son descended, then we probably need to consider here the idea of God-forsakenness or abandonment. It is a real giving-over to the enemy. It was, then, to this realm that the Son knew himself to be passing when he prayed beforehand to be saved from death (5:7), knowing that he was passing beyond the hope of his prayer being heard. There would be no lifeline left to him and no further opportunity to cry out for help, but only his Father's free act of mercy, love, and faithfulness.

Further in the interest of conceptual tidiness there is the temptation to detach Christ's ongoing intercessory ministry (2:17–18) from the cleansing and forgiveness that is described as once-for-all. Why would *atoning* intercession be necessary if a once-for-all offering has already been applied? Perhaps his continued empathetic intercession has a different character, that of encouragement and supply for enduring through temptation and hardship. Certainly the latter are involved, but it is finally difficult—and not only because we are commanded elsewhere to pray for forgiveness (Matt 6:12;

---

2. Attridge, "God in Hebrews," 95–110.

cf. 1 John 1:9)—to exclude the notion that his presence before the Father extends his atoning mediation through the present (2:17–18; 3:14; 4:12–16; 7:25; 9:24; 10:14, 19–22; 12:24; 13:8, 10, 15, 21). It seems necessary to regard his once-for-all offering and his ongoing intercession as two perspectives on the one act whose full inner truth is still hidden.

## Teaching Hebrews 2:10–18

1. Christology and salvation: These are less a matter of conveying truths than telling their story. The beginning of this unit (the "perfecting" of the pioneer) together with its ending (his sympathetic priesthood) is all going to be taken further in 4:14—5:10 as well as what follows. The perfecting (2:10) is the history Jesus obediently accepted (vv. 11–16) for the sake of becoming their salvation in the form of their high priest and offering (vv. 17–18). The effect will be that he is himself perfected and he perfects his brothers and sisters.

That story is embedded in another: He entered the covenantal history of Israel, claimed the seed of Abraham as

In the modern world millions of children are never allowed to come to term. But what is the fate of those that are born? According to a Unicef report, as of 2003, "over 11 million children under the age of 15 living in sub-Saharan Africa have been robbed of one or both parents by HIV/AIDS"; the expectation was that these numbers would only increase (UNICEF, *Africa's Orphaned Generation*). According to an undated posting of Orphan Hope International, "It is estimated there are between 143 million and 210 million orphans worldwide (recent UNICEF report). The UNICEF orphan numbers DON'T include abandonment (millions of children) as well as sold and/or trafficked children. The current population of the United States is just a little over 300 million" (Orphan Hope International, "Facts & Statistics"). Can such a reality be understood? Can we know what this means? Exacerbating all this is a growing feeling of isolation and alienation, fueled by the socially inimical effects of our technological society (see Turkle, *Alone Together*). More philosophically it has been argued that one of the chief characteristics of the Modern tradition has been its "patricidal" impulse, namely, the need to disown and distrust all tradition—metaphorically to kill one's parents—so as to live as an authentic individual (Lundin, "Interpreting Orphans," 5, 12–13). Many types of responses are urgently needed, and, though it is precisely what the modern age has sworn off, Hebrews' message is critical. The vision of a true family of God with a shared history (Israel's), a bodily presence, prolonged attentiveness, sacrificial provision, a supportive environment imbued with forgiveness, and a common hope should be as timely as ever.

his brothers and sisters, freed them from the deserved death they had brought upon themselves, and is bestowing on them his benefits to support them on the way to the glory he won for his family. In this history of Israel the history of humanity and the entire world find their determination (v. 10; 1:2–3). This was the story contained all along in Pss 8 and 110.

Again, 2:5–9 provides another storyline for vv. 10–18: The *humiliation* (descent below the angels), *exaltation* (crowned with glory and honor), and the *final dominion* (all things under his feet):

- The *humiliation* is a matter of becoming wholly like his brothers and sisters, living in solidarity with them, taking full responsibility for their history, acting as their pioneer, ultimately suffering their fate of death;
- The *exaltation* involves the resurrection (implied in breaking the power of the devil) of the Son who is Jesus and his ascent to the divine throne from which he bestows his benefits as a merciful and faithful high priest;
- The *final dominion* is yet awaited, which accounts for the continued suffering of his brothers and sisters on their way, for whom his own suffering qualified him to provide help.
- The benefits of tasting death for everyone, making people holy, breaking the power of the devil, freeing those held in slavery, and making atonement for the sins of the people are less functions of the discrete stages than the fruits of his complete work.

Through all of this the story of the inauguration of the new covenant is lurking (Jer 31 in Heb 8:7–13). Just as God took them by the hand to lead them out of Egypt, he now takes hold of the seed of Abraham, making them his people, to lead them out of slavery into glory. He will forgive their wickedness and remember their sins no more, having "remembered" the Son (2:6). See the introduction to this commentary.

Of course there is yet another story, that of the discouraged and faltering readers on their mean Italian streets. It is the preacher's whole effort to convince them that the above stories comprise the true historical drama in which they are situated and to make it their own by faith (11:1–2).

2. Pioneer and priest. In 2:10–18; 4:14–16; and 5:1–10 Hebrews takes the thought of 1 Cor 10:13 and deepens it: No temptation has seized you except what seized your Lord and was fully met and defeated there, and whose completed victory is now made yours—both in its perfect and irreversible effects to be discovered on his return (9:28) and its life-giving entrance into the present. The difficulty of approaching the divine throne is greater than most admit, but it is the sine qua non of all obedience and the central exhortation of Hebrews. Understanding the fullness of the Son's entrance into, identification with, victory for, and sympathetic representation of our situation is strong help for perseverance.

3. The enemy finally has one weapon, death, which he wields in a great variety of ways, applying it to us directly, drawing it out in torture, threatening our loved ones with it, bringing it to bear on the widest scale in a bid to discourage all hope whatsoever. There is no point to resistance . . . so we think. That one weapon has been cast down and utterly destroyed. It now belongs to us (1 Cor 3:22-23).

4. There are rich potentials for exploring the substance of the *help* provided by our high priest (2:17–18). Merely to illustrate: In the immediate context it would appear to promise courage and wisdom even when circumstances seem to render the promise impossible or persecution and tribulation reach murderous or apocalyptic proportions, as in the examples of 11:1–40 (cf. 5:7–9; Mark 13; 2 Tim 4:16–18; Heb 13:7, 18).

5. All of 2:5–18 was a further rationale for the strong warning of 2:1–4 and can be taught as such.

# 3:1–6

*"If you believed Moses, you would believe me; for he wrote of me."*

## Context

WITH THE END OF chapter two, the sermon has arrived at the borders of its goal, the development of Christ's high priestly ministry. Like Israel in Deuteronomy, the community now pauses on the edge of the land to reflect on their past and future and to receive a warning.[1] We have shifted attention from the Son's journey to their own. The narrative backdrop of 3:1—4:11 will be sweeping—all of history!—but the disaster of Israel in Num 12–14 (cf. Deut 1:19–46) as viewed through Num 12:7 and Ps 95 will be the particular focus, transposed into the key of "these last days." *The setting that requires the theme of Christ as high priest does not alter a bit.* Every line of 3:1—4:11 assumes that entry into the promised resting place requires priestly mediation and a cleansing sacrifice; the whole land before them is "Most Holy Place." But before the priestly identity and work of Christ are explicitly resumed (4:14–16), the story that gives them their rationale will be recounted in what is at once exhortation and exposition.

The naming of Moses in 3:1–6 takes us from the heavenly witness of angels (1:5—2:18) to the earthly stage of the divine drama. Moses was the greatest human figure on the Jewish landscape, but the Son, it has already been made clear, is something else altogether. It is not now the task to show that the Son is greater than Moses, but to understand both Moses and Jesus in relation to each other in history. Moses was great as a servant *in* the house over which the Son presides; great as a *witness* to the things that would be

---

1. One can say that as in Deuteronomy, they are at their second chance relative to Numbers 13–14.

spoken later in and as the Son; the Son alone is the one to whom all glory and honor belong (cf. 13:21). From the vantage point of heaven's history in 1:1—2:18 Moses's name went unmentioned in the single, albeit weighty allusion to him (2:2). We find ourselves now in the wilderness at the point of Israel's great decision with Sinai behind and the promised resting place of the end-time immediately before them. Thus the comparison of Moses to the Son is a comparison of worlds, from the shadow to the reality, with all that this means for the present moment of crisis.

From the vantage point of the entire book it is possible to view 1:5—4:11 as a self-contained movement framed by an emphasis on God's act of speech (1:1-4 and 4:12-13). Within that opening movement as a whole, we may speak of the divine *word* in the Son (1:5—2:18) and the community's *response of faith* (3:1—4:11), though the latter blends both themes (speech and faith) and genres (exhortation and exposition).

Looking forward from 3:1-6, we see how it sets the stage for 3:7—4:11 both in particulars and in general (3:1-6 is to 3:7—4:11 what 2:2 is to 2:3-4). Further down the line, in the comparison of Moses to Jesus the entire exposition of 4:14—10:25 is foreshadowed, and in the expression of Moses's faithfulness we foresee the whole of 11:1-40. The "heavenly calling" anticipates 12:25-29.

The internal thought structure of 3:1-6 is as follows: The exhortation, as in 2:1-4, is briefly stated (v. 1) though in this case the same sentence shades off into the undergirding rationale (vv. 2-6). The latter development places Num 12:7 on the table in v. 2 and carries out an exposition in three interrelated parts that focus different aspects of the imagery of the OT allusion: builder of the house (vv. 3-4), Son and servant vis-à-vis the house (vv. 5-6a), and the house itself (v. 6b).

## Background

The citation of Num 12:7 in Heb 3:5 belongs to two networks. The first is simply the subsequent context of Numbers, as Heb 3:7—4:11 draws on Num 13-14. Secondly, it is also likely that when Num 12:7 was cited as it is here, it was being associated with Exod 33-34 and Deut 34 (cf. Exod 24; Deut 18:15). Other Jewish traditions associated these texts, as do other NT texts (Matt 11:25-30; John 1:1-18; 2 Cor 3:7-18; cf. e.g., Matt 17:1-9; Acts 3:22; 7:37, 40; 1 Cor 13:12; 1 John 4:12; Rev 22:4).[2] A glance at these indicates the

---

2. For Matt 11:25-30 and Hebrews 3-4, see Laansma, *Rest*, 209-51.

unique status of Moses, the glory he encountered and its effects, and the way in which these passages marked the surpassing glory of the Son.[3]

In Jewish traditions Moses was viewed as a priest, and was generally "for later Judaism the most important figure in salvation history thus far."[4] The wider Jewish elaborations were likely known to Hebrews' writer and readers and probably added to the force of what is said, but Hebrew's argument does not incorporate the legendary aspects or use them as a foil for its polemic.[5] Hebrews does not present Moses as a priest, but among other things he sprinkles blood in the passover (11:28), builds the earthly sanctuary according to the heavenly pattern shown him (8:5), inaugurates the old covenant by cleansing everything with blood (9:15–22), and is the lawgiver (7:14; 10:28). His association with the introduction of Jesus' priestly role is natural. At this juncture of the argument, however, it is his role as the one who led Israel out of bondage to the setting of the rebellion in Num 12–14, and then in Deuteronomy (1:1–46; 4:1; 9:22–24; 10:12) warned them against repeating that mistake, that is in the foreground (3:16; cf. 11:24–29).

For *high priest*, see the introduction to the commentary and on 4:14—5:10.

The word *apostle* (3:1) could designate merely a human envoy or delegate of any sort, a prophet of God, Jesus' special group of twelve, Paul, or others.[6] Christ is nowhere else in the NT designated an apostle, though the cognate verb is used of him as one "sent" (e.g., Matt 10:40; 15:24; John 17:3, 8); it is also used of Moses (e.g., Exod 3:10; Acts 7:34–35). In Acts 7:35 Moses is "sent" as Israel's ruler and redeemer in connection with the angel that appeared to him in the burning bush (cf. Heb 2:2, 10). In Heb 3:1 this designation is likely a spontaneous way of summing up 2:5–16 (cf. 10:5–10), while *high priest* captures both how that same journey perfects him as their pioneer and what he does as their priest.

---

3. D'Angelo, *Moses in Hebrews*, 95–149.

4. Jeremias, "Mōusē," 849, cf. 871.

5. Attridge, *Hebrews*, 105. See, e.g., Philo, *Her.* 182; *Sacr.* 130; *Mos.* 1:158; 2:166–89; *Leg.* 3:100–103, 204, 228; Sir 44:22—45:5; *Assumption of Moses*. In rabbinic sources, where Moses could be held higher than the angels, see e.g., *Lev. Rab.* 1:14; *Siphre Zuta* 12:6–8; cf. D'Angelo, *Moses in Hebrews*, 95–149. See also Meeks, *Prophet-King*; Gager, *Moses*.

6. For wider notions of intermediaries between God and humanity, see Attridge, *Hebrews*, 107; Ellingworth, *Epistle to the Hebrews*, 200.

## Comments on Wording

3:1 *holy brothers, you who share in a heavenly calling.* The address expresses affection, reassurance; it encourages trust. Following on from a careful meditation on who made them *brothers (and sisters)* and *holy* and who journeyed from *heaven* to enact the *calling* of God (also 12:25–29), every word also commands them to own that exposition. The language of *sharing* belongs to a network that emphasizes mutual participation of the Son and his family (1:9; 2:14; 3:1, 14; cf. 6:4; 12:8).

*consider Jesus.* Their "confession" stems back to God's own speech as delivered through the Son (2:1–4) and follows the Son's example (2:12). Its audible and public character (cf. Rom 10:9–11; Phil 2:11; Matt 10:22–23) is assumed in the persecution they have endured due to it.

3:2 *faithful to him who appointed him.* Besides Num 12:7, see 1 Chr 17:14, 1 Sam 2:35.[7] In the wake of 2:17—3:1, the thought jumps to that of 5:1–10 where he is *appointed* as high priest. Thus here (v. 6) he is a Son over the house; in 10:21 he is a *great priest* over the house. The Son's faithfulness (trustworthiness) was a basis for his exaltation (2:9; 5:7–10; 10:1–10), grounds for their confidence (2:17–18), and an example to follow (3:7—4:11).

3:3–4 *worthy of more glory than Moses—as much more glory as the builder of a house has more honor than the house itself.* On any reading, Hebrews' wording at this point is indirect. It implies that the Son is not only *over* the house as its first member, but is the house builder; per v. 6, the church is the house. He is one with them, and distinct from them. The Greek wording recalls the glory and honor of 2:9 and anticipates 5:4–5— the high priest who sits at God's right hand—giving the Son a priestly cast (compare 3:6 and 10:21). Given what has already been said about the Son and creation (1:2–3, 8, 10) a statement about God (not the Son directly) as the builder implicates the Son in the same honor. It is a reminder that the covenant carries the cosmos in its wake (1:2; 2:10; 12:25–29) and that "all things" are to be under the Son's feet; it is also an echo of the OT texts where God portrays himself as a house or nation builder (1 Sam 2:35; Num 14:12, 14; 2 Sam 7:11). When Jesus is compared with the *glory* that Moses received, we think of Exod 33–34 (cf. John 1:1–18; 2 Cor 3:7–18). Yet Jesus is also identified with God, whose glory appeared to Moses (cf. Heb 1:3), and it both logically follows and fits with Hebrews' larger scheme that the Son is "what" Moses saw (8:5; cf. 9:8–11; 10:1).

---

7. D'Angelo, *Moses in Hebrews*, 78–81.

*3:5 Moses was faithful in all God's house as a servant.* The Son's light cast backwards enables us to see Moses and his work for what they are; the Son himself is seen by his own light, which includes that cast through Moses. The upshot is v. 5b: Moses was but a *witness* (*to testify*) of the things that would be *spoken* in and as the Son (cf. 8:5; 11:24–27).

*3:6 Christ is faithful over God's house as a son.* The Son over the house here in 3:6 should be seen in the priestly garb of 2:17—3:1 (10:21). He is not an aloof priestly officer, but a brother (7:5) who has opened and pioneered the way, builds the house, and offers sympathetic help. It is likely that the name *Christ* in this context carries its force as Messiah, aligning his identity and work with the prophetic anticipations of Israel.

*we are his house, if indeed we hold fast our confidence and our boasting in our hope.* The ordering of the clauses fronts the strong word of assurance—"whose house we are"—and then pastorally frames the caveat in terms of that which they must do rather than that which they must avoid. *House* is used for the new covenant *household* of Abraham (2:10–16), in which Moses served as a steward and the Levites enacted their symbolic role (7:9–10). The *confidence* and *boasting in hope* are 1) the practice of appropriating the authorization to approach the divine throne (4:14–16) by doing so—that is, by approaching with a clean conscience—and then also 2) the ordering of one's whole life in the church and wider world around that central act of obedience (10:18—13:17).

## Comments on Theological Themes

Hebrews' strong assurance of participation in salvation coupled with its equally strong warnings against apostasy presents a tension that interpreters are tempted to resolve by amplifying divine preservation at the expense of human perseverance or vice versa. Hebrews itself does not succumb to either of those temptations nor attempt a theoretical explanation that reduces the tension. Likewise, it is a testament to our own perversity that a word of assurance given to those who are unduly fearful is twisted into complacency, while a loving word of warning given to those who are complacent or straying is twisted into unfounded fears and "sorrow unto death." We will return to the tension itself in reading 5:11—6:12. For now we can observe that Hebrews does present a practical resolution: With the focus on the "already" of salvation as assurance and provision, and the "not yet" as hope and challenge, we are called to and are made responsible to "hold firmly" the worshipful and public expressions of confidence and the boast of hope. We are called as well to "fix our thoughts on" the Jesus who is "apostle and high priest" and who, as such, is faithful to the one who appointed him; not, that is, to fix our thoughts introspectively on faith, but on him and on his faithfulness as both example and provision. Faith exists, grows, and continues *only* as we hold fast and fix our thoughts on him.

## Teaching Hebrews 3:1–6

1. Who and where are we? We are siblings of the Lord; made holy; those who have a share in the heavenly calling, where "sharing in" is to be understood realistically in association with 2:14 and where heaven's call itself is to be understood as the divine speech in and as the Son. We are the people of these last days approaching the border of the promised resting place. What has been made of us by God according to his free grace in Christ belongs to what is to be believed as gospel. It is "the given," that in which we find ourselves as an already accomplished fact, on which we can only look back, and from which we can only proceed.

2. What are we to do? We will have persistently to distrust the world and our own instincts and understandings insofar as they are not consciously disciplined and remade by the knowledge of Jesus.[8] The world is not what we think it is and we are not who we think we are. We shall have to assume as the singularly true and reliable thing in this world the name of Jesus Christ and the word of forgiveness spoken in him. We are to give ourselves to that activity of concentrated attention daily, privately, corporately, energetically. To do this in the sense of "holding fast our expression of confidence and boast of hope" necessarily involves more than merely intellectual focus but public resolve, proclamation, and life in all the ways illustrated by 11:1–40. It is faith and obedience, which for Hebrews are one and the same.

3. What then is the knowledge of Jesus? We are not to give our attention to Jesus in the way of free speculation according to the dictates of our desires and ideals—even if those are the desires and ideals of an entire civilization—but are to concentrate all our powers of understanding on him as the one who is known only as he is illuminated by his own light through God's speech in the prophets, and above all in Moses. If

---

8. Substantial qualifications and explanations would be necessary to head off misunderstandings of what is intended by this insistence on the centrality of Jesus Christ for all right understanding and knowledge. Suffice it to say that rightly understood this shows all due respect for the modern sciences and all areas of progress in understanding, including with respect to the ways in which all these things properly influence the way we read the Scriptures and so know Christ.

this attention is to proceed in this obedience to the divine word rather than our own fancies it will require careful attention to the divine attestation of Moses as the one who was uniquely glorified by God among all the prophets. We can scarcely be expected to have grasped what can be known of the Son if we have not given our full attention to the one to whom he is compared and who, as God's servant, witnessed to him. This of course requires skill in handling the full canonical witness as unified in the Son.

4. When we *hold firmly* to boldness and the boast of hope (v. 6) we are not shifting our attention from faith's object to faith itself, but only the more resolutely fixing all attention on our apostle and high priest in full obedience and assurance.

5. We are reminded (v. 4) that the Son's rule will extend over the entirety of creation; there will be no escape; there is no neutral ground in which to take refuge. Similarly, Hebrews does not ask permission to include us in the history of Scripture and the Son but imperiously announces that our history is contained there by dint of our relationship to the Son in and as whom God speaks (vv. 2–6). Application is not optional. It has already happened. The question is whether what has been applied has been greeted with faith. Relatedly (v. 6) we understand that a command to believe and a warning against unbelief are the natural forms of address to those made free for obedience. Moreover, the way in which Hebrews coordinates the already and the not yet of salvation elongates the moment of faith so that faith's "utterance" is extended over the whole of one's life. Faith is not a past event that constitutes a signed, finalized contract with God, a coupon clipped, in a drawer, good for redemption on judgment day. It is the script for one's life to the end (3:14), or it has not been uttered at all.

# 3:7–19

*"As for that in the good soil, they are those who, hearing the word, hold it fast in an honest and good heart, and bear fruit with patience."*

## Context

THE SERMON BEGAN BY praising the Son through the lens of christological passages that were central to the church's confession: Pss 2:7; 8:4–6; 110:1. Ps 8 via the angelic witness enabled the two part portrayal of 1) the Son's person exalted over creation from its beginning to its end (1:5–14), and 2) his history of salvation in his descent and ascent (2:5–18). In this history the people of God find their own place as his family. But why is it crucial that he be known as high priest, that being the identity on which all of 1:1—2:18 settled? Because this is the need to which the entire history pointed. The *promise* to Abraham and to his seed finally centered on the *entry* of the family of God into God's own *resting place*, symbolized in Israel by the related images of the creation *sabbath* and the Most Holy Place of the *tabernacle* and temple. This resting place—the city of God, Mount Zion (12:22-24)—is entirely filled with the holy presence of God; it is entirely Most Holy Place. But the people of God are defiled, having sinned, and are prone to sin (3:7–11; 8:9). The promise cannot be fulfilled. It is impossible. That was where the Son's journey came in, entering him in the lists of Israel's struggle. He shouldered Israel's responsibility for its history as one with them, his journey perfecting him as the pioneer for the many sons and daughters God would lead to glory. Having been perfected through that journey he became their high priest, winning for them the way to God, illuminating the path, and supporting them on the way (2:10–18). He himself has arrived at the goal of the promise: Entry into God's resting place, the inheritance. He has won for the people a share already in that salvation by inaugurating the new covenant, but the history of the promise is not yet completed. They themselves have not yet entered. This awaits his second appearance (3:14; 9:28). The new covenant people find themselves in this respect exactly where the people of God of all earlier history were (cf. 11:3–38): They have been led out of bondage (2:14–15; 3:16–18), God has spoken to them (1:1–4; 2:3–4; 3:7–11), the promise remains (4:1, 7, 9). The *same* gospel has been proclaimed to the earlier and the current generations (4:2, 6). *Faith* is the sole possibility left. But will the new covenant people learn from the earlier history the meaning of faith and what is the full catastrophe of unbelief? If they are to learn from it they must understand 1) that this *is* their history, not merely 2) in that the same promise remains and faith is necessary, but 3) in the way that Moses illuminated what was necessary for the entry of the people as made possible by the Son's faith. Heb 3:1–6 touched on all three of these points, while 3:7—4:11 will place almost all its weight on the first and second (impossible without assuming the third) and 4:14—10:25 will develop the third at length.

[Given 3:16], as the Holy Spirit says in Psalm 95, "Today if he speaks, do not harden your hearts

> as they did so that he swore they would not enter his resting place."

Beware, lest you tolerate within you the same heart of unbelief when turning from God

Rather, exhort each other daily

> as long as it is called today
>
>> for you have become partakers of Christ
>>
>>> if you hold the initial posture firm till the end
>
> as long as it is said, "Today, do not harden your hearts
> if you hear him speak."

For who rebelled and did not enter? Those who left Egypt with Moses but disobeyed.

And so we see that they were not able to enter because of unbelief.

## Background

Hebrews 3:7—4:11 begins its exposition of Ps 95 by concentrating on the parallel situations of the current audience and the Israelites in the wilderness

(3:7–19): If God speaks "today" (and he has), do not respond with the same unbelief that Israel did at that time. It then (4:1–11) proceeds to deepen the warning by probing the promise latent in the psalm, its content and history. Because the former assumes the latter, it is advisable to jump ahead to read our treatment of 4:1–11.

From a later point in history associated with David, Ps 95:7–11 makes reference back to the events of Meribah and Massah (Exod 17:1–7; Num 20:1–13; 27:14; Deut 6:16; 9:22; 32:51; 33:8; Ps 81:7; this connection is weakened in the LXX), but unmistakably also to the rebellion of Kadesh Barnea (Num 13–14; Deut 1:19–46; cf. Num 20:1; Deut 9:22–23). The continued history of disobedience following Kadesh is indicated by Hebrews but it becomes clear from Heb 3:7—4:11 that the rebellion of Num 13–14 is certainly in the preacher's mind as Israel's disaster of unbelief on the very borders of the resting place.

Thus, like the earlier generation, the people of the new covenant stand at Kadesh. Or rather, they stand as Moses addresses the people from the perspective of Deuteronomy, looking back on Kadesh and warning against repeating the mistake (Deut 1:19–46). It is into this history that Ps 95 fits, picking up the words of Moses in Deut 12:8–14 as these words wrote the script for Israel's subsequent history (e.g., 2 Sam 7:1–19; 1 Kgs 5:3–5; 8:56; 1 Chr 6:31; 22:9, 18; 23:25; 28:2; 2 Chr 6:41; Ps 132:8, 14; Isa 11:10; 14:3; 28:12; 32:18; 63:14; 66:1; Jer 6:16; 31:2; 50:6; Lam 1:3; 5:5; Mic 2:10). The closing line of the psalm draws from that OT tradition of God's promise of a *resting place* for Israel after he gives them rest from their wanderings and from their enemies; when he has done this for Israel, God himself comes to his resting place in the Most Holy Place of the temple.

From this perspective, Ps 95 is one of the weightiest texts of Israel's history. Its selection is not incidental to Hebrews' entire argument.

## Comments on Wording

3:7 *Therefore, as the Holy Spirit says.* The OT text speaks in the Son *immediately* to the new covenant audience as internal to the "original" audience. It is less for Hebrews that we must first ascertain how the psalm addressed David's contemporaries and then judge how it would apply to us, than that we first discover its subject matter and intent "in and as the Son" and then understand what it will also have meant for David's contemporaries—understanding that they had that gospel in figural form (as a shadow), that the obedience required of them corresponded to that form, and that their obedience belonged to its foreshadowing function (8:5; 9:8). This relates to both details (the sense of *today*, for instance) and the general conception.

*3:9 and saw my works for forty years.* The preacher "edits" the text to associate the forty years with the experience of God's works (compare Neh 9:21, 26) rather than the period of judgment (compare Ps 95:10) so as to accentuate the guilt both realized in and revealed by the history following Kadesh. This also assists in paralleling the church's own situation, they having also had a history of seeing what God did (2:4; 6:4–5; 10:29). In Heb 3:17 he reverts to the psalm's own wording.

*3:11 they shall not enter my rest.* The word translated as *rest* should be translated here and throughout 3:7—4:11 as a local idea, *resting place*. This agrees with the intended sense of Ps 95:11, it fits best with the both the vocabulary used and the OT tradition in which it was situated, and it makes the best sense of Hebrews' argument. Interpreters differ on what the psalmist intended by the resting place, though the simplest understanding is gained through the closely related Ps 81:13–16. The precise wording, *my resting place*, probably unites the ideas of the land as both Israel's and YWHH's, governed from its center in the Most Holy Place, the place of YHWH's throne (e.g., Exod 15:17). It is important to recognize that for Hebrews the psalm refers to the *ultimate* resting place—the city of God, Mount Zion (11:10, 13–16; 12:22–24; 13:14), the place of God's own sabbath celebration prepared from the foundation of the world (4:3; cf. Matt 25:34)—from this mention and throughout 3:7—4:11. It is one and the same "gospel" that was given to the wilderness generation (in shadows, patterns) and to the new covenant people in these last days (4:2, 6).[1]

*3:12 leading you to fall away from the living God.* The language used here echoes Deut 29:18–20, and thus anticipates 5:11—6:12 and 12:15. As an important implication: Even for Jews born and raised under the Mosaic law, to turn from the Son is to turn from God himself. Like Esau, even those of Israel who break faith with the Son have sold their birthright. There are no "two ways." Further then: Disassociated from the Son, the OT is a dead letter permitting endless interpretations.

*3:13 exhort one another every day.* The preacher intends "meaty" words of encouragement on the order of the present sermon (5:11–14; 13:22) and the *daily* encouragement probably assumes daily gatherings (10:25; cf. Acts 2:46). A "churchless" Christianity is impossible. Without what the fellowship is as a gift (2:4; 6:4–5), salvation itself is impossible.

---

1. For all of this in considerably more detail, see Laansma, *Rest*, 41–45, 77–101, 252–358.

*3:14 we have come to share in Christ, if indeed.* Cf. 3:6. The language recalls Christ's initiative in this "sharing in" (2:14) and our share in the heavenly calling (3:1; cf. 6:4) and it anticipates the meditation on what faith is in 11:1–2. The preacher is not trying to make a technical point about proving the authenticity of a *past* event of salvation by means of a *continuing* faith. It is the more basic point of the entire sermon: Faith is necessarily the "utterance" of one's whole life to the end, just as it was for the Son (10:5–10; cf. 2:5–18; 5:7–10; 12:1–3)—this is due as much to his example as to the nature of the salvation he won; his provision and example cannot be separated. Only such faith finally involves participation in Christ and his salvation. The phrase *our original conviction* probably gets at more than the subjective posture; it indicates something closer to the original situation concretized in their life of obedient faith.

3:16–18 Compare 1 Cor 10:1–13. This anticipates Heb 6:4–8, that is, the disturbing reality that a larger group participates in the blessings of salvation than perseveres to the end.

*3:19 they were unable to enter because of unbelief.* Hebrews brings rebellion, sinning, disobedience, and unbelief into the closest of connections. Conversely, "faith" is no mere assent and trust, but full-fledged submission and heart-and-body obedience (cf. 10:22; 11:1–40).

## Comments on Theological Themes

Heb 3:7—4:11 is a key passage for Hebrews in its projection of the goal of salvation history. Notice how the great themes of *entrance* and *promise* make their first explicit appearances here, and how the *faith* of the people of God is likewise first raised in the sermon at this point. The body of the sermon to come in 4:14—10:25 is about to concentrate all its attention on the way in which *entry* is won, both in terms of the Son's already-accomplished entry as priest and sacrifice, which we now have as hope (6:18–20), and our own future and ultimate entry when he returns (9:28). The preacher hinted at the latter theme in 2:17–18, but broke off to remind us of the larger story into which it fits as a key moment. Entry, yes. But *what* is to be entered? When the sermon reaches its conclusion, the vision of *what* is to be entered is reprised in the great climax of 12:18–29. What is before us in 3:7—4:11 is that same locale, that same great destination under the appearance of a theme that bonds together all of Israel's history: the promised resting place, with God's own resting place at its center. It is not that the word for *resting place* actually means "temple" or "Most Holy Place" but that its history is so utterly bound up with God's presence in the temple as the quintessential destination of all Israel's journeying that this vision of the future salvation forms the assumed backdrop of every single line to come in the sermon. *This* is what was promised Abraham and proclaimed through Moses. *This* is that toward which every step of Israel's history strived. *This* is what Moses's tabernacle foreshadowed in its rites that won—imperfectly, parabolically—entry into the Most Holy presence of God himself (9:7–10). *This* is why we needed a great priest and his self-offering. *This* is what the Son has entered and opened for the people of God. *This* is what God had in mind from the foundation of the world. *This* is where he has been waiting for his people, the place of his own sabbath celebration of the completion of his works. And it is that very history in Moses that illuminates how it will be entered: *By faith!* This first half of 3:7—4:11 (3:7–19) concentrates its weight on the reality that God *has* spoken "today"—just as he had through Moses—and that if the community repeats the mistake of the wilderness generation by imitating its unbelief the entire goal of world and salvation history will be lost to it. They stand on its very border! Believe! Which means for "today": Approach the throne, as already made accessible, because we have a great high priest (4:14–16; cf. 2:17–18)!

Another point is important to a commentary with preachers and teachers in mind: Is the Holy Spirit's new voicing of Psalm 95 in this preacher's sermon a new act of revelation beyond what was said by God in the Son (1:2)? Should we expect new revelations given by the Spirit? Not for Hebrews. What the Spirit says is internal to that *one* act of speech already given. God's speech in his Son is an event that confronts us as we move forward in history but never out of the presence of that once-for-all and irreducibly past act of speech in the Son, who is the same yesterday, today, and forever. Any theology of revelation that involved even a slight re-centering of that speech away from this speaking in time in God's Son would cease to have anything whatever to do with Hebrews' theology of the word. Likewise, to tear it away from the written Scriptures, as if they are not integral to this event, would also have us talking about something altogether different, and yet it is just as clear that these writings are not God's word *in themselves*, as if in a self-contained textual dynamic. It is the living speech of God, uttered as the Holy Spirit speaks, whose speech is always and exclusively God's speech "in the Son."

## Teaching Hebrews 3:7–19

1. Unbelief. Israel's history in the wilderness was a laboratory of belief and unbelief, from which we can learn of the insidious, incremental

creep of sin leading to apostasy. A little grumbling. A little desire for those leeks that used to be so plenteous (Num 11:5). We are all babes in the woods. Left to ourselves, we are none of us equal to the deceitfulness of sin. We need our apostle and high priest with all the benefits of his great salvation, not least those benefits he administers through his church.

2. Salvation. Faith is made possible only where God has spoken, and he has spoken "today" in the Son. The "last days" (1:2) that we inhabit are the days addressed by that speech, when salvation is made available. The fault pinpointed in Israel is that of not knowing God's ways (v. 10): ways that lead us into and through the wilderness, richly providing; ways that lead us to an enemy too great but already defeated, a destination unattainable but already won, a salvation inconceivable but now made known; the way that is and has always been his Son. This sermon as a whole is an attempt to illumine those ways—which must then be taken to heart resolutely, firmly, constantly to the end. Those "ways" throw light back over the entire history of God's speaking—particularly with respect to Moses—so that we can see how it all relates and illumines the present.

3. The church is only implicit in this salvation, but it is implicit. This sermon itself is an expression of that provision of fellowship, but the preacher desires for them to involve themselves in this mutual care of meaty exhortation *every day* as they deepen and sustain each other's faith. In fact, 3:14 reminds us that the reality of 3:6—we are his house (if)—is the underlying substance of everything said in 3:7–19. It reminds us that this reality of fellowship is a gift, a work of his, not of ours (3:4; 2:9–10); it is not the creation of faith by the hidden working of psychological and sociological laws (such "laws" are subject to the reality and not its master), but it is what faith receives as already made and already whole, entirely earthly but unassailable and inviolable because heavenly. When faith receives this gift, however, it is a standing protest against all sin-inspired attempts to undo and refashion the good world of God's creation, reconciliation, and redemption. At the heart of this protest is the regular, *bodily* gathering of those who are, both individually and together, sharers of Christ because he shared in their blood and flesh.

4. Christology. It is sometimes observed that 3:7—4:11 makes no overt mention of Christ outside of 3:14 and requires (so it is thought) no specifically Christian commitments as such for it to "work" as an exhortation. Yet when it is seen in context (above) we see how fundamentally

this misunderstands the whole point of everything said. The preacher intends to situate us in a history that necessitates our apostle and high priest if it is to attain its goal. Everything said about the promise itself—the great resting place held forth by God—is owing to the vision of history that surrounds 3:7—4:11 in the sermon. This is not merely about God "speaking" in some general sense, but about what he has said "in and as the Son" (1:2). The Scriptures are breathed forth anew by the Spirit of God (v. 7), now filled with the meaning they always intended as they address the one people of God whose living representatives enjoy the blessings of the new covenant.

5. Without imposing strict rules we can observe that in its exhortations Hebrews tends to place the accent on salvation as future, the place at which we arrive at journey's end. Here it is the promised resting place, a thread that had run through Israel's history, the history which had uncovered both the promise itself and the way it was to be attained. The strong condition of 3:6 is thus resumed in 3:14, as it will be developed later (6:4-8). Yet that future or "not yet" of salvation never presents itself without the "already" of the provision, the priestly ministry and self-offering that hangs over every word between 2:17-18 and 4:14-16. Even the "sharing in Christ" (v. 14) has a present aspect to it (2:3-4; 6:4-6; 10:29) but it can be lost and it is the ultimate achievement that is finally what 3:14 has in mind.

6. What is needed, then, is faith—the "substance" of things hoped for and the proving of things not seen (11:1-2)—which conforms itself heart and body to the word spoken. It does not resist hearing this new speech of God by a hardened heart (cf. Acts 7:39-43, 51-53), it does not give way to discouragement, disillusionment, or distraction, but holds on to its initial enthusiastic form of obedience to the end (cf. 6:9-12; 10:32-35). It receives the vision of the history it inhabits when it receives the promise and makes that history its only history. It does not repeat the history of Kadesh, Massah, and Meribah.

# 4:1–11

*"Come to me, all who labor and are heavy laden, and I will give you rest."*

## Context

SEE THE INTRODUCTION TO 3:7–19. The exhortation and exposition of Ps 95 continues by concentrating on the promise itself in its substance as well as its history. In the course of doing this the preacher deepens and expands the warning. Or again: 3:7–19 has us thinking about how the people were led out of bondage, heard God speak, and died because of unbelief—with the warning not to do that. 4:1–11 has us thinking about what was promised them and is still promised—with the encouragement to enter in. From a wider angle: If the treatment of angels in 1:5—2:16 functions generally like the throne room vision of Rev 4–5, then Heb 4:1–11 (as will 12:18–29) functions much like the vision of the New Jerusalem in Rev 21–22.

The argument of this passage has puzzled most interpreters so we will both lay it out graphically and paraphrase it.

[Given our inclusion in the history of 3:7–19] let us fear lest anyone fall short

> for (or: as long as) a promise to enter God's resting place
> does remain

For we are receiving the gospel just as Moses's generation did

> though the message did not profit them
>> because they did not unite in faith with those who listen

> for we will enter that resting place, being those who believe (i.e., listen)
>
>> just as is said
>>
>>> they will not enter my resting place
>>
>> although his works have been complete since creation
>>
>>> for in Gen 2 he talks about resting after his works
>>>
>>> and in Ps 95 he says they will not enter his resting place
>
> Therefore (given this history) speaking in David much later he appointed "today"
>
>> (for this is not the resting place into which Joshua led the people)
>
> Therefore there remains a sabbath celebration for the people of God,
>
>> for the one who enters God's resting place rests just as God did from his own works

Therefore, let us make every effort to enter that resting place

> (striving in this way) so that no one will follow the example of the Israelites in the wilderness

In sum: We are receiving the same gospel and so share in the same history. Those of Num 13–14 did not unite with the people of God of all ages who listen obediently for otherwise they would have entered. For we who believe even now in these last days will enter God's resting place—which shows that the promise remains and that faith is the necessary condition for entrance. This is made clearer when we read Ps 95 together with Gen 2 and recognize what resting place the promise had in view all along, that it was not Canaan. Since entrance into that greater resting place was God's purpose right from creation, and given the failure of Abraham's seed when this gospel was announced to them (cf. Heb 8:7–13), God appointed the day called "today." (God would not fail to keep his promise. He brought it about in his time.) And the chronology of God's announcements underscores what we said above, to wit, the promise did not concern the resting place into which Joshua eventually led the people but God's own resting place. So we see that the promise remains in force and what it is: Participation in God's sabbath celebration as that which occurs when God's resting place is entered. Therefore—since we inhabit the same history and can see the pitfall—let's do what has to be done to enter that resting place.

## Background

The exposition of Ps 95 in Heb 3:7—4:11 links the tradition of God's *resting place* (see on 3:7–19) with God's *sabbath* in Gen 2:2–3. Though this will be made explicit only with 4:3–5, this way of understanding the promise latent in Ps 95 was built into the exposition as soon as the psalm was cited in 3:7–11.

On the face of it this linkage is due to the serendipitous translation of the LXX, which used Greek cognates for *rest* in both Gen 2:2–3 and Ps 95:11—unlike the Hebrew, which used unrelated stems. The Jewish exegetical technique was a well-known one, *gezerah shawah*, that is, the argument from analogy employed when two passages make use of identical and possibly unique expressions. In reality, once a closer look has been given the OT texts, we find that the narrative of the creation of the cosmos that culminates in God's sabbath (Gen 1–2) is conceptualized as temple building, and the later tabernacle and temple narratives are conceptualized in terms of the creation of the cosmos. The temple is the center of the world and the world's history is bound up with the temple. Both sets of narratives are in conversation with ancient Near Eastern creation myths that culminate in the defeat of the enemies of the deities and the erection of a temple where the deities find rest.[1] The likelihood is that the creation sabbath and the promise of a resting place for Israel and for God in his temple were never fully disassociated. Even though they were never explicitly connected on the surface of the OT text, the fact of the relationship shaped the narratives in ways that a sensitive reading would have intuited if not scientifically exegeted. Ps 95 itself in the verses that precede those quoted in Heb 3:7–11 praises God as creator (Ps 95:4–6), and when it closes with the phrasing *my* [God's] *resting place* as that which will be denied disobedient Israel, it not only brings its conception into closer association with the temple idea as God's resting place but potentially echoes the idea of God's sabbath rest following creation (Exod 20:11). In short, Hebrews' interpretation of Ps 95:11 in terms of the sabbath of Gen 2:2–3 has a deep running rationale built into the OT, whatever the process of exegetical reasoning Hebrews may have followed.

1. Walton, *Ancient Thought*, 196–99; Laansma, *Rest*, 17–101.

Ps 95:11 is not worded as a promise, but Hebrews' exposition is not, by some odd set of exegetical principles, twisting a promise out of it. Rather, the preacher is acknowledging that the psalm, with the rest of the Scriptures, is about the history of that promise. The promise is the proper context of the psalm; a promise of an inheritance that is a resting place for Israel, which has at its center God's own resting place (Deut 12). From the larger context of Hebrews it is likewise clear that the promise to Abraham finally concerned God's purposes for the cosmos from its foundations. This makes the idea of a promise of entrance into God's resting place—the location of God's own sabbath celebration following the completion of his works, bound up with the Most Holy Place—a particularly potent way of expressing that creation's story itself has reached its goal (cf. 12:25–29; 1:2; 2:10). Inexpressible good awaits those who believe the promise. Unspeakable loss awaits those of unbelief.

The idea of post-mortem or salvific *rest* was (and is) of course a commonplace, not least in Judaism and Christianity, so that diverse parallels for Heb 3:7—4:11 have been theorized by interpreters. Among these, there were Jewish expectations of the world to come as "wholly sabbath and rest"; the weekly sabbath as a symbol of the age to come; the post-mortem destiny of the blessed as a place of rest. There are also indications that Ps 95:11 was associated with eschatological hopes in Jewish traditions. Again, there might be links in Christian traditions with Acts 7:48–50 or Matt 11:25—12:14. Some of these strains are of possible but formal and marginal importance for what the preacher actually does in his exposition, which is independently carried out and unique in its contours.[2]

## Comments on Wording

4:2 *For good news came to us just as to them.* The verb for *gospel* is used, which signals as powerfully as possible the *continuity* of the one promise of God delivered to Abraham, through Moses, and finally in and as the Son (1:1–2).

*those who listened.* That is, those who *listen*. The reference is to the people of faith of all ages, including the present (11:1–40).[3] The argument as a whole and v. 8 in particular shows that Joshua and Caleb would be included among those who "listen" but not in the sense that their subsequent

---

2. See Laansma, *Rest*, 102–58, 335–66.
3. The Greek aorist participle indicates this is the case across history, just as the aorist participle and verb do in 4:10.

entrance into Canaan obtained what was promised; what is said in 11:13-16 applies to them, too.

*4:3 For we who have believed enter that rest.* See the paraphrase above; see also 3:7-19: We *will* (the entrance is yet awaited) enter that resting *place*.[4]

4:3-5 See the discussions of contexts above. Notice that the preacher is attempting to *indicate* how in *truth* the OT anticipated all this, but he is not really trying to *prove* it with exegetical *facts*. He is preaching to save lives (which does require good reasoning) more than he is defending a thesis for a PhD committee. By citing the two passages side by side he *gestures* toward the resulting vision for the sake of emotional impact.

4:6-8 Again, see the discussions of contexts above. This telling of the story assumes what will later be said about the need of the new covenant in 8:7-13 (cf. 10:2 and related texts). It is not that the promise of a resting place had gone begging for faith until David and afterwards (see 11:3-32) or that the failure of the wilderness generation had left vacancies in the city that needed filling. Rather, *the history of disobedience revealed what was necessary*, which was precisely the appointment of "today," the day of the Son, so that "those who are called may receive the promised eternal inheritance" (9:15). This is what God had always intended, to which Moses had witnessed in advance (3:5).

*4:9 So then, there remains a sabbath rest.* Rather, the Greek word designates a festive sabbath *celebration*; the idea anticipates 12:22-24.[5] The combination of Ps 95 and Gen 2 is not merely a matter of reinterpreting the *rest* as a *sabbath-rest*, but of projecting onto the screen of hope the vision of God's great creation-sabbath celebration in the place of his rest, the city of God (cf. Ps 132:8, 14; 1 Chr 23:25; 28:2; 2 Chr 6:41).

*4:10 for whoever has entered God's rest.* That is, God's resting *place*. The writer fuses Gen 2:2-3 and Ps 95:11 into a single sentence. The *works* in mind are those of endurance in hardship, works of faith (cf. Rev 6:11; 14:13), fittingly paralleled with God's own works.

*4:11 Let us therefore strive to enter that rest* (resting *place*). In keeping with the background drama of Num 13-14, the preacher is less concerned about individual survival (yes, of course, that too) than the survival of the community, the church. Just as in Num 13 the apostasy of a few (only ten!) drew in its wake the fall of the entire assembly, such is the danger now faced anew. See Heb 12:14-17; cf. 3:13; 10:25; also 5:12; 6:10; 10:32-35; 13:16.

---

4. Verbs of movement are frequently future-referring in the present tense, and the context strongly supports that understanding here.

5. Laansma, *Rest*, 276-77.

## Comments on Theological Themes

The vision of 3:7—4:11 is oriented to the *future* as the preacher paints an apocalyptic-sized canvass of the place promised as their inheritance, the city where God dwells in his holiness (Deut 12:8-14), entrance into which necessitates the great priest over God's house (Heb 3:6; 10:21; cf. 2:17-18; 4:14-16). The resting place is the still future goal of the pilgrimage of the whole people of God.

Because their forerunner has already entered (6:18-20), however, they *already* have access in the form of an approach to the divine throne. It is their greatest need not merely to avail themselves of that access so as to "receive mercy and find grace to help in time of need," but to avail themselves of that access because this is the necessary beginning of and the well-spring of the possibility of all other obedience—just as had been true of Israel's covenantal life in the land. What happens in the sacred precincts is the heartbeat of the nation's whole life.

In this extended sense of a present approach it would be possible to speak of a foretaste of the *rest* associated with this great salvation. This is by no means to be excluded; see below on 5:11—6:3 and 12:4-17. If, however, we wish to hear what the author is most concerned to say in the present context we will preserve the future orientation of the vision as a whole.

## Teaching Hebrews 4:1-11

1. Salvation. For good reason the vision of salvation in terms of *rest* (cf. Matt 11:28-30; Rev 6:11; 13:14; 2 Thess 1:7) and the future sabbath has captured the imagination of the church.[6] The preacher's idea of it as a *place*, as *future*, as a *communal* concern, and, above all, as rooted in the particular history connected to Deut 12 has frequently been overlooked as application rushes in free association to what rest means in more immediately imaginable ways. Rest is a fundamental human experience and is treated by many cultures as a good to be pursued in both its literal and figurative senses. Precisely because it is in fact so rooted as a reality in Israel's hopes as voiced through the psalms and prophets, much of this freer association is fruitful and successful when

---

6. We may set aside the ideas that this passage has anything to do with weekly sabbath observance or a future millennium. It relates to the weekly sabbath only indirectly, inasmuch as it indicates in part that to which Israel's sabbath was always pointing. For discussion of the other NT passages related to rest and sabbath, see Laansma, *Rest*.

it is fertilized with those writings. It will produce its best fruit, however, if it is left in its native environment and received for what it is.

2. Christology. Christ is nowhere named in 4:1–11 but he is the water in which the argument swims, the presence that explains its whole logic. Just as we saw with other passages (e.g., Ps 2:7; 8:4–6) the exposition *begins* with the conviction of *who* is the true subject matter. Ps 95:11 is not even phrased as a promise—it is an oath threatening the withholding of privilege—but the key to all reading is *context*. That context is Christ, which means, the whole history of God's speech in and as the Son. In possession of this truth, the meaning of Ps 95:11 as the signal of a continuing *promise*, the same promise delivered to Abraham, the same promise that Ps 8 already showed concerned the whole cosmos from its foundations, is patent. And because the resting place in question is the promised inheritance where their holy God dwells in their midst in his place of rest—that is, it is *extensively* the Most Holy Place—Christ as our great priest is just what we need (7:26–28; 9:15; 10:19–25). Because it is the end of God's works, his own sabbath, it signals the consummation of creation's history and the enjoyment of salvation forever (12:18–29)—which hangs on the once-for-all offering of Christ.

3. Promise, faith, entrance, rest. The success of the preacher in projecting the vision of salvation in terms of God's creation sabbath in his place of rest—all against the sweeping backdrop of Israel's history, with its considerable potential for fleshing out what the writer does not make explicit—can cause is to overlook that the chief concern is with the promise and faith, by which that entrance will be won in time. Notice that these words themselves—promise, faith (of the people of God), entrance—begin here and recur through the sermon. The resting place is the same place he will later designate as the city of God, Mount Zion, etc., but he will not again use this characterization of resting place. It is potent and unforgettable, but after 4:11 it has done its work. Or we could say that because it is so potent it need not be repeated. It represents the entire goal of Israel's history, as that had been delivered to Abraham in the brief wording of the promise verbalized to him. Because it is bound up with God's holy presence in the tabernacle and temple, as the place of salvation it is completely synonymous with the place of God's throne that occupies the whole central exposition of Ps 110. Under its other names it will appear again, not least in the grand finale of 12:18–29.

# Excursus:
# The Sabbath Celebration in God's Resting Place

THE SABBATH OF GOD in Gen 2:2–3 is illuminated by its own context, Israel's sabbaths (e.g., Exod 20:11), the ancient Near Eastern context (see under Background), and the later Jewish and Christian developments. Taking these together, the resting place is the great sabbath celebration represents joy, the sum of Israel's festivals—her sabbaths, her sabbaths of years, and the years of jubilee whose trumpet was sounded on the Day of Atonement (Lev 25). Of course we must actively resist the conception of the sabbath as a day of mere dour moods and asceticism. The Lord said through Isaiah:

> If you turn back your foot from the Sabbath, from doing your pleasure on my holy day, and call the Sabbath a delight and the holy day of the LORD honorable; if you honor it, not going your own ways, or seeking your own pleasure, or talking idly; then you shall take delight in the LORD, and I will make you ride on the heights of the earth; I will feed you with the heritage of Jacob your father. (Isa 58:13–14)

Sabbath is a celebration of and a full entering into the perfect *shalom* of God—the wholeness, peace, justice, victory, and harmony of creation redeemed to which nothing can be added and from which nothing can be taken away. It is the recognition that in both creation and redemption all is sheer grace, the love of God which has already *given*—simply because he chose to do it—and given all and only what is good. It is the summation of every command to one's own soul, "Bless the Lord, O my soul," the summation of the fellowship of the entire joyful assembly (Heb 12:22–23) and of the praise of all creation.

In keeping with the history of the promise of a resting place, this vision of salvation is one of home, a place and refuge. *All* God's enemies have been irreversibly placed under his feet (2 Sam 7:1; 1 Kgs 5:3-4), and without preference, *all* God's people will benefit. This is a gift not only for the wise, the noble, the powerful and able (Matt 11:25-30; cf. 1 Cor 1:26-31; 3:21-23). In Israel it was for the son and daughter, the servants, the beasts, and foreigners so that they could also rest and be refreshed. This was to be so because both master and slave had been slaves in Egypt and the Lord their God had brought them up out with a mighty hand and an outstretched arm (Deut 5:12-15); both master and slave had been formed by God within their mother's womb (Job 31:13-15). It was therefore a day on which Israel was "to loose the bonds of wickedness, to undo the straps of the yoke, to let the oppressed go free, and to break every yoke"; it was a day to share one's food with the hungry and provide the poor wanderer with shelter, when seeing the naked, to clothe them, and not to turn away from one's own flesh and blood (Isa 58:6-7). For God lives in a high and holy place, "and also with him who is of a contrite and lowly spirit" (Isa 57:15; cf. 66:2). It is thus a day when the people bless the King and arrive home, "joyful and glad of heart for all the goodness that the LORD had shown to David his servant and to Israel his people" (1 Kgs 8:66). It is a day when Isa 32:16-20 is fulfilled.

At the heart of the gift of rest to Israel and as its source was the presence of God, God with us, desiring us to be with him. To Israel he had said that when they had reached their resting place and their inheritance he would choose a place where his Name would dwell. "And there you shall eat before the LORD your God, and you shall rejoice, you and your households, in all that you undertake, in which the LORD your God has blessed you." (Deut 12:7). About Zion he would say, "This is my resting place forever; here I will dwell, for I have desired it. I will abundantly bless her provisions; I will satisfy her poor with bread. Her priests I will clothe with salvation, and her saints will shout for joy. There I will make a horn to sprout for David; I have prepared a lamp for my anointed" (Ps 132:14-17). It was said that there only Israel was to offer her sacrifices. On this all of Hebrews is a commentary: "But when Christ had offered for all time a single sacrifice for sins, he sat down at the right hand of God, waiting from that time until his enemies should be made a footstool for his feet. For by a single offering he has perfected for all time those who are being sanctified. . . . Where there is forgiveness of these, there is no longer any offering for sin." (Heb 10:12-18). And we, therefore, as long as it is "today," are to "go to him outside the camp and bear the reproach he endured. For here we have no lasting city, but we seek the city that is to come. Through him then let us continually offer up a sacrifice of praise to God . . ." (Heb 13:13-15).

In all these things the promised resting place is an end—the end of the journey, the end of resistance; it is completion and achievement. The need, after all, is not only to begin the journey in faith but to "hold fast" all the way to "the end": to attain the goal. And there is an end. Humanity is not merely an evolutionary stage that will pass; the cosmos will not pass through endless cycles; neither reincarnation nor pure physics will have the final say. Instead, " it is appointed for man to die once, and after that comes judgment" (9:27). Jesus' own life of obedience was not merely a stage on a path, a phase with new transformations yet to come, but a definite allotment of time. It had a beginning and a terminus when his story of saving obedience was complete, at which point he sat down and waited. The prophecy of Ps 8 has arrived at the fulfillment—desired but otherwise unattainable in this world—that is given us as a whole so that we can walk in it. Jesus Christ is the same yesterday, today, and forever.

All of this says much about those who harbor such a hope. Even now, how can those who affirm the goodness of that city as a resting place in which that great sabbath is celebrated fail to seek that same *shalom, now* for all people? How can they not be consumed with this mission, which—like their Lord walking through Galilee—overflows with good works wherever it steps? They do not build that city! They do not even seek it here. But since they belong to it they will pursue its peace along with all others and the holiness without which no one will see the Lord. This hope also hints at what their inward character will be when it is purged of all the discontent and vain wanderlust that poisons the present age, above which our imaginations cannot rise and which make the earth that does not yet do the will of God seem preferable to heaven, where his will is done already.

Even more, though the author Hebrews does not mention the name of Jesus anywhere in this passage, all of this magnifies the glory and honor of the one who promises, who is the promise, who keeps the promise, and in whom is all that that promise offers. That one who brings and who is that resting place and its sabbath is the one whom God "appointed the heir of all things, through whom also he created the world. He is the radiance of the glory of God and the exact imprint of his nature, and he upholds the universe by the word of his power. After making purification for sins, he sat down at the right hand of the Majesty on high, having become as much superior to angels as the name he has inherited is more excellent than theirs." (Heb 1:2–4).

# 4:12–13

*"Do not think that I have come to abolish the Law or the Prophets; I have not come to abolish them but to fulfill them."*

## Context

THE WORD THAT GOD spoke in the prophets was striving all along to reveal that Moses's law could not perfect the people and bring them to their resting place while it was simultaneously speaking of the Son who would do these things; by the same word, now spoken in and as the Son, all things will be brought to their goal.

All of 1:5—4:11 has been about God speaking, though 3:1—4:11 brought that to a head by reminding us of Moses, who was a witness to the things that would be said, and by allowing the Holy Spirit to "speak forth the Son" in the words of Ps 95 and Gen 2. God has indeed spoken "today." Unless we have lost the thread, the virtual song of praise to God's speech in 4:12–13 is not surprising but the most fitting of conclusions—almost like a doxology. (It is not actually a "hymn," but is exalted, poetic prose, as was 1:1–4.) It is in fact rounding out the entire opening movement, reprising the exordium of 1:1–4, and transitioning us forward to the theme already announced in 2:17–18, namely, the priestly ministry and offering of Christ as announced in Ps 110. From suggestive echoes of Israel's judgment following Kadesh (v. 12) it transports us to the place of judgment under the throne of the one who is a consuming fire (v. 13; cf. 12:29) so that the renewed appearance of our great and sympathetic high priest (4:14–16) meets us where our need is greatest. The stage has been set. The back-story and the goal of history have been narrated. The Son has been introduced in all his glory.

The central exposition of the Son *as high priest and offering* can occupy all our attention henceforth.

The word of God delivered to Israel had been God's holy presence burning in her midst, a burden too great to bear until a child was born and a Son given.

## Background

1. The impossibility of hiding from the presence and the knowing gaze of God is a well-established OT theme (1 Kgs 8:39; 1 Chr 28:9; Ps 139; Jer 17:9–10; 23:23–24; cf. *1 En.* 9:5; Philo, *Prov.* 2.35), which naturally couples with the power of the divine word (Isa 49:2; 55:11; Jer 23:29; Hos 6:5; cf. Wis 7:22–30; 18:15–16)[1] and the ultimacy and inescapability of the judgment of God; cf. 2:1–4; 12:25–29; Luke 16:2; John 12:48; 1 Cor 4:5; Eph 6:17; 1 Thess 2:4; 1 Pet 1:23; Rev 1:16; 2:12.

2. In a variety of ways, Hebrews comes as close to John's "logos [Word] christology" (John 1:1–5, 14) as any other NT book. Yet not only does Hebrews not use John's phrasing or anything just like it, but saying that Hebrews "has a logos christology" finally proves a distraction. The simplest way to explain how this is so goes outside the boundaries of "backgrounds," but it helps us see both what is not and what is the more helpful backdrop against which to read these verses.

In the Jewish streams that led to John's conception of the Logos, wisdom is prominent. We noted Hebrews' indebtedness to those wisdom conceptions in 1:1–4. In John 1:1–18 this christology is associated with strong ideas of divine identity, personal existence before the incarnation, and the taking on of flesh, as also in Hebrews. In Hebrews it is finally best to understand 1:2 to mean that God spoke not only in or by means of the Son (cf. 2:3) but *as* the Son, and to understand the speech of God in the Son in terms of who the Son is and what he did. The Son is the content of the divine speech. Thus the parallels with John are deep and it may be that in another sermon the preacher behind Hebrews would have used John 1:1's very formulation or something equivalent. In this sermon, however, his interests run along different lines. In 4:12–13 the "word of God" is a dynamic concept that includes but is not limited to the OT Scriptures that have filled so much of 1:1—4:11. Given how Hebrews has presented these

---

1. For additional parallels, including Philo, see Attridge, *Hebrews*, 133–34. Lane, *Hebrews*, 1:103, refers, among others, to *Tg. Neof.* Gen 3:9; 4:14; *Tg. Ps.-J.* Gen 3:9; 24:62.

citations, it is a matter of these Scriptures understood as God's utterance, as gospel; as spoken immediately to "us" by the Holy Spirit through preachers such as our present author; as articulating their true subject matter which is the Son who is Jesus as a fact of history and who takes precedence in his identity as the "radiance of the glory of God and the exact imprint of his nature." The assertion that God's word is "living and active" (cf. Acts 7:38) must have something to do with the way in which the older speech, particularly Moses, is caught up and carried forward in the Son, as well as with the Holy Spirit's presence in this very sort of exposition. *That it penetrates so deeply into the roots of the human person recalls where Israel failed* (3:10). *As such, the characterizations of vv. 12–13 pinpoint what Moses's rites could not touch and what they could not bring about* (7:18; 8:7–9; 9:7–10; 10:1–4) and thus the lack that was filled with Christ's priesthood and offering in the new covenant (9:11–14; 10:11–18, 22)—which was what Moses's rites were saying all along. Once again, the relevant "background" that must be seen so as to grasp this statement about "the word of God" (if vv. 12–13 are to be understood as originally intended) is the history of *the divine promise as God's word* that finally required something beyond imagination if it was to attain its goal. We are on the verge of exploring what that something more is. It is something that was impossible, but we now look back on it as already accomplished: we *have* a great high priest, Jesus the Son of God.

## Comments on Wording

4:12 *sharper than any two-edged sword*. The history of Num 13–14 (Num 14:43) may have suggested the image, but the comparison of the word to a sword also has other parallels (Eph 6:17; Rev 1:16; cf. Isa 49:2; Philo, *Her.* 130–131, 225) and is a transparent figure in its own right. Its double-edge quality signals effectiveness as a weapon. No association with Gen 3:24 seems to be intended, though it would be suggestive and suited to the context so long as the Garden's temple associations are recognized.

*piercing to the division of soul and of spirit, of joints and of marrow*. This is making a point about the total power and authority of the word, not about the "parts" of the human person.

4:13 *no creature is hidden from his sight*. Because the covenant is the inner meaning of the cosmos and determines its history, these constant references to creation as a whole are not incidental (1:2–3, 10; 2:8, 10; 3:4; 4:3–4, 10; cf. 11:3). By their very nature, the work of the Son and his eternal covenant bring history itself and the world itself to their conclusion. See 12:25–29. That nothing created is "hidden" or "invisible" to God reflects

Hebrews' wider interest in the penetration of the Son's word into the secret foundations of reality (heaven itself; the conscience), beyond the merely apparent and tangible.

*all are naked and exposed to the eyes of him*. The imagery could be that of a wrestler or soldier bending back the opponent's neck to achieve submission, or a neck of a person or sacrificial animal bared to a sword.

*to whom we must give account*. This is the most likely sense of the Greek, but the wording allows alternative understandings. For instance, . . . *eyes of him with whom on our behalf is the Word (Jesus)*; or . . . *eyes of him concerning whom we are speaking*.

## Comments on Theological Themes

By its earlier history it was already clear how the word of God was "shaking" the earth (12:18-21, 25-29), judging Israel down to the roots of its heart (3:7-10). By doing so it was revealing what was necessary but also that these things of Moses were not yet that work of God but a witness to that work (3:1-6; 8:7-13); they were copies and shadows (8:5; 9:9, 23-24; 10:1-4). Something else altogether was needed for the ancient promise to reach its end (4:6-7). "Today" was needed. The word was penetrating down into Israel, but it was also striving forward towards its goal in the speech of God in his Son. By the allusion to "creature" and "all" and "we" in 4:13 this history is carried forward to the final shaking of "not only the earth but also the heavens" (12:26, which see). Thus, under the theme of God's speech—his word—the story of salvation and of history has been told in the round in the whole of 1:1—4:13. With 4:14—10:25 the narrative settles on the key moment and work that won entrance for the people of God, and with them the cosmos: Christ as high priest and offering.

## Teaching Hebrews 4:12-13

1. Scripture and word. Heb 4:12-13 is one of the more memorable texts about God's word. Its exalted prose and accessible imagery give it an almost free-standing quality that has accommodated a wide range of understandings and applications. As usual, it is vital that the high regard for God's word that this passage prompts be turned back upon this text as a reverent *respect for its context*. As usual, this might disappoint our fancies but instruct us in far richer knowledge of God and his creation, which then gives our fancies new flight.

2. If we have been listening to what has been said about God's word, his Son, and their history we recognize that there is no escape (2:3; 4:13; 9:28; 12:25–29; 13:17). Nor should we seek or even desire escape, if we have been listening. Psalm 139! The word that pursues us is the "hound of heaven" who loves us, and pursues us with his grace and mercy (4:16; Ps 23:6). That word overran us (3:7–10), but also carried through us to the Son (4:6–7; 2:5–9) who took responsibility for us, became our pioneer, and sits before us at the right hand of God as our high priest forever (2:10–18; 1:1–14). Those who understand this do not hide, mask, excuse and self-justify, nor do they rebel. They stop their flight, turn *toward* the word, and welcome its searching examination, accepting its judgment, holding all the more resolutely in faith to the promise uttered in and as the Son of God. Verses 12–13 are about the history of Israel and therefore the history of humanity, but they are also the history of each of us. In this vein it comes into proximity with 1 Pet 5:17; 1 Cor 11:32; cf. Heb 12:4–11.

3. The preacher is speaking concretely of the word of God as the *preached* Scriptures (the present sermon is an instantiation of what he has in mind, it would seem), as *gospel*, as uttered *by the Holy Spirit*. Human agency is assumed, but its power resides in the living God who speaks, as whose word the proclamation goes forth.

# 4:14–16

*"What do you want me to do for you?"*

## Context

For the thread of thought leading up to 2:17–18 and then through 3:1—4:13 to our present passage, see the introductions to those units. The conjunction "therefore" refers back to the whole of what precedes and 4:12–13 specifically.

Having reached history's end in the entrance into God's resting place and the judgment of 4:13, the narration circles back to the moment of entrance and how it is won. Heb 4:14—10:25 is a long meditation on the history of this moment against the backdrop of all history. We may place it within Hebrews as a whole like so:

1:1–4 Exordium: God has spoken in his Son

1:5—4:11 In praise of the Son who became high priest and the need to listen to what God says

4:12–13 Conclusion to first movement, reprise of exordium

4:14—10:25 Christ as high priest and offering

    *4:14–16 Transition, frame with 10:19–25

    5:1—7:28 Christ is high priest

    8:1—10:18 Christ's high priestly ministry

    *10:19–25 Transition, frame with 4:14–16

10:26—12:29 Exhortations toward faith and progress

13:1–17 Peroration

13:18–25 Closing

This set of limited headings serves merely to enable a view of the whole, and especially of the way in which 4:14–16 and 10:19–25 serve as framing units for the central exposition of Christ as high priest and offering. 4:14–16 is written by way of anticipation and 10:19–25 is enriched with what has been developed in the meantime, but there is substantial overlap between these.

Internally, the thought of 4:14–16 is this:

Therefore (having a great priest) let us hold firmly the confession

  For we have a high priest who was tempted

    Therefore let us approach the throne

      in order that we might receive mercy and find grace to help us in our time of need

While 5:1—10:18 will revolve chiefly—but not only (e.g., 5:11—6:20; 7:19, 25; 10:1, 13–14)—on the once-for-all offering of Christ that "perfects" his people, the beginning and end of the sermon tend to concentrate (not exclusively) on the hard road of endurance in imitation of the Son, the need of perseverance in faith, the understanding of the present as the time when we do not yet see all things in subjection to him but live in the certain knowledge that they will be, the provision of access through our brother-priest, and the central, all-important necessity of *approaching the divine throne*. This dual perspective alternates between the memory of Israel en route, with the accompanying tabernacle, and ultimate arrival at their destination, right into the Most Holy Place which has enveloped the entire city. It alternates between an already-granted approach to the divine throne beyond the veil and an entrance yet to come. It meets the needs of a beleaguered people on the streets of Italy trying to see where they fit in the history of the world, which is the history of God. It has met the needs of a faithful people on the streets of cities of every nation for two millennia.

## Background

For priesthood, see on 5:1–10.

Hebrews' argument works not only with a script for the Son and his family but with a stage, the creation as cosmos (cosmology). Assumptions about cosmology have already been operative but rise closer to the surface in 4:14—10:25, being bound up with the sermon's ideas of the tabernacle.

The oblique reference to this in 4:14—*passed through the heavens*—occasions for us a brief sketch.

Firstly, given the connection between cosmos and tabernacle, we can clarify that though Herod's temple lurks in the background, Hebrews nowhere mentions either it or Solomon's temple (see on 9:1–10 for both of these structures). Hebrews' argument favors rather Moses's *tabernacle* according to Scriptures so as to compare and contrast the Mosaic and the new covenants as well as to parallel Israel still on its way to their resting place. The temple *idea* informs the sermon's imagery throughout, and is plainly implied in connection with 12:18–29. With chapters 11–13 the imagery will shift from the tabernacle to the land and city. Just as in the OT God's choice of a place for his name and the building of the temple awaited the grant of rest from enemies round about (cf. Deut 12; 2 Sam 7; Heb 3:7—4:11), so also—as indicated by Ps 110:1—the heavenly session of Christ awaits the bringing of all his enemies under his feet, at which point the cosmos-temple of God will be established.

Secondly, heaven is that sphere of creation that signals at once both God's continued *presence* within the created world, which he does not relinquish or abandon, and his *separateness* in holiness. It is the place—made by him but not of "this" creation (9:11)—where his throne is, seemingly coterminous with the Most Holy Place of the heavenly tabernacle (e.g., 8:1–2; 9:24).

Thirdly, the heavenly tabernacle imagery seems capable of being rotated from the vertical (1:3; 4:14; 7:26; 8:1–2; cf. 2:5–10) to the horizontal (4:16; 6:18–20; 9:1–14; 10:19–20), being imprecisely related to type and antitype/shadow/pattern (8:1–6; 9:9, 23–24; 10:1–4), or to the past, present, and future of salvation (e.g., 9:6–10; 10:1), or to the "outward" (symbolic) and "inner" (actual) aspects of the human person (9:6–14). A verse like 9:24 can be read as a vertical movement, and yet the immediate contrast, as if a simplified version of 9:1–14, is with the horizontal movement of the earthly priests.

Fourthly, this freedom in the use of the spatial imagery, which is amplified when the sacrificial imagery is considered, discourages us from insisting that the preacher imagined a building with a curtain and throne in heaven and a liturgy with the sprinkling of blood and so forth. In fact, to say *either* a firm yes or no to such a conception is probably already to impose a modern, scientific conception on the preacher's mind, as if he invested the same importance in questions of physical structure that we do. Suffice it to say that it is enough to think that the "pattern" shown Moses (8:5) was the Son, who is also that to which it all pointed (10:1), and that when we arrive at 12:25–29 the entire creation, cleansed and reclaimed, is *all* Most Holy

Place. One thinks of Rev 21:1–3, 22–23, though that writer, too, made rich use of temple imagery in depicting heaven. See the elaboration on this in the introduction to this commentary.

Fifthly, this same set of observations discourages us from assigning discrete priestly and sacrificial functions of Christ to earth or to heaven in any absolute sense. Even in the temple ideas of the Ancient Near East and the Old Testament, the Most Holy Place was a unique location where heaven and earth intersected.[1] For Hebrews, Christ's earthly cross is a place where the heavenly atonement happens, though, again, it is of one piece with the resurrection and ascension/enthronement; without the latter the death would be emptied of its point and power.[2] Yet at points (e.g., 9:11–14, 24) the complex event of the resurrection, ascension, and session seems to be the central moment. In the end, Hebrews' concern is to say something about salvation and the Son, *and the governing side of the comparison between the tabernacle/cosmos and the Son/salvation*, just as it is with Melchizedek (7:3), *is the Son.*

Sixthly, notions of a heavenly temple (e.g., *1 En.* 14; TLevi 5:1; 18:6), or a temple-structured universe (e.g., Isa 66:1–2; Josephus, *A.J.* 3.123, 180–81; Philo, *Spec.* 1.66), or the temple as an allegory for the sense-perceptible vs. unchanging world of ideas (e.g., Philo, *QE* 2.91–96) are attested in diverse Jewish sources.[3] Hebrews' Greek expression, its investment in symbolism, and its combination of spatial and temporal dualities provide tantalizing touch-points for all these parallels, but each proposed "source" for Hebrews' ideas finally constitutes more of a procrustean bed than a well-fitting key. He seems determined to know and to say nothing of these things that is not expressed in the OT Scriptures and understood in terms of the person and history of the Son of God as already known by this writer and audience.

Finally, because of the way in which the tabernacle imagery is integral to the implied cosmology of Hebrews it is important to observe that the contrasts between that which is "heavenly" and that which is "made by human hands" (9:11, 24; cf. 8:2) or that which is a sketch or shadow or antitype (8:5; 9:23–24; 10:1) of the true thing (8:2; 9:24; 10:1), where the true thing

---

1. Walton, *Ancient Thought*, 118–34; Wildberger, *Isaiah 1–12*, 262–63. Notice the cover image of the Sun God, Shamash, on Walton's book and the discussion in Walton, *loc. cit.* For more on the Shamash Plaque, see Woods, "Sun-God Tablet Revisited," 23–103. Thanks to John Walton for input on this.

2. There is still great worth in the long excursus of Hughes, *Commentary on Hebrews*, 329–64. There is a kinship of sorts between attempts to find a strict chronological picture of the end of history in Revelation or a scientific chronicle of beginnings in Gen 1–3, on the one hand, and attempts to find a strict spatial-temporal picture of the priestly work of the Son in Hebrews, on the other.

3. Cf. Attridge, *Hebrews*, 222–24, with many references.

is the model (8:5) shown Moses as well as the good things that are coming (10:1)—all this is less a comment about the cosmos as such, as if it is espousing the metaphysical dualism of the Platonic tradition, than it is about the old covenant and its tabernacle as alongside the new covenant and its great salvation. The problem with the Mosaic tabernacle and its sacrifices was not that they were material and earthly as opposed to something not those things, but that they were by design mere symbols involving animals being sacrificed by defiled human priests within a typological drama as opposed to the actual saving events of the death, resurrection, and ascension of the Son of God who shared fully in the blood and flesh of the seed of Abraham. The Mosaic tabernacle was a divinely designed picture within this creation of what will finally be true of the entire creation, which will be enveloped by heaven, and thus become heavenly (see 12:25–29). If, accordingly, the Mosaic sacrifices were limited to a mere cleansing of the flesh, unable to perfect the worshipper in the true sense, that is, "according to conscience" (9:8–14; 10:1–18), then the greater salvation will not be a bypassing or discarding of the physical body and a salvation of the immaterial soul, but a cleansing of the *whole* person (10:22) and a bodily resurrection (6:2; 11:35; 13:20); the same goes for the whole creation.

## Comments on Wording

4:14 *Since then we have a great high priest who has passed through the heavens, Jesus, the Son of God.* See above on the ascension (cosmological) imagery. This compressed summary is cashing in much of what has already been said about who the Son is, that the Son is Jesus, that he completed his journey, and so forth. It is equally anticipating the expansion on all these things yet to come. It is a teaser.

*let us hold fast our confession.* That is, *to the confession*; see 3:1.

4:15 *unable to sympathize with our weaknesses.* See 5:1–4; 2:10, 14, 17–18; 5:7–10; 12:1–3. Though we frequently fail where he never did, his brotherly sympathetic presence is never withdrawn. Though it defies faith, faith firmly holds to the knowledge that he accompanies us into our darkest failings. This promise stands in exquisite tension with vv. 12–13.

*tempted as we are, yet without sin.* The truth of Jesus' sinlessness is left implicit in the synoptic Gospels. It is symbolized in the stories of the temptation and Gethsemane, signaled by the groundlessness of the accusations in his trials, and attested at points by others (Mark 1:24; Luke 1:35; 23:41). John's Gospel is more direct (7:18; 8:46; 14:30) and it became a theological claim about him (2 Cor 5:21; 1 Pet 1:19; 2:22; 1 John 3:5, 7; cf. 1 Pet 3:18;

Acts 3:14). The association with the unblemished animal is implied by Heb 9:14 though not (explicitly) here or in 7:26; in 1 Pet 2:22 the allusion is to Isa 53:9.[4] In this idea of sinlessness, Hebrews shows no signs of dependence on or derivation from Jewish messianic ideas.[5] Though empirical and theoretical proof for Jesus' sinlessness is left unaddressed by Hebrews, the fact itself is asserted as vital, both as a qualification of his priestly ministry and sacrificial offering, on the one hand, and as his example (12:1–3), on the other. His history is one of simple obedience from start (10:5–10) to finish, uncomplicated and unqualified.

4:16 *Let us then with confidence draw near.* The verb for *draw near* has priestly associations in the OT but Hebrews nowhere explicitly characterizes believers as priests; their priestly character is implied, but he reserves that category for Christ in this sermon. This image of our present approach—which, in terms of the tent imagery, gives access to the divine throne, and not merely the outer precincts of the tabernacle—is generally distinct from that associated with the verb *enter*, which is what Christ has already done, what hope does at present, and what the people of God will do in the future. The linguistic distinction between these terms (*draw near* and *enter*) is sufficiently clear to indicate that through it the tabernacle imagery is being adapted to express, on the one hand, what is true of the Son alone as savior and what is true for his brothers and sisters as a result. On the other hand, it expresses what happened once-and-for-all in the past (his entrance), what will be true when he appears a second time (our entrance), and what is the case in the time between (our drawing near), while he waits for his enemies to be made a footstool for his feet and while we continue in all the contingencies and imperfections that characterize existence this side of the sanctifying transformation to come.

*help in time of need.* It is well to recall the stories of Exod 13:17—14:31; 1 Sam 13:8–10; 23:26–29; Isa 37:1–38; 2 Cor 1:8–11; Heb 5:7–10; 11:1–40. The general logic of 1 Cor 10:1–13 is echoed in the relationship of Heb 3:7—4:13 (= 1 Cor 10:1–12) and 4:14–16 (= 1 Cor 10:13). Whatever the concrete form that help takes, it will have the character of that which brings endurance through hardship on the way to the deliverance of resurrection (5:7–10)—i.e., it enables that which will issue in salvation—more than the removal of hardship (e.g., 2:10; 6:9–12; 10:19–39; 11:1—12:13). That this present help will be mediated through the community and thus take very

---

4. Cf. Jer 23:5–6; 33:15–16; Isa 9:7; 11:1–5.

5. See, e.g., Philo, *Spec.* 1.230; *Fug.* 106–18; *Somn.* 2:185; also *Pss. Sol.* 17:36; Attridge, *Hebrews*, 140; Koester, *Hebrews*, 294.

human forms that ameliorate suffering, is also assumed (3:13; 6:10; 10:25, 33–34; 13:1–7, 16).

## Comments on Theological Themes

The mention of the sinlessness of the Lord in v. 15 in its own way serves to intensify the claim about the fullness of the temptations he endured, marking their extreme limit. Conversely, he alone never succumbed so that he alone knew the full force, intensity, and power of temptation. Indeed, the greater the power of the agent, the greater the power of the temptation that works within. Any suspicion that his sinlessness indicates that he is not really one of us, not really fully human, fails to see that the absence of sin makes him more human, not less, and grounds the very possibility of the redemption of humans *as* humans. Any related supposition that sinlessness was not Jesus' beginning state but that he progressed from failure to success only after struggle is alien to Hebrews; Heb 10:5–10 indicates that his way was one of simple obedience beginning on the eve of the incarnation. Any attempt on our parts to distinguish between divinely willed desires (for food, sleep, sex) and perversions (e.g., to occupy the place of the Father) as a way of understanding what it meant for him to be without sin becomes a distraction both by its failure to recognize that we for our parts have no desires, even created ones, that are not polluted by sin (as if there is a piece of us that does not need forgiveness and sanctification), and by its claim to see further into the mystery of the Son of God than we are permitted. At bottom, sin is anything that is not one with the Father's will of holy love, any disorder in the world or in the person, anything not yet "subjugated" (Pss 8 and 110). Plainly the claim made about Jesus is not that he experienced every particular temptation—he was neither a woman, nor married, nor caught in the swirl of twenty-first-century philosophical, social, economic, ecological, and anthropological disintegration. It is misguided to imagine that he must have experienced the moments of this or that addiction, the effects of a given form of abuse, or the attraction of any imaginable sexual activity. If his trials had not been as limited by his allotment of space and time as any of ours, he would not have been human and he would have been disqualified from the claim to empathy. The claim is rather that he experienced as a human the fullness of the human condition and situation in a world of sin and evil to the extent that it cannot be said by any other human that he, Jesus, cannot and does not understand what they undergo in any particular trial or in the cumulative force of all their trials.

What is accented by the word *sympathize* is that the depths of the human struggle are known to him experientially as a fellow human, and are not despised by him but only qualify and equip him to be a fitting high priest on our behalf. In differing ways we recall Matt 8:17; 9:36; Mark 10:21; John 11:35. In *The Lord of the Rings*, Samwise cannot know Gollum as Frodo does, and Frodo's knowledge, borne of the shared experience of the ring, engenders compassionate understanding; he has felt the ring's work from within and so understands both its power and the ring-bearer's weakness. It is not possible to say that God does not know our suffering. He has taken full responsibility for it, taking it into himself in its fullness. As horrific as our suffering can be, it is closer to the mark to say that we have not known human suffering as he has.

Mercy (kindness expressed for someone in need) and grace (beneficent disposition, if not a practical application of goodwill) capture, and capture without remainder, the unfailing disposition and practical response of the Father when approached through the high priest who is his Son (7:25). The survival and blessing of the one who approaches is accordingly due not even partially to merit and worth, for what is merited and natural is vengeance, punishment, and destruction (Exod 33:20; Isa 6:5). "Faith," then, is the unspoken posture and way of life, whereby *alone* we participate in that which, acting wholly externally to ourselves but on our behalves, makes us holy and the objects of divine favor. Such faith alone honors God as the true God (11:6). See the introduction to this commentary.

## Teaching Hebrews 4:14–16

1. By Christ's "having passed through the heavens" and the authorization of our approach, the once-for-all offering of Christ is implicitly asserted. The emphasis falls however on his presence there as an empathetic priest who reconciles us to the Father so that his promised blessings flow upon us. The rest should be easy but it is Hebrews' insight to grasp that faithfulness in this approach to the divine throne is the most difficult of acts of obedience. It is not firstly the absence of "tangible things to do" (such as would be on hand in the Mosaic rites) that makes it difficult, but the full reality of the direct encounter itself on God's terms. This is the moment of truth, the moment creation was made for. Apostasy starts where the approach hesitates. It is for this reason that Hebrews uses the strong language that it does—*hold fast, draw near with boldness*. At a pre-conscious level, this is what the human heart will not do (Gen 3:8; Isa 6:5; Luke 5:8), and it will be all the

more reluctant when the approach brings it into the all-exposing light of the divine word (vv. 12–13), into the presence of the God who is a consuming fire (12:29). But faith sees there our brother, our great high priest, and knows him as God's Son who atones for our sins (2:17). It therefore not only perseveres but encourages others daily to do the same (3:13), just as the preacher does here. If one does not persevere in this approach, one will not persevere to entrance.

2. It is important to appreciate what was just said for the understanding of Hebrews as a whole. Its exhortations concentrate altogether on the reluctance of the people to move *forward* in this approach, and not at all on a danger of reverting to anything (the synagogue or temple). It is possible that there were at least some in the audience who were tempted to merge quietly back into their pre-Christian Jewish life and society, rationalizing this in ways that may or may not have amounted to a renunciation of their Christian faith in their own imaginations. Even so, the chief problem faced by this audience is not a peculiarly Jewish one, but a *human* one. Whatever their ethnic and religious derivation, whatever their philosophical commitments, the reality before them and us is the holy God of Abraham, Moses, and the prophets, the Father of Jesus Christ. That reality and the nature of approach was revealed through Moses and through the Son. Here is obedience.

3. In this and the related passages of Hebrews the humanity of Christ is revealed more daringly than almost anywhere else in Scripture, not only in terms of his temptation and testing through which he was victoriously perfected—in him, *we* made it!—but in terms of his continued humanity as our resurrected and exalted representative. Reverent wisdom is needed for understanding his struggle with temptation if we are not either to drag Christ down into our defilement or deny the reality of his full share in our blood, flesh, and history. The purpose of what is said is not to attract speculation but to encourage boldness in the approach.

4. This is one of the passages in Hebrews that is like a lightening rod for the teaching of the entire sermon, attracting to itself all that went before and anticipating all that is to come. For those who are not teaching through the letter but merely dipping in, 4:14–16 provides a peak from which to look in almost any direction.

## 5:1–10

*"For I have come down from heaven, not to do
my own will but the will of him who sent me.
And this is the will of him who sent me,
that I should lose nothing of all that he has given me,
but raise it up on the last day."*

### Context

SEE ON 4:14-16. WITHIN 5:1—10:18, the argument proceeds in terms of 1) the fact, nature, and effectiveness of Christ's high priesthood (5:1—7:28), and 2) the ministry he carries out in the heavenly tabernacle (8:1—10:18). Within the first of these, 5:1—7:28, the exposition of Ps 110:4 proceeds in two movements, the first of which (5:1-10) grows so organically out of what precedes that some include it with the earlier material in their outlines. Following this first step in the exposition (5:1-10) the writer pauses to secure this exposition to both the readers' situation and the broader history for which Christ's priesthood is the pivot (5:11—6:20). That done, the exposition will continue uninterrupted to its completion. The second movement of 5:1—7:28 is, then, 7:1-28.

In the nature of this preacher's style it is frequently misguided to reduce a unit to doing just one thing, but with that proviso it is fairly apparent that 5:1-10 and 7:1-28 constitute a running "commentary on" Ps 110:4. Notice how 7:28 reprises the beginning and end of 5:1-10.

4:14—10:25 Christ as high priest and offering

   *4:14-16 Transition, frame with 10:19-25

   5:1—7:28 Christ is high priest

5:1–10 You are a priest

(5:11—6:20 Warning, encouragement, exposition)

7:1–10 According to the order of Melchizedek

7:11–19 Forever

7:20–25 The Lord has sworn and will not change his mind

7:26–28 Summary application

8:1—10:18 Christ's high priestly ministry

*10:19–25 Transition, frame with 4:14–16

There is more to 7:1–28 than suggested by this outline but we will expand when we get there.

The preceding units have accounted for why the exposition of 5:1—10:18 is important: It is because 1) the nature of what was promised not merely to Jews but, through Abraham, to all people required a priesthood and sacrifice that are "according to the Scriptures," 2) the history of the promise and identity of the promise-maker required that the gospel of Christ be satisfyingly situated in that history and reconciled to what was already known of the God who promised, and 3) the slippage of this church required a deepened vision of both the divine word and the response of faith, a vision that would clarify where they were on the way to the inheritance ("How many more miles?"), the need of the hour ("Be patient, we'll be there soon"), and the full provision already made for that need ("Look in the bag I packed for you. It's there in the back seat. But if you don't quit complaining we'll leave you at the next truck stop"). The preacher's chosen strategy has been to take the church's existing confession with its built-in proof-texts of Pss 2, 8, 110, and Jer 31 (among other things) and unfold its latent potentials.

Within 5:1–10 the thought runs as follows:

The qualifications of the true priest are known from the Scriptures concerning the Aaronic priesthood.

    According to these criteria the Messiah was designated "priest"
    by the one who called him Son,

        who (the Son)

            having offered prayers to the one who could save
            him from death

> and having been heard due to his reverence
>
> and although he was Son
>
> learned obedience from what he suffered
>
> and (as a result)
>
>> having been perfected
>
> became the cause of an eternal salvation for those who obey him
>
>> having been designated high priest according to the order of Melchizedek

## Background

Ps 110:1 was widely utilized by the earliest Christians, but no other NT writer does anything with Ps 110:4 (unless Rom 11:29 echoes it) or the figure of Melchizedek. Likewise, there are plenty of priestly characterizations of Jesus elsewhere in the NT (e.g., Matt 8:3–4; 10:32; John 14:16; Rom 8:34; 1 John 2:1; or again, Mark 10:45; Rom 3:25; 8:3; 1 Cor 5:7; Gal 2:20; 1 Pet 2:24; 1 John 2:2; yet again, Rev 1:13),[1] but no other NT writer calls him a priest. There was a great deal of speculation about Melchizedek in Judaism, particularly among the writings found at Qumran, but it is not (in the texts we possess) connected to Ps 110:4, and the latter verse's priestly idea had no significant part in messianic hopes (for further on Melchizedek, see on 7:1–10). It is *possible* that the preacher was the first to wed the priestly identity of Jesus already present in the Christian traditions to Ps 110:4. The way he does so does not stray an inch from the established trajectory of the gospel and the known identity of Christ but it does enable us to "meet him again for the first time."

Apart from Ps 110 and Gen 14, Hebrews' argument relies on the continuities and discontinuities with the Aaronic priesthood. It is the understanding of the discontinuities that Melchizedek facilitates on the way to Jer 31. The continuities with the Levite Aaron, however, are necessary and basic, beginning with 5:1–4 and running pervasively through to 10:18.

Within the OT Ps 110 echoes patterns found outside Israel—particularly in the Canaanite setting of Melchizedek (Gen 14:18–20)—of a combination of the priesthood and kingship in a single figure. Within Israel itself,

---

1. Fletcher-Louis, "High Priestly Messiah: Part 1," 155–75, and "High Priestly Messiah: Part 2," 57–79; Perrin, *Jesus the Priest*.

however, these appointments belonged to separate tribes, Levi and Judah. Though Israelite kings involved themselves in priestly functions—which is what Ps 110:4 presumably had in view—they were emphatically not priests in the full sense. From the time of David the high priesthood belonged to the Aaronic line of Zadok. It is important to note the firm promises of the permanence of these tribal appointments within the OT (Ezek 40-48; Jer 31:14-22, though the latter was probably missing from Hebrews' LXX), promises that must be reflected in Hebrews in the way that Christ's priesthood is continuous with the Levitical-Aaronic office as perfection to shadow. Hebrews is too literate and too honest to have been sweeping these under the rug.[2]

During the period of the Second Temple (see on 9:1-10), particularly from the Maccabees on (see on 11:32-40), the Jewish high priesthood disintegrated in corruption and political wrangling. By the first century AD the high priesthood of Jerusalem was a hollow shell with no connection to Zadok and completely beholden to the powers of the Roman state. With the destruction of the temple in AD 70 its function came to an end. Though Hebrews was probably written to an audience far from Judea (likely prior to AD 70) and though it makes no reference to the temple there, it is possible that this history contributed to the appeal of a faithful high priest duly appointed by God.

During this same period of the institution's disintegration, clouds of speculation grew up related to the past priesthood (e.g., Philo's allegorical reading of Moses in *Fug.* 108-9 and *Somn.* 1.215),[3] present (e.g., a heavenly priesthood), and future (e.g., the expectation of a future priestly figure of messianic character). There is evidence that some in the Maccabean line attempted to justify the arrogation to themselves of both the kingship (though they were Levites) and the high priesthood (they were not of Zadok) by appeal to Ps 110. Some messianic texts seem to show signs of opposition to this very abuse, speaking of two messiahs, a priestly one and a kingly one. Yet other messianic texts meld the offices. Yet again, there were ideas of heavenly liturgies involving angels in priestly roles, which some think to be closer to what is in Hebrews than the alternatives.[4]

Naturally, when all of these disparate lines of speculation revolve within the same society around the same institution and the same Scriptures

---

2. Zech 6:13 is interesting but Hebrews makes little more than a glancing allusion, if at all, to this possible union of priestly and royal prerogatives. Bruce, *Epistle to the Hebrews*, 124-25 n. 33 concludes that two different persons are in view in Zechariah; likewise, Smith, *Micah-Malachi*, 218-19.

3. See Attridge, *Hebrews*, 100; Ellingworth, *Epistle to the Hebrews*, 45-48.

4. Mason, '*You are a Priest Forever*'; Attridge, *Hebrews*, 97-103, 146-47, 192-95.

and when the lines of speculation share other ideas such as that of a heavenly temple, there will be various points of similarity. History is crowding them through a narrow conceptual neck. Not least, the angelic liturgy is suggestive in comparisons with Hebrews. Yet parallels are not automatically signs of derivation,[5] and Hebrews' sources seem chiefly to be 1) the inherited traditions of the gospel concerning the Son who is Jesus, and 2) the OT Scriptures themselves. There are no signs that the preacher is trying to correct deviant understandings of Christ as high priest and no clear indications that he was assuming specific knowledge of these other traditions or engaging them in conversation. Exodus 25:40 (Heb 8:5) and Moses's status (3:1–6) established the Aaronic priesthood as the divinely authorized witness, a copy and shadow of the heavenly original which was Christ. It was only a shadow, but it *was* a shadow. Jeremiah 31 had spoken of a new covenant, which meant a change of law. Psalm 110:4 with Gen 14:18–20 and Ps 110:1—within the context of the received gospel and these other OT texts—supplied another critical element to this story.

Jesus is not remembered as having called himself a priest nor do other NT writers do so, while, as we noted, he plays the part of a priest and is depicted in priestly terms both in the gospels and other NT writings. This is true to such a degree that it warrants the question as to whether this identification originated in the aims of Jesus himself during "the days of his flesh."[6] One may conclude that the balance of probability is that Jesus must have known what he was about in this, conceivably including in his use of Psalm 110, whether or not his followers fully appreciated the implications before Hebrews. One may also conclude that Jesus, under the guidance of the Spirit, with or without his own full or partial comprehension, conformed to a pattern of conduct that was consistent with the truth of the identity, though the designation awaited the divine pronouncement, since "no one takes this honor for himself" (Heb 5:4–5). (Of course, one could also propose that Jesus stumbled into this pattern in ignorance, and that is the whole explanation.) What is most doubtful is that the different NT writers would have on their own authority contrived the image of Christ as priest without naming him as such. Such a subtle stratagem could be laid at the feet of a single writer, but only a conspiracy theorist would lay it at the feet of the separate authors of the gospels and Paul, to name only these. It is more likely that Jesus' life itself indelibly inscribed the pattern on the tradition. It was only a matter of time before the direct identification forced itself into the open.

---

5. Note, for example, Attridge, "Epilogue," 297–307 [299].

6. See Perrin, *Jesus the Priest*, whose work has catalyzed these reflections and to whom, as concerns myself, any credit for insight belongs

## Comments on Wording

**5:1–4** As he does elsewhere (7:1–3; 9:1–7) a quick summary of the OT material sets up an exposition. The summary is built on what preceded and anticipates where this argument is going, so it lets some of that context do the heavy lifting. The preacher had what we are now hearing in mind when he was developing the earlier passages (see further comments below).

**5:1** *from among men*. The writer is not talking about human priesthoods in general, but the Aaronic priesthood as the divinely fashioned copy and shadow. The word *men* in this sentence accordingly connotes family (7:5) and, as such, where the Son is concerned, pointedly indicates the need of a *human* representative from among the children of Abraham (2:10–14). In 7:28, which echoes these verses, there will be a note of distinction added in Christ's case, for he is the Son in the sense of 1:1–13.

**5:2** *deal gently*. Cf. Num 14:5; 16:22; also Num 12:3, related to Moses. The Greek word is built on the same stem as *sympathize* (4:15) and recalls what was said there, though the meaning differs. The *wayward* and *ignorant* people recall 3:10, for which a priest is provision so that there is hope of arriving at the resting place.

*beset with weakness*. In the sense of engendering empathy and gentleness, this parallels Christ (2:17–18; 4:15), but in the sense of the Aaronic priests' failings (5:3; cf. Exod 32:24; Zech 3:3–9) it distinguishes him from them (7:28).

**5:4–5** *no one takes this honor . . . did not exalt himself to be made a high priest*. The honor-glory pairing carries the narrative of the descent, the sharing in blood and flesh with his fellow Abrahamic children, and its perfecting suffering, *because of which* he was crowned with glory and honor (2:5–18). It also signals the copy-perfection relationship with Moses's witness (3:3). *Christ* is likely here *the Christ/Messiah*, underlining the relationship to the prophets and especially Moses (1:1).

**5:5–6** Ps 110:3 in the LXX made its own allusion to sonship (*from the womb, before Morning-star, I brought you forth*), but the pairing of Pss 2:7 and 110:4 has the advantage of recalling the whole presentation of 1:5–13, merely adjusting Ps 110:1 to 110:4.[7] At a stroke this tells us of not only the *fact* of the Son's appointment but his history, qualifications, and authorization as high priest. Verses 4–6 also make a strength of an apparent weakness: There is no tradition of Christ's having claimed the priesthood for himself. For good reason this is so. Had he done so, he would have disqualified himself. He is priest by an oracular declaration (Ps 110:4 is addressed to the

---

7. Does it also recall the beginning (Luke 3:22) and end (Luke 20:41–44) of the gospel narrative?

same individual as 110:1, which Christ explicitly applied to himself) that corresponds to the truth of his identity and history. The psalm itself speaks only of being a *priest*, but as the Son that he is, as being appointed forever, as being alone in his order, and as doing and effecting what he has, he cannot but be the *high* priest.

5:7–10 In 2:5–9 he was crowned with glory and honor *because of the suffering of death*, both as a matter of obedience and perfecting. That logic was signaled by the use of glory-honor in 5:4–5 and is now made explicit.

5:7 *offered up prayers* etc. The having-been-perfected nature of Christ's priesthood is rooted in his total share in the human situation, helpless without God's deliverance, while his priestly representation was already at work in this *offering* (5:1; cf. 13:15) during his life on earth.[8] It is evident that for Hebrews, not least from 10:5–10 (cf. 2:5–18; 9:15; 12:2–3), the Son's prayers for deliverance were not for his own sake alone.

*he was heard*. The resurrection and exaltation were the answer. This passage becomes the key to understanding all prayers for deliverance and promises of blessing (e.g., Pss 34:4–10, 17, 19–20, 22; 37:4) all of which are coupled with the assurance that God does not lie. No prayer is answered outside of first being answered in our pioneer.

5:8 *Although he was a son, he learned obedience*. The reference is not to sonship as such, as if being a true son would naturally involve obedience, which is generally true, but to *the* Son that he was as known from 1:1—2:18, and who himself chose the existence (10:5–10) within which it would be possible for it to be said with authenticity that he *learned* obedience. This *learning* is not a charade any more than his sharing in the blood and flesh of Abraham's seed is a mere appearance (Docetism), though given 10:5–10 we cannot imagine progress from partial (faltering) success to full success in obedience.

5:9 *being made perfect*. See 2:10–18 and the introduction of this commentary. At this point this is a statement of fact whose timing is as hard to pin down as ever in this epistle beyond the complex moment of death, resurrection, exaltation, and session.

*source of eternal salvation to all who obey him*. His once-for-all provision, on the one hand, and his example as pioneer, on the other, are integrated in the one who is Lord with all things under his feet.

5:10 *designated by God*. He did not take the honor on himself, but received it from God who glorified him in recognition of who and what he was in fact. In literary terms this line closes 5:1–10 and marks the spot to

---

8. Attridge, *Hebrews*, 146–47.

which the sermon will return in 7:1, following the extended warning and encouragement of 5:11—6:20.

## Comments on Theological Themes

Being "chosen from among men" (5:1; "men" here = human beings) in the sense intended for the Son—requiring that he share in the humanity of the children (2:10-16) so as to effect the benefits he did—states a necessary condition but not a sufficient one for being the priest he is. If he had been merely human with his fellow children—if God had merely chosen a child of Abraham—he would have been no more suited than they to act as pioneer (see 7:26-28). Accordingly we understand that the whole story of 1:5—2:18 (10:5-10) is assumed in 5:1-4, which is why the preacher adds to v. 1 the words that would be superfluous in application to the sons of Aaron: "chosen from among men (*anthrōpoi*, men, humans)." The Son, who was already Son, had actively to share in their blood and flesh.

Was the Son's history *determined* by the prior givens of creation and the Aaronic priesthood? The question is instructive for understanding Hebrews' argument. The NT makes it doubtful that God found his hands unexpectedly tied by the nature of his creation, forcing the measure of the incarnation if the ship was to be righted. It prefers to speak of our being chosen in Christ before the creation of the world (Eph 1:4; 2 Tim 1:9; cf. John 17:24; 1 Pet 1:20), and of all things being created through him and unto him (Col 1:16; cf. Heb 1:2). What Hebrews for its part does is not only subject the history of all humanity to the Son's history (2:5-9) but it reveals him to be the sole human who not only chose obedience once in existence *but as Son chose to enter into human existence, take to himself the human situation, and take full responsibility for his fellow children as an act of obedience* (10:5-10). Of no other man or woman *could* this be said. As such, his obedience as a human is unequaled and could not be equaled, his status as a human is necessarily first among his fellow children, and his identity as their representative is simply a fact of their created existence. In this light, humanity that accepts his representation in faith cannot claim to have been

> "Man's maker was made man that He, Ruler of the stars, might nurse at His mother's breast; that the Bread might hunger, the Fountain thirst, the Light sleep, the Way be tired on its journey; that Truth might be accused of false witness, the Teacher be beaten with whips, the Foundation be suspended on wood; that Strength might grow weak; that the Healer might be wounded; that Life might die."
>
> —Augustine (*Sermons* 191.1)

unfairly "thrown" into existence with all its consequences, much less renounce that existence. Its existence was self-chosen as an act of obedience unreservedly at one with the Creator's will. Conversely, because he chose this and saw it through, our own creation is just and our hope is secure.

Is Christ a priest? He is not remembered for having made the claim, nor is there a record of others having assigned the title to him. It may be that this combined with his tribal lineage seemed too great an obstacle to outright identification (7:13–14), though the tradition preserved all the ways in which he acted the part and all but gave him the title (see the Background, above). Like "the other disciple" of John 20:4–5 who arrived at the tomb and looked in but did not enter, the other NT writers regarded him in priestly fashion but did not name as him such. But the preacher of Hebrews, like Peter, made bold to go right in. The key was Ps 110:4, and with it the door opened to a treasury of understanding (see the introduction to this commentary). By no less than an oracle of the Lord he was declared priest, and, once this insight was admitted and integrated with Exod 25:40, Jer 31:31–34, and the like, it would be possible to turn the question on its head. Is he a priest? He is *the* priest, the heavenly pattern shown Moses. Rather, were those of Aaron priests? Yes, but only as copies and shadows, and as such they witnessed to what would be true in him.

God's hands were not tied by creation and its history. The initiative was his. The historical-cultural cultic givens of the Israelites' Mesopotamian-Egyptian-Canaanite context, givens forged by sinful hands, became the idiom through which (in the sinful hands of Israel) the God of Israel truthfully revealed and worked what was prior to those givens. He did this through the Mosaic tabernacle. The manner of this act of God is unreserved, unrepentant, and its results fixed—above which and beyond which we cannot get to a deeper, non-cultic grasp of these realities, once we have known them in the Son.

## Teaching Hebrews 5:1–10

1. The Son has been appointed as priest. There is the fact of it and the who of it. That he has been appointed puts beyond dispute that priestly mediation is necessary; what is said about all this in Hebrews is not merely creative theological rhetoric but ontology. That he has been appointed establishes that no other priest is possible. That he has been appointed reveals what a priest finally is and does. That he has been appointed reveals why mediation was necessary and its sheer impossibility outside of what actually took place and outside of who he is.

2. Moderns have to do with the same reality that faced Israel in the holiness of God and the promise of entrance into his presence, though our modernist culture's governing categories are ill-suited to receive or understand these things. As moderns we can put Uzzah's death (2 Sam 6:6–7) on a chart but we cannot account for its cause. No culture, including that of antiquity, can comprehend this reality. It was in order to reveal this whole reality that the Mosaic law gave Israel her tabernacle, priesthood, its rites, and God's presence (his *Shekinah*). Lest, however, we feel handicapped by the parochial narrowness of the modern reduction of what can be known to what is known scientifically we should remember that what they had in all those things was but the shadows and what we now have in the Son is the reality (8:5; 9:23–24; 10:1–4; cf. 1 Pet 1:10–12). We scarcely have grounds to consider ourselves interpretively cheated! Hebrews itself blocks off both the desire and the possibility of a return to that earlier form of revelation. Moreover, at this very point the writer's decision to ground his appeal in the *inscripturated word* of Moses places us just as near those shadows as any Jewish reader of antiquity. What will be somewhat uniquely required of moderns will be a measure of openness to what is being revealed, a disciplined resolve to suspend belief in the creeds of atheism and deism that systemically shape our inner and outer worlds. In short, to think of Hebrews' talk of priesthoods and sacrifices as a matter of taste, and antiquated tastes at that, is to miss that its version of the gospel is the most relevant and necessary for the modern age, relentlessly pressing on us the acknowledgement of the thrice holy God's approaching presence.

3. The characterization of Jesus as *sympathetic* and the true priest as able to *deal gently* has a ready application to all who obey him and not least those granted authority in the church as they live in imitation of him. The characterization of v. 2a represents "the golden mean between indifference and mawkish sentimentality."[9] It "indicates more particularly forbearance and magnanimity on the part of people who are subject to great provocation and who could, if they wished, give way to unmoderated anger and meet the provocation with utmost severity."[10]

4. Was the Son's prayer "to the one who could save him from death" a prayer to be rescued from undergoing the cross or a prayer to be rescued from death's power? We gave the nod to the latter, but only as understood to include the former, or we have failed to see the uniqueness

---

9. Simpson, "Vocabulary," 36–37.
10. Bruce, *Epistle to the Hebrews*, 120.

of his death and resurrection. Death is the enemy to be rejected and renounced (2:14–15; 1 Cor 15:25–26). The prayer, "If it is possible, let this cup pass by me," is not a hitch in obedience or a rhetorical strategy for expressing what was possible, but the positive expression of obedience. It is itself the obedient man's expression of God's fixed, eternal No to death, voiced by the Son who has taken responsibility for Israel's guilt and its consequence. But if that No was to be realized it would be by resurrection at the price of death, death in its reality and God-forsakenness as it was never known and would never be known by anyone other than the Son who accepted it "in behalf of all" (2:9). For all others, resurrection comes easily, freely, but for him, and only for him, it came at its full price. In this unequaled moment the obedience of hope is the abandonment of hope. We are listening to a Trinitarian symphony that harmonizes beyond our range of hearing.

5. Some object to the depiction of divine parental discipline on the grounds that it fuels abusive structures at the expense of victims. In response, a distinction is to be drawn between victims of abuse and those who adopt the role of authoritative interpreters of such texts. As to the latter, a certain kind of sympathy with victims that openly pushes back against Hebrews' depiction of strong parental discipline (5:8; 12:4–11), while understandable, finally views the world backwards—as if the determinative lens was either my own person or that of human society as such, rather than the Son and his Father, through whom the powers of oppression by which we suffer are defeated in the obedience of the Son—and by so doing risks cutting the rope to the only true anchor of hope on offer. Texts like this have certainly been misappropriated by both oppressors and victims, but abuse and oppression are categories of sin that are to be resisted on every side and never confused with the work of the Father and Son. That said, deep sensitivity is called for when assisting victims of abuse in reading such a text. See 12:4–17.

# 5:11—6:3

*"For to everyone who has will more be given,
and he will have an abundance.
But from the one who has not, even what
he has will be taken away."*

## Context

SEE 4:14-16 AND 5:1-10 for the larger context. Fifteen minutes or so into a substantive discourse the preacher pauses both to jolt his listeners to engagement and to spur them on toward love and good deeds—because these (growth in obedience and growth in understanding) depend on each other for progress. At 7:1 he will resume the thread left at 5:10.

Taking 5:11—6:20 as a whole: If what is at stake in the approach to the throne of grace is *the attainment of the entire history of the Abrahamic promise*, an outcome that hinges on the priestly mediation of the Son, then we recognize *the need to fall in line with Abraham's faith in the promise*. The necessity of walking in the footsteps of Abraham's faith is the real burden of 5:11—6:20, a fact that can be lost in the turbulence of 5:11—6:12. When Abraham comes into the argument at 6:13-20 it is not merely as a way to raise the topic of oaths or to bend the thought toward Gen 14 in Heb 7:1-10 so that Melchizedek can be explored. It is because the Son's priesthood, announced in Ps 110:4, was the hidden means by which the promise given Abraham and believed by him would come to fruition. The promise, the priestly order by which it would be realized, and the faith that would receive it were all there at the moment of its entrance (7:4-10) setting the pattern for the entire history to follow. If the readers are unwilling to keep pace in the same faith—that is, to be authentic children of the Abraham who greeted Melchizedek and attested the resurrection—they will never be able to keep pace in understanding, no matter how many words the preacher spills.

This passage (5:11—6:20) begins with the preacher's reservations about whether the audience is up to the subject matter (5:11). He then proceeds to a cycle of arguments in which we do not hear the audience's responses but we sense how the author anticipates their response and presses his attack.

Thus, in 5:12-14 he elaborates on v. 11 by developing the imagery of a child's versus an adult's diet and how someone grows up. He is shaming them into agreement, motivating them to prove that they are ready for the solid food. In 6:1-3, as if convinced that he has won their agreement, he nevertheless gives them to understand that in fact this will mean moving beyond their current limits—they may in fact be ready but the evidence for that is yet to be found. The challenge notwithstanding, they will move on, *if God permits*. That is the thought on which 6:4-8 will hang. The outcome is not to be presumed upon, a fact that should sober them. They are not dealing in ideas or in a society with a revolving door they may use at their whim. They are involved in covenantal relations with the living God with whom one does not trifle. But, having taken them to the edge of the abyss, he assures them that just because of the faithfulness of that covenantal God there is cause for hope (6:9-12). Having sobered and reassured them, he echoes the reservation of 5:11 in 6:12, while turning to the promise that is the subject matter requiring their adult attention (6:13-20), and then finally to the priestly order through which that promise comes to fruition (7:1-28), thereby resuming the thread from 5:10. By now they should understand that what is at stake is not merely a set of ideas to be digested but a history to be lived by faith. When the exposition is completed he will shift his whole rhetorical effort to the obedience of faith (10:19—12:29).

> In the natural course of things everyone passes biologically from childhood through adolescence to adulthood "while they sleep," as it were, but the process of maturation through the same stages in mind and character operates by quite different rules. Any parent or teacher can instinctively appreciate the appropriateness and effectiveness of Hebrews' sort of rhetoric for an audience that has *potential* but is simply unmotivated, sluggish, distracted, and lazy (or even merely is in danger of being so!); all the more so when it is applied to a group that is a mixed bag of attentiveness (6:11) but which must be addressed as an organic whole more than as an aggregate of individuals. In this context it can be entirely fitting to say both that they *are* "sluggish" (5:11) at one point, and then, having let that sink in and do its motivational work, that they must take measures so that they do not *become* "sluggish" (6:12).

## Background

Judging from 6:9–10; 10:25, 32–39; 13:7 it has been years rather than months since this community's reception of the gospel. The list of 6:1–2 tells us nothing, however, about the ethnicity of the original readers.

The pedagogical imagery employed in 5:11–14 uses stock rhetorical devices that cut across diverse strands of popular philosophy of the time (e.g., Epictetus: *Ench.* 51.1; *Diss.* 2.16.39; Philo: *Agr.* 9; Paul: 1 Cor 3:1–2).[1] Of itself it conveys no connection with any particular school, but it does represent the common assumption that virtue, ethical discernment, was a central concern of education. The key to understanding Hebrews' drift will be the covenantal drama that is assumed, particularly as rooted in the disciplining of Israel under God's hand. When the present passage (5:11–14) falls immediately on the heals of the Son's own disciplinary process (5:8), on the one hand, and shares phrasing and ideas with 12:4–11, on the other, we are likely in touch with the writer's animating image: The faithful covenantal God's paternal care for his children (Deut 8:5) and the need actively to submit to that process (Heb 12:9, 12–13) so that the vision of Isa 32:15–18 will come about (see on 12:4–17).[2] Once we have got that far we can begin to see that a substantial part of the hidden portion of Hebrews' theological iceberg is what is gestured toward here: Heb 5:13–14 is about the "peaceful fruit of righteousness" toward which the covenantal Father of 12:4–11 leads them with his disciplinary care, the very righteousness to which the new covenant would give rise (8:8–12; 10:16–17; cf. 6:7–8); the righteousness that is closer to the surface of Paul's concerns when he addresses himself to the law (e.g., Rom 2) than is normally at the surface of Hebrews' concerns when it approaches that same law from the perspective of its cultic rites—though it *is* present (6:7–8, 10; 9:14; 10:24, 32–35; 11:1–40; 12:14–17; 13:1–6, 15–16, 21).

## Comments on Wording

5:11 *hard to explain, since you have become dull of hearing.* They have grown "lazy with respect to" either the act of listening or the message. The word for "lazy" is repeated in 6:12. The problem is both moral and intellectual: He would express the same frustration even if we proved our exegetical

---

1. Attridge, *Hebrews*, 155–65, with many parallels.

2. Similarly, if we juxtapose Ezek 11:18–20 and 14:1–11 we can see how what is viewed from one angle as a simple act of God, as if effecting in an instant a comprehensive change, is from another angle the result of a process of discipline.

mastery of every line of 7:1—10:18 but failed to act out its meaning as in 10:19—13:25. The need is not bookish understanding, but imitation (6:12) of the models of bodily active faith (11:1–40).

5:12 *basic principles of the oracles of God.* These are the essential lessons of the OT (6:1–2) that are necessary to get anywhere with the gospel (7:1—10:18).

*You need milk, not solid food.* Milk is good in itself, suited to an infant, and can be used elsewhere as an image of what all believers should desire (1 Pet 2:2). The preacher's point concerns the need of growth. His assumptions are that when they are not growing they are slipping toward apostasy; that spiritual growth, unlike biological development, does not happen as one sleeps; that growth in understanding depends on growth in obedience; and that his own present effort to instruct them should have been unnecessary. As it is, they are in a prolonged childhood that leaves them unable to cope in a world that requires adults.

5:13 *the word of righteousness.* That is, the ethical-social fruit of the new covenant (see vv. 14, 7–8; 12:4–11), into the world of which the entire surrounding exposition is trying to lead them.

5:14 *distinguish good from evil.* This is the sign of being an adult (Deut 1:39; Isa 7:16). Verse 14 as a whole anticipates 12:4–11; it is a matter of following the Son's example in 5:7–10. Contextually, it is to have become a flourishing growth in the conditions brought into effect by the new covenant (6:7–8), navigating with Solomonic discernment the trying circumstances of their Roman world, discerning what faith-obedience means, remaining alert to the deceitfulness of sin (3:13) and guarding against straying in heart (3:10).

6:1–2 The "foundational" matters of 6:1–2 are characterized as the *elementary teachings about Christ* though on the face of it the Christian slant is not evident beyond the broadly Jewish. The items might gesture toward the gospel of repentance and faith followed by beginning instruction about rites and eschatology in the ways that these are voiced by the OT Scriptures. Hebrews revolves around OT exposition and the OT is a word about Christ; within the OT there is conceptual infrastructure (6:1–2) and advanced teaching (5:1–10; 7:1—10:18). The rhetorical force is akin to what a professor might say to a capable group of graduate students in a physics course: "Come on, people. Let's get beyond two plus two equals four."

6:1 *go on.* The Greek verb in the passive voice is sometimes interpretively rendered, *let us be borne.* The construction can have the active sense: *let us go on to.*[3]

---

3. Attridge, *Hebrews*, 162–63.

*Dead works.* These are more likely acts of disobedience than the ritual works commanded by the law.

*6:2 instruction about washings.* This is probably a catch-all for initiation and cleansing rites, both Christian baptism and Jewish rites (cf. 9:19; 10:22); it is possible that John's baptism was included in the gospel narrative they had received.

## Comments on Theological Themes

Behind this and similar passages in Hebrews are the promises related to the new covenant: Jer 31:33–34; Ezek 11:19–20; 36:24–38; back of these, Deut 4:29–31; 28:1–14; 30:1–10 (cf. Deut 11:11–15). It is these same texts that will underlie Heb 6:7–8. The power to discern and choose is a sign of God's prior act of salvation. It is a *gift*, a grant of *life* and that means *freedom*, which is freedom for *obedience*. The *reception* of this gift is *faith*, the flourishing of God's planting. Israel's history under the Mosaic covenant makes evident that at the heart of all obedience is the approach to the divine throne, on which everything else depends, from which everything else emanates, around which everything else is formed. Hebrews is not lacking in a vision for that larger social-ethical life, even at the level of what is made explicit, but it concentrates its energies on what is most central and urgent in *covenantal* life: Let us draw near.

## Teaching Hebrews 5:11—6:3

1. For Israel the knowledge of God was not something to be discovered first in a bookish sort of way, by studying texts and engineering ideas, but through the way of obedient hearing. The progress for which Hebrews looks is available for the whole people, not merely those of a cerebral bent. Even a child can learn the ways of the city of God if she lives there long enough, and the ways of her parents by being with them. Moreover, the obedience of faith opens powers of reasoning that are available to all. That for which this sermons scolds them is that which is in reach of all, and that which is in the reach of the whole.

2. That said, the expectations regarding the ability to teach (5:12) should be sobering. If we find the world into which Hebrews takes us uninteresting and inaccessible even though we have travelled this "way" for years, we should consider whether we have taken to heart 5:11—6:3. What confronts us is less a matter of studiousness in the stereotyped

sense, than of values and the faith that *seeks* understanding. As for the academics, theology will not be gained in the library—that is necessary and never to be neglected!—but finally in the world. They, especially, must see to it that they do not refuse him who speaks. In *that* way they will not be unacquainted with the teaching about righteousness.

3. Conversely, it is necessary for *all* more or less to cultivate the desire and the disciplines of prolonged concentration and deep attentiveness and, indeed, the habits of study and reflection. The modern technological and image-centered age has had a stupefying effect which only means that we may need to find distinctive ways to adjust our life habits so as to flourish in the word of the gospel.

4. So completely does this writer's vision revolve around the OT Scriptures that even when he speaks of "the elementary doctrine of Christ" he is thinking of those teachings latent in the Scriptures.[4] Because this is true, to be preaching from the apostolic texts is to be preaching the OT as well.

5. What the writer pursues is not finally a matter of mere choice or effort. In the end, only *God permitting* will we move forward. This appended condition reflects the wisdom of Jas 4:15 (cf. 1 Cor 16:7), but seems particularly deliberate, being developed in vv. 4–12.

6. While there is certainly a place in the wide world for churches that are centrally evangelistic in character, whether that means being more welcoming or giving "altar calls," there is a danger if these communities do not actively cultivate the growth of Hebrews' sermon. Without that growth the ground is fertile for apostasy.

---

4. This writer is of course not alone in this. One needs only to remove the chapter break between 2 Tim 3:14–17 and 4:1–5 to recognize that "preaching the word" in 4:2 (= the gospel) is equal to preaching the Scriptures (= contextually the OT Scriptures).

# 6:4–8

*"When the unclean spirit has gone out of a person, it passes through waterless places seeking rest, but finds none. Then it says, 'I will return to my house from which I came.' And when it comes, it finds the house empty, swept, and put in order. Then it goes and brings with it seven other spirits more evil than itself, and they enter and dwell there, and the last state of that person is worse than the first."*

## Context

SEE 5:11—6:3. THE PASSAGE before us is one of the difficult texts of Scripture. In the centuries leading to consensus on Hebrews' canonicity this text's bearing on the question of restoring lapsed Christians to communion complicated Hebrews' inclusion. The question of the text's force has in fact never settled on an enduring consensus.[1] For some, concluding that it denies the possibility of restoration for apostates, Hebrews has simply gone too far as measured against the gospel of Jesus and the apostles.[2] It is never the case that we read without presuppositions but in the case of a text like this the role of our presuppositions necessarily rises nearer the surface. This will be as true for us as anyone, though space limits require that they remain largely implicit for the present commentary.

As for the immediate literary context, 6:4–8 can be viewed as a direct development of the end of 6:3, . . . *if God permits*. It is expanding on the freedom of God to act as he sees fit.

---

1. See, e.g., Bateman, *Warning Passages in Hebrews*.
2. Attridge, *Hebrews*, 172.

> For it is impossible to renew again to repentance
>> those who have participated in salvation
>> and have fallen away
>
>> because they are crucifying the Son to their disadvantage and subjecting him to public ridicule.
>
> For land
>> that drinks in the rain
>> and produces a crop useful to the farmer
>
> receives God's blessing
>> but if it produces thorns and such it is in danger of being cursed and will be burned.

There are other ways to translate and chart the argument but understood like so it seems that the main line of thought is explaining the role of God in the progress of the community relative to 5:11—6:3. Progress depends on God's permission because it is impossible to renew those whom he has rejected. Of course in saying this the preacher is registering a warning—Beware! Show effort!—as well as perhaps his own feeling of urgency in forestalling such a disaster (cf. 2 Tim 4:1–4). But he will immediately proceed to assure them of his own conviction, according to which he does proceed in hope (6:9–12).

## Background

More than Hebrews' other warnings, 6:4–6 *seems* to say that there can be a passing of final judgment before death. This stands in some tension with 9:27, but then strictly speaking 9:27 also stands in tension with 11:5. Assuming that 6:4–6 does mark a point of no return, how might it be understood?

Firstly, cutting across the NT documents is the tension of the already and the not yet of salvation, though some writers place more emphasis on the already (e.g., John) with a corresponding emphasis on God's sovereignty and the assurance of salvation (preservation), while others place emphasis on the not yet with a corresponding emphasis on human responsibility and the caution against presumption (perseverance). Hebrews contains both sides, but in general presents faith as a pilgrimage on the way to salvation, which is a future destination. Technically, one cannot lose "salvation" in this scheme because one has not yet arrived there; faith does not represent a moment of "conversion" but a lifetime of obedient pursuit. This is oversimplified, of course, leaving untouched Hebrews' strong language of present participation in Christ and the Spirit which must correlate in broader ways with the gospel as presented by the rest of the canon. What it does do is caution against presuming that our grasp of the tension of the already-not yet is better than that of the apostolic witness. Hebrews' version of the gospel led naturally and appropriately to the strong warning of 6:4–6. If we would not say what the authors of Scripture did say—assuming we have rightly understood what they were saying and why—we should rethink our own understanding. What we have just said also cautions against over-quick harmonizations of the language of diverse NT writers who may use similar sounding language in different ways and for different ends.

Secondly, the OT itself presents patterns of covenantal relations that could have formed expectations for the new covenant. The "sin with a high hand" (Num 15:30–31; cf. Deut 17:6 and Heb 10:28; 1 Sam 3:14) receives no direct attention from Hebrews and it is doubtful that either here or elsewhere in Hebrews there is a one-to-one correspondence intended. Presumption is condemned in Deut 29:16–21, however, which is cited in Heb 12:15 (3:12 might echo it) and connected to Esau's despising of his birthright. Analogously, in Jer 7:1–29 the people are presuming on the presence of the temple but have not listened so God commands his prophet not to pray for them because he will not listen; in Jer 11:14 and 14:11–12 the prophet is not to pray for the people because God has determined to destroy them.

If we then consider a range of NT passages (1 John 5:16–17; Matt 12:32; 7:22–23; 1 Cor 10:1–13; Jude 5–7; Gal 3:1–4; 4:19; 5:2–4; 1 Tim 1:13, 20; 2 Pet 2:20–22; 3:16–17; John 5:14; Rom 11:21; Rev 2:5; and not overlooking Judas who would have shared in Matt 10:8; cf. Luke 10:17–20) we conclude that for these other NT writers the full blessings of salvation are bestowed unstintingly and without prejudice on a larger number of people than will persevere to the attainment of salvation. Such an understanding should not be surprising for anyone who has paid attention to Jesus' prodigal strewing of his salvation in the form of feedings, healings, and exorcisms, whether or not the recipients persevered in discipleship (e.g., John 6:66). In at least the case of the "sin that won't be forgiven" and possibly in the case of 1 John 5:16–17 (1 Tim 1:20 and 2 Pet 2:20–22?) there are hints that it is indeed possible to fall under irrevocable judgment while still living, just as judgment was passed on Israel while she still lived in the land. If this is along the right lines, then Heb 6:4–8 is not a true outlier. Whatever we are to say regarding a doctrine of a "hidden election," for Hebrews there is in the addressees but one group of people all equally sharing in the same blessings of 6:4–6, some of whom might not persevere to the end and attain salvation, and some of whom could conceivably sin against grace in such a way that it is impossible to renew them to repentance even prior to death. Subjectively, experientially, empirically there is no basis on which a human judge could separate the sheep from the goats. One can but persevere in faith, and thus in perfect confidence.

Thirdly, Jewish authors addressed sins for which no repentance was possible, either because of the judgment of God, because of the person's own perversity, or because of the judgment of the community (Sir 34:26 [31]; m. 'Abot 5:18; t. Sanh. 13:5; 1QS 7:23-24; Philo, *Fug.* 84; *Leg* 3.213; *Spec.* 1.58; Josephus, *B.J.* 2.143-144 [2.8.8143-144]).[3] The overlap with Hebrews is expected and real, though Hebrews operates with its own rationale.

Lastly, with Heb 6:7-8 one thinks of course of Gen 1-3, but probably nearer the surface are the descriptions of Canaan and Israel itself as God's garden (Deut 11:10-12; Isa 5:1-7), and particularly as they were to flourish in the conditions of the new covenant (Isa 32:15-17; 44:1-5; 45:8; 51:3; 55:10-13; 61:11; Jer 31:23-29; Ezek 17:1-24; 34:25-31; 36:8-15, 22-38; Hos 14:5-8; Amos 9:14-15; cf. Deut 28:12; Hos 10:12).[4] The "root of bitterness" (Heb 12:15) that must not be permitted to grow refers to Deut 29:18, where the judgment of God leaves the land of Israel "burned out with brimstone and salt." These OT associations and the near context of Heb 6:4-6 indicate that it is the new covenant blessings that are in mind in the rains that fall, which heightens the tension created by the warning in the light of Deut 30:6-8; Ezek 11:18-21; 36:26-27. Even within the conditions of the new covenant and new creation, for now, while the ages overlap, it is possible to turn back and forfeit all.

## Comments on Wording

6:4 *it is impossible*. The Greek text uses the conjunction *for, since*, connecting the thought back. For both grammatical and logical reasons, those for whom it is impossible cannot be those once enlightened, etc. This leaves God or those attempting pastoral care; our present suggestion is that it is the latter. The empirical cause for the impossibility is not strictly supplied by v. 6b, though it is better translated as "since/because they are crucifying etc."

---

3. For these and similar references, see Attridge, *Hebrews*, 168–69; Koester, *Hebrews*, 319–20, 451; see also Carson, *Divine Sovereignty*, 9–121.

4. The imagery of humans as plants is found in pagan literature; Koester, *Hebrews*, 323, cites Euripides, *Hecuba* 592-99; Quintilian, *Inst.* 5.11.24. Jesus was fond of horticultural imagery (e.g., Matt 7:15-20; 13:1-43; Luke 13:6-9). For a survey of "seed theology" and plant metaphors in Jewish texts, see Elliott, *Survivors*, 314-44.

than "while they are . . . ." It explains the inner meaning of their falling away, but not in a way that is apparent to our own eyes. Left to our own lights, would we have been harder on Esau than Jacob? Would we have determined that Saul's sin was worse than David's, or that Judas was in a different place at the time of his sin than Peter? The explanation of the impossibility, such as it is, comes in vv. 7–8. It is a matter of whether it will happen, which is subject to God's will (6:3, 7–8, 10).

*Once been enlightened.* The word for "once" can mean "once" or "once and for all," but the distinction is less significant in a context that excludes a second repentance of the same order. For the idea of being enlightened, see 10:26, 32; the reference is to the decisive, pivotal event wherein a human perception of and assent to the truth of the gospel is brought about by divine agency.

*tasted the heavenly gift.* This marks full participation in heavenly realities, the whole gift of salvation as granted in the present; cf. 3:1, 14; 8:5; 9:23; 11:1, 16; 12:22.

*shared in the Holy Spirit.* Again, the description concerns what is common to the whole community.

6:5 *powers of the age to come.* Cf. 2:4–5; 10:1; 13:14. *Powers* suggests something experiential (2:4; Gal 3:1–5). In his own categories, Paul indicates how the new creation as the age *to come* is already present and operative (2 Cor 5:17; Gal 6:15). In John, Jesus tells Martha that he is himself the resurrection that she rightly associated with the future (John 11:24–25); in the Son and his benefits the future is present.

6:6 *fallen away.* Cf. 10:29. There is nothing said in the present context that necessarily limits what is intended to a verbal, declared renunciation of their faith; what is said could have in view conduct *that amounts to* a rejection of the blessings just enumerated. Either way, the "falling away" in mind would be an action that uniquely strikes at the very heart of the gospel and faith, in effect if not in intent.

*to restore them again to repentance.* Hebrews takes for granted that all believers continually sin and must therefore approach the throne of grace. The sin that is in view in 6:4–6 is a particular one, that of a comprehensive rebellion against and turning from the gospel: apostasy, the rejection of God's forgiveness in Christ. The "renewal" would be a new inauguration into the life of vv. 4–5, following a complete break with it. The description says nothing of the internal psychological state of the apostate (e.g., would they want to repent, attempt to repent, feel remorse, etc.).

*holding him up to contempt.* The compound verb, *to disgrace someone publicly, expose, make an example of,* is used only here in the NT (the simple form is used Matt 1:19 and Col 2:15), but it is used in the LXX of Num 25:4;

Jer 13:22; Ezek 28:17; Dan 2:5. It is a fitting description of the intent of Roman crucifixions. Having not merely affirmed the atoning effect of the cross but participated fully in its benefits, having seen it for what it is, such ones have renounced (actually or in effect) all that and chosen (actually or in effect) to be numbered with those who in hostility crucify the Son. Contrast 11:26; 12:2; 13:13.

6:8 *near to being cursed*. The meaning of the phrase is likely not that this "land" is simply close to being cursed, but that it is *under* a curse. The fires (10:27; 12:25–29) are those of conclusive judgment rather than purging discipline.

## Comments on Theological Themes

It seems to us advisable not to allow a notion of "individual and effectual election" to determine whether Hebrews espouses a doctrine of an impossibility of a second repentance and whether the blessings of salvation are experienced only by those so elected. If we held to a strong notion of election it would affect how we defined "apostasy" in the context of our systematic theology (it would limit apostasy to the non-elect who at present participate in salvation's blessings equally with the elect), but attempting to bend Hebrews' language to accommodate that idea violates the tension of which we spoke earlier and so threatens to mute the divine witness to the reality itself.

## Teaching Hebrews 6:4–8

1. The temptation to use this passage as a means of frightening people or exercising power over them has probably always been strong, but this abuse must be avoided. Even Jesus in Matthew 12 did not declare that anyone had actually committed the sin that would not be forgiven. He posits it as a real danger, not merely a rhetorical hypothetical, but he goes no further. Likewise, Hebrews. Neither these nor other texts give the authority or the rational basis for making a judgment about particular cases (e.g., a recanting of faith under persecution); these are not texts to be invoked in regards to church discipline (which is marked by the spirit of hope; e.g., 1 Cor 5:4; 2 Cor 2:5–11; 1 Tim 1:20), except as the *warnings* they are and as addressed to the church at large.[5] Much less may this passage be applied to oneself authoritatively.

---

5. For the history of applying this text to church discipline, see Koester, *Hebrews*, 23–25, 40, 318–19.

2. The gravest of dangers is revealed in this text, and a faithful exposition should spare no effort to communicate its truth. Yet the need is equally to teach this text with sensitivity to the applications and fears that have grown up around it, and thus with care to defining the uniqueness of apostasy, speaking courage to fear and grace to guilt, and by all means available seeking to bring about the intended, constructive effect.

3. The preacher indicates no circumstances under which he would give up hope on anyone and cease from any attempt to renew them. Where hope is expressed (6:9–12), however, it has nothing to do with the past participation in the spiritual blessings of 6:4–6, as if these are a grounds for confidence. Hebrews mentions such things as signs of God's offered grace, but these are the things they stand to flout and forfeit. Insofar as hope makes reference to the past of these believers it references their good works and love (fruitful faith), but, above all, it looks to God's righteousness (v. 10).

4. Viewed from the outside it might be hard to imagine a stronger candidate for the sin of apostasy than Peter's thrice repeated and very emphatic denial following an extended and intimate experience with the Lord. Remember David. In both cases the final word was the word of forgiveness. Nevertheless, this passage must be allowed to stand as the unqualified warning that it is. The pastor calls out no one by name, but he walks the entire church up to the edge of the abyss and bids them fear. The point is not to wring our hands wondering or merely to veer back from the edge. The only appropriate application is to head in the exact opposite direction: Approach the throne of grace!

5. At the same time, this text provides occasion for celebrating the good gifts of salvation, and it may belong to the writer's intent indirectly to stir his readers to a greater desire to hold onto and deepen their experiential as well as theoretical understanding of these things. The human heart tends to cherish most those things that it feels itself to be in danger of losing.

# 6:9–12

*"But the one who endures to
the end will be saved."*

## Context

SEE 5:11—6:3 AND 6:4–8.

The reference to laziness in 6:12 echoes the same word in the Greek text of 5:11 suggesting some degree of closure, although v. 12 simultaneously launches the theme of 6:13–20. It is not until v. 20 that the allusion to Ps 110:4 is resumed and the exposition begun in 5:1–10 can continue in 7:1–28. The whole of 5:11—6:20 revolves on a single vision of the progress of the new covenant people of God who live by the faith of Abraham in God's promise—*live* both in the senses of thriving and surviving (persevering) in the new covenant conditions. The signs of faltering faith and the author's instinct that unless he jolts his readers they will fail to realize their potential to engage his exposition have prompted the strong words of 5:11—6:8. He now reassures them that his confidence regarding them is in fact undiminished. He has not spoken as a judge but as a fellow pilgrim who shares in the same realities and the same dangers and who must pull his weight in the responsibility of mutual exhortation (3:12–13; 10:24).

## Background

Among pagan writers the idea of justice as equitably meting out rewards according to the worth of each is widespread (*Rhet. Her.* 3.2.3; Cicero, *Inv.* 2.53 §160[1]). Similarly, among Jews the idea of rewards for righteousness and punishment for sin showed itself in a variety of ways (e.g., Deut 28:1–68;

---

1. Koester, *Hebrews*, 324.

Job 8:3–7; John 9:2, 31; cf. Sir 35:1–26). Though brought into a wholly altered and unique framework (e.g., John 9:3; Luke 13:1–5; Matt 9:9–13; Rom 4:5–8; Eph 2:8–10; Titus 2:11–15; 3:3–7), a judgment according to works is a clear expectation of the gospel writings as well (e.g., Matt 25:31–46; Rom 2:6–10; 2 Tim 1:18; 4:14; Jas 2:12–13, 24; Rev 20:12; 22:12; cf. Heb 10:35; 11:6). In the present context the main connection of thought is with the image of the fruitful land in vv. 7–8. The writer is confident of his readers, and thus encouraged to proceed with his teaching, because the signs are present that the rains of God's covenantal gifts (4:14–16; 6:4–5; 9:11–14; 10:19–25; 12:4–11; 13:10, 20–21) have not been without effect but that under those showers the land (and who created the land?) has borne a crop useful to the one for whom it is farmed (cf. also 10:32–39); as such, one expects that this land stands under God's blessing. That their works are present is necessary; that the writer's deeds, his skillfully wrought stratagems of rhetoric, are active is necessary; but there is no question of where credit is due (cf. Deut 6:10–12; 8:17–18; 1 Chr 29:14–16; Ezek 11:19–20; 34:11–16, 25–31; 36:8–15, 24–36; Hos 11:3; 14:4–9), and of what finally grounds the writer's confidence. See the introduction to this commentary.

## Comments on Wording

*6:9 in your case, beloved, we feel sure of better things.* The Greek refers to *the* better things, meaning the useful crop that receives God's blessing (v. 7). Just for this reason the writer is exhorting them, even if he must resort to severe warnings.

6:10 *God is not unjust so as to overlook.* The negative wording—*God is not unjust*—is litotes, the negative for the positive for the sake of rhetorical exaggeration; as in, "Albert Einstein is not a bad scientist." The understatement continues with the denial that God will *overlook*. The language of "remembering" (2:6; 8:12; 10:17; 13:3) and "forgetting" (ESV = *overlook*) is figurative for *pay close attention to* or *overlook, be inattentive to*, respectively. The implied vantage point from which God "will not overlook" is probably the future judgment (9:27–28); the "salvation" of v. 9 is probably thought of as the future outcome of their pilgrimage more than present participation, though these overlap.

*your work and the love that you have shown for his name.* In the first instance it is the bonds of the community that the writer is keen to shore up with good works toward one another (v. 10b; cf. 3:12–13; 4:11; 10:24–25,

32–34; 12:14–17; 13:1–7, 16–19), but it is evident that his ethical vision is as broad as the righteousness of the new covenant (5:14; 8:10; 12:4–14; cf. 1:9; 7:2; 11:1–40; 13:20–21) and that it is imbued with a missional spirit.[2] They are performing a ministry done for his "people" (*to the saints*) but ultimately it is for God's name; it is expressly covenantal faithfulness.

6:11 *And we desire each one of you to show the same earnestness . . . until the end.* See on 4:11 regarding the concern for perseverance *together*. By alluding to the need of continued earnestness (*diligence, eagerness, zeal*) he is alluding in brief to the enthusiasm that characterized their beginnings (3:14; 10:32–36); it is opposite the sloth against which he warns them (5:11; 6:12). Showing zeal "until the end" is necessary for arriving at all (3:7–19), and necessary lest they forfeit their existing share. See the introduction to this commentary.

*to have the full assurance of hope.* Or, *toward the full assurance of hope*. The allusion could be to the strengthening of hope for the journey (cf. 10:22) or the securing of what is hoped for. In v. 18 the word "hope" signifies that which is hoped for.

6:12 *imitators.* Imitation is a major theme of Hebrews, the center of which is the Son (2:10; 5:7–9; 12:1–3) and the circumference the patriarchs and the other models of faith (11:1–40; 13:7). The focus here is on the patriarchs, especially Abraham; Jesus' example is probably in mind in 6:20.

*through faith and patience.* This might be hendiadys for *faithful perseverance* or *persevering faithfulness*.[3] The "patience" in mind is not a passive waiting, certainly not a "putting up with" God's delay. It is closer to the idea of "endurance" (10:32–36; 12:2); cf. 6:15. Moreover, it is an endurance of continued fruitfulness in faith-obedience.

*inherit the promises.* The allusion could be to the passing on of the promises (6:17; 11:9, 13, 39; cf. 1:14; 4:1, 8) or to the obtaining of what was promised (e.g., either in the past, 6:15; 11:8–9, 33; or ultimately, 9:15; 10:36). The writer uses both senses to make his point: Abraham's faithful endurance led to the reception of what was promised (land, seed), from which we see the necessity of faith and the faithfulness of God. But what was ultimately promised was something they did not receive in full, but continued to look for at the time they died.

---

2. See Laansma, "Hebrews and the Mission," 330–34, 337–38.
3. Attridge, *Hebrews*, 176.

## Comments on Theological Themes

Heb 6:9-12 is so deeply immersed in the knowledge of God's gracious atonement and new covenant blessings that it takes liberties of expression that could not be misunderstood from within this, its proper frame of reference. The intent is, however, easily missed. The seemingly universal appetite for confirmation that there is some truth to the doctrine of karma or independent achievement, to justify our existence and to appease the gods,[4] no doubt predisposes readers to hear strains of merit theology where it was never intended. The connection of thought with v. 7, the studied understatement of v. 10a for the sake of rhetorical effect, and, above all, the theology taken over from the OT of God as the creator and Lord of the covenant—all these things make evident that while obedience is necessary and a reward is promised, God's grace remains prior and incongruous (see the introduction to this commentary).

It is possible that an aspect of the problem detected by the writer of Hebrews was an unhealthy appeal to spiritual experience on the part of the readers. In 2:1-4 the manifestations of divine power are noted as attesting the authenticity and validity of the word that came through the Son (v. 4), and presumably the "divisions of the Holy Spirit" were still in effect, but no mention is made of the continuance of the wonders into the present as a form of comfort and encouragement.[5] Similarly in the present context, 6:4-5 affirms the fact of these experiential aspects of salvation—there is no hint of embarrassment or a desire to diminish them (cf. also 11:32-35; 13:2)—but only by way of establishing the depth and reality of their participation in this salvation. When it comes to the writer's statement of his present confidence there is no appeal to the fact of this experience, but only to the "peaceful fruit of righteousness." Indirectly he appears to be indicating that the mere fact of the shared experience is no sure sign of authenticity and cannot be presumed upon. Their hope is the faithfulness of God, and the need is of perseverance in faith to the end—faith that takes the shape of the righteousness of the new covenant, with God's laws inscribed on their hearts.

## Teaching Hebrews 6:9-12

1. Contextually, Heb 6:9-12 1) gains some of its potency by way of contrast with the uncompromising warning of 6:4-8, 2) concentrates the

---

4. For a local illustration of this, see Arnold, "'I am Astonished,'" 429-49.
5. Koester, *Hebrews*, 211-12.

readers' attention on the urgency of sustaining a zealous life of faith-obedience, 3) begins to bend their thought toward the promise-theology of 6:13–20, and 4) reinforces the truth that faith is not merely how we grasp the promise in the sense of trusting it, but also (and this is the real point of 6:9–12) how we grasp the promise in the sense of *understanding* it at all. Recall that the thought-arc of 5:11—6:20 revolves on that latter point, which is why the writer disrupted his exposition of Ps 110:4. Living in the faith modeled by the patriarchs is the antidote to the sloth that is potentially blocking off their progress into the understanding of and participation in the realities of Christ's priestly service and sacrifice. It is to be the fruit-bearing land that receives God's blessing rather than the curse, and thus receives not merely his permission to advance beyond the elementary teachings but his help in doing so.

2. It probably needs to be made more explicit than it is in the text itself that the concern for "each" of the readers is a concern for each individually, but it is equally a concern for the community as a whole. At the same time, what the writer says in this paragraph (vv. 9–12) reminds us that in addressing a community the "situation" of the letter is complex and multi-layered. The writer is not thinking of the whole church as a single mass, but as a community of members who are faring differently. Those who are less "guilty" need to be reassured lest they become collateral damage of the author's rhetoric. The same discretion is needed in our own teaching.

3. As to "showing the same diligence/zeal to the end," it is fitting to stress that while this human effort of perseverance must be viewed as the merely natural effect of God's creative work and covenantal blessing for his own glory there is no question of taking it with anything less than full seriousness as a matter of human decision and action. This "great salvation" makes us more human, not less (2:5–9), renewing and deepening the meaning of authentic freedom for full obedience, and thus for responsibility. Where faith does not exist in publicly manifested form it does not exist in some hidden and private form. In keeping with this, "diligence" and "laziness" are less a matter of two poles on a spectrum than mutually exclusive spheres; they are two "ways" between which a choice must be made either for life or death.

4. Likewise, the "earnestness" (i.e., that in which they are to be diligent) that is mentioned receives further definition from 1) the earlier conduct of this community (6:10; cf. 3:12–14; 10:32–39), 2) the various exemplars of faith (the community's earlier leaders, 13:7; the Lord, 12:1–3; the models of 11:1–4; Abraham and the other patriarchs), and

3) the righteousness of the law written on their hearts, which is behind the language of 5:14 and 6:7; cf. 12:11. Developing these separately as well as conflating them into a kind of stereoscopic vision of a single, richly complex whole presents several possibilities for exposition.

# 6:13–20

*"There is another who bears witness about me,
and I know that the testimony that he bears
about me is true."*

## Context

FOR THE BROADER FLOW of thought, see 5:11—6:3; 6:4-8, 9-12.

In 5:11—6:20, having raised the Melchizedekian nature of Christ's appointment in 5:1-10, Hebrews is in process of situating Melchizedek in the story of the promise made to Abraham and his seed. Even if up till now Abraham has been named only in 2:16, once we recognize that the promise of God arcs from the patriarch to the entrance beyond the curtain into the resting place, the Most Holy Place of God's temple—and recalling its similar role in the theology of Paul[1]—its (the promise's) structuring role in the whole argument so far becomes apparent. The question is how the promise will be fulfilled, how the whole people of God will do the impossible: enter past the curtain into the inviolable presence of this holy God (Exod 33:20). The answer is that this happens through the priestly ministry and cleansing sacrifice of Christ, after the order of Melchizedek and as parabolically (9:9) foreshadowed in the Aaronic priesthood and Mosaic tabernacle.

This promise and this faith must not and cannot be abstracted from their particular history. At the present juncture the weight of the argument falls on the historical entrance of the promise itself, which brought about the entrance of authentic faith.[2] The faith that concerns the gospel is always

---

1. E.g., Gal 3:6—4:7; cf. Wright, *Justification*, 94-100.

2. When the distinct perspectives of Hebrews and of Paul in Galatians are considered, there is no final conflict with the timing of "faith's" entrance in Gal 3:23, 25; cf. Gal 3:6-9. Also, because the Abrahamic promise concerns the history of the world,

posterior to (following) the word and act of God and is brought about by them, so it cannot be shapeless and general. *That* faith, which is the living model for the faith of the present community, was not only birthed by but was resourced by the promise, and the same promise continues all the more to resource faith for those in the last days who have seen their forerunner enter beyond the curtain on their behalf. *Tapping into that resource and following in the footsteps of Abraham's faith are the need of the hour if the readers' understanding of and participation in the realities of the new covenant are to proceed as the author intends.*

Sketched in brief:

... we want you to show the same zeal to the end that you might become imitators of those who through faith and patience inherit what was promised to Abraham and his seed.

[Things must be this way and can be this way because of the following:]

*For* (when God made the promise) in Gen 22 he swore by himself, the highest possible authority,

> and in this way, exercising the faith-patience you must now show, Abraham obtained the promise.
>
> (And don't overlook the drama of Gen 22 when comparing your endurance to his).

We recognize the significance of that oath if we consider the parallel with human oaths

and that God utilized this human form precisely to make the firmness of his promise clear.

> (Note well: He did this not only with Abraham, but also in Ps 110:4.)

He did this so that we who took hold of hope might have strong encouragement.

> That hope is like an anchor disappearing into the hidden depths beyond the veil
>
>> where our forerunner entered for us
>>
>>> having become high priest forever in Melchizedek's order.

---

Hebrews will back the history of faith up to Abel, Enoch, and Noah in 11:4–7.

## Background

HEBREWS 6:13-20 is a cloak of many metaphors—legal, nautical, cultic, and athletic. They do not master the argument, as if needing to be made consistent with each other, but are freely marshaled to convey meaning and emotional impact.

The citation in v. 14 comes from Gen 22, which will recur in Heb 11:17-19. Abraham's faith echoed the Father's unwillingness to withhold his own Son and the Son's hope of resurrection (5:7-10; 12:1-3; cf. 6:20). It manifested his unflinching confidence in the righteousness and power of the one who promised, which even death could not overcome. Abraham would withhold nothing, not even the tangible son of promise, in obedience to the intangible spoken word (12:25-29) of the promise giver. It is this sort of faith that the author intended by "earnestness" in v. 11.

The *oath* recalls 3:7—4:11 and anticipates 7:20-25. God's constancy and reliability are often affirmed in Scripture (e.g., Num 23:19; 1 Sam 15:29; Ps 145:13; Isa 45:23) and his oath taking was highlighted by other interpreters (e.g., Philo, *Sacr.* 91-94). In everyday life oaths had an important place in business transactions. "A partnership (*koinōnia*) was fixed by an agreement between its members. The agreement was termed a *metochē* [the partners were *metochoi*] and was often in the form of a *homologia* or acknowledgement"[3] (cf. Heb 2:3, 14; 3:1, 14; 4:14; 10:33; 13:16). Along with other terms used by Hebrews the legal, even commercial cast of Hebrews' characterizations are evident as it conveys the serious reality of the new covenant as the Creator and Redeemer's "law of the land" (7:12; 8:10; 10:16-17) in these last days and forever.

The *anchor* is found only here in Scripture as a metaphor but was frequently used in a figurative sense by other writers of the time and would become a favorite of later Christians. Acts 27:29-30 well illustrates the terrors of a lee shore and the security afforded by an anchor. The sea itself as the primordial force of chaos and evil ranged against YHWH can serve as a metaphor for both the state of the individual and a civilization (Isa 17:12; 57:20; Jas 1:6). Besides providing security, the fact that a lowered anchor has passed beyond sight contributes to the aptness of the comparison to Jesus.

A *forerunner* refers to those hurrying on with others following, whether messengers, troops, or athletes; the word is also used of winds and early fruits. The association intended by Hebrews is debated, whether the thought is of an advance warrior (possible associations with 2:10), early fruit, an advance ship (noting possible nautical imagery in 2:1; 6:1, 19; 13:9), or an

---

3. Llewelyn, "Legal Jurisdiction," 45-53 [47-48]; cf. Horsley, *New Documents*, 78-79.

athlete (12:1). Certainly the idea of the Christian life as a "running" is found elsewhere (Acts 20:24; 1 Cor 9:24, 26; Gal 2:2; 5:7; Phil 2:16; 2 Tim 4:7), and might lurk here.

## Comments on Wording

6:15 *Abraham, having patiently waited, obtained the promise.* See 11:8–19. It is this sort of faith that must be imitated if the capacity for understanding (5:11–14) is to be established. As for what he *obtained*, when the allusion is to Gen 22 one could say parabolically that he obtained the promise of a *resurrected* seed (11:19).

6:18 *two unchangeable things.* The two things are the mere word (promise) of God, which needs no oath, and the oath that is added for the sake of human weakness. The *oath* refers back to v. 13 but also anticipates the oath of Ps 110:4 in Heb 7:20–25, both oaths belonging to the organic history of the one promise and the writer, as usual, laying the groundwork in advance for something he intends to say later. The word for *guaranteed* in v. 17 is related to the word for *mediator* (8:6; 9:15; 12:22; cf. 7:22) and conceivably anticipates the Son's role as the embodiment of the promise.[4]

*fled for refuge might have strong encouragement to hold fast to the hope.* Elsewhere it is a matter of fleeing from (2:3; 12:25) whereas here it is *fleeing to* in the sense of the ESV's added words, *for refuge* (e.g., Gen 19:20; Num 35:25; Ps 143:9; Isa 10:3). The idea of 1 Kgs 1:50–51; 2:28 is possible, though different wording is used. The exodus imagery of Heb 3:7—4:11 could be in mind. The *hope* is at once our future entrance and the forerunner himself.

6:19 *enters into the inner place behind the curtain.* See on 4:16 for the distinction between the imagery of *approaching* and *entering* in Hebrews. To date only the forerunner has entered, who is himself our hope and who, like an immoveable anchor hidden from sight in the depths but fastened with an unbreakable cord, secures our lives in the present no matter how great a storm threatens to wreck us on the rocks of the lee shore.

6:20 *where Jesus has gone as a forerunner on our behalf.* Since 6:20b echoes 5:10 it might be that 6:20a echoes 5:7–9 and the trial-filled life of Jesus conceived as a course run by him. The image of running is not used there, but it is so used of the Christian life by Paul and will be applied to the believers in connection with Jesus' example in Heb 12:1–3. As such, the example of Jesus (5:7–9; cf. 2:10; 12:1–3) is added to that of Abraham as that which resources faith (6:12).

---

4. Griffiths, *Divine Speech*, 111–14, 120–21, 162.

## Comments on Theological Themes

It is beneath the dignity of God to give an oath and an affront that we should seek one. His gentleness and mercy are on display in condescending to provide the strongest possible encouragement for a faith that is besieged ultimately by the threat of death itself (2:14–15; 3:12–13; 11:13–16; note the implication of the *sea* in the image of the anchor in v. 19). Conversely, faith owes its existence to the prior word, which creates and nourishes it.

The cash value of anyone's word depends on their character and power. Both of these God has revealed through the history of Israel, at the heart of which is the history of his Son. It is a general insistence of Hebrews that the tangible things in which people place all their stock are dependent on the divine word, to which all things tangible owe their origin and continuance, and whose continuance is limited by that very word (1:2–3, 10–12; 11:3; 12:25–29). In reality God's word is the only thing that is reliable.

## Teaching Hebrews 6:13–20

1. One way to teach this passage might be to unravel its strands to some extent to consider them in turn: Firstly, the way in which it closes the warning and exhortation of 5:11—6:20 and reprises what went before. Secondly, the way in which it points us to the very particular history of the promise as a word of power that creates and resources faith—both in the form of the word of a promise reinforced by God's oath and as a record of the faith it has created beginning with Abraham. Thirdly, the ways in which coming themes of Hebrews are anticipated, particularly as subsequent chapters will take for granted what is said here. The first and second were teased out in the above. For the third see the following topics.

2. There is of course the significance of a divine oath, on which he invites us to meditate so that when he raises it again in 7:20–25 we will see the force of what he says and that the oath of Ps 110:4 is a continuation and elaboration of the promise given to Abraham.

3. The images of an anchor and a forerunner are pregnant and should be allowed to resonate through all the coming exposition. Particularly as a forerunner "for us"[5] we are being pointedly reminded of 2:10, 17–18; 4:14–16; 5:7–9. In this way all through 7:1 and following, not

---

[5]. The ESV translates, *where Jesus has gone as a forerunner on our behalf*, which could be understood to connect *on our behalf* with either *has gone* or with *forerunner*; we are opting for the latter. The NIV translates it as *entered on our behalf*.

only at 7:25, we are not lost in technical matters of exposition—either Hebrews' or our own—but grasp the leading and urgent concern for faith: In his intercessory work he is a *sympathetic* high priest, a priest who deals gently with those who are ignorant and straying, because he shared fully in the blood and flesh of Abraham's seed, suffered, was tempted, and learned obedience.

4. Again, we are meant to notice that the the whole history of the promise was present *in nuce* at its inception. The allusion to Gen 22 contains within it the great threat to and victory of the promise and its faith in the parabolic death and resurrection of Isaac (11:19). In this and other ways we see the overarching theme of the divine word as itself the creator and sustainer of faith, we see the goal on which that promise was always fixed (anticipating the entire exposition of shadow and reality), and we see that it is indeed fixed, unswerving, unchanging, and unconquerable on its way to certain and now accomplished victory.

# 7:1–10

*"Before Abraham was, I am."*

## Context

IF HEB 6:4–8 is one of the most challenging texts of Scripture, 7:1–10 is one of the most puzzling. If a modern student submitted an OT exegetical paper "according to the exegetical order of Melchizedek," she would not receive an encouraging evaluation.

See the introductions to 4:14–16 and 5:1–10 for the larger setting. Those earlier passages brought us to the threshold of several questions: What did it mean to say that the Son belonged to the Melchizedekian order? What were the implications for the law, that is, the covenant? What did it mean for the Son's priestly work and his salvation? These questions are answered together more than separately, and what is ahead requires the exertion to which 5:11—6:20 called us. A few clarifying comments are critical, which we have space only to register.

In 7:1–10 it is the Melchizedekian *order* that is of interest, not the mysterious figure of Melchizedek as such. The latter figure has occupied interpreters to distraction, which is what must not happen. Hebrews is focused on the Son for the sake of encouraging endurance to the end through the real-world costs that mount as we proceed.

As such, the Melchizedek we meet here is the textually inscribed and formed Melchizedek, or, better, it is the textually inscribed *order*. The absence of a father and mother, for instance, is not a comment about a human figure—still less an allegedly angelic one—but on the figure as *textually presented*. Nothing Hebrews says supports the view that Melchizedek himself was taken as anything other than a human person, but it is not the individual as such that matters in any event. The preacher is submitting to the lead of Ps 110:4 by turning to the only other thing the divine author said about Melchizedek: Gen 14:17–20. He reads with expectations that the divine author will have anticipated what he would say in Ps 110:4 and what would be the case in the Son. God would have told the story of Melchizedek in a way that foreshadowed the priestly order that the Son now occupies. That Hebrews reads the text with pre-formed ideas about the Son is patent—he knew what he was looking for in Gen 14, including what was not in the text—and we can speculate about other sources and influences. But the effort of Hebrews to "go the way the words run" must be respected. This is faith seeking understanding, and seeking it in the words of the text.

Involved in this is that the single key "background" for Hebrews' reading of Ps 110:4 and Gen 14:17–20 is the existing confession of the Son as given in 1:1—2:18. Hebrews puts it explicitly in 7:3: Melchizedek is made like the Son. Later, he will put it the other way around (7:15) but this is after the framework has been established and the point is clear that he is using shorthand for the priestly order as such, to wit, that he is high priest "according to" the order of Melchizedek. As in 8:5 and 10:1 and throughout, the Son is both the original and ultimate, for whom Melchizedek serves as the middle link.

If these things are borne in mind, most complaints about Hebrews' logic—that Jesus *did* have a mother, etc.—are shown to be disingenuous or misguided or both. If we do not accept Hebrews' truth claims, we will fault his argument not only here but throughout. If we do accept those claims, this is rather straightforward. In fact, 7:1–10 is not on the margins of NT interpretive practices, but representative of its heart.

Verses 1–10 proceed in two parts: Firstly, vv. 1–3 comprise a single, highly involved Greek sentence built out of the simple statement, "For this Melchizedek remains a priest for all time." Between the subject and predicate of that clause run a whole string of modifiers that are inferences from Gen 14, like so:

For this Melchizedek

> king of Salem
>
> priest of God Most High
>
> who met Abraham when he returned from the slaughter of the kings
>
>> and blessed him
>
> to whom also Abraham gave a tenth from everything

>
> firstly being interpreted as king of righteousness
>
> and then also king of Salem
>
> > which is king of peace
>
> without mother
>
> without father
>
> without genealogy
>
> having neither beginning of days nor end of life
>
> resembling the Son of God
>
>   remains a priest for all time.

There are, then, five pairs with a closing modifier: king-priest, blessing-tithe, righteousness-peace, motherless-fatherless, without genealogy-eternal, resembling the Son. The final modifier qualifies the sense in which he "remains a priest for all time."

Secondly, vv. 4–10 elaborate particularly, though not exclusively, on the matter of the tithe and the blessing—the matters most directly attested by Gen 14—and their implication for the superiority of this priestly order. The closing words echo the beginning, signaling the rounding out of the initial comparison.

## Background

As for the Jewish fascination with Melchizedek,[1] he is in some texts a merely human figure (1QapGen XXII, 12–25; Philo, *Congr.* 99; *Abr.* 235; Josephus, *A.J.* 1.179–82; *B.J.* 6.438; Ps-Eup. [*OTP* 2:880]; cf. *Jub.* 13:25; *b. Ned.* 32b; *Lev. Rab.* 25:6) but these texts would have provided no impetus for Hebrews' exalted descriptors. Several other texts present him as something more than human (e.g., Philo, *Congr.* 99; *Migr.* 29; *Leg.* 3.79–82), yet again the dissimilarities are strongly against derivation.

More promising are those texts among the Qumran Scrolls and related writings that formulated hope of a priestly messiah and that speculated richly on the figure of Melchizedek. "11QMelchizedek presents Melchizedek as a heavenly, eschatological figure in the service of God. He will delivers [sic] the righteous on God's behalf and will execute judgment on Belial

---

1. For the following, see Koester, *Hebrews*, 339–41, whom I am summarizing. For the sake of brevity I leave out *2 Enoch* and gnostic texts, both of which are addressed by Koester.

and his lot. Also, Melchizedek will make atonement for those of his own lot."[2] Yet Hebrews does not present Melchizedek as a heavenly figure and does not understand his appearance to Abraham as an angelophany. Hebrews had more in common with the Qumran sectarians than with Philo but, particularly when attention is paid to the substantial discontinuities, they do not rise to the level of proof for influence.[3]

For perspective, David Hay's comment finally seems to us apt. He observes that for moderns it seems that Hebrews has made far too much of the little we are given about Melchizedek in Gen 14 and Ps 110:4, and opines:

> The marvel about the argument concerning Melchizedek in Heb 5–7 is not that the author has made so much out of so little, but that he has made so little out of so much. It is clear that at least within Judaism large clouds of speculation swirled about Melchizedek, and there can be little doubt that the author of the epistle knew more than he chose to elaborate (cf. 7:1–3). With the most astonishing thrift, or absolute reserve, he determined to know nothing of him that could not be inferred from Gen 14:18–20 and Ps 110:4 (chiefly the latter).[4]

In sum, two main possibilities present themselves, neither of which excludes Hebrews' awareness of the strains we have reviewed or his marshaling of their ideas: The writer, with remarkable skill and deftness, studiously avoided committing himself to any of the strains of speculation, perhaps as a quiet form of polemic against these conceptions. Or the writer was simply focused so intently and single-mindedly on his own subject matter—the Son who is Jesus as high priest according to Ps 110:4—that his overall conception naturally (and non-polemically) differentiates itself. The latter seems to us the simpler hypothesis, even if it could overlap in part with the former.

## Comments on Wording

7:1 *King of Salem*. That is, the Jebusite city that became Jerusalem (Gen 14:18; 2 Sam 5:6–10; Ps 76:2).

---

2. Mason, 'You Are a Priest Forever,' 185; based on a close analysis of 11QMelchizedek (11Q13) and comparisons with *Visions of Amram* (4Q543–4Q549) and *Songs of the Sabbath Sacrifice* (4Q400); cf. 196–8. It is worth noticing the levels of speculation necessarily involved in reaching these conclusions.

3. Mason, 'You Are a Priest Forever,' 203, himself makes no claim of dependence but merely that there are in fact "parallels."

4. Hay, *Glory*, 152–53.

7:2 *by translation of his name.* These interpretations of the names are given primarily by way of heaping up praise; ostensibly this is praise of Melchizedek, but actually it is further praise of the Son to whom Melchizedek points. The interpretations stem from the Hebrew etymologies, which were common knowledge.

*King of righteousness . . . peace.* See 1:3, 5–6, 8–9, 13; 5:11–14; 7:14; 12:11, 28; 13:20.

7:4 *See how great this man was.* Rhetorically the invitation is to focus on Melchizedek but the real intent is the (canonically-textually presented) man as a *figure* of what was to come, and Abraham's *faith* that saw what was to come in what was shown and said to him (just as in 11:8–19).

7:5 *a commandment in the law . . . from the people . . . though these also are descended.* The reference to the law anticipates the need of a change of law, which will come to a head in the citation of Jer 31—he points this out *because of* Jer 31. The Son, too, is descended from Abraham, but—so the writer wants us to ponder—he is such only as Son *of God* (7:28). Moreover, though indubitably a duly appointed priest of the one true God Most High the Son is not a Levite, again, with implications for the law. The final phrase, *though these also are descended from Abraham*, entails the point that will be playfully but earnestly made explicit in vv. 9–10.

7:7 *It is beyond dispute that the inferior is blessed by the superior.* Strictly in terms of word use an inferior can "bless" a superior; Hebrews' claim concerns a particular kind of "blessing." Even so, it is hard to see *formal* features that place Gen 14:19–20 in a special class of benedictory pronouncements. Like the rest of Heb 7:1–10, the exegesis of Gen 14:19–20 is founded on the conviction of its ultimate referent, the Son of God, as figurally presented.

7:8 *by mortal men . . . by one of whom it is testified that he lives.* We take it that the claim is not that the Canaanite priest Melchizedek is immortal alongside the Son, still less that he is the pre-incarnate Son himself, but that the Scriptural-Christological presentation of him serves as a pattern of the Son who has a two-fold claim on indestructible life (to be elaborated pastorally in vv. 11–25), so that Abraham's conduct also manifests the pattern of faith-obedience related to the Son. At the same time, the inability of the Aaronic priests to bring "perfection" is signaled, also in preparation for vv. 11–25.

7:9 *One might even say.* Hebrews is insistent on the human ancestry of Jesus (2:10–14; 7:14), so he was also "in Abraham's loins." Hebrews assumes we understand that the Son both is and is not a descendent of Abraham. Accordingly, if v. 9 is play it is serious play that is merely a closing flourish in the spirit of the *whole* of 7:1–10; the intent of v. 9's opening phrase was probably to signal somewhat more explicitly to the readers the nature of the entire argument.

## Comments on Theological Themes

If we wish to argue that for Hebrews Melchizedek is more than human we cannot stop at treating him as "angelic" on the grounds that an angelic profile aligns with a particular Jewish parallel. Hebrews is much bolder. Melchizedek is on par with the Son, so nothing less than divine. Of course if we go that route we also end up with two eternal priests, which is absurd on Hebrews' own terms. The view that Melchizedek was the pre-incarnate Christ himself is a "solution" that cuts against the whole grain of what Hebrews actually says. For the rest, see above.

At the very birth of the promise in its historical form the whole history is contained *in nuce*. Reading it (Ps 110:4 and Gen 14:17–20 combined) in the light of the Son makes apparent its radical implications for the whole history of the divine word and thus for faith. Primarily, this particular episode in Genesis is pregnant with implications for the Son's priestly identity and role, with entailments for the entire Aaronic priesthood and sacrificial system. Creatively and elegantly expressed for pastoral effect it is this that the writer of Hebrews is intending. The whole of Heb 7:1–10 is praise of the Son through the praise of Melchizedek, but, again, it is praise *of the Son*. It is, no less, a call to imitate Abraham who "through faith and patience" inherited "the promises" (6:12), with sweeping implications for obedience to the whole of the divine word. It is the indirectness of this exposition, fully reliant on the "way the words run" in the Scriptures, that gives it its unique potency so long as it is understood for what it is.

## Teaching Hebrews 7:1–10

1. Scripture and interpretation. A passage whose existence is owed to the lead of the Scriptures has come to be treated by many moderns as an abuse of the Scriptures because it does not align with modern interpretive rules. See on 1:5–14 regarding the writer's entire approach to interpretation and its implications for our own. If we are willing to inhabit Hebrews' own perspective we cannot but marvel at the artistry of the divine Storyteller.

2. Christology. 7:1–10 is written in praise of the Son and for the deepening of faith. Any exposition that departs from these interests is to that

extent disconnected from Hebrews' concerns. Unlike all other priests, the Son does not occupy a priestly order, as if something greater than him. He *is* the order ... of which God spoke in the prophets.

3. Further with respect to staying on topic: It would be a distraction to speculate on whether Hebrews believed that a pagan, Canaanite priest was counted an authentic priest of the true God, still less that a knowledge of the true God would have arisen by some version of natural theology. Parts of the Jewish tradition sampled above understood Melchizedek to be a true priest of the true God,[5] but Hebrews is preoccupied with his canonical function as a figure of the *Son's* priestly *order*. That it is priestly service to the one God Most High is true because it is true of the Son, with Melchizedek being made like (Scripturally *presented* like) the Son; it is the same logic operative for "without father," etc.

4. Likewise: This is not a text about Christian tithing. Tithing plainly has a place in Genesis 14 and in the law of Moses but its function in Heb 7:1–10 is exclusively one of signaling the faith of Abraham and the preeminence of the Son as priest according to the order of Melchizedek.

5. Salvation. 7:1–10 is a key passage in drawing our attention forward to the great salvation to which the law witnessed, but it is as committed as the rest of Hebrews to the proposition that the law was the normative witness. Hebrews does not discount the law, as if happily throwing it into the bin of obsolescence. It is rather establishing the law for what it was and remains, without which faith has no vision of its object. The chief implications for the great salvation of the Son are taken up in the rest of the sermon.

6. Concerning the Son as King of righteousness and peace: The discourse as a whole is concentrated on the point of entry into the land of salvation. But, insofar as that salvation is available already now, it is as if to say, "The land lies open before you. Occupy it. Flourish in its harvest of righteousness and peace. Live as members of this covenantal community and actively bring its conditions to realization. Extend its borders." And indeed, it turns out that doing so is our only hope of finding entrance at all in the end (5:11—6:12).

---

5. Moreover, the biblical tradition itself evidences a complex view of those outside Israel's covenantal relationship, whether of a figure such as Balaam (Num 22–25); a pagan "prophet" (Titus 1:12–13; cf. Acts 17:28); or Abraham himself at the time of his initial summons; cf. Gen 4:26. But what Hebrews thought on these things is neither apparent nor relevant.

7. Faith. Part of what 6:12 and imitating Abraham's faith involves is what 7:1–10 is about. If one wishes to align oneself with the faith that pleases God (11:6), one must align oneself with Abraham's penetrating, even prescient faith in the promise.

# 7:11–28

*"I give them eternal life, and they will never perish,*
*and no one will snatch them out of my hand.*
*My Father, who has given them to me, is greater than all,*
*and no one is able to snatch them out of the Father's hand.*
*I and the Father are one."*

## Context

SEE 4:14–16; 5:1–10; 7:1–10, all of which set the context. As we proceed we have to resist the urge to reduce Hebrews' to a straightforwardly reasoned argument. There is a definite logic, but there are also extras bundled in (e.g., v. 22). The artistry is in pulling this off without clouding the main thread. The key to understanding how this is so is in recognizing that the aim is not the pursuit of ideas but of a vision of the Son and his history. The coherence and the rhetorical force of the whole derive from the larger drama. The text itself is merely a witness and need say no more than is sufficient to bring that drama to mind.

In 7:11–19 it is the change of the epochs, from shadow to perfection, from ineffectual to effectual, that is foremost. To draw this out Jesus' apparent liability is made his greatest asset: That as priest in the Melchizedekian order he is not descended from Levi does not disqualify him. That possibility is not even acknowledged. Rather the point is pressed that the fact of his indestructible life both squares the circle of the diverse OT passages—Ps 110:4 as against the Mosaic law—and uniquely qualifies him to be the one true priest. The Levitical priesthood is thereby put in proper perspective and the way is opened to affirm that a total change of law was the anticipated outcome from the beginning (8:1–13). As becomes evident, that change is actually the removal of the copy so that its prior, its original, which is the true, stands alone. The Son is not subservient to the law, but the law to the Son.

Verses 20-22 cash in what was said about oaths in 6:16-18, underscoring the inviolability of Ps 110:4 as divine intention and reliable promise. The inviolability and permanence of the divine word is complemented by the inviolability and permanence of the Son's life and thus his priesthood (vv. 23-25), whereby he is able to save forever.[1] At the same time we are made to see that the change of law that has been undertaken does not signal a perpetual cycle of changes but is unidirectional and final, representing what was the intention from the very beginning.

The whole is brought to its climax in vv. 26-28 gathering together things previously affirmed and heaping up the praise of the Son in a way calculated to engender trust and obedience fit for him. At the same time, the emphasis of these last verses prepares the way for the shift from the fact and nature of the Son's priestly identity to his work and the location of that work in 8:1—10:18.

## Background

With this passage we enter a world quite removed from ours, some features of which we can at least mention.

Hebrews' strong comments on the limitations of the law's effects depend wholly on his christological commitments and, absent those commitments, would have raised the strongest of objections from those Jews still centered in some fashion on Moses. Moreover, we should assume that for Hebrews the law was a single fabric; it would not have contemplated a change of only part of the law, e.g., the ritual, leaving the rest untouched. Jewish beliefs, in contrast, were that the law was eternal (*Jub.* 13:26); the conviction was that it would continue forever in ways that would be at odds with Hebrews' argument (e.g., *4 Ezra* 9:36-37; *2 Bar.* 77:15; Philo, *Mos.* 2.14-15).[2]

The allusion to the covenant (*diathēkē*) in 7:22 is the first mention of this institution in Hebrews. In the Hellenistic world this word was used of a *last will and testament* (cf. Heb 9:16-17). It had been used by the LXX,

---

1. Quietly affirmed in this paralleling of the inviolability and permanence of both word and Son is the virtual identification of the Son and divine speech, even if not quite in John's fashion; see on 4:12-13.

2. Jesus, according to Matt 5:17-19, on his own terms (finally consistent with Hebrews) insisted on the continuation of the law to the end of world history.

however, to translate *berit*, *covenant* (e.g., Gen 6:18; 15:18; Exod 24:7-8; Deut 4:13), which determined most of its uses in the NT.

In 7:22 the Son is also said to have become the *guarantor* or *surety* of a better covenant. In common practice a surety agreed to assume responsibility for another person's debt if that person should be unable to meet the obligation.[3] It is not a term naturally associated with either the divine covenant or with wills, but in the extended sense of guaranteeing something it follows somewhat naturally from the emphasis on the divine oath. As usual in Hebrews the Son's *being* is closely bound up with the divine *word*; if the Son did not have an "indestructible life" (v. 16) the divine oath would be in vain (hence vv. 23-25). At the same time this characterization (guarantee) anticipates another, that of a *mediator* (8:6; 9:15; 12:24) of the covenant.

In 7:25 the Son's intercessory ministry as a priest is pointedly emphasized. The tradition existed in Judaism of seeking out someone approved by God to bring a request (e.g., Exod 8:8; 1 Sam 7:8). Angels were thought to bring people's requests before God. In secular matters, members of the imperial household were well positioned to gain access to the emperor, or others somehow close to the throne.[4]

Hebrews will observe in 7:27 (cf. 10:11) that the Son does not have need to make *daily* offerings for his *sins* as did the Levitical high priests. In fact the Levitical high priest "officiated as a priest only on festive occasions,"[5] and the sacrifices for a priest's sins were occasional rather than daily (Lev 4:3); the double offering, first for his sins and then for those of the people, was that of the *annual* Day of Atonement. Differing explanations have been given for Hebrews' comment—e.g., he may have conflated the daily offerings (the Tamid offering; Exod 29:38-42; Num 28:3-8; Sir 45:14) with the Day of Atonement because they are sometimes listed together, or he may have been thinking of the meal offering that accompanied each Tamid offering[6]—but the writer may merely have generalized on the idea of *necessity*, apart from whether in fact the need was addressed daily. Another such generalization occurs at 10:11. More broadly, the argument of Hebrews is that the variegated cultus taken as a whole and with the Day of Atonement at its heart foreshadowed the priestly work of the Son. The Mosaic law is like a dispersive prism that separates the colors of the single, unified light of Christ's work.

---

3. Koester, *Hebrews*, 363.
4. Ibid., 365-66.
5. Schürer, *History of the Jewish People*, 275-76.
6. For these and other suggestions, see Attridge, *Hebrews*, 213-14.

## Comments on Wording

*7:11 if perfection had been attainable through the Levitical priesthood.* The claim that is inferential at this point is a straightforward assertion in vv. 18–19 (cf. 9:8–10; 10:1–4), which see. Something that is simply true can and in this case must also be arguably true. For *perfection* see the introduction to this commentary and 2:10–18.

*under it the people received the law.* The ESV's translation is possible, but it is more likely that the sense is, *the law given established that priesthood* (see NIV, 2011).[7] The law is not ignored or twisted through selective treatment by Hebrews; it is met head on. In anticipation of v. 14 and just as in 10:8 Hebrews requires us to see that the *divinely given* law established the temple, its priesthood, and its rites, indicating both their abiding authority and properly limited function within the final saving economy. Putting the law in this light reveals its Author's intent and the form that faith must take in the present.

*7:12 there is necessarily a change in the law as well.* This anticipates 8:1–13. The preacher is rhetorically preparing us for that, creating a sense of drama, but he himself will not have backed into Jer 31 as a solution to Ps 110:4. He interprets the psalm against the backdrop of the promised and now inaugurated new covenant. Yet he is in earnest: By design, the psalm anticipated that there would have to be a change of law.

*7:13 from which [tribe] no one has ever served at the altar.* That is, as a member of the divinely established (Aaronic) priesthood in connection with the Day of Atonement (contrast, e.g., 2 Sam 24:25; 1 Kgs 3:4; 8:22). The OT speaks of the Levitical priesthood continuing into perpetuity (Exod 40:15; Num 18:19; 25:13); see on 5:1–10 and 8:1–6. Priestly genealogies were maintained both before and after AD 70 (Josephus, *C. Ap.* 1.32).

*7:15 This becomes even more evident.* Formally the argument of 7:11–14 was showing that Ps 110:4 indicated from *within* the epoch of the old covenant that this change of order was pending. In actuality that exposition assumed the Son as the subject matter of Ps 110 and read it accordingly. At this point (vv. 15–19) we are merely asked to circle around and look at the same thing from the other side, from the fact of the Son who is known from the Scriptures rather than the Scriptures as known from the Son.

*another priest arises in the likeness of Melchizedek.* The verb for "to arise" here and in v. 11 (*anistēmi*) is elsewhere used of the resurrection, and

---

7. This translation represents a change from the previous edition of the NIV, which read, "for on the basis of it [the priesthood] the law was given to the people." For a defense of the NIV's new and more likely translation, see Koester, *Hebrews*, 353; he translates "the people had been given Law about it."

the play on the latter meaning is likely intentional, particularly in the light of v. 16.

7:16 *not on the basis of a legal requirement concerning bodily descent*. That is, *not according to the law of a fleshly command*; this anticipates 7:23–25, 28; 9:9–10.

*by the power of an indestructible life*. Firstly this is his resurrection life but it is likely (1:1–14; 7:3) that the idea encompasses the life he always possessed. See the introduction to this commentary.

7:18 *a former commandment is set aside*. The language here goes farther than v. 12 in speaking of an annulment (*athetēsis*; cf. the verb in Mark 7:9; Gal 3:15) of the foregoing commandment, where the allusion appears to be to the complex of laws bearing on the Levitical priesthood (see, likewise, 8:13; 10:9)—yet this aspect was of one fabric with the entire law of the covenant. See on 8:1–6.

7:20 *For those who formerly became priests were made such without an oath*. The point concerns individuals, not tribes.

7:22 *the guarantor of a better covenant*. The language of firmness, security, permanence, and so forth is diffused throughout Hebrews (cf. 6:19). Within vv. 20–25 the reassuring guarantee of the promise, on which one may and must stake all, is bound up with its effectual application (vv. 23–25).

7:24 *he holds his priesthood permanently, because he continues forever*. Verses 20–25 are not making two separate points, but are looking at the two complementary sides of one thing: the oath and the contents of the oath in the person of the Son who is Jesus. Had not the Son been who he was, as revealed in 1:1–14 (compare 1:11–12; cf. 13:8), the divine oath would have been empty; conversely, the meaning of the oath is revealed in the Son. Because he abides forever, he can be and is the guarantor of v. 22 who is grounded in the oath.

7:25 *he is able to save to the uttermost those who draw near to God through him, since he always lives to make intercession for them*. The only salvation that interests the writer is not complete unless eternal, and not eternal unless complete. It might be that the rendering *completely* more clearly indicates this for English readers. The phrase *through him* is primarily comfort and encouragement in intent, but it is equally a warning; the exclusivity it involves is not incidental to Hebrews' whole argument. See on 2:17–18.

7:28 *the oath, which came later than the law, appoints a Son who has been made perfect forever*. The "weakness" of the Levitical priests (and *a fortiori* the weakness of any other human priest) inhered at once in their defilement (5:2; 7:27) and mortality (7:23–25), neither of which can be ascribed to the raised Son. While the priests' humanity in 5:1 was a point of similarity with the Son (cf. 2:10–18; 5:5–10), there is a quiet but firm contrast in the present verse when they are characterized as *humans* and he is named the *Son*. He is one of them and not one of them.

## Comments on Theological Themes

In 7:12 there is a *change* of law and in 7:18 (8:13; 10:9) the Mosaic law is *set aside*, annulled—indicating strong *discontinuity* and implying a *new law*. These comments are made with a view to the laws concerning the priesthood and its rituals, but since the law was one seamless fabric it finally has sweeping implications for a whole change of covenant. It is clear from the argument of 8:1–13 that Hebrews draws a direct line from 7:12 through 7:22 to Jer 31. Yet in Jer 31 (Heb 8:7–13) it is a feature of that new covenant that these same, Mosaic laws (again, all of one, seamless fabric) will be put on their minds and written on their hearts—indicating strong *continuity*. The hidden key is the logic of death and resurrection, with its continuity and discontinuity. Nearer the surface is the argument of 8:1–6, which see.

Meanwhile it is critical to observe that for Hebrews the appropriate form of authentic faith before Christ necessarily involved the erection of the tabernacle, sacrifice of animals, and the rest of the priestly rituals—in this way they upheld the gospel. The same faith following Christ necessarily "sets aside" the Mosaic commandments in turning exclusively to the Son as high priest and his once-for-all offering—in this way they uphold Moses's law.

No OT claim (e.g., 1 Sam 15:22; Ps 40:6; Isa 66:3; Hos 6:6) goes as far as does Hebrews in claiming that the divinely ordained institutions were "weak and useless" (7:18–19; cf. 8:4; 9:9–10; 10:1–4, 11), though Hebrews will find a pointer in this direction in Ps 40 (Heb 10:5–10, which see). This claim cannot be sustained on the grounds of historical exegesis of the OT alone but finally only from the revelation of the gospel. Their efficacy as rites was circumscribed by the symbolic drama they enacted (Heb 8:5; 9:6–10, 23–24; 10:1–4), yet when met in faith they were gospel (4:2, 6) and effected full salvation with true forgiveness and cleansing (e.g., Lev 16; Ps 51:1–9; Ps 103:12). *Of themselves* they accomplished nothing of the salvation now revealed, which is the only salvation; *of themselves*, they revealed nothing of the God with whom the Son is identified.[8] To prefer them to the Son is to deny that salvation and that knowledge. It is the achievement of that salvation and its application that is intended by Hebrews when it speaks of "perfection" (for perfection, see on 2:10–18 and the introduction to this commentary).

---

8. This point is expanded and explained in Laansma, "Living and Active Word."

The mention of Christ's ongoing intercessory ministry in 7:25 (cf. 9:24) registers that the claims to a sympathetic high priest (4:14–16; cf. 2:17–18; 5:7–10) were not empty sentiments, for the preacher has now backed up the claim that we do *have* such a priest, duly appointed. It also indicates that the ongoing intercessory work that frames the central exposition (4:14–16; 10:19–25) is integral to everything said in 5:1—10:18. Indeed, 7:25 is the very cap of 5:1–10 and 7:1–25, with 7:26–28 serving as a closing flourish. An implication and clarifying comment follow: Salvation hinges forever on the faithfulness of the Son—nothing else or more—but for just this reason it is secure. While the Son's intercession might seem to imply the reluctance of the Father to forgive and help, this work is in fact a fulfillment of the Father's own promise. As always, human images cannot contain and limit God's acts where the images are used to reveal it.

The strong affirmations of the Son's exaltation, holiness, and separateness in 7:26–28 require us to hold together his full humanity and full deity as developed earlier. Salvation, and particularly Christ's priestly work, had to be a work of one fully human and—because the whole of humanity was hopelessly compromised and impotent (sin) and because the promised benefits were beyond the capacities of the human creature to bestow (finitude)—the work fully of God. In the one who is Son these requirements were met, each without compromise. Of course the revelation that it had to be so came to light only in the event of this salvation itself. See also on 5:1–10.

Finally, regarding 7:28 and its emphasis that the promise of Ps 110:4 came *after the law* (cf. the similar argument of 4:6–9): There is a superficial tension between that claim and Paul's in Gal 3:15–18. Both writers, however, finally view the promise given Abraham as the fundamental and inviolable word from which all that follows must be understood; both agree that the law was not a final word but a shadow of what was coming (Col 2:17).

## Teaching Hebrews 7:11–28

1. In terms of translating and preaching to a Gentile audience: The gospel does not negate and replace the OT but assumes and subsumes it. Hebrews is not a version of the gospel for Jews but for all believers, Jews and Gentiles. We are all sons and daughters of Abraham, heirs of the same promise—the promise of entrance into God's holy resting place—and therefore equally in need of a priest and sacrifice. Jesus is our great high priest and must be known as such. See on 5:1–10. By that same token, the church must recognize that the anti-Judaism

and anti-Semitism that was woven into the church's teaching from the earliest centuries must be repented of as nothing other than paganism. It is the glory of the law to be the servant of the gospel and its dishonor to be anything else, but it does have the glory proper to it (2 Cor 3:7–18; cf. John 1:16–18). It is not any form of human priesthood that is a copy and shadow of the true, but solely this one. We cannot fail to see the abiding necessity of these things for seeing Jesus and his gospel for what they are. We never outgrow the OT revelation, nor do we have the Son without it.

2. Maybe the best counsel for teaching 7:11–28 is to review its formal features. In vv. 11–19 the argument proceeds inferentially first by considering how the word of Ps 110:4—as read in the light of its subject matter, which is the Son—signaled from within the OT itself that "perfection" was not attained through the institutions commanded by Moses in themselves and that what we know as the new covenant was always intended (vv. 11–14); secondly, it shows how the appearance of the Son—as understood through the Scripture of Ps 110:4—established this as obvious and undeniable (vv. 15–19). These are simply two perspectives on the same thing, since each needs the other. It is this salvation that was always the content of the promise given Abraham, the promise that flowered via Moses's covenant and ultimately in the Son and the new covenant.

3. In vv. 20–25 the argument is again fashioned out of complementary perspectives that combine to show a) not only the surpassing-ness, and b) not only the completeness and eternity of this salvation, but c) its unidirectional and final nature. On the one side is the divine oath that distinguishes the Son's priesthood from Aaron's (vv. 20–22); on the other side is the Son himself as the one who abides and so never fails nor abdicates his office. As such, he is the meaning of Ps 110:4's oath and its (for it contains the new covenant) guarantor. For this reason "he is able to save to the uttermost those who draw near to God through him, since he always lives to make intercession for them."

4. Finally, vv. 26–28 at once a) reprise and conclude the first half of the main exposition of Ps 110 (5:1–10 and 7:1–28), b) extend its praise of the Son for the sake of encouraging the faith of obedience, and c) prepare the way for the second half of the exposition in 8:1—10:18.

5. In short, Hebrews as a whole, and not least in 7:11–28, provides nothing less than a panoramic "walk through the Bible" form of biblical theology at its best. It is the Bible doing its own theology. What we

have here are not merely reflections organized into the parts of a system. We have, rather, the organically unfolding drama of God's revelation where its central interests are most at stake. More, Heb 7:11–28 is the announcement of *arrival*, with the greatest possible light shed on the destination of that journey. It is an understanding of the anchor of which the writer spoke in 6:19, the anchor needed in the storms of the present age that threaten to destroy us.

# 8:1–6

*"Something greater than the
temple is here."*

## Context

FOR THE BROADER OUTLINE, see 4:14–16; 5:1–10.

    Hebrews 8:1—10:18 proceeds by weaving Ps 110 together with other OT texts (e.g., Exod 25:40; 24:8; not least, Ps 40; other allusions abound) and uniting the entire fabric with the person of the Son who is Jesus. Chiefly, Jer 31:31–34 will feature prominently in 8:1—10:18, being verbally combined with Psalm 110 at both the beginning (8:1–13) and end (10:11–18). Indeed, Jer 31 had been omnipresent in Hebrews from the very start and broke through to the surface in 7:22. The singular promise to Abraham with its long history finds its meaning and fulfillment in the Son, who is high priest forever in the order of Melchizedek, guarantor and mediator of the better covenant. In that covenant the one promise disperses into promises which are better because they go to the original and ultimate intent of the inheritance vouchsafed to Abraham. In other ways, too, 8:1—10:18 reveals things assumed and operative all through the earlier phases of the sermon.

    Accordingly, with 8:1–6 the writer gathers up his argument thus far and pushes yet deeper into its subject matter, shifting from Ps 110:4 to 110:1. It has been established (5:1—7:28) that we have such a high priest and that with this appointment there necessarily comes a change of law, which means a change of covenant; the OT, freshly understood, had anticipated all this. That new covenant with its better promises is centered on a better offering, the effectual offering in the true tabernacle which is once-for-all in application and which annuls the command to enact a rite whose *raison d'être* was to model and foreshadow this offering. To put it one way: To continue with the Mosaic rites would be to deny the arrival of the true offering, as if something more was to be anticipated; it would be to ascribe the efficacy to the old covenant's goats and calves that belongs to the Son alone. More to the preacher's point: If confidence was placed in these as what was commanded by God, how much more complete can be the confidence placed in that to which they pointed; how much more confidently all can be staked on this offering, where "all" embraces the harsh day-to-day realities faced by them and their families in their Roman world.

Verses 1–6 are bookended by the mention of the priestly ministry of Christ (*leitourgos* [priestly minister] in v. 2, *leitourgia* [priestly ministry] in v. 6) and falls into three parts. Verses 1–2 register the "main point" of the argument so far and announce what will be the new focus, the ministry in the true tabernacle. Verses 3–5 articulate a key premise by restating part of the introduction of 5:1–4 and showing from Exod 25:40 what/where Christ's ministry is, how the Levitical relates to it, and that all this was indicated by the OT. Verse 6 then transitions to the remaining exposition regarding his better ministry, his mediatorial role in the better covenant, and the better promises that enact it. The rest of 8:7—10:18 will take up these subjects of v. 6 in reverse order: The better promises which establish (8:7–13) the better covenant of which he is mediator (9:1—10:10), according to which he has obtained a ministry superior to that of the Levitical priests (10:11–18).

## Background

Relating to the priesthood, see on 5:1–10. For Hebrews' preference for the heavenly tabernacle (vs. temple), its cosmology, and the relation between these, see on 4:14–16; for more on the Ancient Near Eastern background of the tabernacle and its relation to the cosmos, see on 3:7—4:11. More about the Mosaic tabernacle will be said at 9:1–10.

To repeat only part of that: In speaking as it does of the earthly and heavenly tabernacles (8:2, 5; 9:9, 11, 23–24; 10:1) the language of Greek philosophers[1] is utilized in ways that accentuate the security, permanence, and stability of the object of Christian faith and hope. Hebrews' rhetorical employment of the language of his day is to be observed and celebrated; it attests the translatability of the gospel. It is critical to notice, however, that words like *copy*, etc. are applied to the Mosaic tabernacle as a way of communicating its provisional, subordinate place in covenantal history. It is not a matter of firstly adhering to metaphysical claims about the cosmos and then applying them to the Mosaic tabernacle—which would leave his

---

1. E.g., Philo, *Mos.* 2.74; cf. Attridge, *Hebrews*, 222–24.

argument collapsing in on itself—but of first understanding the history of the covenants and the relation of the Mosaic tabernacle to Christ and then seeing in that history a revelation of the history of the cosmos. As goes the tabernacle and the covenant, so goes the world. It is not as if the author *thought* he was doing what we describe but had *actually* been taken captive by Greek metaphysics; what we have described is the way the argument actually works.

## Comments on Wording

8:2 *the holy places, in the true tent that the Lord set up*. To take this language literalistically would be no less a modernist misreading than to attempt to bypass it by seeking some sort of scientifically acceptable knowledge concealed in their antiquated mythological fancies. We must inhabit the world as imaged-forth. As one aspect of this, notice that he speaks of the heavenly things as *made*; "heaven" is not external to creation; God works *within* and *for* his creation; salvation is not an escape from created things.

8:3 restates part of 5:1–4. (See 5:1–4).

8:4 *if he were on earth, he would not be a priest*. Rhetorically the argument of vv. 3–4 seems to subordinate Christ's offering to the Mosaic pattern: Priests must make offerings and the Levitical priests have their system; Christ cannot encroach on their domain so a different offering in a different locale must be found for him. Actually, in the end the theological logic works in the opposite direction, recalling 7:12 and the need of a change of law. It is not that the Levitical priests have proprietary rights over earth, so Christ must operate in a different domain. His rights always covered heaven *and* earth, and theirs was a visible and temporary copy and pointer to him; they were tenants, stewards. To have carried out another priestly work on their plane (merely earthly, in the nature of copies) would have 1) set God against his own word (he had promised that role to them forever), and 2) been as ineffectual as their work precisely because it was not heavenly (heaven always takes precedence, always rules; history always proceeds from there to earth—but it does proceed to earth). Or again, it is true that the law of the old covenant does establish the institutions of the Jewish tabernacle and temple. Another earthly tabernacle and offering would merely be a rival and a violation of God's command, of no more legitimacy than Jeroboam's altar—*that* is the sort of move that would amount to another priesthood "on earth." Though Hebrews will speak of annulment (7:18; 10:9), it will do so only on certain terms carefully constructed and consistently maintained. It will not tolerate a simple setting aside of the command of God. If, however, it is the case that the offerings commanded by Moses were from their very inception only the echo of the thing and event themselves, merely the "copy and shadow" of the true tabernacle, and if Christ's offering (which was very much *on earth*, as far as the cross) is the offering of that original and true tabernacle, then so far from being a rival and a violation it is the case that his offering needs no justification; it is in fact prior; it is what gave legitimacy to the offerings commanded by Moses, and the two systems are properly related—indeed, they are related as old covenant to new covenant. It is from this angle alone that we properly use the language of "annulment." It is also clear from this that the language of "copy and shadow" is at once vertical (earthly-heavenly) and horizontal (then and now) in orientation, for with the historical event of the death and ascension of Christ the "copy and shadow" has reached the end of its purpose and usefulness. The heavenly has become the earthly.

8:5 *a copy and shadow . . . . make everything according to the pattern*. Only insofar as it did correspond did it have purpose and meaning as a parabolic pointer to the genuine. It is of particular importance that the readers see that this was all *expressly* built into the old covenant so that they see that what has come about in Christ does not violate the divine speaker's intent but brings it to its goal (1:1–2).

8:6 *the covenant he mediates*. This verse serves to transition to the citation of Jeremiah 31 and the remaining exposition of 9:1—10:18. The high priest whom "we have" has obtained not a rival ministry nor merely a replacement, but a *superior* one, the original and genuine ministry after which Moses's ministry was fashioned and for which his served as a copy and shadow. That superiority was again anticipated and elaborated within the OT itself in the prophecy of a new covenant, of which he is the mediator (one who mediates between two parties to remove a disagreement or reach a common goal; 9:15: 12:24; cf. 2:3; 1 Tim 2:5). The way in which he is the mediator will be elaborated in 9:15–22, but first Jer 31 itself will be cited to show how this covenant is "better."

*it is enacted on better promises*. This bears on the change of law signaled in 7:11–12. "Better promises" indicates both the fact of arrival at the original intent of the Abrahamic promise (dispersed here into promises) and the contrast with the promises of the Mosaic covenant that concerned shadows and copies.

## Comments on Theological Themes

8:4 states that if Christ "were on earth, he would not be a priest." Pressed literalistically, this could mean that Christ is a priest only "in heaven" as spatially conceived. This could be made to mean that he was not a priest until after the ascension; it could also be made to mean that his offering could only transpire in the locale of heaven (e.g., the presentation of blood in the heavenly tent), not "on earth" (i.e., the cross). Such an argument not only misses the intent of Hebrews' words in context as we have understood them but is out of keeping with the larger vision of Hebrews, which includes Christ's incarnation and death within the act of self-offering and views heaven and earth as having joined in him. When Hebrews uses the phrase "on earth," the vertical contrast implied is finally at one with that of prior pattern (above) and subsequent copy (below), that which foreshadows and the eschatological thing itself, old covenant and new covenant, the present age and the age to come, the whole contrast of 12:18–29 (cf. 12:25); there is a vertical contrast, but never merely that. The conceptual tidiness of arguing that what occurred to Christ "on earth" cannot have been part of his offering is finally alien to Hebrews' thought.

## Teaching Hebrews 8:1–6

1. If we are preaching or teaching verse-by-verse we might proceed like so: verses 1–2—the state of the question—brings the entire exposition to a head (we *have* such a high priest; we have *such* a high priest; we have such a *high priest*) and announces the next step: Christ is a priestly minister in the genuine tent pitched by God himself.

2. Verses 3–5—the heart of the question—strikes at the heart of matters by reminding us from Moses himself that his cultic system, and the entire covenant of which it was an element, was a copy and shadow of a heavenly pattern, which was and is the genuine tabernacle and genuine act of atonement. The implication is as potent as it is clear: For God to be faithful to his own word (1:1–2) the only system over which Christ *could* preside as high priest is that of the original and authentic tabernacle; anything else would be a rival and betrayal. This is indeed the "change of law" (7:12) that was shown to be necessary if God was to be faithful to his own word (4:6–7; 7:11–19; 8:7–13). It is accordingly a change that is a step "backwards" (to what preceded, commissioned, and authorized) and "upwards" (toward the divine act as such, which is always oriented from "above" to "below") as much as

it "forwards" (to what is historically new and final). As such it changes nothing and changes everything. It changes nothing in the sense that so far from saying that the Mosaic system was wrong-headed and intrinsically mistaken, Christ establishes it; it is forever necessary (for believers of any ethnic and national stripe) to view the authentic through Moses. It changes everything by ushering us through and past the Mosaic directly into the authentic tabernacle and commanding us to make that journey. What grace gives—immediate access to the divine throne in the genuine tabernacle—it gives as a command and with ultimate seriousness.

3. Finally, v. 6—the pursuit of the question—outlines how this will be developed and the inner logic of the whole argument to come in 8:7—10:18. The better promises on the basis of which the new covenant is legally enacted (8:7-13) reveal the extent to which it is a better covenant of which he is the mediator (9:1—10:10) in accordance with which we affirm that he has obtained a superior ministry (10:11-18). All the weight of what follows 10:18 falls on the necessity of unreserved obedience to this ministry (cf. 5:9).

4. In Hebrews itself these six verses, immediately on the heels of the earlier exposition, would have taken only a couple of minutes themselves and before long the discourse would be into the implications (10:19—13:17). Any exposition that sets up camp here necessarily requires that we make explicit the drama within which Moses, the Son, and those of faith fit. Our lives are being translated into this drama because it concerns the whole of creation whose story is at its end; because Jesus the Son is the hinge on which everything turns; because Jesus' history is the history of God's promise passing through Moses; because Moses is the divinely chosen witness; because God who does not lie must be found faithful to his own word; because through Moses we see our great salvation. Because of all that we see that faith is possible, and we see that and how it is possible to inherit what was promised.

# 8:7–13

*"It is written in the Prophets, 'And they will all be taught by God.'"*

## Context

THE WHOLE OF 5:1—10:18 was overviewed at 4:14-16 and 5:1-10, which see. The specific development of 8:1—10:18 was overviewed with 8:1-6. Having observed that the oracle of Ps 110:4, its background narrative in Gen 14, and the "rise" of the Son who is Jesus combine to signal a change of law (5:1-10; 7:1-28) the preacher proceeded with great economy to show that the logic of the covenants left nowhere to look but to the pattern shown Moses in Exod 25 (8:1-6). The law of the original tabernacle, that after which Moses's tabernacle was fashioned, is the law of the new covenant, and the promises of the new covenant merely bring to full blossom the singular promise to Abraham, a promise that concerned the history of creation itself. Moses's law and covenant belong to that historical development as a copy of the original and a foreshadowing of the thing itself. As such its system was designed to point, not itself to effect the perfection promised. This limitation of both intent and effect was signaled from inside the old covenant when Jeremiah spoke of the new covenant and conveyed its "better promises" on which is based the enactment of the better covenant. It is this that the writer will assert in 8:7-13, though its logic has been operative from the sermon's beginning. Mainly he will do so by quoting Jeremiah's own words, but the brief introduction of vv. 7-8a and the equally brief concluding comment of v. 13 pack a punch. Having got that far, the argument will proceed to show at greater length that Christ is in fact the mediator of a covenant that is better (9:1—10:10) and that to that extent he obtained a superior ministry (10:11-18). This whole logic was summarized in 8:6.

But is the citation of Jer 31 at this juncture a rehearsal of its promises? Hebrews' brief comments that precede and follow the citation in vv. 8 and 13 concentrate on the defects of what preceded the announcement of a new covenant and the implication that the old is thereby set aside. Even so, the bulk of the citation—the longest in the NT—expresses the positive promise of the new and its mention of the defects serves mainly to highlight the jewel's beauty by placing it on a black cloth. To speak of "better promises" entails the need to address in what sense the good divine promises of the old covenant were deficient, not yet bringing perfection—all to the glory of the new and to the end of greater encouragement. Both sides of this will be explored through 9:1—10:10, before returning to Jer 31 and highlighting only its positive side (10:11–18).

See further the introduction to this commentary.

## Background

Jer 31:31–34 is rarely cited in the older Jewish midrashim,[1] and though the new covenant was important for the Qumran sectarians (CD 6:19; 8:21; 20:12) the passage from Jer 31 is not cited in these contexts. Ellingworth comments that for the sectarians the new covenant "was understood as a more rigorous re-establishment of Torah observance, with additional rules. The spiritualization of the idea of sacrifice contrasts with the realistic centrality of the death of Christ in Hebrews' treatment of the new covenant."[2] Nor is this passage from Jeremiah quoted elsewhere in the NT, though its presence is felt: Matt 26:28 (Mark 14:24; Luke 22:20); John 6:45; 1 Cor 11:25; 2 Cor 3:3, 6; Rom 11:27 (cf. 1 Thess 4:9; Acts 10:43). Its place in the liturgy of the eucharist would have planted it deep within the church's theology and experience.

Jer 31:31–34 falls within an extended prophecy of restoration to the land for exiled Israel (Jer 30–33). It is the only OT passage that makes explicit reference to a "new" covenant, though Isa 54:13 (cf. John 6:45) and Ezek 11:17–21 and 36:16–38 (cf. 2 Cor 3:1–3) overlap in substance; cf. Deut 4:29–31; 30:1–10; Isa 59:20–21; 27:9. A whole string of ideas from the context of Jer 30–33 would seem amenable to Hebrews' outlook (e.g., 30:8, 10; 31:2, 25; 32:37–39; 33:8, 15–18, 19–22), arguably because Hebrews represents a broader investment in the prophet's vision. His immediate pastoral ends require a disciplined argument, and his focus gets at the center of a larger reality.

1. Cf. Ellingworth, *Epistle to the Hebrews*, 414.
2. Ibid., 415.

In all, as proof texts go, the writer of Hebrews has Jer 31:31–34 on his side. His most dramatic infusion is, however, undeniably transformative in the total conflation of its words with the Son who is Jesus and all that is true in him (which involves the other OT texts and themes, including Exod 24:8 in 9:20 and Ps 40 in 10:5–10).

## Comments on Wording

8:7 *if that first covenant had been faultless, there would have been no occasion to look for a second.* The emphasis falls on the latter half: A second was in fact being looked for; therefore something lacked in the first. The assumed agent is God, since the initiative lies with God in what follows (cf. 4:6–8).

8:8 *he finds fault with them when he says.* The *fault* (cognates are used in vv. 7–8) shifts from the first covenant (v. 7) to the people, but only by equivocation in the sense of "fault." The rhetorical logic of vv. 7–8 anticipates that of v. 9, which begins with the assertion of a change of covenant to something different (meaning better, hence in place of something deficient), and goes on to give the reason as the unfaithfulness of the people. The differences indicated for the new covenant then address the root of unfaithfulness in the people. As the surrounding argument makes clear, the first covenant was not designed to bring perfection (thus its "fault") but to witness to that which does so. Meanwhile, the need of the greater priest and offering was made all the more clear by the disobedience (fault) of the people.

8:9 *not like the covenant.* In highlighting the earlier disobedience as well as the appointment of a new day the exposition of Ps 95 is recalled (3:7—4:11). But whereas there the emphasis fell on the continuity of the promise as heard (= gospel; 4:2, 6) so that their disobedience could serve as a negative example, here the emphasis falls on the new act of God in unilaterally establishing the event of salvation in these last days.

8:10 *I will put my laws into their minds* etc. The law that is written on the heart is ultimately the law of which Moses was a shadow, the law of the heavenly tabernacle (7:12) which was the pattern shown him (8:5); that *this* law is written on the heart does not ignore or reject Moses but attains the end of his witness and so removes Moses's law (7:18). The leading respect in which this inward inscription is developed in the following context is the effect on the conscience (e.g., 9:9–10, 13–14), with the result of obedience in the bold approach to God's throne. From that central act of obedience all else follows in covenant life.

8:11 *they shall not teach, each one his neighbor.* Both the context of Jeremiah and that of Hebrews assume that the new covenant involves continued priestly mediation (for Hebrews that is Christ's role exclusively) as well as the role of teachers in the community. See John 6:44-45.

**8:13** *In speaking of a new covenant, he makes the first one obsolete. And what is becoming obsolete and growing old is ready to vanish away.* The time frame intended could be that of the prophet, which would mean that Moses's covenant has now "vanished away" (the Greek wording allows this). It is possible, however, that the logic of 12:18-29 is quietly operative. Because the covenant is the inner basis of the cosmos and the cosmos the external basis of the covenant—because the temple is the center of the world and the world's history is bound up with it—there is an acknowledgement that the story of the old covenant and the cosmos aligned with it is not yet terminated. That awaits the second appearance of the Son (9:28) and the final shaking of not only earth but also heaven. A reference to the destruction of Herod's temple in AD 70 or to the waning of Judaism is unlikely.

## Comments on Theological Themes

The idea of 8:7 is not merely that so long as the first covenant functioned effectively there was no need of a second, as if the first had of itself the potential of bringing perfection and until proven otherwise there was no room for a competing system; this understanding does not give sufficient weight to 7:18-19; 8:4; 9:9-10; 10:1-4, 11. Blame is in fact predicated of the first covenant in a context that is asserting the intrinsic limits of that covenant. Certainly blame is laid at the feet of the people (vv. 8a, 9), but only in company with an insistence on the limits of the first covenant's intent. This is strong language which Hebrews allows to stand without qualification (contrast Rom 7:11-13). Or rather, the whole discourse explains it, making evident that the law was God's own, inviolable in keeping with its intent (e.g., 8:4), and accordingly was only good. The overall argument is not from bad to good, but from good to better (without which the "good" is nothing).

In speaking of the new covenant in 8:9 it is said that it will be "not like the covenant" God made at Sinai. There was more than one *renewal* of the Sinai covenant over the course of Israel's history but Jer 31 as interpreted by Hebrews cannot be grouped with them. The whole argument of Hebrews is against this grouping, with particular passages most pointedly registering the difference: 7:11-19; 8:4; 9:15-22; 10:1-4. Once these are probed it is evident that the step from old covenant to new covenant involves a break as complete as death itself, which does not merely symbolize but *is* the most complete form of termination in created existence. Resurrection at once overcomes and assumes this break and termination, but it does assume and establish it. None of the Sinai covenant renewals is of this order. Clearly, at the same time, resurrection is a matter of radical continuity, but its discontinuity must be acknowledged. Moreover, to treat the new covenant—as announced in Hebrews—as another renewal of Sinai is to reject that which gave Sinai its only rationale and authority; it is to reject the pattern shown Moses and to absolutize the shadow and copy.

## Teaching Hebrews 8:7–13

1. The nature of the first covenant, particularly its intention and limitations. Care must be taken to appreciate the old covenant for what it was and for its aims. Only in this way can the language of annulment, obsolescence, and the like be rightly understood, and only in this way can the new covenant and the Son himself be rightly received.

2. The weakness of Israel, and thus our own weakness. If all nations do not find themselves unreservedly in Israel's history, not least her failure, they will never find themselves in her blessings. Hebrews does not speak of grace in the same ways that other NT writers do, but on its own terms the exclusivity of God's grace in salvation is no less clearly marked. Hebrews presents yet another telling of the same story. See the introduction to this commentary.

3. The better promises, based on which the better covenant has been enacted. Hebrews gets at much of this through implication—negatively by highlighting the failures of Israel as something that is put in the past and made impossible, positively by leaving a bread crumb trail to wider streams of OT texts associated with Jer 31 (see under Background). That it is the law which was the pattern for Moses that is written on the heart has implications for the Christian's appropriation of Moses's law comprehensively—not only its "ritualistic" aspects, but also its "moral" and "civic" aspects. For the preacher's immediate ends, however, he centers the weight of his exposition on the Son as the pattern shown Moses and thus effectual, and he concentrates its effects in the cleansing and forgiveness it brings and the corresponding act of obedience on which everything else hangs: the approach to the divine throne.

4. The announcement that the turning of the ages has begun and will continue inexorably to its conclusion. The new covenant has been inaugurated (9:15–22); the great high priest has been installed (5:1–10; 7:1–28); the once for all offering has been executed (9:1—10:10); the Son sits on the divine throne and waits for his enemies to be made a

footstool for his feed (10:11–18; 12:18–29); the resulting possibility is solely that of faith-obedience that inhabits this drama of the covenants and the cosmos (10:19—13:17).

5. How the appearance of the Son who is Jesus speaks to all these things and brings them to their goal. This was the burden of 1:1—4:13, which is woven into all of 4:14—10:25.

6. What this must mean for our lives on our own streets. This emerges particularly through the direct exhortations of the book.

7. The deepened recognition of how this reading of Jer 31 accounts for the truth of 1:1–4.

# 9:1–10

*"I am the way."*

## Context

SEE 4:14-16; 5:1-10; 8:1-6.

4:14—10:25 Christ as high priest and offering

    *4:14-16 Transition, frame with 10:19-25

    5:1—7:28 Christ is high priest

    8:1—10:18 Christ's high priestly ministry

        8:1-6 Introduction: The tabernacles, priesthoods, and covenants

        8:7-13 The better promises of the new covenant

        9:1—10:10 The covenant of which Christ is mediator

            9:1-10 The first covenant as copy and anticipation

            9:11-14 The second covenant as accomplishment

            9:15-22 The inaugural mediation of the second covenant

            9:23-28 The eternal, heavenly, and final character of Christ's ministry (divine drama)

            10:1-10 The bodily offering that accomplished God's will (human drama)

        10:11-18 Conclusion: The better ministry

    *10:19-25 Transition, frame with 4:14-16

Without putting too fine a point on it, 8:6 lays out the internal logic of 8:7—10:18. Concerning the five sections of 9:1—10:10: The first two address the copy-actual contrast in broad terms, while the latter three address the same thing from a more dramatic perspective, from inauguration to consummation and the central element of the bodily offering.

Having signaled that the change of priesthood anticipated by Ps 110 entailed a change of law, and having shown that Exod 25 (8:1-6) and Jer 31 (8:7-13) indicated what that change involved and how Moses related to it, the argument proceeds to show how the Mosaic system itself was revealing these things (9:1-10) and that the accomplishment was achieved in Christ (9:11-14). That 9:1-14 carries forward the point about the change of law is evident from 9:1, 10 (cf. 8:4), though when we get to vv. 11-14 the reference to "regulations" drops out and there is no effort to draw a one-to-one correspondence with the tabernacle's arrangements and rites as laid out in 9:1-10. Instead the argument goes straight to the nature of Christ's service, its location, and its effects. It may be that in part the contrast of a somewhat mechanical apparatus with many elements and constant repetition as against the single masterstroke of the one Lord belongs to the essence of the contrast. The emphasis falls on the service that takes place in the holy place, in keeping with 8:6 and 10:11-18. The architectural design and furniture of the holy place have significance only to the degree that they symbolize the salvation at work in making access to God's presence possible.

Within 9:1-10: Following the opening assertion that the first covenant had regulations of service and a holy place (9:1) the unit proceeds to describe these in reverse order: the holy place (9:2-5) and the service (9:6-7). Finally, it is asserted that by these very things the Holy Spirit was indicating their place in the larger workings of God (9:8-10): they were prophetic, provisional, and of limited effect.

## Background

According to the biblical narrative, after entering the land and before it came to Jerusalem and into Solomon's temple the ark of the covenant resided at various sites (Bethel, Shiloh, Kiriath Jearim, Gibeon). Beyond this the data do not permit sure conclusions about the history of the ark's locations or whether the ark and tabernacle were separately at different sites at times; nor does the history concern Hebrews' argument. Solomon's temple, built in the mid-10th century BC, was destroyed by the Babylonians in 586 BC; the ark was lost to history.[1] The rebuilding of the temple following the exile was

---

1. For traditions concerning the ark, see Bruce, *Epistle to the Hebrews*, 202.

completed by 515/16 BC (Ezra-Nehemiah). Herod's temple was built from 20–19 BC on the same site (Josephus, *A.J.* 15.11.1–2.390; *B.J.* 1.21.1.401; cf. John 2:20) and was destroyed by the Romans in AD 70 (Josephus, *B.J.* 7.1.1.1–3); it has not since been rebuilt. The history from Ezra through AD 70 is commonly referred to as the Second Temple period.

Hebrews' description of the original tabernacle of Moses is summarized with allusions that scatter across Exodus, Leviticus, Numbers, and Deuteronomy. The summary indicates no direct acquaintance Herod's temple in Judaism; it appears to reflect the writer's knowledge of the OT with the influence of other traditions. The only features that will receive comment in Hebrews' exposition are the holy place, the Most Holy Place, and the curtain that separated them.

A close examination of Hebrews' description raises several questions—particularly regarding the location of the incense altar and the contents of the ark—that have been thoroughly examined by many with differing conclusions. Merely to explain the problems let alone the proposed explanations would take us well beyond our limits.[2] It is not clear that decisions on these points have had much bearing on the interpretation of Hebrews overall, so it would seem better to follow the preacher's lead in not being distracted by them.[3]

---

2. See Cockerill, *Epistle to the Hebrews*, 373–74; Bruce, *Epistle to the Hebrews*, 199–204; Attridge, *Hebrews*, 233–38; Boyd, "Ark," 165–68.

3. Line drawings from Bateman, *Charts*, 79–80.

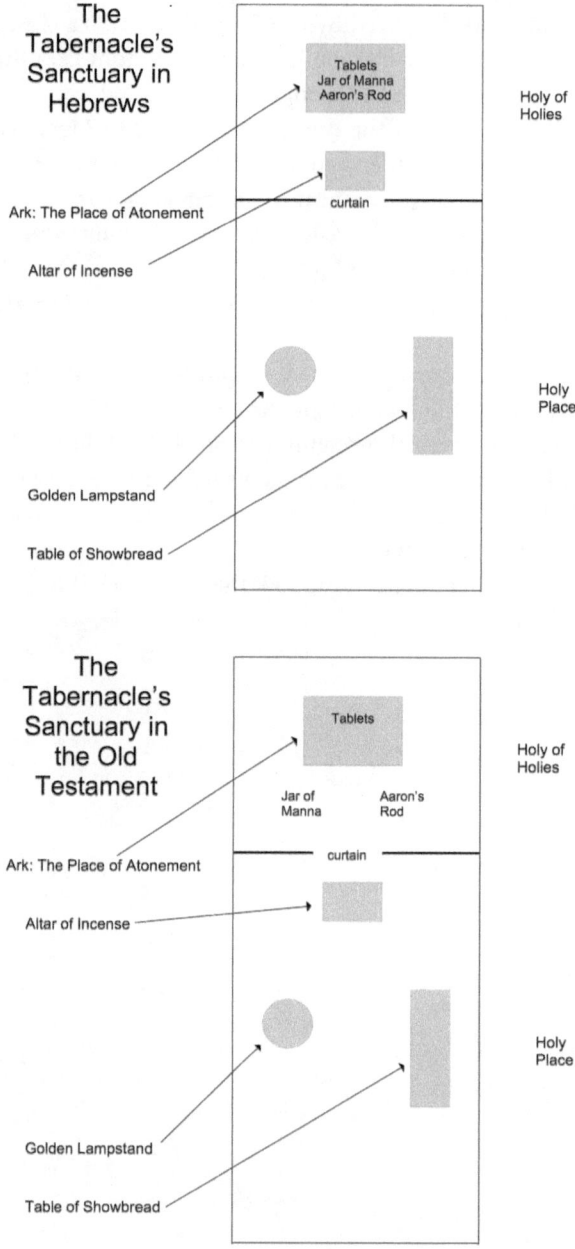

Hebrews' Tabernacle and the Old Testament Tabernacle

As it stands it is apparently the writer's intention to paint a picture with enough detail to call the whole tabernacle and its system to mind—visualization is part of his overall rhetorical strategy—while concentrating all his energies on the central salvation communicated through the covenant as a whole and the Day of Atonement in particular. It is helpful to remember that in all likelihood few if any of the readers had been to Herod's temple in Jerusalem, which may or may not have been standing at the time of writing, and relatively few would have direct and personal access to the Scriptural texts (aside from access to scrolls, literacy rates in the general population of the Roman world appear to have been somewhat lower than in most modern societies). A description of the tabernacle that gave the general picture, especially for Gentile converts accustomed to pagan temples, would be in keeping with the discourse's ends.

## Comments on Wording

9:2–5 Any good study Bible will elaborate on the significance of the furniture and features listed here; most of the particulars do not resurface in Hebrews' exposition: The *tabernacle* as such, Exod 26:1—27:19; 36:8–38; 38:1–20; 39:32—40:38; *the lampstand*, Exod 25:31–40; 37:17–24; 40:24–25; *the table and the bread of the Presence*, Exod 25:23–30; 37:10–16; *the curtains*, Exod 26:31–37; 36:35–38; *the golden altar of incense*, Exod 30:1–10; 37:25–29; 40:26–27; *ark of the covenant covered on all sides with gold*, Exod 25:10–22; 37:1–9; 40:20–21; *golden urn holding the manna*, Exod 16:32–34; *Aaron's staff that budded*, Num 17:10; *the tablet of the covenant*, Exod 32:15–16, 19; 34:1–4; Lev 16:13; *the cherubim of the Glory*, Exod 25:18–22; 37:7–9; Num 7:89; Ps 18:10; Ezek 10:10–14 (cf. Ezek 1:5–13);[4] 1 Sam 4:4; *the mercy seat*, Exod 25:17–22; 37:6–9; 39:35; Lev 16:2, 13–15; Num 7:89. The last-mentioned feature provides the climax, concerning as it does the ritual of the Day of Atonement.

9:6 *the priests go regularly into the first section, performing their ritual duties.*[5] The broader interest of Hebrews is in the repetition of the act, which was simultaneously based on and evidence of the rites' ineffectual nature (7:27; 10:11; cf. 9:25; 10:1–4, 11); here in vv. 6–10 the present verse (v. 6) helps underscore the limited access to the Most Holy Place in v. 7. For the

---

4. On the cherubim in later tradition, see also Bruce, *Epistle to the Hebrews*, 204–5.

5. The Greek uses present tense forms for this activity, which do not serve as evidence of whether the rites were still ongoing at the time of writing. Likewise elsewhere, where the present tense is used for things that are conceived as practiced in principle based on Scripture: 5:1–4; 7:5, 8; 8:3, 5; 9:25; 10:1.

priestly responsibilities for the outer tent we otherwise refer again to the following passages, among others: Exod 27:20-21; 29:38-43; 30:7-8; Lev 6:8-30; 24:1-9; Num 28:1-15; cf. Luke 1:8-22.[6]

9:7 *into the second only the high priest goes, and he but once a year*. For the Day of Atonement, see Exod 30:10 and Lev 16. The writer of Hebrews can use both the endless repetition of rites (v. 6) and the limitation of access to one priest only once a year (here) to illustrate the ineffectual and typological nature of the Mosaic system. For Hebrews, the Day of Atonement represents the ultimate destination of Israel's journey in faith, which, in accordance with the promises of the new covenant, takes the people of God into the immediate presence of God, that is, into his resting place (3:7—4:11). In one stroke—the single, once-for-all bodily self-offering of the Son—that covenant has been both inaugurated and consummated (9:11-28).

*Not without taking blood*. Blood will from this point become thematic (9:7, 12-14, 18-22, 25; 10:4, 19, 29; 11:28; 12:4, 24; 13:11-12, 20; cf. 2:14); the other goat used in the Day of Atonement ritual does not figure into Hebrews' present exposition.

*[Blood] which he offers for himself and for the unintentional sins of the people*. Cf. 7:26-28; also 4:15; 5:2-3. The reference to sins committed in ignorance is often thought to derive from the OT's distinction between sins committed unintentionally and those done "with a high hand" (Num 15:22, 30-31; cf. Lev 4:1—5:19; also 1 Macc 13:39; Sir 23:2; Tob 3:3; 1QS 9:1). Another possibility, however, is that the writer intends no thoroughgoing distinction between "sins" and "sins of ignorance"; the matter of ignorance is raised as a reminder of 3:10 and the people's perversity.[7] Either way, Hebrews excludes no sins from the forgiveness effected in Christ while he does allow that there is a particular post-baptismal sin, that of apostasy, that can render renewal to repentance impossible (6:4-6).

9:8 *By this the Holy Spirit indicates*. Elsewhere the Spirit is made the speaker of Scripture (3:7; 10:15), though here it is not specifically the text but the tabernacle and its rites as ideally enacted through which the Spirit was and is communicating. The counterpart of this mention of the Spirit comes in v. 14.

*the way into the holy places is not yet opened as long as the first section is still standing*. The Greek text has perplexed interpreters. Merely to state our conclusion: With v. 8 the writer has conflated the ideas of the first and second covenants (8:7—9:1) with the ideas of the Mosaic (first) and heavenly

---

6. How Hebrews would understand Exod 30:7 in connection with the outer room would depend in part on Heb 9:4 and the location of the incense altar.

7. Cockerill, *Epistle to the Hebrews*, 380.

(second) tabernacles. The upshot is that as long as the *first* (the Mosaic) *tabernacle* was operative, the way into the (second, the genuine and heavenly) *Most Holy Place* had not been disclosed. Whether and how long the first was to be operative was not a matter of its physical presence and ritual activities (i.e., whether it was standing and operational in the mechanical sense), but the declaration of God. The way into the genuine sanctuary has now been disclosed, and so displaces the first system. This seems the most likely sense and the Greek wording used is picked up in the summary of 10:19. The (limited) access of the Aaronic high priest represents in parabolic form (v. 9) the genuine access of the Melchizedekian high priest—therein is its continuity—but the very way in which the Aaronic and wider Levitical priestly access is structured (including the high priest's need to atone for his own sins) was intended to show from its very inception that it was emphatically not the genuine priesthood and could never bring about the access of which it was only a copy (its discontinuity). It could only witness to it (3:5). The latter is the point of v. 8. But the Mosaic system, and it alone of all humanly conceived cultic systems, did witness to it, and that was the glory of the Mosaic system.

9:9 *which is symbolic for the present age*. It is a *parable* (*parabolē*, a *type*, *symbol*; 11:19); cf. 10:1–4. This can be compared to 1 Cor 10:6, 11; Rom 5:14; cf. 1 Cor 9:10. The entire Mosaic system was divine speech in "parabolic" or figurative form.

9:9–10 *gifts and sacrifices are offered that cannot perfect the conscience of the worshiper . . . regulations for the body*. The gifts and sacrifices are offered that are never able *to perfect* (see 2:10 and the introduction of this commentary) the worshippers with respect to the conscience. They are merely *regulations of flesh* (ESV = *for the body*; cf. 7:16; 9:13); they are matters of an earthly system that was intrinsically limited to symbolic functions, pointing toward the heavenly system of which they are copies. The reference to *regulations* creates a bookend with 9:1; being *of the flesh* correlates them with a merely *earthly* sanctuary (9:1; but see on 8:1–6 for this language); together they go to the change of law that corresponds with the shift from the Mosaic copy to the heavenly original and its Melchizedekian high priest. The latter brings the *perfection* that the Mosaic system did not and could not bring (7:11, 19), i.e., the genuine cleansing and transformation that effects eternally the intended ultimate ends of the divine promise. The perfected conscience is one that is sanctified and grounded so as to have complete confidence in the approach to the divine throne (4:14–16; 9:13–14; 10:22).

9:10 *imposed until the time of reformation*. This recalls the strong language of 7:18, which see. The same faith that enacted the laws of Moses is now commanded to enact the law of the pattern that Moses copied. Moses is not thereby negated but established, and established precisely through annulment (see 8:1-6).

## Comments on Theological Themes

For Hebrews the salvation of Christ is effected through the whole act of his obedience, from incarnation to enthronement. Its correlation with Moses's tabernacle, however, brings the imagery of blood to the forefront, raising questions about blood's specific role. Among other things, interpreters debate whether blood symbolizes the offered *life* or *death*.[8] A final decision is elusive because Scripture never directly explains the theory behind the use of blood and different texts suggest different possible answers (Exod 12:21-23; 24:8; Lev 17:11; Deut 12:23).[9] Within the NT more broadly[10] and Hebrews in particular (esp. 9:15-22, 23-28) blood is associated with Christ's death, but there are also ways in Hebrews that the blood offering corresponds to the heavenly presentation in the Most Holy Place, so seemingly with an offered life. In 9:15-28 these currents run together. There is a logic at work that is intractably personal and cultic, bound up with the life of God with his creation, before it is anything scientific and conceptual. Nor, in any event, is it Hebrews' purpose to draw up a conceptually tidy philosophy of salvation. Instead the author patterns his expositional exhortation after the personal-dramatic-cultic lines that he inherits and he does so as a form of witness more than as a dissecting description that lays bare cause and effect like billiard balls interacting on a table. Hebrews' interest is to advance *that* Christ's blood—the personal application of his self-offering—effects cleansing and forgiveness rather than to explore *how* it does. See on 9:12, 15-22; 10:1-10.

The allusion to the *conscience* in 9:9 introduces a new motif that will be repeated (9:14; 10:2, 22; cf. 13:18). Hebrews' use of this motif—which is distinctive vis-à-vis Paul's use, though complementary to it—correlates at once with the pairings of earthly vs. heavenly, old covenant vs. new covenant, etc.; it is thus a matter of parable/symbol (= merely of the flesh) vs. achievement of the divinely intended cleansing (= of the conscience). In other words, Hebrews' mention of the conscience does not stand on its own but represents another way of getting at the same thing that the

---

8. See Attridge, *Hebrews*, 248.
9. Lewis, "Covenant and Blood Rituals," 341-50.
10. E.g., Matt 26:28; Rom 5:8-10; 1 Cor 11:25-26; Col 1:20, 22; 1 Pet 1:19; Rev 5:9. In the following Christ's death is atoning: Col 2:14; 1 Pet 2:24; 3:18. The death of the first human and the sentence of the law lurk in Rom 5:12-21; Gal 3:10-14.

rest of the discourse is getting at: genuine rather than figurative cleansing. There is no escaping the implication of the *subjective* experience which was previously lacking and now present (10:2, 22), which almost certainly is intended to echo the promises of Jer 31:31–34 and the law written *on the heart* (cf. 10:22)—that is, the heavenly law of which Moses's was a copy and shadow. But it is just as clear that for Hebrews the point about the conscience pertains to what is *objectively* the case with the turn of the ages *before* it is subjective; moreover, it is patently clear from the fact of the entire discourse that it is subjectively real not automatically but only where faith is active (11:1, 6; cf. 3:12–15). The subjective experience is therefore necessary, precisely because faith is necessary, though the *experience* (not the objective fact of cleansing) depends on faith rather than faith on it; faith, for its part, depends on the prior word of God. On these terms, the lack of the experience is the denial of the truth of God and the rejection of the word he has spoken in the Son in these last days.

## Teaching Hebrews 9:1–10

1. The whole preceding discourse both assumed and clarified what was said in 1:1–4 bearing on the truth that the same God who previously spoke in the prophets has now spoken in and as the Son. The ways in which this is so were elaborated in our exposition of 1:1—4:13; 4:14–16; 7:1–10; and 8:1–6 (not to be repeated here). What is before us in 9:1–10 is the application of this teaching in ways that are out of step with both modernist approaches to strictly historical exegesis (no modern would write 9:8–9 in an exegetical essay) and many allegorical practices of Judaism and the church (note Hebrews' sober restraint in interpreting the tabernacle's features). This helps us to see what Scripture is as divine speech—which is necessary if we are to receive Hebrews' teaching—and what we can aspire to as best practices in our own cultural setting.

2. Related to this, it becomes clear through vv. 8–10 that it was not only the text as such that served as a pattern of Christ but the form of life that arose in Israel's obedience. That is, what Hebrews develops in vv. 6–7 is not a textual citation (compare 2:5–9) but the actual practices of the Levitical priesthood with respect to the Mosaic tabernacle. It is the latter, according to vv. 8–10, by which the Spirit was disclosing the truth of things. Thus the "literal" obedience of the Jews in offering animal sacrifices was not a deficiency of faith, as if they stubbornly misunderstood what God required; it was precisely what God required

and what faith enacted. When it was faith-obedience it participated in the offering of Christ and perfected their conscience while it simultaneously—and in perfect harmony with the word of God—witnessed to the truth of 9:8–10 (cf. 9:15, 26; 11:1–40).

3. Thus we can see that claims like 9:8–9 (9:14; 10:2, 22) are neither denying the truth of texts like Lev 16:16, 30, 34; Pss 51:1–9; 103:12 for OT believers, nor asserting that true new covenant believers do not struggle with a "guilty conscience." It is for Christians a matter firstly of the objective act of God in history as conveyed to us through the preached word; the *time of reformation* has in fact come. It is then a matter of faith, in the sense of 11:1–2. The cleansed or perfected conscience is finally by faith an experience grounded in reality, which is a real sharing in Christ (3:14) and the Holy Spirit (6:4–5; 10:29). But everything hangs on faith, so the experience is not optional after all.

4. All of this reinforces our vision of salvation and the Son. The ultimate goal of Israel's journey involved entrance into the Most Holy Place of God's own presence, there to celebrate the great "sabbath of sabbaths" (Lev 16:31). The Mosaic law—particularly as now seen in the light of the Son—made this clear, revealed how it would come about, and showed that the arrival had not yet come nor could it come about through that system. As 9:11–28 will elaborate, the Son—known by his own history as seen through Moses (not through just any human religious system) and Ps 110:4—brought all this about in once-for-all fashion. He thereby brought about the new covenant of the heavenly tabernacle of which Moses's tabernacle was a copy and shadow (8:1–13). Faith is a matter of staking everything on this word.

5. If attention is lagging by this time, it may be appropriate to return to the kick-in-the-pants that was 5:11—6:3.

# 9:11–14

*"It is the Spirit who gives life; the flesh is no help at all. The words that I have spoken to you are spirit and life."*

## Context

See 8:1–6 and 9:1–10.

4:14—10:25 Christ as high priest and offering

   \*4:14–16 Transition, frame with 10:19–25

   5:1—7:28 Christ is high priest

   8:1—10:18 Christ's high priestly ministry

      8:1–6 Introduction: The tabernacles, priesthoods, and covenants

      8:7–13 The better promises of the new covenant

      9:1—10:10 The covenant of which Christ is mediator

         9:1–10 The first covenant as copy and anticipation

         9:11–14 The second covenant as accomplishment

         9:15–22 The inaugural mediation of the second covenant

         9:23–28 The eternal, heavenly, and final character of Christ's ministry (divine drama)

         10:1–10 The bodily offering that accomplished God's will (human drama)

      10:11–18 Conclusion: The better ministry

   \*10:19–25 Transition, frame with 4:14–16

Having signaled that the change of priesthood anticipated by Ps 110 entailed a change of law, and having shown that Exod 25 and Jer 31 indicated what that change involved and how Moses related to it, the argument proceeded to show how the earthly system itself was revealing these things (9:1–10). Now it shows that Christ has accomplished the great salvation to which Moses witnessed (9:11–14); he is the priest of the good things that are now here, that is, the priest of v. 10's *time of reformation.*

The Greek text of these verses has two complex sentences which amount to two perspectives on the same thing.

Verses 11–12 assert particularly what Christ did vis-à-vis the Levitical priests of vv. 1–10: Appearing as the priest of the new order he entered the true sanctuary, that is, the actual Most Holy Place, once-for-all (vs. once a year), and through his own blood. In so doing he brought about the great salvation promised by God.

Christ

> appearing as high priest of the good things that have come about—the new order of v. 10
>
> through the greater and more perfect tent not made with hands (i.e., not of this creation)
>
> neither through the blood of goats and calves
>
> but through his own blood

entered once-for-all into the sanctuary

> finding eternal redemption

Verses 13–14 restate this with the emphasis on the effectiveness of Christ's blood in bringing about the benefits God intended for his people.

For

> if the blood of bulls and goats etc. sprinkled on the unclean sanctified toward the cleansing of flesh

how much more will the blood of Christ

> who through the eternal Spirit offered himself blameless to God

cleanse our conscience from dead works unto the service of the living God?

A few more orienting comments: Firstly, these verses take up what was first announced in connection with his identity as priest in 7:27 and so answer the need posed in 8:3: The Son is both priest *and offering*. This of course roots in the basic confession (2:5-18; 5:7-10). Indeed, these verses are finally a passing of all of 1:1—4:13 through the prism of Moses's tabernacle and another stage in the flowering out of 4:14-16.

Secondly, the whole passage picks up on the better promises of the new covenant (8:6-13), particularly concerning the forgiveness achieved in these last days and, via the reference to the conscience, the law written on the heart and mind (cf. 10:16-17). The pattern shown Moses has come to earth and baptized us with heaven.

Thirdly, as a matter of rhetorical strategy these lines are a matter of theological assertion rather than textual exposition. In them the preacher piles up images in ways that 1) conflate a variety of rites as if to gesture toward the entire Mosaic system, though the center is the Day of Atonement, 2) resist assigning particular effects to particular moments of Christ's history, 3) collapse the once-for-all and ongoing intercessory aspects of Christ's work, and 4) utilize the tabernacle as a lens but preserve the primacy of the Son's history as the controlling reality.

Fourthly, the mention of the Spirit in v. 14, which is closely bound to the person of Christ and the efficacy of his blood, echoes the reference to the Holy Spirit active in the divine speech of vv. 8-10. The Spirit who testified through the Mosaic system was instrumental in the accomplishment of Christ's redemption. Equally notable is the Trinitarian harmony of v. 14b: through the *Spirit* he offered *himself* to God.[1]

## Background

Much of the background required here has been supplied in connection with the discussion of the priesthood (5:1-10), the heavenly sanctuary (8:1-6), the earthly sanctuary, blood, and the conscience (9:1-10). On the language of cleansing, perfection, and sanctification, see the introduction to this commentary.

If we judge by the wording of the LXX, of the animals listed in vv. 12-13 only the calf (*moschos*, young bull, bull) figures into the Day of Atonement rite of Lev 16; the same animal is mentioned for other rites (e.g., Lev 4:1-35). The male goat (*tragos*) is used as an offering in the Pentateuch only in connection with the offerings of Num 7:12-88; the latter passage, however, culminates with Moses entering the tent of meeting and hearing

---

1. Attridge, *Hebrews*, 250-51, opposes Trinitarian ideas here.

"the voice speaking to him from above the mercy seat that was on the ark of the testimony, from between the two cherubim" (7:89). The bull, designated as a *tauros*, is never used as an offering in the LXX of the Pentateuch, though the word could otherwise be used interchangeably with *moschos*.[2] In other passages, however, there is mention of the "blood of bulls and goats," which God declares he does not want (Isa 1:11; cf. Ps 50:13). The mention of the ashes of the heifer refers to the rite of Num 19:1–22 (on which see any good Study Bible), which is not associated with the Day of Atonement in the law,[3] but which is classed as a sin offering (Num 19:9; cf. Heb 13:12–13).

## The Day of Atonement[4]

| Questions | Leviticus 16 | Reference in Hebrews |
|---|---|---|
| Who officiates? | As the levitical high priest, he alone enters a tabernacle made with human hands (16:2–3, 17 ; cp. Exod 25–26). | As regal high priest, Jesus alone enters the heavenly tabernacle (9:12, 25–28 ; 10:1–3, 10:14). |
| What is needed? | 1. A young bull is needed for a sin offering (16:3, 6, 11, 14, 18–19) | 1. One person is needed: Jesus (9:11–14). |
| | 2. Two male goats are needed (16:5, 7–10): one as a sin offering (16:3, 15, 18–19), one as a scapegoat (16:5, 8, 10, 20–22). | 2. Compare the concept of human atonement in Rom 9:3. |
| What happens to the animals? | 1. The bull is sacrificed as a sin offering and its blood is sprinkled on the atonement plate (16:6, 11, 14). | Jesus Death on the cross serves as atonement in the heavenly holy of holies (9:11–12; 10:4–10). |
| | 2. The sin offering goat is sacrificed and its blood is sprinkled on the atonement plate (16:15). | Some may argue that Jesus dies and offers his own blood in the heavenly sanctuary. |
| | 3. The scapegoat is sent into the wilderness (16:10, 21–22). | |

---

2. Bruce, *Epistle to the Hebrews*, 213.

3. But see Ellingworth, *Epistle to the Hebrews*, 454, and Bruce, *Epistle to the Hebrews*, 216.

4. Adapted from Bateman, *Charts*, 83.

| Questions | Leviticus 16 | Reference in Hebrews |
|---|---|---|
| Who benefits? | 1. The blood of the sacrificed bull benefits the high priest and his household (16:6, 11–14) | 1. The blood of Jesus benefits all who are called (9:15). |
| | 2. The blood of the sacrificed goat benefits the people (16:15). | 2. The blood of Jesus benefits all who eagerly await him (9:28). |
| | 3. The blood of the sacrificed bull and goat benefits the tabernacle (16:18–19). | 3. Compare: The sufferings of Jesus benefit all who obey him (5:9). |
| | 4. The scapegoat benefits the community (16:21–22). | |
| How often is this to occur? | 1. On the Day of Atonement, the high priest enters the holy of holies three times on behalf of himself, the people, and then the tabernacle (16:11, 15, 18–19, 33) | 4. Jesus enters the heavenly holy of holies *once* for all people (9:28). |
| | 2. The Day of Atonement and its expectations were repetitious and needed to practiced annually (16:29, 34). | 5. Jesus enters the heavenly holy of holies *once* for all, never to be repeated (9:11–12, 25–28; 10:1–3, 10–14). |

## Old Testament Offerings[5]

| Name | Portion Burnt | Other Portions | Animals | Occasion or Reason | Reference |
|---|---|---|---|---|---|
| Burnt Offering | All | None | Male without blemish; animal according to wealth | Propitiation for general sin; demonstrates dedication | Lev 1 (see also Num 7:12–88) |
| Meal Offering or Tribute Offering | Token portion | Eaten by priest | Unleavened cakes or grains, must be salted | General thankfulness for first fruits | Lev 2 (see also Num 7:12–88) |

---

5. Adapted from Walton, *Charts*, 22.

| Name | Portion Burnt | Other Portions | Animals | Occasion or Reason | Reference |
|---|---|---|---|---|---|
| Peace Offering<br>a. Thank Offering<br>b. Vow Offering<br>c. Freewill Offering | Fat portions | Shared in fellowship meal by priest and offerer | Male or female without blemish according to wealth; freewill: slight blemish allowed | Fellowship<br>a. For an unexpected blessing<br>b. For deliverance when a vow was made on that condition<br>c. For general thankfulness | Lev 3<br>Lev 22:18–30 (see also Num 7:12–88) |
| Sin Offering | Fat portions | Eaten by priest | Priest or congregation: bull<br>king: he-goat<br>individual: she-goat | Applies basically to situation where purification is needed | Lev 4 (see also Num 19:1–22; 7:12–88) |
| Guilt Offering | Fat portions | Eaten by priest | Ram without blemish | Applies to situation where there has been desecration or de-sacrilization of something holy or where there is objective guilt | Lev 5–6:7 |

On the one hand, as he does elsewhere, the writer is drawing together from the spectrum of Mosaic rites to make a singular point about the one offering of Christ. Collectively, the Mosaic offerings worked as a copy and shadow of his single, once-for-all offering and the genuine cleansing it brings. Here again is warning against pressing the work of Christ into the mold of any one rite, even the Day of Atonement rite by itself. On the other hand, the writer is quietly gesturing toward the climax of Num 7:89 (cf. Heb 9:2–5) and the polemic of Isa 1:11 (cf. Heb 10:5–10).

Is the echo of the the polemic of Isa 1:11—if such it is—an indication that for Hebrews the sacrifices of 9:12–13 are in some measure idolatrous? There are things to say in favor of this but it seems unlikely in the context of Hebrews' "greater than" argument, wherein he does not typically disparage the former things but assumes their legitimacy as commanded by God (7:11–14; 10:8) and asserts that they highlight the greater glory of Christ. The use of the adjective "made with hands" is explained not by reference to idolatry but as Hebrews itself explains it, "that is to say, is not a part of this creation."

## Comments on Wording

*9:11 appeared as a high priest of the good things that have come.* In other words, the *time of reformation* of v. 10 is now upon us, with its new covenant and new tabernacle.

*through the greater and more perfect tent.* Cf. 4:14.[6] The idea at present might be less spatial than instrumental, however, relating to the two aspects of 9:1: He entered and found redemption through the instrumentality of the heavenly tabernacle and that of his own blood, as opposed to the instrumentality of the earthly sanctuary and the blood of goats and calves.

*not made with hands, that is to say, not of this creation.* The language used here is a reminder of the typological point of 8:4–5 with no debt to metaphysical dualisms. The heavenly things, too, are *made* (8:2; 11:10), the Son's offering is inseparable from his humanity (10:5–10), the people of God are grouped with the heavenly things (9:23), and the final vision of salvation as a realm incorporates the cosmos (12:25–29). The logic of the present claim goes to the union of covenantal and creation history, where the present creation is correlated with the old covenant and the age to come with the new covenant. Another system cannot be established for the present age without violating the first covenant (8:4).

*9:12 by means of his own blood.* As his blood it is human and representative (2:10–16); it is an act of obedience (5:7–10; 10:5–10); it is pure and thus fitted to the need (7:26–28). The association of blood with Christ's death is traditional (e.g., Matt 27:4, 6, 24–25; John 19:34; Acts 20:28; Rom 3:25; 5:9; 1 Pet 1:2, 19). In the present context it is used interchangeably with Christ's offering of *himself* and it is correlated with the *eternal Spirit*. It comes to the fore not because crucifixion was an extraordinarily bloody form of execution nor because the preacher had independent knowledge of a heavenly event involving blood rituals, but because of the existing patterns

---

6. Bruce, *Epistle to the Hebrews*, 212–13, unconvincingly identifies the tabernacle at this point with the people of God. A variety of other identifications that have been proposed from the patristic period on are listed by Attridge, *Hebrews*, 246, with whose demurrals we sympathize.

of use and meaning inscribed in the law and the present effort to understand Christ through that witness.

*thus securing an eternal redemption.* "Eternal" (cf. 5:9) looks both forwards and back (9:26). It was in this sense already accomplished when the pattern was shown Moses on the mountain (8:5). It is characterized as a *redemption* or *ransom* (*lytrōsis*; compare *apolytrōsis* in 9:15; cf. 11:35), an idea that pertains to the experience of being liberated from an oppressive situation. Elsewhere in the NT see, e.g., Mark 10:45; Luke 24:21; Acts 7:35; Rom 3:24; Titus 2:14; 1 Pet 1:18; in the OT, see, e.g., Exod 6:6; Lev 25:48; Pss 107:2; 130:7-8; Hos 13:14.

9:14 *the blood of Christ.* See v. 12. In the Day of Atonement the blood would be presented after entrance into the Most Holy Place, but Hebrews does not make that controlling for the understanding of the significance of Christ's cross and ascension. The preacher merges the Day of Atonement rite with all the required sacrifices combined (cf. vv. 12-13) simply to signal full access once-for-all.

*offered himself without blemish to God.* Cf. 4:15; 5:7-10; 7:26-27. The animals chosen for the Day of Atonement were to be *without blemish* (*amōmos*; cf. Num 29:8); the same characterization applies to other offerings (e.g., Lev 1:3; 3:1; 4:3); cf. 1 Pet 1:19. In 9:24 the tabernacle imagery momentarily disappears to speak more simply of entering heaven itself to appear before the face of God; the present verse, correlating with v. 12, does the same more concisely.

*purify our conscience from dead works.* On the conscience, see 9:1-10. The dead works are acts of disobedience rather than the ritual acts of the first covenant. Note, as well, how the terms *perfect* (9:9), *sanctify* (9:13), and *purify* (9:14) can be used to some extent interchangeably. See the introduction to this commentary.

*to serve the living God.* That is to say, so that we may serve *him* who is in truth the living God (3:12), so that we may be *qualified* by him and know ourselves to be qualified to serve him, and so that we may serve him *acceptably* (for the last, see 12:18-29; 13:1-17). The verb (*latreuō*) bears especially on the service of worshippers in a cultic setting, redounding to the praise of God (8:5; 9:9; 10:2; 12:28; 13:10; cf. the noun in 9:1, 6). This reference recalls 4:15-16 and anticipates 12:28 and 13:15-16; there is no implication here or elsewhere of a "Christian cultus" surrounding the Eucharist.

## Comments on Theological Themes

There is a clustering of much of the language for salvation (cleansing/purification, sanctification/consecration, perfecting/completing, forgiveness/liberation, salvation, redemption) in 9:1-28. See the introduction of this commentary for a general overview.

The contrast of these verses is not between physical blood and something "spiritual" (= non-physical) but between the blood of non-willing animals and the human blood of the obedient Son, offered through the Spirit to God.

Verse 12 characterizes the results of Christ's work as a finding of *redemption*. This is not terminology used with the Day of Atonement in the LXX, but once the latter is seen as the means of arrival at the goal of salvation the conflation of images is natural. In Hebrews we think back to the slavery involved in fear of death of 2:15 and the release that Christ won. In the nearer context (9:15) the association is with the transgressions committed under the first covenant, transgressions that merited punishment, even death (2:2; 10:28). In the first instance this is the story of Israel in her fatal disobedience, but it is finally the story of all nations. No doubt this implied story partially illuminates the rationale of blood and death in the atonement.

In 9:13 it is said that the Mosaic sprinkling of blood in its rites *sanctifies* and brings *purification of the flesh*. The negative statements of 7:19; 9:8-10; 10:1-4, 11 do not contradict but rather complement the claim made here, noting its limitation. Those sacrifices were not partially effectual for forgiveness, with Christ's sacrifice somehow making up the deficit.[7] With respect to the great salvation they did *nothing* and *everything*; nothing in the sense of 9:8; 10:4; etc., but everything inasmuch they were the gospel (4:2, 6) received in the faith of 11:1-40. Within the terms of the shadowy, parabolic drama they enacted they qualified (sanctified) both priests and people to live in God's presence in the land.

9:14 refers to the *eternal Spirit*, which we have taken to be the Holy Spirit.[8] The context suggests more than one association. In the closer context the contrast is with the instrumentality of the Mosaic sanctuary and

---

7. Hebrews' point applies equally to all forms of sin and impurity (both ritual and moral) within the Mosaic system. What is said about the uselessness and impotence of OT rites (7:11, 18-19; 9:9-10; 10:1-4) has reference to all offerings up to and including the Day of Atonement. What is said of Christ's cleansing, etc. applies to all of the aspects of existence to which those rites—both moral and ritual—pointed. See the introduction to this commentary.

8. The phrase is famously difficult. For the history of interpretation, see McGrath, *Eternal Spirit*.

its service, and the correlation is with the instrumentality of the heavenly sanctuary and Christ's own blood. The contrast of "flesh" (v. 13) and Spirit is also too clear to be unintentional (cf. 12:9); as such, it does not derive from a metaphysical opposition of matter and idea but is rooted in the discourse's own contrasts of copy and thing itself, external and internal, and so forth.[9] The same Spirit who conveyed the true (limited) status and function of the Mosaic tabernacle was active in Christ's offering, the effects of which were accordingly genuine and eternal; the effects are both inner and outer, rather than outer only (10:22). In other words, this phrase is a pregnant one whose chief function is to contribute to the general contrast of the first covenant as copy and the second covenant as salvation itself and as eternally effectual.

If the preacher thinks realistically of a "sprinkling" of Jesus' blood on the heavenly things (9:13–14, 19, 21; 10:22; 11:28; 12:24), it was a matter of Jesus' own sin-bearing body (9:28; cf. 2:10–18) in which believers share (2:14; 3:14).

## Teaching Hebrews 9:11–14

1. Hebrews has a knack for advancing an argument while gilding it with allusions either to the immediate context or to wider theological currents shared with his audience. Heb 9:11–14 puts this on full display, presenting both potentials and challenges. The central ideas are that 1) Christ entered once-for-all, and 2) his blood cleanses our consciences, these two ideas corresponding to the sanctuary and service of 9:1 and showcasing the new law/covenant as articulated in Jer 31. The rest functions to carry forward the argument but primarily to stimulate confidence and faith in the face of persecution and temptation.

2. Blood can become either an object of morbid theological fascination or an embarrassing residue of a mythologically minded culture. It is plainly symbolic, having been lodged in the history of Israel's cultus and the church's proclamation before Hebrews took it up. It is just as plainly realistic, having a concrete referent in the death and ascension of Jesus the Son. In Hebrews the inbuilt logic already in place in the OT does its own work in accounting for blood's role. There is no attempt to dissect how it works, as if delving into a magician's powers. Yet even this image is not allowed to obscure what is the real focus, which is the history of the Son. Blood has no independent power, even as an image, and it can be replaced by the simpler statement that

---

9. For other associations, see Isa 31:3; John 3:6; 6:63; Phil 3:3.

Christ offered *himself*. Beyond this, the associations in this context are with obedience, death, representation, redemption, personal application (sprinkling), the eternal Spirit, and the effect of perfecting the worshippers.

3. Regarding the need of an unblemished offering, J. Denney's words (cited by Bruce), which go beyond what Hebrews explicitly claims, might stimulate good theological reflection: "Only one who knew no sin could take any responsibility in regard to it which would create a new situation for sinners.... Christ's offering of Himself without spot to God had an absolute or ideal character; it was something beyond which nothing could be, or could be conceived to be, as a response to God's mind and requirements in relation to sin."[10] See further on 10:5–10.

4. This is not airy theological stuff, unsuited for material problems of life in the "real world." The great crowd of believers comprises the nation of Israel on the journey to the promised inheritance, beset by all the mundane temptations, pressures, needs, and threats faced by Israel between Egypt and Canaan. The pressures against faith faced by every individual of Moses's generation were as down-to-earth as any faced by a believer in first-century Italy or twenty-first-century America, Asia, or elsewhere. They loved their children and needed footwear just as much. They experienced thirst and insecurity just the same. In making the Israelites of Moses's day his people, assuming full responsibility for them (including for their bodies), God placed *himself* at their center. Without that center the rest was idolatry. With that center all these other things were added (Matt 6:33; Luke 12:32). The provision made for Israel to sustain her on that way is made now—with one, singular qualification: *how much more!* Therefore, let us draw near.

---

10. Cited in Bruce, *Epistle to the Hebrews*, 218.

# 9:15–22

*"this is my blood of the covenant, which is poured out for many for the forgiveness of sins."*

## Context

SEE 8:1–6 AND 9:1–10 for the overview.

4:14—10:25 Christ as high priest and offering

    *4:14–16 Transition, frame with 10:19–25

    5:1—7:28 Christ is high priest

    8:1—10:18 Christ's high priestly ministry

        8:1–6 Introduction: The tabernacles, priesthoods, and covenants

        8:7–13 The better promises of the new covenant

        9:1—10:10 The covenant of which Christ is mediator

            9:1–10 The first covenant as copy and anticipation

            9:11–14 The second covenant as accomplishment

            9:15–22 The inaugural mediation of the second covenant

            9:23–28 The eternal, heavenly, and final character of Christ's ministry (divine drama)

            10:1–10 The bodily offering that accomplished God's will (human drama)

        10:11–18 Conclusion: The better ministry

    *10:19–25 Transition, frame with 4:14–16

The preacher has shown that Christ's ministry accomplishes what the first covenant and its earthly ministry did not. He did so in terms of the heavenly ministry of the new covenant but he now will back up from the rituals of the covenant to what was assumed: the inauguration of the new covenant itself. This move will takes us yet deeper into the understanding of the atonement and its history.

Heb 9:15–22 unfolds in four steps: 1) A transitional comment restates vv. 11–14, substituting *death* for *blood*, and also expands it by reintroducing the role of the mediator from 8:6 and connecting it to the inheritance (v. 15). 2) The mediatorial role is explained by the role of the testator's death in the activation of the will (vv. 16–17). 3) The blood principle (assumed in the death of this testator) is transferred to the covenant inauguration ceremony, with particular reference to Exod 24:8 (vv. 18–21); 4) A closing statement generalizes on the rule that without the pouring out of blood there is no forgiveness (v. 22). This last verse is less the conclusion than the linchpin: We see that the new covenant's promise of forgiveness (8:12; 10:18) had anticipated Christ's death as its necessary means, that this was why blood had played the role it did in the inauguration of Moses's covenant, and that with Christ's death the new covenant has been enacted and the inheritance distributed. The argument of vv. 15–21 works because the separate elements have a place in the drama of Christ, by whose blood we have forgiveness. The key thing, however, is not to admire its logic but to be swept along in renewed confidence by what it reveals.

Thus we experience a shift within the field of the varied shadows and copies, a shift from the Day of Atonement (grouped with the other rites) to the inaugurations of the two covenants. This is unexpected so long as the Mosaic rites are viewed as controlling, particularly given how seamless is the movement from 9:11–14 to v. 15. If the "blood" is the blood of the Day of Atonement (though it was not the blood of that rite alone but the whole, varied system) then how is it also the blood of the covenant *inauguration* ceremony? Once we absorb the full implications of 1:1–4 and 8:1–6, however, we recognize the priority of the Son. In that one Christ-event is accomplished the entire drama that unfolded through the history of the first covenant. The various rituals of Moses are the dispersed colors of the single light concentrated in the Son; conversely, the Son accounts for the logic of the first covenant's entire ministry.

A backgrounds comment related to this bears on the internal structure of the passage: Hebrews is about to play on the Greek word for *covenant* (*diathēkē*), which was in normal usage the word for a *last will and testament*. It will not do so, however, as an exegetical slight of hand, but on the sound footing of both a theological and thematic nature. Only because it is firstly *christologically* sound to do so does the writer of Hebrews make this move (see immediately above), and only secondarily does he do it because the Greek language he employs permits it. The linguistic tail is not wagging the exegetical dog. From that same angle it is evident that 1) an offering that is "eternal" and "once-for-all" is naturally not only the end of the matter but the beginning, and, given the principle of v. 22; and 2) the sacrifices that inaugurated the covenant were continuous with those of the annual rite (Lev 16:33). It was to show that none of them could bring perfection that the annual repetition followed the inauguration (Heb 9:9–10). It is *thematically* appropriate to do this, as well, given the indissoluble association of promise, inheritance, and covenant in the earlier history (e.g., Exod 15:17; 32:13; Deut 12:8–14; Isa 49:8). Nowhere in the OT are they brought together as here but the image of the inheritance was embedded in the structure of Israel's covenantal world, and an inheritance is as a rule dependent on the death of the testator.[1]

## Background

For the covenant inauguration ceremony of Exod 24, see the OT context in any good Study Bible or commentary. In it death is necessary as part of a ceremony that symbolizes the people's binding participation in the covenant agreement (thus to its blessings and curses), but how the blood "works" or what is its relation to other sacrifices is left unexplained.[2] It may be that Gen 15:1–21 (cf. Jer 34:18), by which God gave his oath to Abraham concerning the covenant and the inheritance (15:3–5, 18), is in the background of Exod 24 and/or Hebrews' appropriation but this is unclear and even doubtful.

As to the image of the will: The identity of Israel as God's family is basic to the OT, as well as to Hebrews (e.g., 1:14; 2:10–16; 3:6; 12:4–11). The original recipients of Hebrews live in their Roman world as people with no abiding city, being deprived of their property and freedom (10:32–34). As the seed of Abraham their hope is that of the inheritance promised him, which has come in its totality to the Son (1:2). A will was the legally binding instrument by which someone declared for the disposition of their possessions and assets on the occasion of the testator's death, and typically with a

---

1. Koester, *Hebrews*, 425, is right to clarify, however, that there is no assumed argument that the image of the inheritance of itself *required* the death of the Son of God; there is no such logical necessity at work. This would, again, assume that the thing which is a copy and shadow controls the pattern. Rather, Jesus' death is assumed, and the testamentary genre assists in explaining it, indicating at this point the full intent of the divine speaker in his use of the copies and shadows.

2. On this difficult question, see Lewis, "Covenant and Blood Rituals," 341–50.

view to one's biological descendants; as a rule, the economic importance for the heirs was great.

> "A testament had to be filed properly with a notary in the presence of witnesses while the testator was alive for it to be valid at the time of death . . . . The unusual statement that a testament "becomes valid" upon death arises from the coupling of legal practice with biblical covenant traditions . . . . Provisions of a testament commonly took effect upon the testator's death: "So long as I survive I am to have power over my property. . . . But if I die with this will unaltered I leave . . . ."[3]

## Comments on Wording

9:15 *Therefore he is the mediator of a new covenant.* Verses 16–22 favor understanding the mediatorial role as that of covenant inaugurator. The word *therefore* could indicate final cause as in 2:10—*for the sake of doing what he does in 9:11–14 he is mediator of a new covenant*—with the purpose idea made explicit and reworked in the following clause. And yet, the very way in which the purpose clause is expressed indicates that the covenant inauguration is being thought of as an atonement sacrifice a la vv. 11–14 (this is clear from vv. 18–22 as well). Thus it is fair to say that on the merits of the better offering (9:23) of vv. 11–14 Christ is the mediator (8:6) of the new covenant prophesied by Jeremiah, and as such the guarantor (7:22) of the covenantal promises of God. By this means the obstacle posed by self-defilement and self-cursing of the covenant partners is removed so that they can receive the inheritance and the promise can be realized—for all nations. By attending to this logic we can anticipate as well that the "heavenly things" of 9:23 includes (likely focuses on) the populace associated with the heavenly tabernacle (cf. v. 19).

*since a death has occurred that redeems them* etc. The argument concerning *blood* in what precedes (vv. 11–14) and what follows (vv. 18–22) is converted to *death* as a transition to the following point about the death of the testator.

9:16–17 *where a will is involved.* The shift of imagery from covenant to will is no more a threat to conceptual unity than the shift from the blood of the Day of Atonement with the other rites to that of the covenant inauguration and back again. Other interpretations favor retaining

---

3. Koester, *Hebrews*, 418, 424–26, who anticipates most of the objections posed by Cockerill, *Epistle to the Hebrews*, 404–5.

the translation of *covenant*, either in the sense of a self-curse involved in the establishment of a covenant (in inaugurating the covenant the participants put their lives on the line should they break covenant) or in the sense of what must be done when a covenant is broken (since Israel broke the covenant her death must be executed, and is in fact "borne" by the Son; if a death is not borne the covenant was a sham).[4] By shifting to the idea of a will the argument unites covenant, inheritance, death, blood, and forgiveness in the story of the promise.

9:18 *not even the first covenant was inaugurated without blood.* Given the interchangeability of *blood* and *death*, the thread concerning atoning *blood* is resumed from 9:11–14.

9:19 *he took the blood of calves* etc. *and sprinkled both the book itself and all the people.* As in vv. 12–13 and on the same basis Hebrews conflates the inauguration ritual of Exodus 24 with other ceremonies, primarily to emphasize the ubiquity of blood in cleansing rites. Sprinkled water, scarlet wool, and hyssop are not mentioned in Exod 24; for these see Exod 12:22; Lev 14:4-6, 49-52; Num 19:1-10, 17-18 (cf. Heb 9:13); Ps 51:7. Hebrews says that the scroll/book was sprinkled. It is in fact the altar that Moses sprinkles in Exod 24:6, after which he takes the *book* and reads it; the two were no doubt one in Hebrews' conception. It is also possible that here, too, Hebrews has conflated the rites, so that the sprinkling of the blood on the atonement cover in the Day of Atonement rite (Lev 16:14-15) was equivalent to the sprinkling of the scroll of the covenant (Exod 20:1-17; 21:1—23:33), since the tablets were inside the ark (see 9:4).

9:21 *he sprinkled with the blood both the tent and all the vessels used.* The tabernacle and its paraphernalia were not yet in place at the time of Exod 24 and they were dedicated with oil in Exod 40:9-11. In Lev 8-9, however, when Aaron and his sons are ordained, the altar is sprinkled with blood (Lev 8:15, 19, 24; 9:9, 12, 18) as well as the garments of the priests (Lev 8:30). In the Day of Atonement ritual blood is sprinkled on and in front of the atonement cover and on the altar. In this way the anointed priest is to "make atonement for the holy sanctuary, and . . . make atonement for the tent of meeting and for the altar, and . . . make atonement for the priests and for all the people of the assembly." (Lev 16:33). Hebrews is probably again conflating the rites in a single conception along the lines of the general principle of Heb 9:16-18 and 22. Josephus (*A.J.* 3.205-6) similarly conflates Lev 8-9 and Exod 40.

---

4. See Cockerill, *Epistle to the Hebrews*, 404–6.

## Comments on Theological Themes

Hebrews does not give enough thematic development to a *call* (9:15; cf. 3:1; 5:4; 11:8) to justify associating it with all that Paul may ascribe to the word. It is firstly the seed of Abraham who are called—not necessarily only those who respond in faith—but the call finally embraces all humankind as addressed in God's speech (1:1–2; 4:12–13; 12:25–29).

The assumed premise of the redeeming (liberating) death in 9:15 (cf. v. 12) is that Israel brought on herself the sentence of death and disqualified herself from inheriting what had been promised (8:7). God refuses to let her go or surrender his promise, however, and so liberates her at his own cost. Both the switch from *blood* to *death* and the association with Israel's transgressions (cf. 2:2; 10:28) firmly associate the atoning blood with the *cross* of Christ; a substitutionary idea is probably assumed (2:5–16; 10:1–10). The retroactive (9:26), once-for-all scope of Christ's atoning death is entailed (cf. Rom 3:21–26). The reference to the *transgressions committed under the first covenant* is not intended as limiting, however—as if *only* for Israel's sins within that history. The entire discourse views world history through God's promise concerning all creation (cf. 1:2–3; 2:5–9; 12:25–29), which found entrance through Abraham and its history in the covenants of Israel. Because the Son's death is once-for-all and cosmic in scope (1:3), and because Israel's history is a shadow and copy of the Son's, we recognize that Israel's history is our own.

No matter how vv. 16–17 are understood, the death in mind is that of Jesus, who could be representing God as the testator,[5] Israel as the covenant breaker, or conceivably both (see on 9:16–17). Just as in 4:3–5 the preacher accelerates through to the application leaving us to wonder.

Assuming that *purification* and *forgiveness* in v. 22 are coextensive in effectiveness, that verse's internal logic must represent a progression of thought from a generalization about the OT (22a) to a larger claim founded on something yet more basic (22b). The atoning power of blood was axiomatic (Lev 17:11; *b. Yoma* 5a; *b. Menah.* 93b; *b. Zebah.* 6a; Philo, *Spec.* 1.205) and does seem to express the rule of the OT, whatever exceptions can be cited both from the OT and post-AD 70 Judaism.[6] Even so, that this postulate is applied firmly and without distinction to the array of rites that have been incorporated into 9:11–21 supports thinking that the preacher is working from the

---

5. Hughes, *Commentary on Hebrews*, 370–71.

6. Thanks to Andrew Hill, Michael Graves, Michael Morales, and John Walton for help on this question. Could it be argued that our own *insistence* on this particular blood principle and *finding* it at work in the OT derive from Hebrews and the rest of the NT, and less clearly from the OT on its own?

conviction that all the lines of the OT cultus converged in the Son in whose blood alone all forgiveness is *in fact* worked.[7] At a certain level that amounts to an historical claim about the blood of Exod 24—that in the aims of God the blood of Moses's inauguration rite was in fact associated with the death of the testator as necessary for the promises of the covenant to come to fruition and that it was for the sake of foreshadowing the cleansing of the "heavenly things"—but it may be doubted that this excludes the possibility that in its original setting the blood of that rite had other aspects to its logic.

## Teaching Hebrews 9:15–22

1. The new covenant prophesied by Jeremiah *has been* inaugurated. In our teaching, the fact of its inauguration should be both established and celebrated. The first covenant had come with a storm, the second in a whisper. The gospel announced the presence of the age to come yet history seemed not to have missed a stride. Seeing the drama for what it actually is comprises the burden of much of Hebrews' rhetorical effort; see on 2:1–4.

2. Verses 15–22 begin and end with the words *redemption* and *forgiveness*, words that make clear where the writer's attention is focused: Christ's benefits *for his people*.[8] It is how Moses witnesses to this that is important for Hebrews. The preacher accounts for this christologically and covenantally but moderns prefer to ground things in theories of history and language. The challenge is to translate it in ways that are meaningful for a modern audience without compromising its argument or altering its message and losing its truth.

3. Paraphrasing the whole of 8:1—9:22 can be a helpful exercise: We have such a high priest who is a minister of the true tabernacle which the Lord pitched. Now, the present age already had a priesthood and ministry ordained by God... which are a copy and shadow of the heavenly pattern shown Moses; that is, the true tabernacle itself. Christ obtained a better ministry by as much as he is mediator of a better covenant founded on better promises. For the prophecy of the new covenant with its better promises, not least the promise of forgiveness, already made evident that the Mosaic covenant could not bring perfection and

---

7. For the challenge of discerning the differing rationales behind various blood ceremonies, not all of which have to do with cleansing, see Lewis, "Covenant and Blood Rituals," 341–50.

8. Noting this contextual focus on the *people* of the covenant will aid in understanding 9:23, i.e., what are the heavenly things needing cleansing.

would give way to the new. Therefore, the first covenant had its regulations and sanctuary as a witness to Christ but they also witnessed to their own limits and thus to the need of the new covenant; as long as that system was operative the Spirit himself was showing that the way into the true tabernacle had not yet appeared. Now Christ, the high priest of the new order, has done what that system could not and has perfected the people: He entered the true tabernacle which is not of this age, did it with his own blood, did it once for all, and obtained redemption for his brothers and sisters. He cleanses them authentically so that they can serve the living God. It is for this very end that he is the mediator of the new covenant, so that through his death on their behalf they might receive the promised inheritance which they had forfeited at the cost of their own lives. For the blood that inaugurates the covenant is the blood of cleansing and forgiveness that triggers the distribution of the inheritance—it is the death that became necessary if the inheritance was to be gained. For without the pouring out of blood there is no forgiveness.

# 9:23–28

*"It is finished."*

## Context

See 8:1–6 and 9:1–10 for the overview.

4:14—10:25 Christ as high priest and offering

    *4:14–16 Transition, frame with 10:19–25

    5:1—7:28 Christ is high priest

    8:1—10:18 Christ's high priestly ministry

        8:1–6 Introduction: The tabernacles, priesthoods, and covenants

        8:7–13 The better promises of the new covenant

        9:1—10:10 The covenant of which Christ is mediator

            9:1–10 The first covenant as copy and anticipation

            9:11–14 The second covenant as accomplishment

            9:15–22 The inaugural mediation of the second covenant

            9:23–28 The eternal, heavenly, and final character of Christ's ministry (divine drama)

            10:1–10 The bodily offering that accomplished God's will (human drama)

        10:11–18 Conclusion: The better ministry

    *10:19–25 Transition, frame with 4:14–16

Following a general comparison of the sanctuaries and services of Moses and Christ revolving chiefly (but not exclusively) on the Day of Atonement (9:1–14), the argument concentrated on the covenant inauguration ceremony (yet again, not exclusively so) with a view to the blood principle of v. 22 (9:15–22). Verses 23–28 will proceed to sharpen the claims about Christ's ministry with special reference to its heavenly, eternal, and complete nature with respect to sin. The final movement of 10:1–10 will concentrate on the bodily (whole person and perfect) quality of Christ's offering as the achievement of God's will. Like Monet's water lilies, these units are successive visions of one subject, each capturing something more.

Given the relationship between blood and forgiveness, the prefiguring blood of animals had been necessary for the cleansing of the copies, both in the inauguration and then in regular repetitions of the sacrifices. Clearly, if the heavenly things themselves were to be cleansed the sacrifice would have to be of a different order (v. 23). For Christ was entering the presence of God himself in a way that brought an end to sin (vv. 24–26). Having accomplished this there remains only the expectation of salvation (vv. 27–28). Thus Christ appeared before the face of God in behalf of us (v. 24), he has appeared at the end of the age to remove sin (vv. 25–26), and he will appear once again for salvation (vv. 27–28). In all this the preacher is like a painter who wishes to do more than represent a particular subject and so fills the canvas with touches that hint at wider stories and truths that also make up this single, unified drama.

## Background

For the heavenly temple and the language of copies and antitypes, see on 4:14–16; 8:1–6. On blood, see 9:1–10, 15–22; for the Day of Atonement, see Lev 16 and on Heb 9:1–14.

Regarding Heb 9:27, the observation that the fate of death awaits all was a Jewish (Eccl 2:15–16) and Greek (*Epigr. Graec.* 416.6;[1] cf. Homer, *Odyssey* 12.22) commonplace. In some currents of Greek mythology there is the idea of a post-mortem judgment of the soul.[2]

Regarding 9:28, OT texts such as Jer 31:33–34; Ezek 11:18–21; 36:24–32 (cf. Deut 30:6; Isa 2:1–5; Dan 9:24) encourage the idea that the

---

1. Cited with translation by Attridge, *Hebrews*, 265, who notes the phrasing echoes traditional Greek notions.

2. Attridge, *Hebrews*, 265, noting Plato, *Rep.* 10.614B–621D; Plutarch, *Fac. lun.* 27–30 (942D–945D); cf. Wright, *Resurrection*, 32–84, for differing strands of pagan thought related to post-mortem existence.

age to come would see an end to sin. In second-temple texts the idea also finds expression. According to Levi 18, the Lord will raise up a new priest, "And in his priesthood the Gentiles shall be multiplied in knowledge upon the earth, and enlightened through the grace of the Lord: In his priesthood shall sin come to an end, and the lawless shall cease to do evil" (18:9; cf. *Pss. Sol.* 17:36, 41).

It is appropriate, as well, to hear an echo of the servant songs of Isaiah (cf. Isa 53:12) in Heb 9:28 as these were taken up in the Christian liturgical tradition (e.g., 1 Pet 2:24; cf. 1 Pet 1:17–25; Mark 10:45; Matt 8:17). Hebrews' presentation of the gospel is unique in the NT but it is recognizably the same gospel at work.

## Comments on Wording

*9:23–24 copies . . . heavenly things themselves . . . made with hands . . . copies of the true things . . . heaven itself.* See 8:4–5; 9:11. Unlike other NT writers who speak of the OT precedents as types (*typoi, patterns*) of Christ (Rom 5:14; 1 Cor 10:6; 1 Pet 3:21), Hebrews, based on the LXX of Exod 25:40, pushes the *typos* back to the heavenly original and the OT precedent becomes the *antitypos* (cf. Acts 7:44), translated in v. 24 by the ESV as *copies*. For Hebrews, Christ and his work correspond to the pattern (*typos*) that was shown Moses, which is at once eternal and eschatological/once-for-all.

*the heavenly things themselves with better sacrifices than these.* The plural *sacrifices* is almost certainly part of the generalization and refers to the single offering of Christ (just conceivably the different aspects of Christ's offering); it does not evidence a churchly liturgy, the repetition of which would directly contradict the immediate argument. The phrase *heavenly things* has been interpreted with reference to heaven—the expulsion of Satan or the idea of Job 15:15 (cf. *1 Clem.* 39:5; Ign. *Smyrn.* 6:1; cf. Eph 6:12; Col 1:20)—or possibly the cleansing of the cosmos as God's temple. Alternatively, the *cleansing* has been reconstrued as dedication or inauguration, but this does not suit the context or word choice. The context has entirely to do with the cleansing of God's *people* (9:14–15, 22, 24–28) in parallel with the blood ceremony of the old covenant (9:19). The *people* are those who have received the heavenly calling (3:1), are called God's house (3:6) share in Christ and the heavenly gift (3:14; 6:4), and are members of the heavenly Jerusalem (12:22–24, 25–29). The new covenant people are heavenly, the very aspect of the heavenly reality patently in need of cleansing. In the first instance, then, the people are the heavenly things. Their cleansing is both interior and bodily (10:5-10, 22). Ultimately the cosmos is incorporated (12:25-29).

9:24 *now to appear in the presence of God on our behalf.* That he at present appears before the face of God *on our behalf* most naturally recalls his intercessory ministry (2:18; 4:15; 7:25; 10:19-25; cf. 9:14), but since that work is finally a different perspective on the once-for-all offering and the present phrasing is a generalized and imprecise use of imagery (the Day of Atonement parallel breaks down here) we should not suppose that this wording intends only a limited aspect of his work.

9:26 *he would have had to suffer repeatedly since the foundation of the world* etc. The exposition has generally been telling the story of the world from within the story of the promise to Abraham and its history in the Mosaic covenant, but it has been all along the story of creation and all nations (see on 1:1-4; 2:5-9, 16; 4:3-5; 11:1-7). By pushing the effects of Christ's offering back to creation, v. 26 raises what was an assumption to the surface. The pattern shown Moses was that of an already completed offering. That Christ *put away sin* certainly involves the removal of its defiling effects, but probably also envisions the writing of God's law on the heart. Grace abhors a vacuum.

9:28 *offered once to bear the sins of many.* Either "many" intends "all" (2:9) under the influence of Isa 53:11-12 and traditional phrasing (compare Mark 10:45 and 1 Tim 2:6); or it is used as in 2:10 to celebrate the abundant grace shown so many through the generations since the foundation of the world. The phrasing that seems to echo Isa 53:11-12 includes the verb *anapherō*, which can have the sense of taking on oneself the burden that another should have borne, thus to *assume* the sins of many.[3] This is not the only place where a substitutionary idea is implied in Hebrews (cf. 2:5-9; 9:15).

*will appear a second time.* It is possible though not clear that this thought is associated with the reappearance of the high priest after he had gone behind the veil into the Most Holy Place (Lev 16:18; Sir 50:5).

## Comments on Theological Themes

Firstly, the once-for-all nature of Christ's offering and its being at the end of the ages for the removal of sin would seem to be interdependent: because it was once-for-all, it necessarily brought the end of the ages; if it had not brought the end, sin would have had a subsequent history and another sacrifice would have been necessary. Even the world history of these last two

---

3. BDAG, "*anapherō*," 75.

millennia belongs to its past, to the ages that came to an end. Conversely, the Day of Atonement offering was carried out but once in a year, covering the whole history of sin of the preceding year. Christ's fell at the end of "history's year," covering all its sin with no history to follow, and so was once-for-all history. Sin had done all it could, its history was exhausted, it was present as a single, integrated whole, and judgment had been rendered which was final: forgiveness. Again, once the sentence of death has been executed it is finished. History is unidirectional; there is no double jeopardy in God's judgment. Therefore Christ will appear a second time—with nothing more to do with sin—for those who await him for their salvation.

Secondly, by this point Hebrews is drawing from itself for its own "background," which involves its own view of what history is. For example, the thrice repeated "appearance" motif (vv. 24, 26, 28) recalls the "we do not see" and "we do see" of 2:5–9, a passage, in turn, that addresses the question of sin and suffering that continue seemingly unaffected after Christ's death and ascension; it anticipates what faith "sees" that is not at present visible in 11:1–40. The riptide to faith presented by the normalcy of suffering is not of concern only to the framing chapters of 1:1—4:13 and 10:19—13:25, but also the central exposition of Christ's offering. In 9:23–28 we gain a glimpse into why the apparent impotence of Christ's work is constitutive of its fundamental, world-ending potency. That is to say: When we agree that revelation and salvation, indeed, the very course of history, originate only in heaven and descend only downward from there, then we rest secure in the knowledge that since the event has been accomplished there the rest of history cannot and will not escape (12:25–29; cf. 2:1–4). It had to be heavenly first, and so hidden, but being heavenly it will certainly be conclusively earthly.

Thirdly, Heb 9:27 in context registers the point that if Jesus is in fact human, the idea of a repeated death (v. 26) is necessarily excluded. Yet further, in a context that arcs from v. 26 to v. 28, which is to say that it arcs historically from creation to consummation, the reader naturally recalls the sentence of death standing over the first parents and the final judgment to come (cf. 10:26–31). Then again, the immediate context situates Christ's death within the historical drama of Israel's covenantal history (9:15). It is accordingly appropriate to find in the proverbial phrasing of 9:27 an indirect reference to an historically comprehensive and not merely individual judgment (Dan 12:2; Matt 24–25; Rom 2:16; 1 Cor 6:2; 2 Thess 1:6–10; 2 Pet 3:3–13; Rev 20). Hebrews shares with other NT writers the belief in bodily resurrection (6:2; 11:35; 13:20); though it is not explicit here, the judgment would be associated with it (4:13; 6:2; 10:30–31; but note Luke 16:22–23; Wis 3:1–4).

Fourthly, there might seem to be a tension between Hebrews' insistence on but one death and Revelation's "second death" (Rev 2:11; 20:6, 14; 21:8). The latter, however, is merely Revelation's way of distinguishing those who are condemned in the post-mortem judgment from those who died and are raised to life.

## Teaching Hebrews 9:23–28

1. Showing that what was said in the prophets and in the Son (1:1–2) is in fact one history is necessary, but above all Hebrews shows how that history with its copies and shadows illuminates the present for what it is, namely the last days wherein the offering of Christ has brought perfection with the corresponding urgency of faith-obedience. All of this is not firstly about what Moses was not, but about who and what the Son and his salvation are.

2. Heb 9:23–28 is an opportunity to press the point that if we are not thoroughly *heavenly minded* we can be of *no earthly good*, because if something is not first of all heavenly it will never be earthly. Cf. Jas 1:17. History itself proceeds from heaven. The rebellion occurred there before it did on earth, and salvation necessarily originates and did originate there from whence *inexorably* it comes to earth. Hope is established; the anchor, hidden from sight, is firm (6:18–20). Just as 1:1—2:18 moved from heaven to earth so 9:23–28 turns our eyes upward to the heavenly work of Christ and 10:1–10 to his incarnation.

3. By the same token an answer is given to the persistent problem of our weakness, both in the face of persecution and temptation. That concern pulses through Hebrews as it was evidently the challenge that had eroded faith and precipitated a drawing back. We are never given to believe that what is present to our senses is somehow less real, only illusory; our *perceptions* and *interpretations* of this life can be illusory, as they always are for unbelief, but this world itself is certainly not a lesser reality, as if along the lines of the philosophers' dualism. We are given to understand, rather, that what seems the greatest deficiency of the gospel—its invisibility and futurity—is its greatest strength; it is the source of all that ever has been and ever will be real. Hebrews does not directly address the question of *why* there is a delay between the first and the second appearances of Christ beyond his waiting for all his enemies to be made a footstool for his feet, though its hints are in the direction of leaving space for the right response of creation to God's

glory (12:28; 13:15–16), exemplified in the Son's faith and extended through mission.[4] It does press the point that in our very experience of continuing weakness we are more clearly to see that salvation had to be and is in fact heavenly and thus invisible but for just that reason more certainly *real* and *inevitable* for history. Where faith is active, that salvation is no longer merely invisible and future, but here and now precisely in our weakness (11:1; cf. 6:4–5).

4. Above all, 9:23–28 is an occasion for announcing the good news that sin has been done away with; its history—for all humanity, for all the cosmos, and certainly for me—is *past*. It has no future. No sin of mine, even today's or even tomorrow's, is in the future respective to Christ's once-for-all offering. By accepting that, I have accepted the hope only of forgiveness; never of a forgiveness beyond which there might be yet more sin, but only of a "having been forgiven." So when he appears it will be not to ransom from sin, which has been done once-for-all, but only for salvation.

5. Accordingly we place no stock in the systems and institutions of this world, whether political or religious, for they are past and we see their weakness and ineffectiveness. Here we have no abiding city, then, but we seek the city that is coming, confessing its reality, inhabiting it now from within the cities of this age in a way that is out of keeping with them and irreconcilable with their ways, engendering their opposition. While we live this way our witness brings those opponents to bow at the name of Jesus and acknowledge him as Lord, that his enemies might be made a footstool for his feet.

---

4. Presumably something along the same lines must be said in explanation of why salvation involved the whole, long history from Abel to Christ, not least the history of Moses. Why not cut to the chase at a far earlier point? There is something inherent to *upholding* creation for what it is, and especially the human creature, rather than negating it by forcibly clamping "salvation" down on it (which would not be salvation at all). Space and time are given to the human creature fully to enact its part, for obedience or disastrous disobedience.

# 10:1–10

*"This is my body, which is given for you."*

## Context

SEE THE INTRODUCTIONS TO 4:14-16; 5:1-10; 8:1-6; 9:1-10. The two-part exposition of 5:1—10:18 is located between a review of history's drama whose center is the Son as promised by God (1:5—4:13) and a command faithfully to play our part in that drama (10:26—13:25). Having shown that we do have a great high priest (5:1—7:28) we have been guided through a meditation on his world-ending and world-birthing offering in keeping with God's promises (8:1—10:18). Thus:

4:14—10:25 Christ as high priest and offering

    *4:14-16 Transition, frame with 10:19-25

    5:1—7:28 Christ is high priest

    8:1—10:18 Christ's high priestly ministry

        8:1-6 Introduction: The tabernacles, priesthoods, and covenants

        8:7-13 The better promises of the new covenant

        9:1—10:10 The covenant of which Christ is mediator

            9:1-10 The first covenant as copy and anticipation

            9:11-14 The second covenant as accomplishment

            9:15-22 The inaugural mediation of the second covenant

            9:23-28 The eternal, heavenly, and final character of Christ's ministry (divine drama)

10:1–10 The bodily offering that accomplished God's will (human drama)

10:11–18 Conclusion: The better ministry

*10:19–25 Transition, frame with 4:14–16

Many readers may feel that 10:1–10 involves a bit of redundancy, and the preacher does reiterate things said earlier. But to a significant degree the feeling of redundancy has to do with the fact that in the earlier exposition we so frequently had to reach ahead to borrow from what is said here. In its own way this is a keystone in the arch, artfully withheld till now. This is the better sacrifice of 9:23. That it is through his own body-and-soul sacrifice rather than the blood of another creature (9:25–26) will now be explained through Ps 40. This text will highlight what it is that set Christ's offering apart as effectual relative to the other offerings (7:11, 18–19, 27; 8:4–5; 9:9–11). From heaven (9:23–28) we move to earth. Still more, rounding out the exposition of the Son's offering by highlighting the Son's perfect obedience to his Father's saving will, even to the point of willingly placing his body at the service of that will, perfectly captures the decision of faith-obedience that confronts the readers themselves (cf. Heb 12:1–4); it is to that response that the discourse is about to turn (10:19—12:29). The echo of Rom 12:1–2 is not merely superficial.

The internal logic of 10:1–10 is thus in outline: The ineffectual copies and shadows (vv. 1–4) required and anticipated the offering of the Son who is Jesus; he spoke the words of Ps 40:7–9 in the act of his incarnation (vv. 5–7); his words announced the change of law wherein he, in history, would carry out the will of God by which we are sanctified through the offering of his body once for all (vv. 8–10).

## Background

For the *shadow-thing itself* contrast, see on 8:1–6. For the *conscience* and for *blood*, see on 9:1–10. For the animals offered, see on 9:11–14. For the idea of *perfection*, see 2:10; 5:9; 7:11, 19, 28; 9:9 and the introduction to this commentary. Ps 40's use is extremely important and requires careful attention for the immediate argument and its wider implications.

Ps 40 is quoted only here in the NT; for possible allusions or echoes see John 1:17; Eph 5:2; Rev 14:3. The Hebrew wording of Ps 40:6 is difficult and English translations differ. It is most likely that Hebrews' LXX source was as he quoted it, a wording that corresponded to the incarnation (2:10–18).

The general sense is that the psalmist stands ready to obey with all that he is: "You gave me ears to hear and obey, you fashioned my body, I am yours, wholly yours to do your will, O God" (cf. Isa 50:4–5).

The voice of the psalmist seems to be the king's, conceivably David, celebrating the Lord's deliverance from Israel's enemies and anticipating a crisis to come. He is thinking of the sacrifices that he, the king, would have offered both before and after a military campaign. It is as if he recalls Saul's failings at just this point before and after the battles of 1 Sam 13 and 15, and Samuel's words of 1 Sam 15:22–23. The king remembers as well that the scroll of the law had spoken about the king when it commanded him to make a copy of the law and read it all the days of his life, learning to revere and obey the Lord and not to consider himself better than his fellow Israelites (Deut 17:18–20). So the king writes, as Hebrews recalls it: "Sacrifices and offerings you have not desired, but a body have you prepared for me; in burnt offerings and sin offerings you have taken no pleasure. Then I said, 'Behold, I have come to do your will, O God, as it is written of me in the scroll of the book.'"

Yet Hebrews and Ps 40 share more than just the words quoted. We are implicitly invited at once to stand in Ps 40 and look forward to the Son, and to stand with the Son and look back to Ps 40. Word limits permit only a list at present: Note Ps 40:13–17 and its relevance to an audience experiencing persecution, along with the Son's willingness to descend below the angels to taste death for all and be made perfect through sufferings. The Lord's deliverance in Ps 40:1–2 is like resurrection from the dead; cf. Heb 5:7–10. The king's heart of obedience—particularly in the wording of the LXX at Ps 40:7–8—anticipates Jeremiah's law written on the heart. Again, compare the references to a confession in the great assembly in Ps 40:7–10 with Heb 2:12–13.

The ease with which these parallels are observed and the naturalness of their associations support the conclusion that Ps 40:6–7 was not merely an isolated proof-text due to the convenient wording of the Greek version that was Hebrews' source but was the subject of wider christological meditation.[1] It serves as a fitting complement to the earlier citations of Hebrews and as a climax to the exposition.

To adopt Hebrews' own outlook, the psalmist's words belonged to the figurative (9:9–10) speech of the shadows and copies; its intent in the earlier covenantal setting could only have conformed to the divine word it was given, the word that was a shadowy witness to the good things that were coming. In that context, a simple renunciation of the Levitical

---

1. See also Koester, *Hebrews*, 438–39.

sacrifices could only have been rebellion, nor is that what the psalmist intended. His language was poetic; a strong way of saying that sacrifice that did not proceed from a heart of obedience was worse than no sacrifice at all. Yet precisely by upholding the Mosaic regulations that faith response was witnessing to the Son's doing away with them (3:5; 9:8–10; 10:1–4); it was attesting its own nature as a shadow and copy (8:4–5), which means, its faith was a *pointer*. If that is understood then this should be evident: Appearances notwithstanding, Hebrews is not exploiting the wording of the psalm to make it say something different than the psalmist intended, nor is it necessary to ascribe a kind of ecstatically induced direct prophecy to the psalmist in order to harmonize the canon. As the speech of the God who has now spoken in and as the Son, the earlier speech, precisely as a shadow and copy, *in fact* finds its subject matter in the Son. Having already made these things plain in the earlier parts of its argument, Hebrews' concern is not at this point to prove that claim but pastorally to enable the readers to hear it pointedly for faith's sake. The writer therefore goes straight to the conclusion in asserting that the psalm, which was the speech of the Son, did away with the first covenant and established the second.

## Comments on Wording

10:1 *the law has but a shadow of the good things to come instead of the true form of these realities.* See on 8:4–5. *Shadow* does not mean less real; it relates to effectiveness and aim; it is firstly about the tabernacle and only derivatively about the cosmos. The word *realities* translates *eikōn* (*form*) in the sense of the thing that casts the shadow.[2] In 8:5 the shadow was, as it were, cast downward from above (thus pointing upward and back to what already existed, from which it derived), whereas here it is cast backward from what is ahead (and so points forward); either way, the Son and his offering are the actual (effectual) event and constitute the person and act of God himself. *The good things to come* have both arrived and await their consummation.

*by the same sacrifices that are continually offered every year.* See 9:6–10.

*make perfect those who draw near.* For *perfection*, see 2:10 and the introduction to this commentary; also 7:11–19, 25; 9:6–14, 15. Objectively, the failure to perfect the worshippers(*those who draw near*; here not the priests only) is due to 10:4.

10:2 *since the worshipers, having once been cleansed, would no longer have any consciousness of sins.* The Greek wording speaks of the *conscience*

---

2. On the language see Attridge, *Hebrews*, 270–71. (We do not follow his own interpretation entirely). Also, Koester, *Hebrews*, 430, 437.

and its *cleansing*. For the force of this language in relation to the two covenants and the experience of faith, see on 9:1–10.

10:3 *But in these sacrifices there is a reminder of sins every year*. Contrast 8:12; 10:17; cf. Philo, *Plant*. 108; *Mos*. 2.107. They are a reminder objectively speaking, in the sense of 9:8–10.[3]

10:4 *it is impossible for the blood of bulls and goats to take away sins*.[4] See 7:18–19; 9:9–14. This claim is grounded in the fact of Christ's own offering as the speech of the God who also spoke through the prophets; from that vantage point the Holy Spirit's intent is now made clear (9:9–10). This is not a renunciation of blood sacrifices or material sacrifices, for Christ's offering was all of these.[5] Nor is this in tension with 9:9–10, 13, as if the earlier verses attributed partial efficacy to the animal offerings where this verse denies any efficacy; see on 9:11–14, 15–22.

10:5 *when Christ came into the world, he said*. The phrasing is imprecise as to exact timing of Christ's utterance beyond the correlation of the *utterance* and the *event* of the incarnation. It seems safe to say, however, that the Son's perfect obedience was complete from its inception (see 4:15). This verse also assumes continuity of identity of the pre-incarnate Son and the Son of earthly history.[6] More to the point, Ps 40 so captures the drama of the atonement as it had to take place and did take place and so pulls together the prior exposition's themes that we can only suppose that the whole exposition has been anticipating this passage. The "scroll" is the book of the law (9:19) which was a shadow of the pattern shown Moses (8:5) and of the good things coming (10:1); as such, it spoke of Christ (10:7), revealing that to which Moses obediently (10:8b; cf. 3:1–6; 8:5) but merely pointed—Moses's law with its bulls and goats (10:4) not being *in itself* what God willed (10:5–6, 8)—and which represented God's actual and ultimate saving will, namely, the simple and full faith-obedience of his human creature and atonement for its wrong so that it may enter his resting place (3:7—4:11; 12:22–24). This was the pattern shown Moses and the Son has now come to put it into effect, thereby supplanting the copy and witness; he must become greater, while Moses becomes less (10:9). The Son who within Hebrews has already been made equal with God accordingly volunteers himself to carry out God's will, for which end he accepts the human body prepared for him—he steps into the place of God's human creature, taking

---

3. This line sits uneasily with a Christian ritual that treats the Eucharist as a sacrifice; Hebrews' endeavor seems to be the more radical one of seizing once and for all on Christ's once-for-all sacrifice.

4. Regarding sacrifices among first century pagans, see Koester, *Hebrews*, 438.

5. Contra Bruce, *Epistle to the Hebrews*, 238.

6. Koester, *Hebrews*, 104–5.

responsibility for its history (cf. 2:5-18). The will of God—Father and Son as one—is thereby achieved (10:10). Moreover, that the heavenly offering (8:1-4) was an emphatically earthly one is here made more explicit than elsewhere.

10:5-8 *Sacrifice and offering . . . burnt offerings and sin offerings . . .* As elsewhere in Hebrews this gathers up the whole sacrificial system.

*you have not desired . . . you have taken no pleasure . . . I have come to do your will . . . these are offered according to the law.* That God willed (desired) them is a truth which Hebrews emphasizes rather than suppresses (cf. 7:11)—but on Hebrews' terms he did not will those rituals as the means of atonement (10:4; 9:22). See further under Background. Hebrews is not opposing obedience to sacrifice (9:22, 26; 10:10!), but setting before us the obedient sacrifice intended by God.

10:8-9 *When he said . . . . Then he added . . . . He does away with the first in order to establish the second.* Similarly to 2:5-9 what were complementary statements in the psalm are made antithetical. This is not literary ignorance but theological exposition. For the strong language of annulment and the intended sense, see 7:11-28; 8:1-13. Hebrews' "annulment" *establishes* Moses's law, and so coheres fully with Matt 5:17-20 when both are understood.

10:10 *And by that will.* That is, by the will of God; implicitly, of course, the Son's own will is in perfect harmony with his Father's, as is the Father's will with the Son's.[7] Further, the totality of the act of obedience requires its interiority but if that is made its essence in some limiting sense the full humanness of it is lost and the atonement with it. Blood (v. 4), body, and the divine will of Father and Son are one.

*through the offering of the body of Jesus Christ once for all.* The allusion is pointedly to Calvary. This is the first time the names *Jesus* and *Christ* are brought together in Hebrews, which might intentionally correspond with the intersection of earth and heaven in this passage.[8] This is the last time the term for *once for all* is used in this sense, contributing to the climactic quality of 10:1-10 in 9:1—10:10. The successful completion of redemptive history, as *history* (cosmic, bodily, and heavenly), is signaled; see on 9:12, 23-28.

---

7. In Hebrews we are saved by Jesus' faith (10:5-10; cf. 12:1-3), certainly, and we are saved by reposing all salvific things in him alone. That Hebrews nowhere formulates as does Paul—faith *in* Jesus—is a formally accurate point that can miss the forest for the trees *if* it denies that the *idea* is not operative.

8. Cf. Attridge, *Hebrews*, 277.

## Comments on Theological Themes

The body prepared speaks at once of the Son's incarnation (10:5) and offering (10:10), and the former is continuous with the latter (2:5–18). Further, it signifies not mere physicality but all that it means to be human emotionally, sexually, economically, etc. Moreover, it cannot be human if it is not particular, within a particular history and its identity. It is the body of fallen Israel, heir to the promises of Ps 8. It is under the sentence of death (9:15, 27; cf. Rom 7:24; 2 Cor 5:21; Gal 3:13). The body that he chose was the body of his self-offering in obedience for cleansing in the completion of his Father's will.

It is therefore a body that is fashioned for the doing of God's will. It is an end to sacrifice in a way that the psalmist could only speak of figuratively. The psalmist (cf. Ps 51:16–17; Isa 1:11–15; 66:3; Jer 7:21–23; Hos 6:6; Amos 5:22–24; Mic 6:6–8) was not at that time instituting the new covenant with its perfection. It is just as plain that what the sacrifices offered by David prefigured—the reality to which they pointed—was no mere *idea* or "*spiritualized*" accomplishment of God's will. The wording is, *sacrifice you have not desired*, but the meaning is "the *animal* sacrifices commanded through Moses you have not desired." It spoke of a death that could be prefigured ultimately only in the commandment to Abraham that he offer his own son, the son of promise (Gen 22; Heb 6:13–15; 11:17–19). It is also the body of the resurrection, the body offered to God alive as the one who had died, who stands before God and intercedes for us *as one of us*, forever. It was our contemptible weakness that he assumed, bore to death, and cleansed, now interceding for us as our brother with gentleness and empathy.

The faith of the Son with which this text has to do (12:1–3; cf. 2:10) is both provision and example. The Son's faith-obedience forges the reality of the law written on the human heart and accomplishes our atonement. Our faith, toward which the whole sermon is bending, is finally a communion with the relation between Father and Son; an obedient echo of the Father's willingness to offer his Son; an echo of the Son's response of absolute trust and obedience as a true child. In imitation and participation every true child declares, "A body have you prepared for me." It is thus irreducibly a body in mission, at one with this Father's will (cf. 10:35–36; 13:20–21).[9]

---

9. For this missional pattern of imitation in Paul, see Conzelmann, *1 Corinthians*, 92.

## Teaching Hebrews 10:1-10

1. The preacher did not "do random" or add thoughts as if forgetting what he had said previously. Hebrews is not in the genre of Pascal's *Pensées*. So when we come to 10:1-10 we are looking at the same history covered in 1:1—2:18 and 5:1—9:28; what was said there assumed what is said here. Because of Israel's disobedience and its defilement forgiveness is necessary, without the pouring out of blood there is no forgiveness, and it is impossible for the blood of the animals offered in obedience to God's command to remove sin. Therefore the one who was Son, the radiance of God's glory, descended below the angels, shared fully in the blood and flesh of Abraham's seed taking responsibility for their history, and so worked sanctification. The history of the promise was realized in the obedience of this man, God's Son, for the blessing of all nations and the attainment of the inheritance. In so doing, all the other claims made of him and his salvation heretofore were established. Again, 8:3-4 is answered not through something "unearthly" but through the taking of a body. See on 5:1-10.

2. To isolate christology within that, the pre-incarnate existence of the Son and the continuity of personal identity in his history are of course assumed. Only God could work salvation. To dig deeper, that a human sacrifice was required is an unavoidable inference from what is said, which can only be accounted for in Hebrews' world by the disobedience of Israel through whom the promise was to be channeled to the nations; it would seem to follow that her death was required as a penalty, which would be the death undergone by the Son in taking a body. To express this in terms of a *body* is merely to express through the language of Ps 40 what was said in broader compass in 2:5-18 and 5:7-10. That the Son's blood was cleansing and sanctifying, working forgiveness, is patent, but that it was also substitutionary seems built into the logic (cf. 9:15). The Son bore our sin (9:28) while, as one of us, perfectly doing God's will. Again, this passage reinforces the conviction that the pattern shown Moses (8:5) was nothing other than the Son himself.

3. Likewise, to isolate salvation, earlier teachings on the relationship of Moses to Christ and vice versa are reiterated and deepened in 10:1-10. Among other things, that we expressed the above in terms of the history of Israel is not to reduce Hebrews to parochial interests but to remind ourselves that as goes Israel (her promise, her tabernacle) so goes the world; the covenant is the internal basis of creation. Further,

the Son's choice of becoming-human has implications not only for himself and salvation but for what it is to be human, for with him we choose our creation and the will of God for his creation. We choose that will to the uttermost. We do so, however, only as those led by God to the glory of his resting place behind our leader who was perfected through suffering (2:10) and whose offering sanctified us (10:10; 2:11).

4. When we celebrate those words, *a body have you prepared for me*, we are finally saying something about our own bodies, our own lives, the lives of those cleansed and forgiven, the lives of those who look to this high priest—whose lives and bodies are represented by and bound up with his body, and therefore with his mission (cf. Heb 13:11–16; Rom 12:1–2).

5. This passage can also occasion wider reflections on living pagan sacrificial systems, their relationship to the Mosaic system, and thus to Christ's offering. There are living cultures where sacrifice is still practiced, yielding unique challenges and advantages for understanding the gospel. The message of Hebrews can speak with a special immediacy and potency to such a setting, and our brothers and sisters in these cultural contexts can potentially open fresh understanding for all of us.[10] Yet care must be taken to put no pagan system on the same plane as Israel's, which, for all its parallels in the Ancient Near East, existed uniquely as a shadow and copy of the pattern shown Moses (8:5) and a shadow of the good things of Christ (10:1).

---

10. Compare Ngewa, "Traditional Sacrifices," 1502–3.

# 10:11–18

*"Your sins are forgiven."*

## Context

SEE 4:14-16; 5:1-10; 8:1-6 and succeeding units. We have reached the end of the central exposition of Hebrews:

4:14—10:25 Christ as high priest and offering

    *4:14-16 Transition, frame with 10:19-25

    5:1—7:28 Christ is high priest

    8:1—10:18 Christ's high priestly ministry

        8:1-6 Introduction: The tabernacles, priesthoods, and covenants

        8:7-13 The better promises of the new covenant

        9:1—10:10 The covenant of which Christ is mediator

            9:1-10 The first covenant as copy and anticipation

            9:11-14 The second covenant as accomplishment

            9:15-22 The inaugural mediation of the second covenant

            9:23-28 The eternal, heavenly, and final character of Christ's ministry (divine drama)

            10:1-10 The bodily offering that accomplished God's will (human drama)

        10:11-18 Conclusion: The better ministry

    *10:19-25 Transition, frame with 4:14-16

10:26—12:29 Exhortations toward faith and progress

13:1–17 Peroration

13:18–25 Closing

If we were to arrive at the goal of the promise delivered to Abraham of entrance into the holy presence of God in his resting place, we were in need of cleansing, sanctification, forgiveness. It was the Son who, having worked this cleansing, sat at the right hand of God, waiting for his enemies to be made a footstool for his feet. That drama had been presented from differing angles in 1:1—4:13 under the theme of God's speech, his *word* in and as the Son. The pivotal moment of that history centered on the appointment of the Son as our great high priest (5:1—7:28) according to the Scriptures, which means, according to the shadows and copies of Moses's tabernacle that had been fashioned after the heavenly original which was the Son. The Son's great salvation as both priest and offering was elaborated especially on the basis of Exod 24–25, Jer 31, Lev 16, and Ps 40. It is a matter of the better promises which establish (8:7–13) the better covenant of which Christ is mediator (9:1—10:10), according to which he has obtained a ministry superior to that of the Levitical priests (10:11–18). Jer 31, which launched 8:7—10:18, will now close it by announcing the gospel's *word* of forgiveness on which everything stands or falls.

10:11–18 will thus draw together the major themes around the key texts of Ps 110:1 and Jer 31:31–34, reiterate from the exordium (1:1–4; cf. 8:1) and cash in the significance of the Son's act of sitting down, foreground the testimony of the Holy Spirit in the matter of writing the divine laws on the heart, and condense it all into the formula: *Where there is forgiveness of these, there is no longer any offering for sin* (v. 18). Henceforth, though teaching and exposition will continue the discourse will turn primarily to exhortation to faith and faithfulness. See further the introduction to this commentary.

Internally, Heb 10:11–18 divides in two. Verses 11–14 pick up on the theme of constant repetition of ineffectual offerings, pointedly symbolized by the fact that the priests *stand* in offering them. The Son, by contrast, having offered one eternally effective offering *sat*, and only waits for his enemies to be made a footstool for his feet, for he has made perfect his worshippers. That kingly act ends matters, and signals as well the end of the central exposition. To that heavenly event corresponds in vv. 15–18 the immanent witness of the Spirit in the words of Jer 31:33, implicitly picking up on the cleansing and perfecting of the conscience as the sign, or rather the accomplishment of the authentic, full, and effectual atonement. The closing comment of v. 18—which could be treated as a third part, a kind of concluding epigram—is a masterstroke, containing both exhortation (10:19-25) and warning (10:26-31). This forgiveness is sovereign, holding implications for all without remainder.

## Background

See the preceding units.

## Comments on Wording

10:11 *And every priest stands daily at his service.* Cf. Deut 10:8; 18:7. See on 7:27 for the writer's penchant for generalizations about the priesthood. The contrast is built on the many-vs.-one template that has been developed in differing ways (many [mortal] priests and many offerings vs. one [eternal] priest and one offering) with the standing-seated opposition rhetorically underscoring 1) the finality and comprehensive effectiveness of Christ's self-offering of 10:1-10, 2) the rounding out of the exposition of Ps 110 by a return to the exordium (1:3), 3) a nod in the direction of the pending appeal for faithfulness (a right response while he "waits"), and 4) an emphasis on his session as a basis for 10:19-25.

10:12 *he sat down.*[1] The priests' standing was a position of honor but also a sign of what was said in 7:11-19 and 9:9-10. The subjugation of Israel's enemies was closely related to the promise of rest (Deut 12:8-14; 2 Sam 7:1-2; 1 Kgs 5:3), so that the present reference to Ps 110:4 would recall the promise of Heb 3:7—4:11. Moreover, the divine rule involved in sitting on the throne recalls 1:3 and the "bearing" of all things, which see.

10:13 *waiting from that time until his enemies should be made a footstool.* This refrain speaks to vindication (13:5-6; cf. 1:8-9; 5:7-10; 6:2; 7:2; 9:27; 10:19-39; 11:6, 32-39; 12:1-3, 25-29; 13:7, 20-21), as well as to the character of the in-between time (2:5-9) for a people who have lost perspective. The imagery is probably not intended in a purely negative sense but includes the positive mission.

10:18 *Where there is forgiveness of these, there is no longer any offering for sin.* See 10:8-9. Hebrews' more characteristic language for salvation is that of cleansing, sanctification, and perfecting; nor is *forgiveness* terminology used with the Day of Atonement ritual in the OT (aside from the *release*

---

1. For the tradition of a continuous heavenly sacrifice that developed from the Vulgate's translation of 10:12 as well as disagreements over the Mass and Christ's sacrifice as it bears on this verse, see Attridge, *Hebrews*, 280.

of the goat, Lev 16:26). The noun used here, *aphesis*, is used by other NT writers for *forgiveness of sins* (e.g., Matt 26:28; Mark 1:4; Luke 1:77; Eph 1:7; cf. Josephus, *B.J.* 1.24.4.481), but this is not characteristic of the LXX where the noun is usually used for *release* from debt and bondage, especially in connection with the seventh year and the Year of Jubilees (Lev 25; 27; Deut 15; 31:10; cf. Luke 4:18). In Hebrews the noun is used at 9:22 and here; the idea lurks elsewhere (e.g., 2:17-18; 4:14-16; 6:1; 9:15, 26-28; 12:17); in the present verse it rephrases Jer 31:33. It is probably used by Hebrews, then, under the influence of Christian tradition, likely in association with the *ransom* language of 9:12, 15 (cf. Eph 1:7; Col 1:14; cf. Lev 25; 27); possibly with connotations of Jubilees or at least remission, release, and freedom from debt and bondage (cf. 2:14-15). The assertion is not strictly that a sacrifice (offering) *is no longer necessary*, but that *there is no longer any offering for sin*, in the sense that no other offering exists or is possible. *All* sin has been atoned for here.

## Comments on Theological Themes

The state of *perfection* in 10:14 (see 2:10) consists in the cleansed conscience (signifying authentic and whole cleansing of the person, inner and outer) grounded in a finished, once for all work (6:18-20; 9:9-14; 10:1-10) making worshippers objectively fit to approach the divine presence (cf. 2:10; 5:9). The *being sanctified* is not directly a matter of incremental growth in obedience (progressive sanctification) but more of continued participation in God's active grace (2:11).[2]

There is enough on the Spirit (10:15) in Hebrews to affirm that the writer operated with a personal conception of the Holy Spirit (see on 2:4; 3:7), but Hebrews has nothing like the fullness of Paul's and Luke's writings. Yet 1) knowing that other apostolic writings closely associate the Spirit and reception of the gospel (e.g., John 15:5-16; 1 Cor 2:6-16; 2 Cor 3:1-6; 1 John 2:18-27; 5:6-12), and 2) noting the way in which the present comment about the Spirit's witness generally correlates in Hebrews with the sustained concern with a cleansed/perfected conscience as the internal effect of the new covenant gospel (= the law written on the heart), it is a fair inference that the writer assumes here that the Spirit is the internal witness, the presence of God in the application of the new covenant blessings; contrast the Spirit's witness in the old covenant (9:9-10). Within 10:11-18 the Spirit's

---

2. Cockerill, *Epistle to the Hebrews*, 452-53. The present passive participle used admits of other interpretations.

witness signals the shift from the heavenly event of vv. 11–14 to the immanent application and experience of it in vv. 15–18.

## Teaching Hebrews 10:11–18

1. Humans of seemingly every culture have devised means of all sorts to cope with the stubborn realities of guilt and defilement, whether those means are cultic, psychological, social, or philosophical. Excusing, blaming, rationalizing, delay, denial, willful amnesia, restitution, doing good and more all ameliorate guilt and dictate the terms by which right and wrong are understood and the wrong is erased. What came to light in the gospel—the *good* news—was the comprehensiveness of the disaster and impossibility of atonement... apart from the death of the Son of God. To put it simply: It was only when we saw the price paid, by whom it was paid and how, that we understood the debt owed—but by then it was already paid. We saw, too, that forgiveness could not have been won by us. Atonement depended solely on God's will *not to remember our sins and lawless acts*; it is the word of forgiveness spoken in *and as* the Son. Rightly understood, Moses's law pointed to the same truth (7:11–19; 9:9–10; 10:1–4). The gospel is "good" news in part in that this knowledge comes to light only as part of the past that has already died, already been buried, already assigned to oblivion. It was never known otherwise; we were never actually suspended perplexed over the abyss. The only response can be the acknowledgement, recognition, and confession that things are so, which is necessarily a form of life constructed on this threefold act from the ground up—in a word, faith.

2. Whether or not other canonical texts encourage the devising of churchly rites of atonement and the positing of other intermediaries to whom prayers can be offered, Hebrews knows none of these. Its argument all but excludes the very possibility that they should exist. One word has been spoken in and as the Son and all that can be done has been done. One priest exists through whom we make our approach to the divine throne. Therefore... (vv. 19–25).

3. As we said at the outset (1:1–4) if Hebrews had begun with the claims of 10:11–18 we would have asked how these things could be so and on what grounds they should be accepted as true. We are hearing what has been accomplished, but it depends for its force on all that has proceeded as a revelation of the Son and his history in the history of the

word of God. As it stands here we celebrate that he has done it and that the new age—sin and guilt forever in the past, God's righteousness reigning inwardly and outwardly forevermore—has been birthed. Or rather faith alone celebrates it from within the continuation of the present weakness, knowing that nothing remains but the eager expectation along with him of the subjugation of all his enemies.

# 10:19–25

*"If anyone enters by me, he will be saved."*

## Context

WHETHER DUE TO DISCOURAGEMENT, distraction, desire, inattention, pride, or other causes many who begin the journey of faith do not finish it. Hebrews is a book about *finishing the journey*. By adopting a heavenly perspective it issues a call to its original readers for gritty, this-worldly faithfulness on their Italian streets. The reward is coming (10:35; 11:6) but if their Lord waits (10:13) their obedience must submit to the same delay—they must accept the present for what it is without illusion or fantasy, which means inhabiting the realities that have been revealed in the gospel. Waiting is not a lazy, selfish, or pouting withdrawal, but an active filling of the present, endurance in growth, an engaged accompanying of the promise as it builds toward its goal.

The whole exposition of 1:1—10:18 is now brought to bear in a prolonged series of exhortations and warnings (10:19—13:25). The accent has shifted from applicable doctrine to doctrinal application. For all of this, 10:19-25 is transitional. "You began well!," the author says (3:14; 6:9-10; 10:32-34; cf. Gal 3:3; 5:7). But "Everything hangs on finishing the journey, so . . . ." *So*: "Get a firm grip on reality and resolutely conduct yourself accordingly!" That is 10:19-25 in a nutshell.

Structurally speaking, if we group the exordium (1:1-4) with the first movement of Hebrews and the closing verses (13:18-25) with the last, Hebrews falls into three main parts with the central section bookended by transitional paragraphs:

1:1—4:13 Opening frame: a review of history's drama whose center is the
    Son as promised by God

4:14–16 Exhortation transitioning into the central exposition

5:1—10:18 Central exposition

10:19–25 Exhortation transitioning out of the central exposition

10:26—13:25 Closing frame: the command faithfully to play our part in God's drama

There is considerable similarity between 4:14–16 and 10:19–25, though of course by this point the exhortation can deck itself out in language colored with the developments of the preceding exposition. A barebones charting of its thought looks like this:[1]

Therefore
> having boldness toward the entrance
>> which he inaugurated as a new and living way
>
> [and having] a great priest over God's house

let us approach [God's holy presence]
> with a genuine heart
>
> in assurance of faith
>
> having our hearts sprinkled
>
> having our bodies washed.

Let us hold fast the confession of the hope
> for the promiser is faithful,

and let us give thought to one another toward the end of provoking love and good deeds
> not neglecting the act of gathering together
>
> but increasingly exhorting each other with an eye to the approaching day.

## Background

See on 4:14–16 regarding the tabernacle imagery and cosmology.

---

1. For a rhetorical analysis, see Koester, *Hebrews*, 447.

The phrase "great priest" in 10:21 is a literal rendering of the more common expression used in the OT for the high priest (e.g., Lev 21:10; Num 35:25, 28).

For the "day" that is drawing nearer (10:25) in Christian traditions, see Mark 13; John 21:22-23; Acts 1:1-11; Phil 3:20-21; 1 Thess 1:10; 4:13—5:11; 2 Thess 2:1-12; Jas 5:3, 7-9; 1 Pet 4:7—5:11; 2 Pet 3:1-16; 1 John 3:2; Jude; Revelation. The expression probably draws from the "day of the Lord" tradition, which is firstly a day of God's self-vindication, involving both judgment and salvation for creation (e.g., Joel 3:14-16; Amos 5:18-20; 8:9-14; Zech 14:1-11). In the NT it can be used of the present (Acts 2:16-21) and the future (e.g., 1 Thess 5:1-11; 2 Pet 3:1-16).

## Comments on Wording

10:19 *we have confidence.* See on 3:6; 4:16. The word (*parrēsia*) frequently denotes a boldness that involves freedom of speech and uninhibited behavior, associations that suit an approach to the divine throne that seeks mercy and grace to help. In 10:35, as in 3:6, it relates to the social sphere.

10:20 *by the new and living way that he opened for us.* This summarizes the whole of 8:1—10:18. The word for *opened*, (*engainizō*), was used in 9:18 for the inauguration of the first covenant; here his blood has inaugurated the new covenant. This way into the Most Holy Place was "not previously existing," thus it is *new* or *recent*; cf. 8:7-13. If the old covenant faithful (11:1-40) persevered though the "day" was further distant and the word given them concerned only shadows and copies, then how much more must we for whom this new way has been inaugurated. It is *living* not merely by being somehow dynamic and active but as God (3:12; 9:14; 10:31; 12:22), the word (4:12), and the risen Son (7:25) are living, being bound up with the risen Son's life-giving, eternal, once-for-all cleansing offering and unending sympathetic intercession.

*through the curtain, that is, through his flesh.*[2] The Greek phrasing (which uses the word usually translated *flesh*, *sarx*, rather than *body*, *sōma*) has been understood in markedly different ways. Compare the NIV: *opened for us through the curtain, that is, his body.* It is most likely that *flesh* functions here as *blood* and *himself* do elsewhere, that is, signifying the means of his entrance (= his self-offering): ". . . a new and living way through the curtain, this is, [through = by means] of his flesh." *Blood* (v. 19) and *flesh*

---

2. There is no evidence of knowledge of the rending of veil that took place upon Jesus' crucifixion (Mark 15:38) on the part of Hebrews. The imagery used is not that of a removed or torn veil, but access through it in the normal fashion of the high priest. It is arguable, nonetheless, that the traditions are getting at the same basic idea; cf. Bruce, *Epistle to the Hebrews*, 251.

(here) might be paired as an echo of 2:14. Attridge captures what is the likely intent: Hebrews here suggests, "... that Christ entered that realm and made it possible for others to do so, not by a heavenly journey through a supernal veil, but by means of his obedient bodily response to God's will,"[3] specifically in his self-offering.

10:21 *a great priest over the house of God.* If it it is a dreadful thing to fall into the hands of the living God (v. 31) it is salvation itself to have a great priest. This summarizes the whole of 5:1—7:28. Its phrasing also recalls at once 4:14-16 and 3:1-6, and with the latter the earlier familial language of 2:11-16. What has been formed is the new nation of God whose cultic center is the Most Holy Place of the heavenly tabernacle. Our own blood and flesh brother is our high priest. The allusion to 3:1-6 is also a reminder of Moses's role as a *witness* of the things that would be spoken (3:5; 8:5). The one to whom all that pointed, the Son who is *over* God's house, is now here.

10:22 *let us draw near.* The magnitude of newness and privilege in this simple exhortation—freed of the fixed times and conditions of 9:7—cannot be over-appreciated. If we say that the event in mind is not "just prayer, such as David and others had available to them," we risk misunderstanding but it might be a risk worth taking to underscore the historic newness of what is intended. For, *draw near*, and its relationship to *entering*, see 4:16 (translated there as *approach*). The terminological distinction is both respected and blurred in 10:19-22.[4]

*with a true heart.* The idea of a *true heart* can be used of a heart that is sincere, faithful, and trustworthy (Isa 38:3; cf. Matt 5:8). Given Hebrews' other uses of the term *alēthinos* (8:2; 9:24) it might signify a heart that has undergone the promised cleansing and been made of a piece with the heavenly gift (cf. Ezek 11:18-21; 36:26-32); it is *genuine*, the law of God having been written thereon. Such a heart knows God's ways, especially his new way, and will enter his resting place (3:10, 12).

*with our hearts sprinkled clean from an evil conscience.* For the *conscience* and its cleansing, see on 9:1-10. What is in that context (cf. 9:11-14) something objectively given is here a matter of appropriation. It cannot be made more true or real or complete than it is as a gift, but it can be refused and neglected (2:3) through unbelief. This comment assists in clarifying that the cleansing of the heavenly things in 9:23 centers on the cleansing of the worshippers who partake in the heavenly summons (cf. 3:1).

*and our bodies washed with pure water.* This is undoubtably in part an allusion to baptism, though it contains the same imprecision as 6:2 and probably picks up on other references to cleansing rites using water (9:10,

---

3. Attridge, *Hebrews*, 287.

4. Where the ESV translates with "to enter" in 10:19, the Greek uses the phrase *eis tēn eisodon* rather than the verb *eiserchomai*.

19). Cf. Ezek 36:25–26. The metaphor bears on bodily conduct and the hope of the resurrection.

10:23 *Let us hold fast the confession of our hope without wavering*. We *have* (vv. 19, 21) and so must *hold fast*. This is a firm grip that will not release this hope for anything desirable for which one might grasp, nor relax its hold for fear or despair or inattention as a rock climber might do. It seems also to convey the positive idea of contemplating, cherishing, understanding more deeply what has been (superficially) confessed (see 2:4). As in 3:1; 4:14 the *confession* no doubt has a public quality. The grounding of this resoluteness is the character and being of the one who promises, assuming familiarity with the history through which he has revealed himself; see on 4:1–11 and 6:13–20.

10:25 *not neglecting to meet together*. The participle for *not neglecting* often has the sense of *forsake, abandon* (e.g., Matt 27:46; Acts 2:27; 2 Tim 4:10, 16; Heb 13:5), and might imply in the present context an abdication of responsibility for the gathering. The *meeting together* implies the regular *scattering* in mission.

## Comments on Theological Themes

The three exhortations feature faith, hope, and love in turn, gesturing toward a comprehensive obedience and drawing together the entire image of the household of God over which stands its brother-priest. The commanded *approach* itself represents the sum of Israel's hopes to "dwell in the house of the Lord forever" (Ps 23:6; cf. 27:4–6) and, consistent with that center, to live in full covenantal faithfulness with our siblings (Ps 15; 101:5–8; Isa 33:15–16; 58:1–14; Jer 7:2–11). It is a matter of bringing what is hoped for into the present through faith and love. Both attention to and the neglect of salvation are, by their very nature, self-perpetuating activities. The *approach* and the bodily *meeting together* represent a wealth of gifts that span the inner and outer summons for holiness of life and perseverance in faith.

What is conveyed in 10:22's mention of water is the gospel's claim on the whole person, inner and outer, with a view to a break with the past and obedience moving forward. Hebrews locates all cleansing in the body and blood of Christ himself and lends no direct support to a developed sacramental theology of baptism and the Lord's Supper. Naturally, however, a sacramental interpretation of these verses could be richly rewarding, less due to the words of Hebrews than the assumed sacramental referent.

The Day that is approaching marks the clean break between the present age and the age to come (2:5; 3:14; 9:28; 10:13). Hebrews focuses less on the question of its timing than its certainty and implications for the present. The implication, however, is that the date has been set, the outcome is known, and, like a child waiting for a holiday, the more time that transpires the more excitement mounts. Radical commitment does not diminish but grows. Those who stand firm till the end will be saved.

## Teaching Hebrews 10:19–25

1. The passages of exposition and exhortation within Hebrews are distinguishable, but they are two ways of talking about one thing, and can run together for stretches as they do in 10:19—13:17. Knowing what things are includes knowing what we must choose in obedience, and understanding the way things are is contained in the commands, that is, in obedience to them (5:11–14). With 10:19-25 our expositional translation must shift its accent so as to carry forward the letter's teaching as the communication of Christ's benefits in the form of commands.

2. None of the benefits of Christ were sought but once they are graciously given, so that we *have* them, they make faith, hope, and love possible. The preacher here heaps up the praise of Christ, each phrase a summary of the preceding exposition, resting all things in Christ so that our confidence is secured. We are like troops on a battle field who felt overwhelmed and who had despaired but have now felt the tide turn in their favor. Or like an entrepreneur who had lost confidence in her vision, her abilities, and her backing, and had suddenly been assured of them all. Or like a parched wanderer in a desert finding a trickle of water and knowing that it need only be followed to its source.

3. The whole of Hebrews orients salvation on the copy and shadow of the Sinaic covenant and particularly on the heart of that covenant in the fulfillment of the promise that takes place with the entrance into God's resting place, his holy presence. But that center has a circumference, that is, a whole people, a nation, gathered around that center, occupying a place that is given, and flourishing in a harvest of righteousness and peace. It is this whole that is always intended even if the argument concentrates on its center. That communal and social aspect is assumed throughout (see, e.g., on 4:1–11; 5:11–14; 6:7–8) and breaks through at points (cf. 6:9–10; 10:32–34; 13:1–8) as it does also in 10:24–25. For that larger world to exist it must have at its heart what was at the heart of Israel, on which her whole world turned, to which she always faced, and from which issued her life: the sanctuary.

4. "Spurring" each other to love and good deeds will not be meddling or judgmental if it happens only where there already exists a relationship of genuine rather than pro forma sibling love Where charity exists it

will be a craft and an art. If one wishes to "spur" one will need first to take the time to love. It will be most effective where we have been heeding the commands ourselves. It can never regard anyone as if what vv. 19–23 have just summarized are not the most determinative realities of all human existence—as if one's fellows can be understood and honored simply as human beings apart from these things.

5. Left to ourselves the centrifugal forces of ego-centrism are always greater than the centripetal force of Christ-centrism. *Meeting together* in the sense intended here is not natural. On top of this the scientific, technological age has made finitude a problem—seen in the frustration of only local presence and influence—and encouraged the quixotic dream of running to and fro (or at least digitally being in many places) in the hopes of saving the whole world. It belongs to the gift of salvation that the Son took to himself our blood and flesh with all its limits and praised God with us in the midst of the assembly (2:11–14), and it belongs to the gift that we have this family, which for me means, this particular local church gathered around the one Leader who has already opened up the world's salvation—and ours, if we will endure in these very exhortations. Being bodily means being *here* together, being real together, being bound together, being here for each other for the long haul, and all the more as we see the Day approaching.

6. The resolve to "attend church" consistently has, in the minds of many, come to be associated with misguided "religion." It is an empty effort at merit, a false salve to one's conscience, a substitute for real righteousness and love, a superstitious confidence in spiritual effects, a bid for appearance over substance, something unnecessary to real "relationship with God." To value consistency in this matter of attendance is to prove one's "Pharisaic" identity. That such consistency (cf. 3:13; *Didache* 4:2) could represent the heart of faith as envisioned by the whole of Hebrews' summons is an alien thought. From the viewpoint of this apostolic word of encouragement, however, the consistent participation in the gatherings—assuming a church to be authentic, but also assuming an authentic church to be flawed—is the sign of a cleansed community doing what comes naturally in worship; it is where all the benefits of Christ concentrate for us and through us, propelling us forward and outward in worship and mission. Its neglect is a sign of faithlessness, the forfeiture of what is necessary for the pilgrimage to the place of salvation, and the abdication of responsibility toward one's fellow pilgrims.

## 10:26–31

*"What will the owner of the vineyard do?"*

### Context

SEE ON 10:19–25. As we move forward with the exhortation, the preceding exposition is cashed in and supplemented with fresh reflections on faith, covenantal family, and the culmination and resolution of the history of God's promise.

A variety of textual features suggest for us the following structural guide for the final chapters. Since 10:19–25 is transitional we will include it in this perspective. As we have stressed already, any outline of Hebrews should admit that Hebrews' rhetoric is driven more by the desire for effect than orderly arrangement so that disagreement among proposed outlines will and should persist:

- 10:19–31 Exhortation to faith and warning against apostasy (reusing 10:19–25)
    - 10:19–25 There is now forgiveness (10:18), so approach!
    - 10:26–31 There is no other or further offering for sin (10:18), so do not refuse the one given!
- 10:32—12:3 Enduring in the great contest of faith in the promise
- 12:4–17 Enduring as the genuine children of the covenantal Father
- 12:18–29 The grand finale: closing vision of the promised inheritance, the peril of refusing the promiser, and a final warning/exhortation
- 13:1–17 Peroration

The sermon may have been going on for about thirty minutes by this point.[1] Just as in 5:11—6:20 a strong warning will be used to reboot their attention (vv. 26–31), balanced immediately by reminders and reassurances (vv. 32–39).

The dominant note to be heard henceforth is that of a positive urging forward in faith, but this is not a pastor reluctant to state that there are terrible consequences for unbelief. The concern for the moment is that that judgment will turn on Jesus, and most pointedly on continuance in the total acknowledgement, recognition, and confession of the forgiveness rendered in him in the light of its once-for-all nature and its identification with the singular and irrevocable promise of God.

This warning of vv. 26–31 is connected to 10:19–25. It provides a rationale—it begins with the conjunction *for* (*gar*), picking up particularly but not only on the approaching "Day" of reckoning (v. 25; cf. 4:13)—and alludes back to v. 18's mention of the once-for-all and exclusively effectual offering for sin. Internally it divides into a general statement of the warning (vv. 26–27), an elaboration based on the model of the Mosaic system (vv. 28–29), a broader reference to the self-characterizations of God in Scripture (v. 30), and a concluding statement (v. 31).

## Background

For background see the previous warnings, especially 6:4–6. The "enemies" that are in the foreground of Hebrews are apostates, those who believed and then sinned as in 4:4–6 and here in 10:26–31. It is the judgment of "the people of God" that is of concern (10:31; cf. 12:25–29). Ultimately, however, it is evident that the "adversaries" are all those who refuse him who speaks, who are not of the faith of the word spoken in the Son as it has been objectively addressed to the whole of creation. Hebrews does operate with the idea of post-mortem personal existence and judgment for all (9:27). Does it hold a doctrine of annihilationism or perhaps an ultimate redemption of all people after a period of post-mortem judgment? The idea of an ultimate extinction of the wicked seems to have existed among some Jews (e.g., possibly, 1QS IV, 11–14), and could be inferred from Heb 10:27; 12:29. It is, however, merely speculative to assign either of the above ideas (annihilation or universalism) to Hebrews. Its formulations are consistent with the idea of an eternal judgment, that is, suffering and loss without end (6:2; 9:27; 12:25–29).

---

1. Koester, *Hebrews*, 455.

## Comments on Wording

**10:26** *For if we go on sinning deliberately after receiving the knowledge of the truth, there no longer remains a sacrifice for sins.* For the "sin with a high hand" in Num 15:30–31 see on Heb 6:4–6. The terminology used in Num 15 differs from that of Hebrews and there is no other way in which Hebrews directly develops the distinction of that OT text. What is meant by *deliberately* is indicated by 6:4–6; 10:28–29; 12:16–17; as well as by the present reference to *receiving the knowledge of the truth*, which is equivalent to being enlightened in 6:4; 10:32 (cf. 2 Pet 2:21). Minimally, this sin is a knowing, willful renunciation from within the acknowledged and real work of grace. That they *go on sinning* is an interpretive rendering of a present tense participle, which does not necessarily represent something repeated or continuing.

**10:27** *a fearful expectation of judgment, and a fury of fire that will consume the adversaries.* The participle translated as *will* may imply menacing proximity ("is about to") in the light of vv. 25, 37. For *fire* in judgment, see 6:8; 12:29; also, e.g., Matt 3:10, 12; 5:22; 25:41; Rev 20:10, 14–15; cf. Lev 10:2, 6; Num 11:1–3; etc.

**10:28** *Anyone who has set aside the law of Moses* etc. For this "greater than" warning, see 2:1–4; 12:25–29. The verb for *set aside* (*atheteō*) recalls the noun used for the *removal* (*athetēsis*) in 7:18 of the Mosaic command and highlights the crucial distinction in the writer's thought between a simple violation and a properly conceived annulment (see on 8:1–6). That they *die without mercy* highlights the ultimate forfeiture of God's mercy and especially here the irrevocable sentence (Deut 19:13, 21; cf. Deut 13:8–9; 25:12; Lev 24:14–16). The mention of *two or three witnesses* (Deut 17:6; 19:15; cf. Num 35:30) is a rhetorical way of underscoring the threefold description of v. 29 and probably contrasts the Mosaic process (Deut 19:15–21), based on fallible and untrustworthy human witnesses, with the immediacy and directness of God's personal judgment of his people (Heb 10:30), who purges the evil ones from among them. The allusion to Deut 17:6 in particular may indicate further that the sin that Hebrews has in mind is equivalent to worshipping other gods (cf. Heb 3:12).

**10:29** *How much worse punishment, do you think, will be deserved.*[2] What follows are neither separate conditions (as if each one represents a fatal step in itself) nor a list of items that must be exhausted but rather different facets of one integrated act of apostasy. For the noun *punishment*, which runs counter to modern sensibilities, see Prov 19:29; 24:22; cf. also Acts 22:5; 26:11.

---

2. Cf. Philo, *Fug.* 84; *Spec.* 2.255, cited in Attridge, *Hebrews*, 293.

*trampled underfoot the Son of God*. The verb for *trampled* is often used in military contexts for complete subjugation (1 Sam 14:48; 17:53), and in related ways. It can be used as a way of saying that not only was something defaced and destroyed but that it was treated with utter contempt and desecrated: "These men, therefore, trampled upon all the laws of man, and laughed at the laws of God; and for the oracles of the prophets, they ridiculed them as the tricks of jugglers" (Josephus, *B.J.* 4.6.3.386; cf. 6.2.4.126). It is used in particular of the treatment of the temple by foreigners (1 Macc 3:45, 51; 4:60). In 3 Macc 2:13-19 the high priest mourns their oppression at the hands of the enemy; that the holy place has been insulted by the presumptuous; that the enemies boast at having trampled down the house of consecration.

*profaned the blood of the covenant by which he was sanctified*. Christ's blood (on which see 9:1–22) is for them common, profane, unclean (*koinos*; Mark 7:2, 5; Acts 10:14; Rom 14:14; Rev 21:27) rather than holy. The phrase, *the blood of the covenant*, is a compact way expressing the full range of benefits of Christ's blood (8:7—10:18). They treat it—that is, *consider, regard* it—as mere human blood, no more; he, then, cannot be for them the Son of God.

*outraged the Spirit of grace*. This is the last mention of the Holy Spirit in the discourse; it is fittingly included here in this strategic summary. Though definite ties to Matt 12:32 or Acts 7:51 are unclear, it reminds of these contexts; see on 6:4-6. *Insulted, mocked, outraged*, might be a reminder of the treatment Jesus received (Matt 26:67–68; 27:27–31, 39-44; cf. Heb 6:6). Grace is thereby rejected, of course, which is to leave one without hope since there is no alternative—and the contrast of insolence and grace makes clear where the fault lies—but the action described here is more especially a personal affront to God, his grace being one with his own person, act, and presence.

10:30 *For we know him who said, "Vengeance is mine; I will repay." And again, "The Lord will judge his people."* This is not an unknown god, underscoring that they are without excuse (3:7–11). Both allusions are firstly to Deut 32 (32:35-36), though the idea of the Lord's vindication of himself and his people is pervasive in Scripture (e.g., Ps 135:14 [LXX 134:14]; Isa 35:4). In Hebrews' context the point is not about church discipline (1 Cor 5:1–13) or non-retaliation (Rom 12:19) but neither is it opposed to these. The immediate concern is that the Lord most assuredly will act as judge on the appointed Day.

## Comments on Theological Themes

See 6:4–6.

Much of the history of interpretation of this and related passages of Hebrews turned on whether a second repentance was possible after failure (especially related to sexual sin), whether a more "rigorist" view was required that allowed no second repentance, or whether a system of penance was appropriate to provide for an indefinite number of opportunities for repentance.[3] The entire development, so far as it related to Hebrews' warnings, misunderstood the argument of Hebrews which held forth an all-sufficient atonement for sins past, present, and future—all but the sin of rejecting that atonement. 10:26–31 asserts the objective fact that rejecting this sacrifice is to leave one with no sacrifice, since there is no other; it does not explicitly repeat the threat of the impossibility of repentance (6:4–6).

The context of Deut 32 (cf. Heb 10:30) suggests a judgment for the sake of Israel, though even there and certainly in Heb 10 it is a sword that falls through his people. The mention of Deut 32:35–36 recalls Heb 1:6, with its reference to Deut 32:43. That verse reads in the LXX, "Rejoice, Heavens, with him, and let all sons of God worship him. Rejoice, Nations, with his people, and let all angels of God prevail for him. Because the blood of his sons he will avenge and he will take revenge and repay justice to the enemies, and he will repay those who hate, and the Lord will cleanse the land of his people." God's salvation and judgment are bound up with the now (ascended and exalted) and future (coming) priest-king.

## Teaching Hebrews 10:26–31

1. Much of what was said at 6:4–8 applies here, allowing for the differing emphases. Knowing and loving our audience will make any exposition life giving, as is its intent. Respecting the truth will compel us to acknowledge the warning that is fixed at the heart of the gospel (Matt 7:23, 27; 23:1–39; 25:30, 41, 46). Wisdom will guide us in adapting a message designed for a community in particular circumstances (Hebrews' original audience) for another that is currently in a different place.

2. Verses 26–27: The good news of this gospel in the shape of the once-for-all atonement accomplished and open for faith (5:1—10:18) entails the reality that rejecting that offering necessarily leaves one where there is no atonement and so leaves only the consuming fire of God's holy presence. There is no neutral place, there is no "giving back one's

---

3. Cf. Bruce, *Epistle to the Hebrews*, 262–64.

ticket," there is no possibility of escaping the claim of this Creator and Redeemer. It is the staggeringly incomprehensible gift of God that he has fashioned his human creature with this potential and he honors the creature by doing only what he has promised.

3. Verses 28–29: Not only the tabernacle and the ministry belonged to the copies and shadows but the judgments that fell on Israel for unfaithfulness. She had been freely chosen and nothing that could be done for her was left undone (Isa 5:1–7). She had borne no responsibility for her election and how fateful for her that election had been. Though the nation apostatized she could not undo her election and its consequences. There was no escape. All these things, both the blessings and the curses were copies and shadows of the drama that is *so much greater*.

4. Verse 30: These citations from Deuteronomy are not about an endless oscillation of injustice and justice, oppression and rescue. There is one great drama moving inexorably—better, *faithfully*—and swiftly to its goal, which is the great day of salvation (9:28). But that Day is the approach of God himself, the consuming fire (12:29). Hebrews can be paralleled in this respect to Paul's second letter to the Corinthians. By every means possible—a harsh letter, painful discipline, deeply vulnerable and honest displays of love, the sending of a delegate in his place, a deliberately slowed approach, a long and emotional argument—he works for their salvation and joy so that upon his arrival (his *parousia*, 2 Cor 10:10–11) there will be joy rather than harshness (2 Cor 12:11—13:10). But he will not postpone his arrival forever, and he will exercise his authority when the day comes.

5. Verse 31: The understatement of this line opens the way for a panoramic display of the whole history of Israel following on from Deut 32, both in God's judgment of the nations and of Israel. There is nothing abstract about this formulation, nor does it require speculative theology to tease it out. The climax is the deliverance of the Son himself as a ransom, so that falling into the hands of the living God can mean salvation, as is intended.

# 10:32–39

*"Rejoice and be glad, for your reward is great in heaven, for so they persecuted the prophets who were before you."*

## Context

FOR A GENERAL OVERVIEW of 10:26—12:29 see the introduction to 10:26-31. The following expands the outline given there:

10:19-31 Exhortation to faith and warning against apostasy (reusing 10:19-25)

10:32—12:3 Enduring in the great contest of faith in the promise

    10:32-39 A call to endure based on their earlier history and the promise of Habakkuk and Isaiah

    11:1-40 Examples of enduring faith from Israel's history

    12:1-3 A call to endure based on the example of Jesus

    12:4-17 Enduring as the genuine children of the covenantal Father

    12:18-29 The grand finale: closing vision of the promised inheritance, the peril of refusing the promiser, and a final warning/ exhortation

13:1-17 Peroration

On the one hand, 10:32–39 recalls the earlier references to the pre-history of the community and it puts flesh on the summons of 10:19-25, not least the call to look out for each other and persevere in the gatherings. As well, the reminder of their past faithfulness tempers the warning of 10:26-31, just as 6:9-12 tempered 6:4-8. On the other hand, and primarily

vv. 32-39 is launching us ahead to a new development centered on endurance in the great contest of faith. He is using their own past as an example of the sort of faith that is needed to the end.

Into this reminder he sprinkles the language of an athletic contest and a spectacle before exhorting them not to throw away their confidence but persevere in faith. Following the protracted list of examples of such faith (11:1-40) he resumes this imagery by placing them on the racetrack of a Roman stadium surrounded by a great cloud of witnesses (12:1). They are to fix their eyes on Jesus who endured the opposition of sinners for the joy (cf. 10:34) set before him. The bridging thought is that of a great contest of faith and the need to finish the course.

Internally, 10:32-39 fall out as follows:

10:32-34 Remember your faith that accepted lesser and temporary loss for greater and enduring gain.

10:35-39 Understand that good beginnings count for nothing if the course is not run to the end.

>10:35 That earlier *boldness* of hope? Good stuff that, bringing a reward. Don't cast that aside.

>10:36 Why? Because *endurance* in doing God's will is necessary if the promise is to be obtained.

>10:37-38 How do we know? *Because God said so* in Habakkuk and Isaiah.

>10:39 Who are we? We *not* timid quitters. We *are* those who stand pat in faith for the long haul.

## Background

For *confidence* (*parrēsia*), see on 3:6; 4:16; 10:19. For *faith*, see on 11:1-7.

Based on the NT alone—especially Acts, the letters of Paul, 1 Peter, Revelation—one would conclude that persecutions of the earliest Christians and other acts of organized or spasmodic resistance to their teaching through the first several decades were intermittently constant and localized.[1] The specific situation that Hebrews has in mind can only be guessed. William Lane has argued in some detail that it was the edict of the emperor

---

1. Potter, "Persecution," 231-35; Schnabel, *Early Christian Mission*, 2:1533-38.

Claudius expelling the Jews from Rome in AD 49 (cf. Acts 18:2) that gives us this history, which is possible.[2]

One prominent feature of the first century world that was exploited both by the persecutors and the preacher is the pairing of honor and shame. For modern western cultures, while public honor and shame play a part in social settings, they are often balanced if not eclipsed by other values such as self-expression, profit, pleasure, or pure notoriety. For Aristotle, however, there were two motives for choosing a course of action, pleasure and honor, and the greater of these was honor (e.g., *Eth. nic.* 3.1.11). Honor could be received through parentage, citizenship, and office, or it could be achieved, for instance, through exceptional manifestation of virtues such as courage in battle. Honor could be lost as well, for instance, by failing to respond to a challenge issued by someone in a public setting. In such a setting one would be hard-wired to seek social approval and avoid disapproval (save face). Shame was a potent weapon by which to bring societal deviants—such as these Christians—back into line. David deSilva observes,

> Sensitive himself to matters of honor, Chrysostom perceives [Hebrew's] strategic use of this [athletic] image, by which he turns an experience of disgrace and marginalization into a competition for honor. . . . Persevering against the blows of the opponents becomes the manifestation of courage and the path to victory, while yielding or giving up signals defeat and shame. The very path that would lead back to esteem in the eyes of unbelievers is thereby transformed into a path of cowardice and 'true' disgrace, an admission of weakness and defeat.[3]

Elsewhere in Judaism "lists of loving works include showing hospitality and visiting the sick, though not visiting prisoners," though presumably the latter would not have been omitted "in times of persecution when the pious were detained for their faith."[4] Hebrews makes two direct references to visiting fellow believers in prison (10:34; 13:3) and at least two other mentions of the topic (11:36; 13:23). That some—possibly leaders, as we tend to see in Acts—had been imprisoned is evidence of the public character of their witness and a local hostility greater than disapprobation. In general, Roman prisons were overcrowded, noxious, dangerous, and dark.[5] Prisoners were

---

2. Lane, *Hebrews*, 1:lxiv–lxvi. Attridge, *Hebrews*, 299, discusses the difficulty of assigning Hebrews' language to any known event.

3. deSilva, *Persevering in Gratitude*, 359–61. Cf. deSilva, *Honor*, 23–42; Koester, *Hebrews*, 464.

4. Keener, *Matthew*, 605.

5. Rapske, *Paul*, 196–206.

often uncared for, unless by friends and family. The process of arrest and incarceration was intentionally shaming with a stigma that could follow a person for life and that could infect those associated with them. In many cases, openly associating with those imprisoned was to place oneself in bodily danger.

As already noted, a metaphor exploited by Hebrews is that of the athletic contest. Physical training had always been important to the Greeks, and as Greek culture made inroads into Judaism it met with mixed reception.[6] Athletic competitions do not feature in the OT[7] or in Jesus' teaching but they were a potent image for NT writers communicating the gospel to the pagan world (e.g., 1 Cor 9:24–27; Gal 5:7; Phil 3:14; Col 4:12; 1 Tim 4:8; 6:12; 2 Tim 2:5; 4:7–8; cf. Jas 1:12; Rev 2:10) as they also were among popular moralists and philosophers. Hebrews commends the self-discipline and courage of the athlete who would be ashamed to succumb either to the weaknesses of the body, the beating inflicted from without, or the taunts of the onlookers; such a one would sooner undergo collapse than forfeit the victor's wreath.

The interpretive challenges posed by the citation from Hab 2:3–4 (cf. Rom 1:17; Gal 3:11) can be roughly appreciated by setting provisional translations of the Hebrew, LXX, and Hebrews side by side:

Hebrew OT

Though it [the appointed time] linger, wait for it; it will certainly come and will not delay. See, the enemy is puffed up; his desires are not upright

but the righteous person will live by his faithfulness.

LXX

If he [presumably the deliverer] tarries, wait for him, because coming he will come and will not delay.

If he [the deliverer] draws back[8] my soul will not be pleased in him.

But the righteous one [the deliverer] will live by my faithfulness.

---

6. For this paragraph, see Ferguson, *Backgrounds*, 91–96.

7. The handful of possible references to "athletics" (e.g., Ps 19:5; Eccl 9:11; Jer 12:5) may not allude to games in the sense that we see them in other cultures so much as to military training or feats.

8. For this translation of the Hebrew, see Bruce, *Epistle to the Hebrews*, 272–73; Attridge, *Hebrews*, 302.

Hebrews

... the one who is coming will come and will not delay

But my righteous one will live by faithfulness,

and if he draws back my soul will not be pleased in him.

It is possible that indirect knowledge of the sense of the Hebrew shaped Hebrews' interpretation of the LXX so that the righteous one lives by his faithfulness (vs. God's, as in the LXX) and is then identified with the one who draws back.[9] The clauses are reordered as a result of reading the text in terms of the warning of 10:26-31 whereby those who are now believers, if they apostatize, become God's enemies (v. 27). The *one who is coming* is aligned with the messianic sense of Ps 118:26 (Matt 21:9; 23:39; cf. 3:11; Luke 7:19); it is no great step from the coming *time* to the coming of God himself. Finally, the words of the LXX of Isa. 26:20, *in just a little while*, are employed since the time that was distant from the perspective of the prophet is fast drawing near (Heb 10:25). As at other points, Hebrews is breathing the gospel through the OT text in the conviction that this was always its authorial intent. Rhetorically, the citation is not lodging an exegetical proof (as if they had to be convinced that this was the correct interpretation of Habakkuk) but reinforcing shared understanding.

It may be that for Hebrews—possibly also for Paul in Gal 3:11—the historical timing of Habakkuk's word was significant for its meaning. It is not a matter of prooftexting, that is, as if exploiting Habakkuk's wording without regard for its contextual sense, but precisely of noting that these lines about faith, *pistis*, fall at a point in history by which time the failure of Israel to bring the law to its goal has been conclusively demonstrated. For Paul's contrast of christological faith vs. law works this carries its own point, which may or may not echo behind Hebrews' usage. For Hebrews itself, the argument of 8:7-13 is nearer the surface. The promise has been straining toward its goal, and all along it has looked for faith. History itself has pressed that point in the examples of 11:1-14, in the fault revealed in Israel and the first covenant (8:7-13), and above all in the revelation of the new covenant.

Likewise, the insertion of the words from Isaiah 26 probably carried contextual associations that Hebrews meant to be heard. Though Israel had undergone God's discipline she had given "birth to the wind" and had

---

9. As we noted elsewhere, it is gratuitous to assume that Hebrews had no contact with other Christian readings of at least some OT texts. Further, God's faithfulness (assuming the phrase *my faithfulness* was in Hebrews' LXX source) is understood to mandate a reciprocal response from the human partner in covenant (cf. Heb 10:23; 6:12-20).

"accomplished no deliverance in the earth" (26:16-18); the Abrahamic promise, which would bring a blessing to all nations, had not attained its goal. There will be a resurrection for God's people, however, though for now it is a time of cosmic judgment (26:19-21; cf. Isa 24:1-23; Heb 12:25-29). It is a matter of knowing which hour is being struck on history's clock.

## Comments on Wording

10:34 *you had compassion on those in prison*. Hebrews does not ask the readers to take the identical high profile role in the public square, any more than Paul seems to have expected rank and file converts to adopt the role that had led to his arrests. The willingness to *have compassion on* uses the same verb that described Jesus in 4:15 (*sympatheō*); it most likely indicates bodily service performed for the prisoners (Matt 25:36; Phil 2:25; 2 Tim 1:15-18; 4:9-18).

*joyfully accepted the plundering of your property* etc. Coming themes (11:1-2, 10, 13-16, 24-26; 12:2; 13:14) are sounded. They are not renouncing earthly possessions but holding them lightly while holding firmly to the promised inheritance; cf. 13:1-6, 16. The nature of the *plundering*—whether legal or illegal—is not indicated.

10:35 *Therefore do not throw away your confidence, which has a great reward*. The boldness that was provided in the access to the divine presence (10:19) corresponds on the earthly plane to a boldness in public conduct, which is a form of confession; cf. Acts 4:13. The bold approach to the divine throne (4:16; 10:19) serves the boldness of their public witness.

10:36 *when you have done the will of God*. That divine will is not a matter of self-preservation—endurance for the sake of one's own salvation—but is a missional will; cf. 10:5-10; 13:13, 21. Their faith corresponds to the Son's not merely in resolve and constancy but in its content and orientation.

10:38 *my righteous one shall live by faith*. These *shall live* both in the sense of "live by faith now" (cf. 11:1-40) and ultimately "inherit life through that faith" (cf. 10:39); the present life is a participation in the future. This *faith* is certainly a matter of trustful believing in God and his promise. As well, the Son—as the content of that promise and its salvation, the guarantor and mediator of the covenant, the model of faith, the one to whom obedience is owed (5:9), and the one who is himself God—is at once *the* righteous one who lives by faith and the object of faith. The real emphasis, however, is on the readers' endurance in covenantally righteous living (cf. 1:8-9; 5:11-14; 7:2; 12:11), faithfulness in the face of all contradiction—as was the case for Habakkuk's audience.

**10:39** *But we are not of those who shrink back and are destroyed, but of those who have faith and preserve their souls.* Through this expression of identification and confidence (cf. 3:1; 6:9) he is not making a final claim on their behalves but is inviting them to side with this view of things and live accordingly. In compressed form this line contains both the promise with its exhortation of 10:19–25, 32–35 (cf. Luke 21:19), and the warning of 10:26–31 (cf. Heb 6:4–8).

## Comments on Theological Themes

The mention of a reward (v. 35; cf. 11:6) in connection with faith is superficially in tension with Paul's sharp opposition of faith and works/wages (Rom 4:4). On this, however, see the introduction to this commentary. For Hebrews, faith is a matter of being in covenant, modeled on the covenantal life of the Israelites on the way to the place of salvation. God rewards, but what he rewards is not achievement or self-atonement but *faith*: the total acceptance of what is *given*, the total investment in what is promised, the total reliance on the one who promises, the total hope for and desire for that inheritance in the understanding that "here"—here and now—"we have no abiding city." It belongs to what is *given* that full humanity thrives precisely as human agency and thus actively strives with the promise and finds this God's joyful and celebratory *reward*. What more it involves is what is explored in 11:1–40.

## Teaching Hebrews 10:32–39

1. The contrast of this passage between an initial enthusiasm and a subsequent malaise can prompt thoughts about youth and old age both in literal and metaphorical senses. Only a little reflection can raise both the advantages and disadvantages of youth, and the same for being elderly. The power of Christian faith, however, consists in none of these sociological and anthropological considerations as such but in its object, which respects neither sex, race, economic class, nor age (cf. e.g., Isa 40:30–31; 2 Cor 4:16). Where faith is active the power of God is active. Faith does not constitute or create that power but inhabits and receives it, and in faith, at the pleasure of God, that power is made real and present in the world as a witness.

2. In part the sloth that has taken hold in Hebrews' community—the diminished industry of faith—follows the well-worn path of a youthful

simplicity and adrenalized enthusiasm in crisis that gives way to fatigue as the costs mount and the resistance is as constant as gravity. Few would speak crassly of a cash value of faith, but most succumb sooner or later to its underlying sentiment. If saving miracles do not disrupt the smoothly flowing surface of our history, then why should we believe that anything at all has happened? Or that we should expect anything different? The answer was given in 2:10; 5:7–10 and will be the theme of 11:1—12:3.

3. Faith as a way of living receives its form from its object, who was an object of reproach. It bears his reproach (13:13; cf. 11:25–26), which means it is *his* reproach and the church really does *bear* it. It is not the former suffering of vv. 32–34 that the preacher exhorts the readers to perpetuate, however, but the faith that engenders the conduct of righteousness.

4. Faith seeks only obedience, never suffering, though suffering is the expected experience. Both the triggers and the "language" of suffering differ from one culture to the next and from one individual to the next. Whether employing the carrot or the stick, like water finding its way through a roof if there is a way to be found, the way of opposition into the believer's soul will be found and faith will be slowly diluted or choked. The answer to all this is what the whole of Hebrews is giving, pointedly in its exhortations. At its heart, this is 4:14–16 and 10:19–25.

5. Faith in Hebrews is not a past event effecting a permanent contract that irrevocably secures benefits. What went before is good and even a cause for encouragement but only if its agent does not shrink back. It is no different with the teaching of Jesus (Matt 7:21–23; 10:22; 13:3–23; 24:13) or Paul (1 Cor 10:1–13; 2 Cor 13:5; Gal 3:1–4; 4:11, 19; 5:2–4) or Peter (1 Pet 3:10–12; 2 Pet 1:3–11; 2:20–22).

# 11:1-7

*"Do you believe that I am able to do this?"*

## Context

See on 10:19-25, 26-31, and 32-39.

There is a continuity that runs from 10:32 through 12:3 that can be lost in the forest of examples that lies between. That continuity can be seen in the following sketch:

10:19-31 Exhortation to faith and warning against apostasy (reusing 10:19-25)

10:32—12:3 Enduring in the great contest of faith in the promise

    10:32-39 A call to endure based on their earlier history and the promise of Habakkuk and Isaiah

    11:1-40 Examples of enduring faith from Israel's history

    12:1-3 A call to endure based on the example of Jesus

12:4-17 Enduring as the genuine children of the covenantal Father

12:18-29 The grand finale: closing vision of the promised inheritance, the peril of refusing the promiser, and a final warning/exhortation

13:1-17 Peroration

Internally, 11:1-40 and vv. 1-7 fall out as follows:

11:1-2 Opening thesis: What faith does.

11:3-7 Faith and the biblical story before the patriarchs (Gen 1-11).

11:3 Faith and the word of creation.

11:4 Abel's faith through which he was attested to be righteous.

11:5–6 Enoch's faith by which he pleased God and because of which he did not see death.

11:7 Noah's faith by which he became an heir of righteousness.

11:8–22 The patriarchs (Gen 12–50).

11:23–31 Moses, the exodus, and the conquest (Exodus—Joshua).

11:32–38 Faith in the remaining history of the old covenant (Judges and following).

11:39–40 Closing summary.

The faith commended in Hebrews is not a human potential but a divinely created one that can exist only where the divine promise has been heard. All other "faith" is misplaced and so is not faith but merely willful, self-authorized optimism or wish.

In 5:1—10:18 the argument of Hebrews emphasized the *discontinuity* that inheres in the continuity of the earlier history, utilizing the imagery of shadow and thing itself. That it is the one, continuous promise of the one God, however, was essential to that very argument and it is the *continuity* that inheres in that discontinuity that Hebrews now raises to the surface and exploits to impress on the readers the history and thus the nature of faith. The one faith can be expressed only in ways that conform to the form of the word (the one, unified word) that is given, whether that means offering the blood of bulls and goats in the tabernacle or not offering those sacrifices on the basis of the once-for-all offering to which they pointed as copies and which has now been historically enacted—but it remains the *one* faith. There is accordingly a unified people whose conduct in this faith instantiates within its epoch the single promise and its transformative in-breaking in their midst.

The biblical narrative is a smorgasbord of lessons on faith for those with eyes to see, and the overall effect of 11:1–40 is won through allowing these vignettes to accumulate. The real unity lies in a historically, anthropologically, and covenantally unified story of the divine word which had a definite content and concerned a definite history whose representative actors endured the evils of the present, acknowledged God's atonement, and will pass through resurrection to the inheritance.

Outside of connecting faith with Gen 1–11 there is no evident attempt to unify the examples of vv. 3–7 around a single idea, or rather the attempt is to allow the overall picture we sketched in above to be seen in these moments. Beyond this, it can be observed that the first (v. 3) and last (v. 7) examples draw out the relationship of faith to what is not seen, while the latter three stress that faith is rewarded by rescue from death. Again, Abel and Noah highlight the association of faith with righteousness. Strikingly, none of the vocabulary for faith occurs in these chapters of the LXX (the first occurrence is Gen 15:6), a lack that is addressed by v. 6. The writer's point is not tied to the occurrence of words but to the presence of the activity of faith. Faith was active because the promise held sway over history from the foundation of the world (4:3–5; 9:26).

## Background

The opening "thesis" (vv. 1–2) in its wording is taken by some to reflect a commitment to a Greek metaphysical dualism such that faith is aligned on the transcendent world of stability and permanence, the invisible heavenly realm of true existence as opposed to the visible earthly realm of shadows and impermanence. The key to faith, however, is not a metaphysical contrast between heaven and earth in the philosophical sense but the reliability of the divine promise in this sense: In perfect faithfulness God brings world history ineluctably to its goal in resurrection and the grant of the eternal inheritance; see on 8:1–6. What opposes faith is not matter (material creation, particularly as if less real and merely shadowy) as such but all that competes with the promise for our faith or actively discourages investing all in what is promised, all that is not yet in subjection to the Son, not least death (2:5–16). It is a matter of the drama of God and a creation that has fallen into disorder and revolt (thus under conclusive judgment) for which the only salvation can be an act of God that he carried out in the Son (issuing in a new world; 2:5; 12:18–29). Every human effort, including cultic devisings at God's own command, is merely a manipulation of that disorder and revolt and no answer to it; in Hebrews' parlance it is merely "made with human hands."

Verse 3 is not a straightforward assertion of creation *ex nihilo*—an idea that is found elsewhere in Judaism (e.g., 2 Macc 7:28)—though it is consistent with that idea. The phrasing of v. 3b is an allusion to the divine word mentioned in the first half of the verse, perhaps partly with an eye on the LXX of Gen 1:2–3 and partly with an eye on the thesis that faith deals in "things not seen," thus with the unseen origin of the universe The further point may be intended that if the readers take refuge in what is seen now rather than what is promised in the divine word they are clinging to what is derivative rather than its source, to which that source granted only limited time (1:10–12). Moreover, they are clinging to what is only derivative without an understanding of its significance in the purpose of that word (1:1–4).[1]

The OT gives no explicit indication of why Abel's sacrifice was superior to Cain's, it does not mention his faith or righteousness, and it mentions only that Abel's blood cried out from the ground. Jewish tradition speculated on these things, for instance the relative quality of the offerings, their differing beliefs about God, Abel's righteousness (cf. Matt 23:35; 1 John 3:12), and Abel's post-mortem intercession. It is possible that Hebrews is aware of some or all of this, though his point is thoroughly shaped by his own christological commitments in conversation with the OT text.

The OT figure of Enoch (Luke 3:37–38; Jude 14) was the subject of considerable speculation in Jewish interpretive traditions (e.g., *1–2 Enoch*) and his inclusion in Hebrews' catalog is probably owing to that popularity. Hebrews' interpretation of Enoch's "transfer" (Gen 5:24; Heb 11:5) as a matter of not seeing death represents a widespread understanding among Jews (e.g., *1 En.* 12:3; 15:1; *2 En.* 22:8; *Jub.* 4:23; Philo, *Mut.* 38; Josephus, *A.J.* 1.3.4.85). The LXX does say that he "pleased" God, and Hebrews, reasoning deductively, argues that this evidences faith (11:6). Beyond this there is no hint of the legendary features that had attached to him, a silence that may or may not be a quiet renunciation. Enoch is for Hebrews another human who acted on faith and evidenced God's reward, particularly with respect to rescue from death.

Noah, who was said to have found favor with God (Gen 6:8) and to have been pleasing to God (cf. Heb 11:6), was designated by Scripture a righteous man —the first individual so designated by Scripture—and indeed perfect (*teleios*) in his generation (Gen 6:9; 7:1; cf. Ezek 14:14, 20). That Noah was "warned" (cf. Heb 8:5; 12:25) and "acted reverently" (cf. 5:7; 12:28) in "faith" concerning "things not yet seen" (cf. 11:3) resulting in "salvation" (1:14; 2:3, 10; 5:9; 6:9; 9:28) for his "house" (3:2–6; 8:8, 10; 10:21) are all Hebrews' own stylizing of the story in keeping with its larger point. Hebrews adds, further, the claims that in all this the world was condemned and that Noah became "an heir of the righteousness that comes by faith." No doubt behind this is the same sort of typological understanding at work in 1 Pet 3:20–21; 2 Pet 3:5–7, even if Hebrews does not develop the correspondences.[2]

---

1. Among others, Attridge, *Hebrews*, 316, unconvincingly finds a "Platonic cosmogonic model" behind this verse. Lane, *Hebrews*, 2:332, reads this verse as a polemic against such a cosmology.

2. Cf. Matt 24:37–38; and compare Gen 6:11–13 (LXX) with Rev 11:18.

## Comments on Wording

**11:1** *Now faith is.* In fact this chapter describes what faith *does* as encountered in the history of the old covenant narratives, a summary of which follows in vv. 3–38. This logic is made explicit by v. 2.

*the assurance of things hoped for.* Given the wider use of the noun translated as *assurance* (*hypostasis*; 1:3; 3:14; elsewhere in the NT, 2 Cor 9:4; 11:17) it more likely denotes something like *realization* or *substance* (KJV). The writer's intent is to assert the way that the life of the future, which comes to us as a yet-to-be-fulfilled promise (thus *not* of the present and thus still unseen), breaks into the present (cf. 6:4–5), particularly through a form of obedience that conforms to it and cuts against the grain of the present evil age. Involved in this is a participation in "heavenly" realities (10:19–25). Such people "do not merely live under the promise, which could be said of all men. They live in and with and by the promise. They seize it. They apprehend it. They conform themselves to it. And therefore in their present life they live as those who belong to the future."[3] They are sharers of Christ (3:14).

*the conviction of things not seen.* The word translated as *conviction* (*elenchos*) denotes rather the act of *proving* something to be the case, involving both their life's attestation of the divine promise and God's attestation of their life. Verse 2 and the examples of vv. 3–38 follow naturally on such an idea.

**11:4** *By faith Abel offered to God a more acceptable sacrifice.* Abel is selected as the first in sequence probably because his "faith" represents the first act of obedience, the first sacrifice of Scripture, and the first martyrdom. The crying out of his blood also made him a pregnant illustration. Hebrews does not speculate on what made Abel's offering "more acceptable"; the divine attestation (cf. 2:4) shows that he represents faith (as in vv. 1–2 and 6) and that this will have been at the root of the divine approval, which was itself tantamount to an ascription of righteousness.

*And through his faith . . . he still speaks.* The reference could be to the speaking of his blood (12:24; cf. Gen 4:10), the witness of his sacrifice, or the more general idea that he acted in faith. If Gen 4:10 is in mind it could be a creative allusion to the justice of God on which the faithful are to wait (Heb 10:30; 12:29; 13:5–6; cf. Rev 6:9–11). It could be that the "better than" comparison that applies to Moses's offerings (Heb 3:5) is being applied to Abel's. Either way, this comment provides a general if only potential association with the themes of 1) faith, death, resurrection, and inheritance; 2) the

---

3. Barth, *CD* IV/1:120 (not in reference to Hebrews 11).

better offering of Christ; 3) the suffering of the righteous faithful; and 4) Jesus' own post-resurrection intercessory ministry. A hint is enough. The theme is faith and the writer carries on with the other examples.

11:5 *By faith Enoch*. Enoch stands out in this list in that Hebrews rehearses nothing at all of either his conduct or a reception of a divine word. What is said of him by Hebrews is said by way of inference from God's approval and a general understanding of what faith involves. The popular legends surrounding him presumably gave his name punch and he provides a springboard for saying something important about faith.

11:7 *By this he condemned the world*. It was Noah's faith-actions that were a form of faith-speech pronouncing condemnation on the surrounding world of unbelief. Hebrews may be aware of traditions of Noah's preaching,[4] but has kept his expression close to what the Scriptural text actually says.

*became an heir of the righteousness that comes by faith*. Formally, *righteousness* closes the rhetorical circle with vv. 3-4 and *heir* opens the circle with the patriarchs to follow (11:8-22). The context of Hebrews favors understanding the righteousness in view as a form of life that is in keeping with (*comes by*) faith (Gen 6:9; 7:1; cf. Ezek 14:14, 20); Noah represents Hab 2:4 in Heb 10:38.[5] The statement seems to assert both Noah's participation through his faith-action in the inheritance (*heir* looks ahead to 11:10, 13-16, 39-40) already during his life and also his ultimate reward, in keeping with the thesis of 11:1, 6. Of course Noah is also the recipient of the first Scriptural covenant (Gen 6:18; 9:9-17) and the new world he enters following the flood smacks of a new act of creation (Gen 9:1-17); without going openly into typological correspondences that may also be intended. In this sense, too, it could be said that he came already into the inheritance of righteousness.

## Comments on Theological Themes

In using these examples to which the biblical text does not explicitly assign faith Hebrews is not interested in proving faith's presence in them but in showing how those who are attested as moving along the way of God illuminated the character and power of God as well as the obedience that characterizes faith. It is a life that sees "him who is invisible" (v. 27), often against the grain of what is visible (that is, open to testing, as moderns would say) if

---

4. E.g., *Sib. Or.* 1.125-36; *1 Clem.* 7:6. See Attridge, *Hebrews*, 319.

5. If the preacher is conversant in Paul's idea of "justification by faith," he has at most refrained from actively suppressing it, but it does not seem to be what he positively asserts in this verse or elsewhere.

not in the face of outright resistance. These verses are not an ode to faith, as if it possesses its own powers, so much as a reflection on the divine promise by a reflection on the faith that is engendered by and echoes the promise.

In v. 6 the strong affirmation of the *existence* of God is striking, since this is not otherwise a question in Hebrews.[6] It fits with the need to see the invisible. Is the writer suggesting further the need to resist a kind of functional atheism involved in the denial of the God who is revealed in Jesus Christ (cf. 3:12)? Is the charge against Christians of atheism already in the air (e.g., *Mart. Pol.* 3:2; 9:2) and part of the rhetoric of their persecutors, and is this verse somehow an echo of that viewpoint? Perhaps the reference is to the divine name, YHWH (Exod 3:14), and thus to the right knowledge of this God. Certainly for this writer, the word *theos, God* denotes no mere concept or category. To say that this God *is* is necessarily to indicate much more than the mere fact of existence. This God is living and active, faithful to his self-revelation. To say that this God *is* in the context of Hebrews 11 is less like saying that there is such a thing as fire, and more like saying that the room in which we are standing is on fire. This God is never an inert quantity but a presence-in-action as Lord, YHWH. For the *reward*, see on 10:32–39 and the introduction to this commentary. For *seeking* God, see, e.g., Deut 4:29; 1 Chr 28:9; 2 Chr 7:14; Ezra 6:21; Ps 14:2.

## Teaching Hebrews 11:1–7

1. Teach it in its original context. Faith in the abstract or as a virtue is of no interest. Even assuming an understanding of faith as situated in Paul's gospel can distract from the attempt to learn from Hebrews. Here it is a matter of life in conformity to the gospel as told in Hebrews. Again, explicitly contrasting this faith with all modern objects (self, science, etc.) and goals (happiness, achievement, etc.) of "faith" can sharpen the focus and clarify how these alternatives are idolatrous.

2. Faith is not something to look at but along. Faith has nothing it itself but finds all things in God to whom it looks. Moreover, we are taught

---

6. If v. 6 is merely to justify the claim that Enoch himself exercised faith, it makes Enoch more of an embarrassment than a positive contributor to this list of examples. To take v. 6 minimalistically as an echo of standard convictions, both pagan and Jewish, about the *sine qua non* for a knowledge of God (Attridge, *Hebrews*, 318) is not convincing either if it is to be the final word. Such an insertion of an abstract doctrine into a warm pastoral appeal would be strange and would further highlight the oddity of injecting Enoch into this list at all. It is more likely that v. 6 is addressed to the readers of Hebrews itself as if to point out what is essential for their faith too, and that in a somewhat more developed way.

to look where these figures looked in faith, in the same way that they looked. In so doing we are drawn to see what they saw and value it as they did. And in so doing we see what is visible in a wholly new light.

3. In their own way, vv. 3–7 are an entire telling of the story, from creation and sacrifice to resurrection, final judgment, and a new world. In Abel and Noah, the active opposition of sinful humanity is present. In Abel's triumph over death, Enoch's removal so as not to see death, and Noah's salvation from the death that swept over the world the ultimate challenge and threat to the promise is met (cf. 2:14–15). In Abel we see that faith need not be offensive to trigger murderous opposition; it need only do the right thing. In Enoch we see that the entire sum of a person's life reduces to the question of faith; his story is eloquent in its brevity. In Noah we see how irreconcilable faith's obedience is with unbelief's experience and its reasoning, building a home that makes no sense as things are and thus announcing the demise of what is; this is the great sermon of faith. At the outset of the list of instantiations of faith (11:3) we recognize the primacy of the divine word over the visible realm it created and are reminded that we do not live by bread alone, but by every word that proceeds from God's mouth (Deut 8:3), whose word is eternal (Isa 40:6–8; 1 Pet 1:24–25). From here we think ahead to the example of Esau who traded away an eternal banquet of food that satisfies for a single meal that leaves one hungry after a couple of hours (12:16–17). At the heart of these verses (11:5–6) we recognize that faith is the *sine qua non* of pleasing God, for it sees him, it sees him as he is, and it conforms itself and its way to him. Moreover, we appreciate that God will not keep his pleasure to himself, but shares it with those who please him (10:38).

> "Though Christ offers us in the Gospel," says Calvin (Instit. ii. 9, 3), "a present plenitude of spiritual blessings, yet the enjoyment of them always lies hid under the custody of hope till we are divested of our corruptible body and transfigured into the glory of Him who is our first-fruits, our forerunner. In the meantime, the Spirit commands us to rely on the promises. Nor, indeed, have we otherwise any enjoyment of Christ any further than we embrace Him, as He is garbed in His promises. By which it comes to pass that *He Himself now dwells in our hearts* and yet we *live like pilgrims at a distance from Him*, because we walk by faith and not by sight."
>
> —John Calvin.[7]

---

7. Epigraph in Karl Barth, *The Resurrection of the Dead* (Eugene, Oregon: Wipf and Stock Publishers, 1933).

That conforming of one's entire life to what is not seen and what is hoped for is to enact (realize) and thus evidence (prove) these things here and now (11:1). To live with the grain of God's promise is inevitably to live against the grain of the world as it is. It is to sing a song that won't harmonize with the present world's controlling melody, to the great annoyance of the rest of the choir. But it will prove to have been the right song, the song on which they depended in spite of their refusal to join it, and the only song that endures.

4. We are beautiful creatures in which beauty and good are to be found. Yet we are also jerks. Hard, coarse, self-serving, vindictive, vengeful jerks smugly consumed with our own business, yet loving, hurting, and beautiful in a story—so we believe—without God or god(s). Ask any squirrel in the local park: Humans are both generous and messy. This can be dramatized best not when the script's interest is in making the theological point, but when what is portrayed is neither the extreme of evil, nor of heroism, nor of love, but just humanity as if it is in fact a world without God. It is best displayed when the story and the people are ordinary. It can be dramatized best in that fashion, as if in accidental confession, but the unadorned observation of the prophets cannot be improved: "There is no fear of God before their eyes." One must "believe that he exists."

# 11:8–22

*"Your father Abraham rejoiced that he would
see my day. He saw it and was glad."*

## Context

SEE ON 10:32–39 AND 11:1–7. Abraham is more than merely another example of faith. The promise given him is the promise that occupies Hebrews' whole story; the drama enacted in his faith is a microcosm of faith's history in the sacrificial "offering" of a son and his "resurrection" as well as in other ways. The attention he receives makes him the centerpiece of this collection. Abraham's was a peculiar moment.

## Background

Treating Abraham as an ideal figure, speculating on motives behind reported actions, attributing to him prophetic expectations, observing his faith and patience—all these are not surprisingly paralleled elsewhere in Judaism.[1] The idea of the heavenly Jerusalem was known from Jewish and Christian apocalyptic (2 *Bar.* 4:1–7; Gal 4:26; Rev 3:12; 21:2).[2] For Hebrews it would be of a piece with the "pattern" shown Moses (8:5).

Verses 17–19 refer to the "binding of Isaac" in Gen 22, one of the most striking passages of Scripture and one that attracted no little attention in Jewish (e.g., 4 Macc 14:20; 15:28; 16:20) as well as Christian traditions, both for what the biblical narrative said and left unsaid.[3] Naturally what Hebrews says contains touch points with those traditions but as with the specula-

---

1. Attridge, *Hebrews*, 322–23, 329.
2. Ibid., 324 with further references.
3. Ibid., 333–34. Cf. Spiegel, *Last Trial*, and Swetnam, *Jesus and Isaac*.

tion swirling around Melchizedek Hebrews' brief exposition does not stray a millimeter from its focus on Christ and the gospel.

One of the difficulties of this passage concerns the language which seems to be used of Sarah in v. 11 but which would be improperly applied to the female partner. The phrase, *katabolēn spermatos* (ESV: [Sarah received power] *to conceive*), in common speech was not used to refer to the woman's part in procreation; it referred to the male's part in "sowing seed." Both ancient scribes and modern interpreters have proposed a variety of solutions. As it stands, the ESV adapts this to Sarah. One alternative is to read the reference to Sarah as a parenthesis that includes the word *barren* (*steira*) so that the phrase in question refers to Abraham: *by faith (and Sarah herself barren!) he received the power for the sowing of seed*. Another omits the word *steira* as not part of the original (for sound reasons, based on the textual evidence) and emends the case forms for Sarah from nominative to dative of accompaniment (easily confused in the process of copying): *by faith, along with Sarah, he received the power . . . .*[4] Some such solution appears necessary.

The imagery of being strangers and temporary residents on earth (vv. 13-16) has formal parallels in philosophically driven writers who wish to characterize bodied human life on earth as somehow less appropriate to the human soul than existence in a heavenly or immaterial world more proper to it; for them it gets at the experience of cosmic alienation and the soul's migration (e.g., Plato, *Ap.* 41A; Philo, *Her.* 82, 267; *Conf.* 81; *Somn.* 1.181). The writer and readers of Hebrews were probably aware of these associations but in the context of Hebrews there is none of this dualistic and anti-cosmic element. That from which they are alienated is the disorder and uncleanness of the present state of the world brought about through disobedience, and that in which they are wholly invested is the world contained in the promise of God, a world that will not be less than the present creation cleansed and reconstituted as God's own dwelling. Hebrews' conception pivots not on the principle of dualism but on the history of atoning death and bodily resurrection. It concerns a world that, as such, proceeds from God to humanity, thus from heaven to earth, and is thus heavenly. One thinks of the similar language of 1 Pet 1:1, 17; 2:11, where some think the primary allusion is to social alienation in their Greco-Roman setting.[5] Social and economic implications are certainly at play in Heb 11 (cf. 10:32-34; 11:9, 26; 12:3; 13:13-14) though in vv. 13-16 the leading contrast from which they derive is the world as it is and the world as promised by God.

---

4. Attridge, *Hebrews*, 321.
5. Jobes, *1 Peter*, 62.

The patriarchs were welcoming the things promised "*from afar,* and having acknowledged that they were strangers and exiles *on the earth*" (11:13); they "desire a better country, that is, a *heavenly one*" (11:16); for "we seek the city *that is to come*" (13:14). In 11:9 the social and theological dynamics balance each other (cf. 11:10).

## Comments on Wording

11:10 *the city that has foundations, whose designer and builder is God.* Cf. Isa 54:11; Ps 87:1. The foundations signify a contrast with the tents of v. 9 and thus anticipate the emphasis on the permanence and stability of what is promised (12:25–29). The Son has already been depicted as the one who laid the foundations of the earth (1:10 referring to Ps 102:25); God is the one who builds all things (3:4) and who pitched the true tabernacle (8:2). The language of designer (*technitēs*) and builder (*dēmiourgos*) is not used of God in the OT but was commonly used of him in hellenistic Jewish writings (e.g., Wis 13:1; Philo, *Leg.* 3:98–99; *Gig.* 23; *Congr.* 105; Josephus, *A.J.* 1.7.1.155). It parallels language associated with the construction of the tabernacle and temple (e.g., Exod 28:11; 35:35; 2 Kgs 12:12; 1 Chr 22:15; cf. 1 Cor 3:10), in keeping with the idea that this would be not a city as such but a particular city of a particular character, the heavenly Jerusalem (12:22).

11:12 *as many as the stars of heaven and as many as the innumerable grains of sand by the seashore.* Cf. Gen 22:17; Dan 3:36 (LXX).

11:13 *having acknowledged that they were strangers and exiles on the earth.* Gen 23:3; 1 Chr 29:15; Ps 39:12. The meaning of Abraham's words in Gen 23 is for Hebrews based on the larger and determinative context of the Scriptural drama in which he acted. The assumed element of this verse is the resurrection.

11:14 *People who speak thus.* See the OT texts of the previous note.
*seeking a homeland.* See 12:22–24; 13:14.

11:16 *God is not ashamed to be called their God.* Cf. 2:11; Exod 3:6 and parallels. This is striking wording that goes to the way in which faith honors and rightly proclaims this God.

11:17 *was in the act of offering up his only son.* Isaac was Abraham's "only son" not in the strict sense (Ishmael had already been born) but in being the son of the promise and being specially loved; Hebrews is not alone in this manner of speaking (Josephus, *A.J.* 1.13.1.222; Philo, *Deo* 4). The characterization anticipates the true Son to come (see the following note).

1:18 *of whom it was said, "Through Isaac shall your offspring be named."* Hebrews stops at implying its point: Isaac, upon whom the promise of a seed depends, will be figuratively put to death and resurrected as a foreshadowing of the promised seed, God's own Son, who would actually be put to death and resurrected and so bring the promise to its realization. It was to be through Jesus the Son that Abraham's offspring would be reckoned (cf. 2:16).

**11:19** *He considered.* Hebrews' artful and indirect exposition elsewhere in this context gives reason to doubt that it is claiming special knowledge of Abraham's conscious deliberations, which are not recorded in Gen 22. The Scriptural record of his actions within the larger drama of the story that would culminate in the Son was enough to warrant this depiction. The intent is to draw out the inner meaning of the act of faith within that larger context.

*from which, figuratively speaking, he did receive him back.* The phrase, *figuratively speaking*, uses the Greek word *parabolē* as did 9:9 to characterize the form of prophetic speech that anticipated the person and work of the Son: it was parabolic or figurative in form. It is possible that this claim of Abraham's resurrection faith consciously echoes Jewish traditions,[6] but that parallel is not a necessary explanation for Hebrews' formulation which is owing to the christological association by which he reads the Scripture and for which he carries out his exposition.

**11:21** *bowing in worship over the head of his staff.* The LXX of Gen 47:31, cited by Hebrews, differs from the Hebrew text if the latter is rendered, *Israel bowed down at the head of his bed*, but the differences are not material to Hebrews' point.[7] The allusion is more likely to the Genesis context in which Jacob looks to the fulfillment of God's promise beyond his own death. Along with the following illustration (Heb 11:22) the allusion to the staff makes for a colorful way of bringing a story to mind and thereby hinting at the resurrection, reprising the idea of 11:13–16 as well as anticipating 11:39–40. Granting this interpretation, its indirectness is a revealing illustration of Hebrews' allusive style, which should be borne in mind elsewhere.

## Comments on Theological Themes

Because the hope that is commended pivots on resurrection, the land and children represent the (partial) fulfillment of the promise to Abraham in a real and not merely typological sense, without reduction to the ultimate

---

6. Attridge, *Hebrews*, 335, referring to the Eighteen Benedictions among other things.

7. Patristic and later exegetes did find allegorical significance in the language; cf. Attridge, *Hebrews*, 336.

content of the promise that they did indeed foreshadow. The ultimate gift would include rather than replace these earlier installments

The social situation of the patriarchs (they were "resident aliens" in their contemporary social setting) is itself a pattern of the ultimate hope of all the people of God, but it is equally true that a faith oriented on what was ultimately promised (being "aliens" in the sense that the heavenly city is our true home) entails the acceptance of social and economic alienation in the present orders (10:32–34; 11:24–26; 13:13–14). In v. 9, *living in tents* epitomizes that existence.

What is foregrounded at several points in vv. 8–22, not least in vv. 11–12, is the way the story of Abraham and Sarah instantiated and illustrated the certainty of the divine promise such that all humanly perceived boundaries of probability and possibility are broken and powerless in its face.[8] What God has promised he will do, and what he has promised is located beyond all the boundaries of the present creation. The ultimate boundary is death, which is more than hinted at in v. 12. Resurrection is the underlying reality.

The image of the "city" and "country" looks to something future but only as an organizing vision for the present and very tangible social existence of the readers. Because that future "country" is that for which the old covenant was a shadow, its ethos and its history can be taken as known and applied as an identity-forming allegiance (NT ethics are fundamentally continuous with the righteousness revealed through Moses). Further, that city is "better" because it is guaranteed, good, and grounded, none of which applies to the world that has not yet undergone death and resurrection.

Gen 22 and the binding of Isaac has shocked, if not disgusted many readers, but what Hebrews does with it is not merely an allegorical spin on an otherwise morally dubious story. Rather, what is revealed in the event of the Son is for Hebrews what was always the center of gravity in both the command given Abraham and his obedience. The offense of the story went much deeper than Gen 22. The burden both of what was required of Abraham and his obedience would fall to God himself and God alone, but it goes to the essence of faith (here, Abraham's faith) that it participates with full abandonment in the very heart of God. God is therefore not ashamed to be called their God.

---

8. For Philo (*Abr.* 111) and Paul (Rom 4:19), Abraham was by this time decisively past the time of fathering children, in spite of Gen 25:1.

## Teaching Hebrews 11:8-22

1. The word that confronted Abraham differed from that spoken to Noah and so as a response his faith was differently formed. The readers of Hebrews could not content themselves with some sort of generalized involvement in Abraham's obedience of faith while either rushing along with the general current of their Roman society or uniting with the Jewish synagogue. For them, too, faith would require a form of living that publicly placed them at odds with their neighbors. Not least, their faith would mark a step forward from the word spoken through Moses, precisely because it was a step forward with the history of that same word (8:7-13). It would be a movement forward with the living God who was taking his people on a journey whose destination had both reached its goal (the "already") and was reaching its goal (the "not yet") in the Son.

2. That said, in the light of the Son, Abraham's faith is uniquely instructive for all faith as a witness to the genuine act of revelation and atonement. Abraham, having been the first to have been openly greeted by the divine promise, responded with a faith commensurate with the content of the promise and the character of the promise giver. Faith does what it believes. In him the very story of the promise was enacted in miniature. In patient endurance he obtained what had been promised (6:12-20). In Melchizedek, he acknowledged our Great Priest (7:1-10). In setting out from Haran without knowing where he was going, believing the promise of an heir in spite of biology, taking a knife while standing over his bound son, and, along with Jacob and Joseph, looking for the promise beyond his own death, in all this both the promise and the faith that would be realized in the history of the Son of God found their telling. Almost the whole story of salvation was dramatized in the faith-obedience that was required of him.

3. Pointedly—so as to teach this productively—such a faith seeks security neither in the Jewish cultic and national institutions whose only rationale was in their temporary witness to the Son's priestly identity and work nor in the protection and provisions of Rome. Nor does it deny these things their continuing place, as if outrunning the history of the word itself. Like the patriarchs in their tents, it dwells within the present structures without giving them any claim on itself and thereby witnesses to the only promise given to all (1 Cor 7:29-31). Naturally this raises the ire of the world structures it has rejected and whose end it announces. In the face of that opposition it assembles together with

others of the same faith who encourage each other daily (10:25; 3:13), serve the saints, cheerfully suffer the loss of possessions, care for those imprisoned as if themselves imprisoned, and offer up sacrifices pleasing to God. At the heart of this, its national life, both in celebrating its final goal and drawing from its provision for the present, it holds fast a confidence that leads to free participation in the great Day of Atonement, the entrance into the Most Holy Place by the blood of Jesus.

4. Teaching this text finally means taking our place within its drama, our own place in our own time and so going forward with its script to its conclusion.

# 11:23-31

*"I tell you, my friends, do not fear those who kill the body, and after that have nothing more that they can do."*

## Context

SEE ON 10:32-39 AND 11:1-7. Just as 11:8-22 revolved chiefly on Abraham while including others down to Joseph (Gen 12-50), so 11:23-31 features Moses while mentioning the beginnings of the conquest and the Gentile prostitute, Rahab, in particular (thus Exodus through Joshua).

Moses was first mentioned by name in 3:1-6 and then several times thereafter (3:16; 7:14; 8:5; 9:19; 10:28; cf. 12:21), but looms behind the entire treatment of the first covenant and its law. None of these passages highlights the "doing" vs "faith" contrast that occurs in Gal 3:12 and Rom 10:5 nor the inclusion of Gentiles on the basis of faith alone. Even so, placing the lawgiver under the sign of faith not only makes for an arresting example but marks out the way in which his lead is rightfully followed, to wit, by keeping pace with the divine word by means of a submissive faith. The net result is not far from Paul. In the same vein, it is possible that the mention of Rahab gestures toward the Gentile mission.

As with the whole of 11:1-40, no one aspect of faith controls the illustrations of vv. 23-31 beyond its constant accompanying of the divine word. As such it is courageous in the face of opposition, resolute in its single-minded allegiance, victorious in its attachment to the inexorably advancing word, and rewarded in contrast to the destruction of the disobedient. It sees past what alone is visible for unbelief and sees what is for the present invisible (11:1), choosing the temporary suffering, loss, and reproach that menace for the sake of the promised deliverance (cf. 12:1-3, 16-17). The note of economic deprivation and social alienation is striking (vv. 23-27) as is the emphasis on risky affiliation with the people of God (vv. 24–25, 31); both of these are highlighted with an eye on Hebrews' audience (3:13; 4:2; 6:10; 10:25, 32–35; 13:1–6, 7, 10, 14, 16–19, 24). The theme of atoning and protecting blood is sounded (v. 28) as well as deliverance from death threatened or symbolized (e.g, v. 29). Just as Abraham's faith had drawn him into the christological drama (vv. 17–19), so also Moses's faith (vv. 25–26). Faith does what it believes.

A series of vignettes utilize seven occurrences of the phrase *by faith* (*pistei*; vv. 23, 24, 27, 28, 29, 30, 31), the first four of which attach to Moses and the last three of which attach elsewhere; this parallels the treatment of Abraham in vv. 8–22 (vv. 8, 9, 11, 17, 20, 21, 22). A slavish adherence to structural parallels is, however, sacrificed for the sake of the pastorally motivated exposition.

## Background

See on 3:1–6. The detail about Moses's appearance as an infant derives from Exod 2:2 LXX (cf. Philo, *Mos.* 1:9). Hebrews makes it half of the rationale for his parents' decision to hide him, probably meaning to hint that they saw what was yet future (unseen) in him (11:1) and therefore did not fear Pharaoh's command. If Jesus' infancy stories as told by Matthew were known (Matt 2) they would come to mind,

> Philo comments, "Accordingly as the child Moses, as soon as he was born, displayed a more beautiful and noble form than usual, his parents resolved, as far as was in their power, to disregard the proclamations of the tyrant. Accordingly they say that for three months continuously they kept him at home, feeding him on milk, without its coming to the knowledge of the multitude." (*Mos.* 1:9 [Colson, LCL])

but that is the most that can be said. Aside from making explicit that Moses's parents did not fear the king Hebrews stops at what is said in Exod 2, while other Jewish traditions elaborated on Moses's remarkable appearance (e.g., Josephus, *A.J.* 2.9.6.231) or referred to other portents given to the parents and the content of their faith (e.g., Josephus, *A.J.* 2.9.3.212–2.9.4.219). Likewise, while other traditions elaborate on Moses's exalted status (Acts 7:22; Philo, *Mos.* 1.32; Josephus, *A.J.* 2.10.1.238–2.10.2.253), Hebrews is more interested in what he saw and chose positively than in what he left behind.

The idea of vv. 24–26 comparing a transient pleasure and a permanent good is a commonplace in biblical traditions (e.g., Ps 73; cf. Job 8:13–18; Rom 8:18) and would naturally come to expression in passages about martyrdom (4 Macc 15:8, 23). Hebrews' application of this reasoning to Moses is a possible inference from Exod 2:11–13 but is not obvious given Exod 2:14–15; 3:1—4:20. As elsewhere, Hebrews is aligning Moses's intentions with the arc of the divine word that his life followed; that is to say, Moses's intentions are inferred from that larger context. For Hebrews, where a life is decisively plotted on that arc faith is at work.

Thinking of vv. 26–27, one thinks of the foresight attributed to other OT figures by NT texts (John 8:56; Acts 2:30–31; 1 Pet 1:10–11). Moses was characterized as a prophet (Deut 18:15, 18; 34:10; cf. Num 12:6–8), an identity that was developed in some Jewish traditions that conceivably contribute to the characterization of Hebrews.[1] Within Hebrews Moses was said to have been a witness to the things that would be spoken (3:5) in a passage that recalls the vision of Exod 33–34, while in 8:5 (cf. Exod 25:40) he saw the heavenly pattern that in the larger argument of Hebrews is identical to the reality of Christ. If Hebrews' narration in 11:25–27 is following the chronology of Exodus and v. 27 refers to Exod 2:11–25, then there is no correlation with a specific vision of Exodus; otherwise we might think of Exod 3:1—4:17; 5:22—6:12; 6:28—7:7; etc., which precede the first Passover mentioned in Heb 11:28.

## Comments on Wording

11:23 *because . . . they were not afraid of the king's edict*. This is a fair assessment of their conduct though no OT text makes these claims (cf. Exod 1:17, 21; 2:2). It might reflect the social situation of Hebrews' readers. Thematically, Hebrews is hinting at the evidence for the claim that they acted *in faith* by noting what they *saw* and by hinting (negatively) at the general theme of reverent *fear* of God (4:1; 5:7; 10:31; 12:28; cf. 10:38–39).

11:25 *choosing rather to be mistreated with the people of God*. Cf. Exod 2:11–14; Acts 7:23–29. The phrase *people of God* in Hebrews reaches beyond the setting of Exod 2 to the larger community of faith spanning the history of the divine promise (4:9; 8:10; cf. 4:2; 10:30; 11:39–40; 13:12).

11:26 *the reproach of Christ*. See on 10:32–39. A necessary challenge for faith is to adopt a completely altered understanding of whose approval bestows honor and what conduct merits it, yet to do so in the midst of a social order that is hostile to faith's commitments (11:1).

11:27 *By faith he left Egypt, not being afraid of the anger of the king*. In the final analysis, Moses's fear notwithstanding (Exod 2:14), he did not submit to the authority and threat of Egypt but moved resolutely—not

---

1. D'Angelo, *Moses in Hebrews*, 95–149.

perfectly—on a path that corresponded to the divine promise. Alternatively the "departure" is conceptualized broadly to include the ultimate exodus.

## Comments on Theological Themes

Particularly if v. 25 is an allusion to Exod 2 it is unlikely that Hebrews is ignoring Moses's act of murder in that episode any more than Hebrews is attempting to sweep the more unseemly conduct of some of the figures of 11:32 (let alone those of the patriarchs) under the rug. The vision of salvation throughout Hebrews is grounded in nothing other than Christ's once-for-all self-offering. Moreover, a theologian-pastor who would write Heb 5:11—6:12 to his present readers would not likely be making a judgment on the ultimate faithfulness of those he chronicles in this chapter. He summons them for the example attested by the Scriptural record.

Verses 24–29 allude to the suffering Moses accepted in his decisions of faith. Nothing in Hebrews hints at a spirit of asceticism at work in the author's appeal. The material losses that faith accepts among the Christian readers may be due in part to restraint in the pursuit of wealth (13:5–6), but are evidently due chiefly to the depredations of their unbelieving neighbors (10:32–34). Whatever its immediate triggers the fact of implacable hostility as a constant is built into the tradition of Ps 110:1 and Ps 8:6 and is everywhere in evidence in the history of faith's obedience to the divine promise, above all in the history of the Son (2:9–10; 12:3). Finally for Hebrews, it is a matter of gesturing to the offense and shame of Jesus' Roman cross in which all evil is concentrated and defeated (13:13; cf. 12:3; 2:14). To participate in that drama is to suffer the fate of the Son, to bear his disgrace.

In v. 30 the walls of Jericho fell by the power of the divine word, but faith was involved in the obedience of the Israelites in marching around the city. This illustration is helpful in clarifying that it is not faith's exploits that advance the salvation of God—as if the power of faith is latent in the human activity as such—but God's powerful word.

Verse 31 marks the end of the main list of examples (11:3–31); what follows has a different character (11:32–38). It is possible that Rahab is a literary device, a way of referencing the end of the account of Jericho's fall (Josh 6:22–25), though her presence elsewhere in Christian traditions (Matt 1:5; Jas 2:25; cf. *1 Clem.* 12) and the things said in this verse favor the conclusion that punctuating the list with her example was a matter of thematic emphasis. As a Gentile she might gesture toward the ultimate composition of the people of God whose boundaries are marked by this faith. The referencing of her history as a prostitute quietly attests the cleansing power of the divine promise of which she partook. Her risky affiliation with the people of God would challenge readers who have been neglecting the assembly (10:25; cf. 10:32–35; 12:14; 13:2–3, 20). Her obedience serves as another illustration of the ultimate fate of faith vs. disobedience (3:16–19; cf. 2:1–3; 4:6, 11; 10:26–31, 38–39; 12:14–17, 25–29; 13:3, 7).

## Teaching Hebrews 11:23–31

1. In teaching Hebrews' conception of faith we have already cautioned against overdoing the contrast with Paul's teaching, not least because Paul is also concerned with faith's activity. Yet faith as faithfulness, as obedience in terms of the new covenant promises of Hebrews' exposition, is where our teaching should center.

2. We also cautioned against making faith into a general principle rather than obedience to the word given, yet certain patterns do emerge from the examples cited: Faith is courageous in the face of opposition, resolute in its single-minded allegiance, victorious in its attachment to the inexorably advancing word, and ultimately rewarded in contrast to the destruction of the disobedient. A twofold transformation is required in our application that involves, first, locating ourselves in the drama of the covenants and, second, locating ourselves specifically in the social settings of our own 21$^{st}$ century lives. Underscoring the latter, it was their lives in their mean city streets where this missional drama unfolded, lives of marriages (13:4), homes, commerce, and Roman laws.

3. Among the striking features of faith in these lines of Hebrews, it sees past what alone is visible for unbelief and sees what is for the present invisible (11:1), choosing the temporary suffering, loss, and reproach that menace for the sake of the promised deliverance (cf. 12:1–3, 16–17). If need be, it accepts economic deprivation and social alienation (vv. 23–27). Though the risk is great it affiliates with the people of God (11:24–25, 31; cf. 3:13; 4:2; 6:10; 10:25, 32–35; 13:1–6, 7, 10, 14, 16–19, 24). Nor will it do so in some sort of spiritual abstraction from its particular social setting, as if sin and evil ever exist in abstraction. Faith cannot be a way of living "religiously" or "spiritually" as if on a plane detached from one's life in the world. Such a dualism has nothing to do with Hebrews' outlook. Where a society turns on a group, as it did it Hitler's Germany, in the Jim Crow south, in the conquest of Native Americans, in apartheid, or in any of its myriad forms, those of faith will conform to a different world.

4. In all of this, Hebrews requires us resolutely to inhabit and commend the drama of the cleansing sacrifice that alone brings salvation for all people. Thus, in this reflection on Moses's faith the theme of atoning and protecting blood is sounded (v. 28). Likewise, deliverance from death threatened or symbolized (e.g, v. 29), is signaled. The entirely this-worldly form of faith finds its rationale in and strains toward the promise of a different city, a heavenly one, for here we have no abiding city.

5. Finally, once again, faith finds its center and ultimate form in the christological drama. Just as Abraham's faith had done this (vv. 17–19), so also Moses's faith (vv. 25–26). All contemplation of faith finds its beginning and end there, and all that is not conformed to the faith of the Son is not faith at all as Hebrews' commends it.

# 11:32–40

*"I am the resurrection and the life.*
*Whoever believes in me, though he die, yet shall he live,*
*and everyone who lives and believes in me shall never die.*
*Do you believe this?"*

## Context

SEE 10:32–39 AND 11:1–7 for the chapter as a whole in context.

With the biblical history through Jericho completed the preacher parades names and exploits that carry the history from Judges into the Second Temple period of Judaism.

Grammatically, vv. 32–40 string several verbs without conjunctions. In contents it has the character of a litany of examples that fuse the stories of past and present in suggestive ways:

11:32 Introduction to the finale

11:33–37 Description of faith's exploits

    11:33–34 Faith in past deliverances

    11:35 Death and resurrection: faith's reward

    11:36–38 Faith in weakness and hope

        11:36–37a Beatings, imprisonment, execution: faith's endurance

        11:37b–38 Refused a place in the life of the city: faith's resting place

11:39–40 Conclusion to 11:1–40

Following the transitional summary of v. 32, vv. 33–34 register the advance of the divine word and thus of faith. Verse 35 posits that death holds no final power and faith looks beyond it for what is promised. Internal to v. 35 is a shift from strength in past deliverances to faith's endurance in weakness with an other-worldly hope; the latter carries through the rest of vv. 36–38. Verses 36–37a allude to the attempts of societies to force submission and quell faith. From there the thought moves seamlessly into the existence of those who are people without a country, civically and economically out of place (cf. 11:9, 14; 13:9–16). Our outline's use of the phrase, "faith's *resting place*," is meant to recall the image of 3:7—4:11, which pictured the future country of the people of God against the backdrop of Canaan as the promised place of security, permanence, and fullness of life in the presence of God (12:22–24). Having prompted this image by mentioning its opposite, the way is prepared for vv. 39–40 which serve as a conclusion both to this final unit and to the whole of 11:3–38.

## Background

What is of interest in this passage is the lot of those who invested all in single-minded faith in the promise that culminated in the history of the Son. As a bridge to the present the depictions extend to include Jewish retellings of the biblical stories, exploits associated with the Maccabean period, and possibly the experiences of the earliest Christians—filtered and recast to speak directly to Hebrews' own audience.

The Maccabean period takes its name from the Jewish leader, the

> It happened also that seven brothers and their mother were arrested and were being compelled by the king, under torture with whips and thongs, to partake of unlawful swine's flesh.... The mother was especially admirable and worthy of honorable memory. Although she saw her seven sons perish within a single day, she bore it with good courage because of her hope in the Lord. She encouraged each of them in the language of their ancestors.... Antiochus felt that he was being treated with contempt, and he was suspicious of her reproachful tone. The youngest brother being still alive, Antiochus not only appealed to him in words, but promised with oaths that he would make him rich and enviable if he would turn from the ways of his ancestors, and that he would take him for his Friend and entrust him with public affairs. Since the young man would not listen to him at all, the king called the mother to him and urged her to advise the youth to save himself. After much urging on his part, she undertook to persuade her son. But, leaning close to him, she spoke in their native language as follows, deriding the cruel tyrant: "My son, have pity on me. I carried you nine months in my womb, and nursed you for three years, and have reared you and brought you up to this point in your life, and have taken care of you. I beg you, my child, to look at the heaven and the earth and see everything that is in them, and recognize that God did not make them out of things that existed. And in the same way the human race came into being. Do not fear this butcher, but prove worthy of your brothers. Accept death, so that in God's mercy I may get you back again along with your brothers." (2 Macc 7:1–29 NRSV)

Hasmonean Judas Maccabeus. The history in broad strokes is this: The Babylonian exile (2 Kgs 25), came to a close when the Persians came to power and Cyrus issued the decree of 2 Chr 36:22–23 (cf. Ezra 1:1–4). The Jerusalem temple, destroyed by the Babylonians, was rebuilt, as narrated in Ezra. (The temple standing at the time of Jesus and destroyed by the Romans in AD 70, Herod's temple, was yet a new structure, but the whole period from Ezra on is referred to as the Second Temple Period.) Persian rule gave way to the Greeks in the wake of Alexander the Great's conquests and then his death in 323 BC. What followed was a crucible for Judaism that left her changed both internally and externally. The natural process of hellenization of Judaism—roughly, "Greek-izing"—became an aggressive policy under Antiochus IV Epiphanes. Jewish responses ranged from active cooperation with hellenizing policies to violent opposition. The turning point came in 167 BC in the city of Modein when a priest of the Hasmonean family, Mattathias, killed another Jew who attempted to offer a pagan sacrifice in Mattathias's place (1 Macc 2:23–26). An all-out rebellion against the Greek overlords spiraled from there, led first after his death by Mattathias's son, Judas who was subsequently given the surname Maccabeus. A significant degree of autonomy was eventually won for Judea, giving way to decline until the beginning of Roman rule in 63 BC. Further detail is unnecessary for the present purposes, particularly as the story can be read in 1–2 Macc and the first book of Josephus's *Jewish Wars*. It is from the wealth of stories surrounding the Maccabean history that some of Heb 11:33–38 seems to draw. For instance, 11:35 reminds many of 2 Macc 7:1–29; cf. 2 Macc 6:18–31.

These and other stories were well known and inspiring for first century AD Jews.

> Eleazar, one of the scribes in high position, a man now advanced in age and of noble presence, was being forced to open his mouth to eat swine's flesh. But he, welcoming death with honor rather than life with pollution, went up to the rack of his own accord, spitting out the flesh, as all ought to go who have the courage to refuse things that it is not right to taste, even for the natural love of life. Those who were in charge of that unlawful sacrifice took the man aside... and privately urged him to bring meat of his own providing, proper for him to use, and to pretend that he was eating the flesh of the sacrificial meal that had been commanded by the king.... But... he declared himself quickly, telling them to send him to Hades.... When he had said this, he went at once to the rack.... When he was about to die under the blows, he groaned aloud and said: "It is clear to the Lord in his holy knowledge that, though I might have been saved from death, I am enduring terrible sufferings in my body under this beating, but in my soul I am glad to suffer these things because I fear him." So in this way he died, leaving in his death an example of nobility and a memorial of courage, not only to the young but to the great body of his nation. (2 Macc 6:18–31 NRSV)

Hebrews' echoing of them is limited to the way in which they vividly illustrate the heroic resolve of faithfulness to the divine word in the face of violent, death-dealing persecution. There is nothing here to support the conclusion that Hebrews was endorsing the program of the Maccabean revolt or putting itself in the position of God making an ultimate judgment on the lives of these martyrs. The rest of Hebrews makes clear enough the line of obedience commended.

## Comments on Wording

11:32 *Gideon, Barak, Samson, Jephthah, of David and Samuel and the prophets.* The three pairs of names are each in chronologically reverse order; it is a bit of poetic license in what is merely a sampling that should remind of other names from the same history.

11:35 *Women received back their dead by resurrection.* Cf. 11:19; 1 Kgs 17:22; 2 Kgs 4:32-35; Luke 7:11-17; John 11:1-40; Acts 9:36-43.

*Some were tortured, refusing to accept release, so that they might rise again to a better life.* See above; Dan 3:17-18; 12:13; 2 Macc 7:14, 23, 36. The word translated *tortured* (*tympanizō*) originally referred to a process of stretching a person and beating them like a drum (*tympanon*) until they died, but by the time of Hebrews it referred to torture and execution more generally.

11:37 *They were stoned, they were sawn in two, they were killed with the sword.* 2 Chr 24:21; Jer 26:23; cf. Matt 21:35; 23:34-39. In later traditions Jeremiah was stoned to death (Tertullian, *Scorp.* 8; Hippolytus, *De antichr.* 31; Jerome, *C. Jovin.* 2.37) and Isaiah was sawn in two (*Mart. Ascen. Isa.* 5:11-14; Justin, *Dial.* 120; Tertullian, *De patientia* 14; Jerome *Comm. In. Isa.* 57.2 [*PL* 24.546]; *b. Sanh.* 103b). Hebrews' interest is limited to generic representations of extreme faith.

11:37b-38 *They went about in skins of sheep and goats . . . dens and caves of the earth.* Judg 6:2; 1 Sam 22:1; 23:13-14; 24:1-3; 1 Kgs 18:4, 13; 19:4, 9, 11-18; 2 Kgs 1:8; 2:8, 13-14; Isa 20:2; Zech 13:4; Matt 8:20; 2 Cor 11:26; 1 Macc 2:28, 31; 2 Macc 5:27; 6:11; 10:6. The cumulative imagery of these two verses is probably meant to be evocative of much broader causes, circumstances, and conditions surrounding the life of those who are either outcasts or separated by personal choice from the levers of power, the comforts, and the protections of their particular society (10:33-34; 11:9, 24-26; 13:3, 5-6, 7-17).

11:39-40 At a stroke, these verses draw together 10:11-15, 10:36, 11:2, 11:13, and 11:33. They are a hinge from the illustrations of 11:3-37 to the exhortations of 12:1-29. As such, though descriptive in form they are prescriptive in force. There is a statement of fact: That "all these" did not obtain the promise was due to the intention of God to bring about the perfecting of his people in the history of his Son. But as 11:13–16 made explicit—and those verses are meant to be recalled here—their very death in faith was a confession of the promise and a call to us to follow their lead. It was necessary for them to wait for the better thing God provided for us, but it was necessary for us that the commendation of their faith should be provided so that we might walk in it. The exhortation of 12:1 follows naturally and makes this explicit. The passive form of *be made perfect* assumes the offering of Christ as its agent (10:14) and anticipates the exhortation to *look to Jesus* who is both the provision and pattern of faith.

**11:39** *all these . . . did not receive what was promised.* Contrast v. 33; compare vv. 13–15.

## Comments on Theological Themes

The names listed in v. 32, let alone others that seem to be included in the broader allusion, raise the question of how some of these are exemplary as "heroes of faith," given their conduct as recorded in the Scriptures. Our hesitation, however, probably reflects both a different understanding of the gospel than was taught by this writer and a misunderstanding of how he intends these examples. Abraham and Moses were not included because they were relatively more righteous and therefore worthy, but because their lives—as attested by Scripture—followed the arc of the divine promise, as did Barak's, Samson's, and Jephthah's, and through them the reliability of the promise and the promiser was proven (11:1–2). In any event, Hebrews makes no definitive pronouncement on the ultimate fate of those listed, who would have been as subject to the warning of 5:11—6:12 and 10:26–31 as Hebrews' own audience.

The examples of vv. 33–35a would seem in accord with a triumphalist gospel, as if the writer was hinting that the readers should expect (if not actively work toward) immediate social vindication and economic conquest—miracles of deliverance. Nothing in the context supports that conclusion; indeed, the writer seems confident that he can cite these without danger of that misunderstanding. That this writer—who everywhere expects that the lives of his readers will follow the way of suffering—can unblushingly include vv. 33–35a is in reality consistent with his rejection of a dualism and "spiritualizing" tendency that came to govern so much of subsequent Christian thought. He does not foresee a "merely spiritual" outcome to this history. That a day of punishment and reward would come is everywhere the witness of the NT and that expectation leaves no aspect of what it means to be human out of its reckoning—i.e., it is not less than a bodily, fully creational outcome. The triumphs of faith in vv. 33–35a are both signs and foretastes of that outcome and are rightly cherished as such.

Verses 37b–38 evoke the stranger's life of 11:9–10, 13–16, 24–27 (cf. 13:14) not with a view to social disenfranchisement generally but with a view to a life situation brought about because of deliberate faith in the divine promise. By that same token, if any people ever had a basis for nationalistic enthusiasm it is the Jewish nation, including Jewish Christians. And yet this is not only missing but positively opposed to the outlook of Hebrews, which insists—emphatically with an eye on Jerusalem in Judea—that the believer's homeland is elsewhere. And if not Jerusalem, *a fortiori* not Rome or any other capital.

Verse 40 raises questions as to when its "perfecting" takes place, whether that of OT believers specifically (did they exist in a post-mortem state of imperfection until Christ?) or all believers. In our view the language of vv. 39–40 is reiterating 11:13 and so intends that these earlier people of faith *died* not having obtained the promise; the history of the promise had not yet reached its goal at that stage. The "something better" is to be taken as the once-for-all great salvation (2:3) which is already accomplished from the viewpoint of Hebrews, but the "perfecting" is probably finally understood to encompass both the present achievement enjoyed by new covenant believers (10:11–14) and the yet future arrival of the whole people of God at the city of the living God (10:36; 12:22–29; 13:14; cf. 11:10, 13–16). The imagery of 11:40 collapses the "already-not yet" understanding of salvation into a single moment, possibly with 13:8 assumed.[1] It is after all the powers *of the coming age* that are already given to believers (6:5); insofar as there is participation in perfection now it is a matter of arriving ahead of time at the future goal. In any event, vv. 39–40 make an important point about salvation history without speculating on the so-called intermediate state of those who died before Christ.

---

1. We should admit that the ultimate arrival may be in the "future" only from the viewpoint of those still living in the present age. For all we know, that "future" arrival may be simultaneous for the believers of all earthly ages, though somehow mysteriously accounting for the appearance during this history of those already deceased (Samuel to Saul; Moses and Elijah to Jesus and the three disciples); cf. Polkinghorne, "Eschatology," 40.

## Teaching Hebrews 11:32–40

1. Each of the figures mentioned in these verses carries potentials for exposition, taking each in its OT context. It would be in keeping with Hebrews' intention simply to turn to Judges etc. and teach directly from the complete stories. For it to proceed as an exposition *of Hebrews*, however, it is necessary to plot these stories on the dramatic arc of the history of the promise that forms the backbone of its entire reading of the OT. It is less a matter of evaluating particular episodes within Samson's life, weighing each vignette in terms of right or wrong, wisdom or folly, than of observing how and where his life followed the sovereign lead of the divine promise, particularly with a view to his willing participation in its advance.

2. We will be reminded that our lives will err perhaps worse than theirs. It will be an evil to withhold obedience for fear of the inevitable evil we will do, however. By disregarding all but a straining ahead to where our forerunner awaits us and from where he already intercedes for us there will be a clearly defined trajectory to one's life that finally makes the things hoped for real in the present and proves the reality and truth of the things not seen (11:1–2). It is a matter of striving to plot one's own life as resolutely as possible on the line of the divine word that was previously spoken through the prophets and finally spoken in and as the Son who is our high priest and offering.

3. In this there is an improper but also a proper triumphalism that we must not be shy to uphold, the firm conviction that God's righteousness (not ours!) will overcome and finally, in his time and through faith (!), conquer kingdoms etc. Even now, if it serves God's ends, he may do these things. But our hope in this is in another city and, like those who went before and above all like our Brother, we reach only for that promised city with single-minded obedience. On that, faith waits patiently.

4. The depictions of vv. 35b–38 will more directly characterize the experiences of faith, giving the external appearance of failure but marking the confidence of salvation. Some already experience these things in their host society and find here strong encouragement. For a Christian culture that has grown accustomed to security the teachings of this passage will be strong meat, and not entirely welcome. For those caught in the transition from being tolerated to being opposed there will need to be a reckoning of what the great salvation of Hebrews finally means, and what the faith that it commands requires.

5. The battles of 11:33–35a confronted the enemy at the periphery of the true struggle of history; the people of the last day confront it at the center. More, we have a confidence that they were not granted, confidence to approach the divine throne with boldness already now, to approach the city of the living God as those on behalf of whom a forerunner has already entered and who intercedes for them. To this "other-worldly" orientation there corresponds a radically "this-worldly" form of living that is thoroughly *engaged* with every aspect of life in the world (11:35b–38; cf. 10:25, 33–34; 11:9–10, 13–16, 24–26, 31; 12:11, 14; 13:1–19). This is a vision largely lost to a church that has settled down in the world and accepted things as they are; it may be reluctant to surrender a "peace" that is to its own advantage; it may have become dull to the incompatibility of Christ and Belial. But faith is different, for faith is the realization of things hoped for, the proving of things not seen.

6. To the casual reader and to anyone in contact with biblically influenced traditions, the figures of Abraham, Moses, David, and Jesus loom as large as any figures of human history. No doubt they were great figures with much to be said in their favor as "great" human beings. Some scholarship devoted to them has sought to amplify these human virtues by way of explaining their successes, playing up their savvy, their learning, their deft politicking, and other attributes that would seem to explain success in their historical setting. But there is a great truth that is as plain as day but as easily overlooked as sunlight: If we eliminated the divine witness, if in fact history could be given a do-over without that witness, we would never know of the existence of these figures. They were no-accounts by worldly standards. The isolated inscription, the debated literary allusion, these shadowy clues that are so amplified for us because we already know to whom they point (or, at least, might point) would not for a moment distract our attention from the significant figures and events of the great world empires. The historical evidence is so slight that proving their very existence outside of the biblical record is a challenge. That must be said so that we may say this: Jesus counseled a very public righteousness, to the glory of God, but at the same time and for the same reason a *hidden* righteousness, not paraded on the street. The left hand was not to know what the right hand was doing. Charity was to be shown those who would be in no position to repay, which in that historical context would have meant not only monetary repayment but the repayment of public honor. One was to invest one's all in what

would essentially be a black hole, a point of no return. Nothing of value, whether gain, glory, or other satisfaction, would come, a loss to which death would only add its exclamation point. This is not a formula for educational, professional, or social advancement, to be sure. Not only this, but many of us do not have even the satisfaction of knowing that we are doing great but hidden things out of our great personal and material resources. We know ourselves to have precious little capital of finance, intellect, strength, influence, and respect. We identify more with the widow and her small change (Mark 12:42) or the grieving tax collector (Luke 18:13) than with David or Paul. For some in this situation, reading the biblical record can have something of the effect of social media, only feeding the sense that, "I don't measure up." Perhaps God really does favor the "great." No. What we should hear in these biblical testimonies is what confirms what Jesus counseled: What the biblical record attests is not that God favors the "great," but that he notices and will (!) honor the very motley crew of nameless ones that Hebrews lists in 11:35b–38. The biblical record is a witness given us already within the present history that God will keep the promise of these verses if we submit to the wisdom of God (1 Cor 1:18–2:5; Matt 11:25–30), which is utter folly in the eyes of the world. Living as if this is true, living this truth out, requires and is *faith*. Having got that far we can add this too: By the power of that divine word of witness, by which he bears all things—that witness that is stubbornly lodged in the heart of a history that would have willfully buried it forever—their weakness has been the power of salvation for the world. That weakness found its epicenter in the reproach of Christ (11:24–26; 13:13). Therefore, there is nothing to fear.

# 12:1–3

*"If anyone would come after me,
let him deny himself and take up his cross and follow me.
For whoever would save his life will lose it,
but whoever loses his life for my sake will find it."*

## Context

See 10:19–25, 26–31, and 32–39.

10:19–31 Exhortation to faith and warning against apostasy (reusing 10:19–25)

10:32—12:3 Enduring in the great contest of faith in the promise

    10:32–39 A call to endure based on their earlier history and the promise of Habakkuk and Isaiah

    11:1–40 Examples of enduring faith from Israel's history

    12:1–3 A call to endure based on the example of Jesus

12:4–17 Enduring as the genuine children of the covenantal Father

12:18–29 The grand finale: closing vision of the promised inheritance, the peril of refusing the promiser, and a final warning/exhortation

13:1–17 Peroration

The imagery of the athletic contest that was prominent in 10:32–39 is resumed in 12:1 as the many examples of 11:3–38 condense and form into the cloud of witnesses that encompasses the runners. There is continuity with what proceeds but also a shift of focus and form, as also a leaning ahead into 12:4–17.

The retrospective of 10:32–34 was capped in 10:34b by a reference to the calculation of one who would sell everything to purchase a field for the sake of the treasure there (Matt 13:44), or who would compare the present suffering and future glory on a scale (Rom 8:18). That thought reaches its climax with 12:2–3. Likewise, the exhortation of 10:35–39 culminated in the call to identify with "my righteous one" who would live by faith and so obtain salvation. The example of the righteous one *par excellence* is what we have in 12:1–3. This connection also clarifies the specificity of the idea of *the will of God* in 10:36. As the path blazed by the Son and required of his siblings that phrase is alluding to the will of God of which Ps 40 spoke (Heb 10:5–10). It is an irreducibly *missional* will. This, too, is what it will mean to go with him outside the camp, bearing his disgrace (13:12–13).

In this history of faith Jesus stands alone. In him faith first properly exists and attains its goal. Because of this he sits on the divine throne, like the anchor that passes into the invisible depths beyond the veil. He is not merely a splendid illustration of the principle that faith is rewarded but the source of the strong encouragement given us (6:18–20; cf. 4:14–16; 10:19–25). The stress of 12:1–3 is on Jesus as example, but not without his identity as provision, which would be impossible. Contextualized like so, there is good reason not to "grow weary or fainthearted."

## Background

Paul's use of the imagery of a race is well-known (see on 10:32–39; also 1 Cor 9:24–26; Gal 2:2; 5:7; Phil 2:16; 2 Tim 4:7; cf. Acts 20:24) and Hebrews briefly signaled this idea at 6:20. 4 Macc 13:27—14:5 relates the endurance of seven Jewish brothers through persecution, who were "despising" their agonies and "running the course toward immortality" (cf. 4 Macc 17:10, 12, 14, 17). The hope celebrated in this latter narrative is unlike that of Hebrews, but the manner of applying the athletic imagery to the martyr's path was evidently a cultural habit.

In Heb 12:2 (cf. 6:6) the supreme example of endurance is Jesus' cross. The frequency of allusions to the Roman cross in the NT coupled with its prominence in the whole of the Christian tradition might cause us to forget its offensiveness in the first century context—and the peculiarity of Christian usage. A now-classic study of this form of execution, rich in citations of primary sources, is that of Martin Hengel, whose very chapter headings are suggestive: "Crucifixion as a 'barbaric' form of execution of utmost cruelty";

"Crucifixion as the supreme Roman penalty"; "The 'slaves' punishment."[1] About it Seneca wrote:

> Can anyone be found who would prefer wasting away in pain dying limb by limb, or letting out his life drop by drop, rather than expiring once for all? Can any man be found willing to be fastened to the accursed tree, long sickly, already deformed, swelling with ugly weals on shoulders and chest, and drawing the breath of life amid long-drawn-out agony? He would have many excuses for dying even before mounting the cross.[2]

Cicero described it as the "ultimate punishment" (*summum supplicium*). The "Roman world was largely unanimous that crucifixion was a horrific, disgusting business," so much so that it was for many an unmentionable: "Crucifixion was widespread and frequent, above all in Roman times, but the cultured literary world wanted to have nothing to do with it, and as a rule kept quiet about it."[3] There were assuredly deeper wounds in the event for Jesus—hell's very anguish—but it would be a weak view of the incarnation, a weak anthropology, and a failure to appreciate the force of Hebrews' argument to reduce or look past the raw human enmity, suffering, and shame attached to this instrument and its place at the heart of our atonement.

## Comments on Wording

12:1 *surrounded by so great cloud of witnesses.* On the one hand and primarily, the use of witnessing language in 11:2, 4, 5, 39 is God's attestation of those who lived in faith. Against that wider context, 12:1 is a cloud of those who gave testimony (martyrs?) about God to others derivatively, as a result of God's testimony. They are those who by their faith realized what was hoped for and proved what was not seen; they saw the invisible (11:1–2, 27). On the other hand, in that identity the many of 11:3–38 are "witnesses" (spectators) of the believers now running the race, who are to be conscious of the example of these others. This sense of the word *martyrs* is generally attested[4] and suits the cloud and race imagery of the immediate context. Even so, we are more conscious of them than they of us. It is doubtful that the writer

---

1. Hengel, *Crucifixion*.
2. Ibid., 30–31, citing Seneca, *Dialogue* 3 (*De ira* 1) 2.2.
3. Hengel, *Crucifixion*, 37–38, noting exceptions to this rule.
4. BDAG, "*martys*," 619:2b. Not using this word but employing the image, cf. 4 Macc 17:14.

intends us to imagine these witnesses in heavenly bleachers looking on, still less imagine anything so realistic that it would contribute to a veneration of the saints. Our eyes, like theirs, are to be fixed on one figure (v. 2).

*let us also lay aside every weight, and sin which clings so closely.* Cf. 3:7–19; 4:2, 6, 11; 5:7–14; 6:11–12; 10:22–25, 39. *Every weight* and *sin which clings so closely* could be two ways of getting at the same thing, or the former could be a broader category of things not sinful in themselves (1 Cor 7:32, 35; 2 Tim 2:3–6). The "laying aside" is not a matter of achieving sinlessness but of the resoluteness of the obedient approach to the divine throne that forms the center and wellspring of all further obedience.

12:2 *looking to Jesus, the founder and perfecter of our faith.* Jesus' name, emphatically placed in the Greek word order, is probably used to emphasize his human fellowship with his brothers and sisters (2:5–18; 5:7–10). The words for *founder* (*archēgos*, 2:10) and *perfector* (*teleiōtēs*) play off the ideas of beginning and end (cf. 1:1–2; 2:10; 7:3). It is difficult to know for sure how the first, *archēgos*, was intended, whether as *originator/founder* or *leader/forerunner* (cf. 6:20), but given the play just noted the former is probably primary and, in any event, entails the latter in this context.

*endured the cross, despising the shame.* The Greek phrasing has no article with *cross*,[5] giving it qualitative emphasis more like the English *endured a cross* without diminishing the reference to the uniqueness of his particular cross (*the* cross).

12:3 *Consider him who endured from sinners such hostility.* The reference is to the opposition expressed in the cross though it may include the entire history leading to that event, depending on how much of that history the readers had heard.

## Comments on Theological Themes

The Son as the originator/founder of faith draws from the depths of Hebrews' characterization of the Son as eternal, the one through whom all things were made, without beginning of days, the same yesterday, and so forth. It is not merely that faith reaches its quintessential expression in him but that the way of salvation followed by all those of chapter 11 was forged by him who went before them (2:10) and is the object of their hope.

Crucifixion sealed one's person and life with the words "failure," "loser," "rejected," and "nothing."[6] Not merely some personal nemesis but

---

5. The article is present in a few manuscripts ($\mathfrak{P}^{13,46}$ D*.c).

6. We are focusing on the public dimensions of the cross because this is where 12:1–3 seems to focus. The deeper movements of the event in being abandoned by his

the world as such pronounces its settled verdict wishing its victim to hear this declaration as its last conscious experience and in that knowledge to die. Its message to all on-lookers: "Let all see and take this to heart!" If the world's court has any validity there is no room for doubt. The attention given to boasting, the praise of people, and the scandal of the cross (e.g., Matt 6:1–6; 23:5–7; John 5:44; 12:43; 1 Cor 1:10—4:21) demonstrates the conviction of the NT writers that here we have to do with one of the primal fears of the human person and one of the most basic of motivations for action. Only one human soul in history has faced the full measure of this public disapprobation and enmity, and he alone because (though not for this reason alone) he alone resisted it fully without wilting or breaking. The cross was a communicative act, a society's (and all societies') declaration whose echoes could be felt in the opposition these readers experienced in their own lives (12:3–4).[7] As such Jesus' cross flooded light on the reality of those very experiences, showing them for what they were: Their sufferings were participation in the way of the Son, their brother; fellowship with him in his flesh, as he had shared in theirs (2:10–18); it was a matter of bearing his disgrace (13:13). Viewed this way, there is a rather natural transition to the verses that follow (12:4–11), recalling that this had been the way of the Son in 5:7–10. He became like us so we would become like him. At the heart of that being-like-him is walking in his faith.

That Jesus despised the shame of the cross does not mean he treated its suffering as illusory or somehow exercised mind over matter; this was not a philosopher's trick. The suffering was real, full, and endured to its full measure. He refused rather to relinquish his confidence or accept his tormentors' verdict and in obedience entrusted himself to God, thus acknowledging only the honor bestowed by God (2:5–9; 5:1–10). This is the way of a child of God, the learning of obedience through suffering in a manner that echoes the Son's pattern (cf. 5:9: "for all who obey him"), this being a dimension of the process of being perfected/made holy. The idea of victory over opposition also contained in 12:3 reminds in turn of 2:14–16 and the victory over the tyrant that held the seed of Abraham in slavery.

---

Father and yet trusting him for deliverance are indicated elsewhere (e.g., 5:7–10), as also the depths of the victory won (2:14–15).

7. Purely from the viewpoint of human penal systems, suffering, and the like, it does not finally matter if in some sense it could be shown that there are other instruments of torture and execution that inflict greater suffering—however that could be measured and generalized. Crucifixion was the supreme expression to hand for the Jews and Romans; other societies would have utilized their own devices to make the same point. That his death was in fact going to be by crucifixion was prophetically anticipated, of course.

A final note on crucifixion acknowledges its political aspect. The crucifixion of Jesus was a lawful act of the Roman state. "If you resist us, we will hurt you." The point of Hebrews, however, is not to vie with the government on its own terms; the point of 13:13–14 is not to migrate to another part of earth or lead a political revolution. Whatever the relation between the gospel and the political activity of Christians and the church, Hebrews' call to faith draws no *direct* line to such activity. The action of the state in public executions is viewed as an instantiation of a larger struggle between God's kingdom and the "enemies" not yet under the Son's feet. It became a governmental revolt against God in the crucifixion of Jesus (Psalm 2), and the expectation of the gospel is that this history will repeat itself (Revelation). For most of these believers that hostility would have instantiated itself in the act of a neighbor or family member; for some it meant suffering at the hands of the state (10:34; 13:3). The call to believers was and remains to accept God's kingdom as God's, and to await it from within the world's structures as its citizens (among other texts, 1 Cor 7:17–24 signals more than one possibility in these regards), which means in accordance with God's kingdom's ways and norms. This is not a passive waiting; God is on the offensive, and his people with him, but the remainder of our exposition elaborates this. For the rest, in God's time, on the occasion of his direct and final intervention, his will will be fully done on earth as in heaven (12:25–29). Even now, while the "until" of Psalm 110 holds, the effect of the life of faith may be to reduce the sum of society's and the state's evil, at the least by bringing it into the light. If so, this is not preparing for God's salvation, but drawing from it; if it does not reduce evil's sway, faith endures.

## Teaching Hebrews 12:1–3

1. Any leader knows that both panic and courage are infectious. Hebrews would have us hold examples of the latter before our eyes. They—those of 11:1—12:3—were attested. Their faith was vindicated in spite of death. The something better, perfection, was obtained by the leader and perfector of faith (11:39–40). *Therefore* the way is clear, it can be run, it must be run.

2. The "cloud of witnesses" is imagery, but because of the resurrection this cloud is no mere figure any more than Elisha's horses and chariots were mere figures (2 Kgs 6:16–17). We are to see things as they really are. Again, for Thomas Jefferson, "The earth belongs to the living." But for those of resurrection faith, the dead in Christ remain among

the living, among those with whom we fellowship. Their lives remain relevant to ours.

3. Keep your eye on Jesus. If we would understand faith anywhere else we must first understand it here in its character, object, and achievement. It is here that we learn with what fury the enemies of God will oppose and the terrors they will wield if faith dares raise its head—and the truth that their powers are in fact only a sham, for they have been broken.

4. It ain't over till it's over. Whether one's allotment is long or short the race is to be run to its end. The need is to go deeper into the confession than we have so that when evil reaches its full measure, as it did for Jesus in the cross, we are not lost but endure to the end.

5. Run to win. Life comes down to faith. This faith is the runner who breaks down every phase of the race from start to finish, crafting a stride and step and training every fiber of the body to move in precisely the correct way until it is instinct and reflex. It is in this way that the competitor strips away the sin of life, which means, everything that slows, distracts, discourages, or potentially disqualifies in the singular pursuit of the way of Jesus.

6. In this, Jesus is not only pattern but also provision. The way is hard. The powers that stand in our path appear invincible. But he has broken them and they will submit. They cannot bar our way because he has already forged the way through. He summons us into the light of his searching word (4:12–13) to approach his throne of grace to receive mercy and find grace (4:14–16). This provision, which was more directly expressed in the earlier chapters of Hebrews is at work in these verses too, being hinted at in Jesus' identity as the originator and perfector of faith and in his having been seated at the right hand of God. The joy set before him was the joy of sharing his salvation with his brothers and sisters (2:5–18). Verses 2–3 are accounting for the realization of the *something better* and the being *made perfect* of 11:40. Right there in the heart of his way of endurance is where we find his fellowship and his support. Right there is where we approach the throne. To go to the cross is to go to the place of suffering . . . and empowering victory.

7. Fixing our eyes singularly on Jesus reminds us that it is not righteousness, justice, peace that are as such the objects of our pursuit—either for ourselves or for others. The object that is our goal is Jesus himself who sits on the divine throne. But this is not to surrender righteousness,

justice, and peace, which are the concern of the one who sits on the throne (1:8–9; 7:2). Thus a right orientation vouchsafes and secures the rest. Life breeds life.

# 12:4–17

*"I am the true vine, and my Father is the vinedresser.*
*Every branch in me that does not bear fruit he takes away,*
*and every branch that does bear fruit he prunes,*
*that it may bear more fruit."*

## Context

SEE 10:19–25, 26–31, 32–39.

Hebrews' exhortation moves naturally from the examples of 10:32—12:3 to what it means to endure as the genuine children of our covenantal Father. One need merely lay 5:7–10 over 12:1–3 to reveal the internal thought that leads so naturally from the latter to the learning of obedience (5:8) that all who obey the Son (5:9) must undergo in 12:4–11.[1] The Son's learning of obedience finds its extension in the paternal discipline of the sons and daughters. The thought of vv. 4–11 continues with vv. 12–13, which resume 12:3. The exhortation that begins with v. 14 is not a new departure but a call to pursue the peace and holiness that come with discipline (12:11); that is, actively to cooperate with that process and live in its fruit. That Greek sentence begun in v. 14 continues unbroken through v. 16 with important references to Deut 29 and Esau's foolish forfeiture of his place in the covenantal family. Verse 17 is the capper: It is an assertion in form, but by implication one of the most potent and punchy exhortations of the discourse. The whole passage concerns the ongoing pilgrimage of the new

---

1. The fact and significance of the Son's death has been repeatedly stressed in the discourse but 5:7–10 is the place where his suffering is particularly developed (cf. 2:9, 10, 18; 4:15) and so the clearest indication of that on which the readers are to focus when considering the one who endured in 12:2–3. Both 5:7–10 and 12:1–3 are followed by passages about growing up that, in turn, both culminate with related thoughts (5:14 and 12:11).

covenant family of God, both those who receive discipline and live and those who are cast out because of their faithlessness.

Thus:

10:19–31 Exhortation to faith and warning against apostasy (reusing 10:19–25)

10:32—12:3 Enduring in the great contest of faith in the promise

12:4–17 Enduring as the genuine children of the covenantal Father

    12:4–11 Developing the image: Undergoing hardship as authentic children of the covenantal Father

    12:12–17 Applying the image: Live as strong-bodied, stout-hearted children of the covenant, secure in your place, pursuing its life, taking care of the family, and cherishing your birthright

12:18–29 The grand finale: closing vision of the promised inheritance, the peril of refusing the promiser, and a final warning/exhortation

13:1–17 Peroration

There is more OT drama lurking behind vv. 12–17 than meets the eye so we should be sure to recognize that the imagined world within which the writer intends his language is that of the covenant community patterned on the shadows of Moses. The shadows and patterns (8:5; 9:23; 10:1) had a center—the tabernacle or temple—but they also had a perimeter, which is the whole community surrounding and oriented on that temple. This circle encompassed the totality of their lives, sexually, socially, economically, internationally, etc. It is not a matter of direct reinforcements of the old covenant stipulations of community conduct, though this new covenant life is vitally continuous with that earlier vision of life around God's throne. The life of Israel as commanded through Moses is a shadowy, "parabolic" (9:9; 11:19) revelation of what must be the life of the new covenant community now approaching the divine throne at its center through the Son (7:25).

## Background

In ways that go beyond the direct citations within vv. 4–17, the preacher's frame of reference for this passage is the OT story of Israel in covenant with God, particularly as God's disciplining hand was bringing her to his promised goal and as this story was told through Deuteronomy, Isaiah, and Jeremiah, among others. It both assumes and reinforces the idea that these Christians are in fact the true covenantal seed of Abraham, members of God's new covenant family—a by no means obvious and possibly a contested claim. There is no other covenant or family of God. They are to embrace that identity, inhabit it, and cherish it. It must not be treated with the contempt of Esau.

Taking Isaiah as it stands, it has been characterized as answering the question, "what would become of the promises of God?" The answer: "There would have to be a purging of the nation because God is holy. Before the nation could inherit the promises made to the fathers, it would have to be made holy. So God would use the pagan nations to chasten Israel for its sins and cleanse it from iniquity.... On the basis of such cleansing and purification, God would then establish the golden age, a time of peace and prosperity that the world has never known."[2] It should not be difficult to see how completely this vision comports with Hebrews as a whole, and 12:4–17 specifically.

Heb 12:12 echoes Isa 35:3 but a much larger network of parallels compels us to recognize a broader indebtedness For instance: Isa 28:12 (cf. Heb 3:7—4:11); 30:9, 15, 26 (the last drawing from sabbath ideas; cf. 66:23); 32:3, 15–18; 33:14, 16; 35:1–4, 8 (cf. 40:3); 40:21–31; 57:14–15; 66:1–2, 10, 18, 22–23.

In other words, in citing Prov 3:11–12 and other OT passages and in utilizing the imagery of a path to be travelled Hebrews is not merely making a general moral appeal with vivid OT imagery that resonates with Greco-Roman household and pedagogical institutions. The preacher is situating his readers in the grand story of salvation that had been told by the prophets (Heb 1:1–2), and, indeed, at its very climax. It is unnecessary to posit a knowing echo of the Baptist's preaching (Mark 1:3) if we suggest that both the Baptist and Hebrews were thinking of the same "way of the Lord" in their common dependence on Isaiah; cf. Jer 31:2–14.[3] It is a summons to inhabit *that* story, boldly to take their place in it, and to bring the new covenant promises to their full realization (Heb 11:1–2).

Back of this is the narrative of the exodus journey that is basic to both Hebrews (cf. 3:7—4:11) and Isaiah: Deut 8:2, 5; cf. Ps 94:12. It is the story of God's covenantal choice of Israel and his paternal raising of his

---

2. Ross, "Introduction to Isaiah."

3. We are taking our cues from the contextual reliance on the Pentateuch and Isaiah but we certainly do not mean to say that only these parts of the OT stand behind this idea of the race/pilgrimage; cf. Jer 31:2–14, where the return of the exiles is a new exodus and the announcement of the new covenant follows.

child to adulthood so as to be fit for the inheritance. What the wording of Prov 3:11–12 facilitates is not merely the general encouragement that one can take the fact of discipline as a sign of fatherly love but the deeper message of *who qualifies as Abraham's offspring* (Heb 2:16; 3:16–19; 4:1–11; 6:7–8; 11:18; 12:15–17; 13:10), placing the accent on the positive point that these believers as members of the new covenant assuredly are those children—if they walk in faith to the end (3:14)—and on the blessings that attend that privilege.

In Heb 12:15 the preacher appropriates Deut 29:17 as a part of the larger indebtedness to the whole situation of Israel in the setting of Deuteronomy and its anticipation of the new covenant.[4] Deut 27–32 (cf. 4:27–31; Jer 31:31–34; Ezek 11:18–20; 36:26–27) carries several parallels to Hebrews, reinforcing what we have just said.

The allusion to the story of Esau in Heb 12:16–17 is particularly potent, marking a division within the natural seed of Abraham. The terminology for inheritance—expressing a theme so controlling for Hebrews—is last used here in 12:17. Though the idea of the inheritance permeates Heb 12:4–29, 12:17 puts the question sharply: Who is the heir? It may be that by naming Isaac Abraham's *only* child in 11:17–18 (in spite of Ishmael) the preacher had been hinting at something like Paul's principle of Rom 9:6–13. The allusion to the blessing of Jacob *and Esau* in 11:20, in turn, was probably thinking ahead to 12:15–17 and Esau's "apostasy."[5] Now in 12:15–17 it is the story of Esau and Jacob that is summoned at the moment when Esau forfeited his birthright, making himself a pattern of all (even if they be Abraham's children) who would forfeit their obtaining of the promise for the sake of transient relief from suffering.

## Comments on Wording

**12:4** *In your struggle against sin you have not yet resisted to the point of shedding your blood.* The word for *struggle* has associations with boxing or wrestling; that they have not resisted *until blood* might play off that further if it is a way of saying that they have not got fully into the fight.[6]

**12:5** *that addresses you as sons.* The way this OT text is made to speak directly to the new covenant recipients of Hebrews recalls 3:7. The wording contains the implication of an assertion: You *are* sons (and daughters)—not merely in a general sense, but specifically as the seed of Abraham in the

---

4. See Allen, *Deuteronomy and Hebrews*.
5. Cockerill, *Epistle to the Hebrews*, 560.
6. Attridge, *Hebrews*, 360.

tradition of Israel. The fact of this relationship was already established by 2:5–18 and 8:7–13. See on the Background above.

12:7 *God is treating you as sons* etc. The argument hooks back via 12:1–3 to 5:7–10 and 2:5–18, in other words, to a christological basis for this identity; derivatively, Prov 3:11–12 can be brought in as a witness. In its reference to normal patterns of parents and children it is not distracted by particulars (dysfunctional homes) but appeals to best practices.

12:9 *Shall we not much more be subject to the Father of spirits and live?* The fallible human parents are a foil; the positive model is God's identity as a Father to Israel. The referent of *the spirits* (= *our* spirits[7]) is the people of the covenant, his children, whom the Father is raising to perfection (12:23). The phrasing ("spirits") is in part the writer's own way of stressing "full and ultimate" vs. "partial and imperfect," in keeping with the general associations of conscience and flesh, above and below, now and future, etc. The expression, "God of the spirits of all flesh" occurs in Num 16:22 and 27:16 (cf. 1QS 3:25; 2 Macc 3:24–25; *1 En.* 37–41). God's transcendent authority and paternal care are underlined.

12:10 *but he disciplines us for our good, that we may share his holiness.* Compare, e.g., Deut 8:5; 2 Sam 7:14; Ps 94:12; Job 5:17; Jer 35:12–16; Mal 1:6; Matt 7:9–11. For the particular history assumed, see above.

12:11 *For the moment all discipline seems painful rather than pleasant.* The word *pleasant* is the word for *joy*, linking the thought back to 12:2; cf. 10:34.

*yields the peaceful fruit of righteousness to those who have been trained by it.*[8] The word for *being trained* continues the athletic theme (10:32–33; 12:1, 4). In the Greek word order *righteousness* is emphatic, probably recalling 10:38 along with 11:4, 7, etc.; accordingly, the theme is still the way of faith.

12:12–13 *Therefore lift your drooping hands . . . but rather be healed.* See on the dramatic background above. The athletic imagery (cf. 12:1–2) hints either at a fighter letting the arms drop or the more general fatigue and discouragement of a traveller. Verse 13 appropriates Prov 4:26 (cf. Isa 40:3–4, though the image differs). Either this amounts to staying on the path or simply avoiding further injury. Either way it amounts to receiving God's discipline as resilient, assured children of the covenant who cooperate with their Father's intentions both personally and corporately.

---

7. Cockerill, *Epistle to the Hebrews*, 624–25; regarding the article, he is dependent on Bruce, *Epistle to the Hebrews*, 344.

8. It may be that *righteousness* is a genitive of source: *peaceable fruit that comes from being in right relationship to God*; so Cockerill, *Epistle to the Hebrews*, 628.

12:14 *Strive for peace with everyone* etc. This is an exhortation to cooperate with the process of vv. 4–11 so as to bear fruit and arrive at the goal of the Way of God (Isa 35:1–10). Here the reference is to "holiness" instead of "righteousness" (v. 11) in correspondence to 12:10 and 4:14—10:26. As in 11:9 the prepositional phrase *with everyone* is better taken as modifying the verb:[9] *in company with everyone pursue peace and (the) holiness* etc. Verses 15–17 follow naturally. Thus, *peace* and *holiness* are understood firstly in line with 12:10–11, though there is no need to restrict their scope precisely (cf. Ps 34:15; Jer 29:7; 1 Pet 3:11).

*no one will see the Lord.* Cf. Exod 34; Num 12:6–8; Deut 4:15–31; 34:10; Ps 27:4; Isa 6:1–13; Matt 5:8; John 1:18; 1 Cor 13:12; 2 Cor 3:7–18; 4:6; 1 Tim 6:16; 1 John 3:2; 4:12; Rev 22:4. Considering that Heb 12:12 just made the allusion to Isa 35:3 it may be that Isa 35:2 is part of the allusion here: "They shall see the glory of the LORD, the majesty of our God." See on the background above.

12:15 *See to it that no one fails to obtain the grace of God; that no "root of bitterness" springs up and causes trouble, and by it many become defiled.* Cf. Deut 29:18 and on the background above; see also 3:7—4:11; 5:11—6:8. In Deut 29 the people are situated imaginatively on the way leading from Egypt to Canaan and are made to recall the images and idols of the other nations. They are to make sure that no one among them turns from the Lord to worship these other gods, presuming themselves to be safe by association with the covenant community (cf. Jer 7:1–29). For *grace* see the introduction to this commentary.

12:16 *that no one is sexually immoral or unholy like Esau.* This characterization derives in part from Esau's cavalier treatment of his birthright (Gen 25:29–34) and probably in part from Esau's choice of wives (Gen 26:34; 27:46—28:1; 28:6–9; cf. Philo, *Virt.* 208) against the larger backdrop of the association of sexual immorality and covenantal faithlessness (note Deut 29:18 in v. 15; see, e.g., Num 25:1–18; Deut 31:16; Judg 2:17; 1 Kgs 11:1–13; Prov 5–7; Jer 2:20; Ezek 16; Hosea); no doubt it also has an eye on the more immediate context of Hebrews' audience (13:1–6).

12:17 *For you know that afterward, when he desired to inherit the blessing, he was rejected* etc. Cf. 5:11—6:8 and 10:26–31 (cf. 2:1–4; 3:7—4:11).

## Comments on Theological Themes

We can be confident that the phrase to *share his holiness* in 12:10 alludes back to the whole development of 1:1–4; 2:5–18; and 4:14—10:26, though

9. Ibid., 633–34.

the wording of 12:10 is left at a general level and interpreters disagree over its specific reference. A sharp distinction between whether the act of "sharing" in his holiness is a present concern (favored by vv. 1, 4, 11, 14–16; cf. 13:1–25; 5:11–14) or another way of saying, "that we may arrive at the ultimate goal" (in the immediate context the play on "joy" and "pain" in v. 11, which echoes 12:2, suggests this) is probably forced. Here, too, anything realized in the present is a sharing in the powers of the age to come (6:5). It may be that in part this line means that God actively guides us to participate in the "approach" to the divine throne that is of the essence of faith.

As to the general idea of v. 11: Hebrews' driving concern with the priestly work and sacrifice of Christ carries with it the larger vision of the flourishing life of the new covenant people around his throne (1:8–9; 3:13; 5:11–14; 6:7–10; 7:2; 10:22, 25, 26, 32–34, 38; 13:1–25; etc.). Possible echoes or allusions in v. 11 include Ps 85:10–11; Isa 11:1–9. Its center of gravity, however, is in Isa 32:17–18[10] where peace, quietness, and confidence allude to the way of faith in the midst of opposition and danger (Isa 28:12; 30:15–16; 32:17–18). Isaiah's theme of *rest* raises afresh what was not an incidental development back in 3:7—4:11.[11] Moreover, there is an inner correspondence between Isa 32:15–20 and 35:1–10, and Hebrews is about to draw from the latter (Isa 35:3 in Heb 12:12). The message is to endure in faith on the great Way of God (Isa 35:8). It should also be observed that the language of v. 11 not incidentally recalls Heb 5:14. Both 5:11–14 and 12:4–11 are getting at the process of maturation within God's covenantal household. In the use of agricultural imagery v. 11 further recalls 6:7–8 (cf. 12:15) and its exploitation of the prophetic characterization of the last days as days of flourishing under God's unprecedented blessing.

In their own ways, 4:12–13; 12:4–17; and 12:25–29 are all getting at the judgment already going on in the world, including in the community of faith. As heavenly as their drama is, it is assuredly earthly. It has already involved the body and blood of their Lord, and could involve their own (12:4).

## Teaching Hebrews 12:4–17

1. This passage deepens a sense of identity as the true seed of Abraham, true members of God's eternal covenant (13:20), who are positioned with the entire preceding throng of pilgrims (11:3—12:3) at the

---

10. The LXX of Isa 32:17 refers to the "works" (*erga*) of righteousness, but the context of Isa 32 (cf. Isa 35) utilizes agricultural imagery. "Works" is often used in classical texts to refer to tilled lands (Liddell-Scott, "*ergon*," 682–83).

11. Laansma, *Rest*, 46–53.

threshold of the promised inheritance, the great destination (12:22–24). We are these children in this history. Involved in this is the positive claim that we are indeed the true children of Abraham, though without dwelling on the negative implications (compare Gal 4:21–31; 5:11; 6:12–16; John 8:31–59).[12] Chiefly it is a matter of understanding, embracing, and cherishing that identity.

2. Verses 4–11 are not about parental discipline as such. Attempts to apply it to that realm must translate it wisely.[13] These verses do address the "problem of pain" in the life of faith, which may have been a key obstacle for the original audience as it has been for subsequent readers. For those of God's family there is no condemnation or judgment involved (cf. Rom 8:1; 1 Cor 11:32; cf. 1 Pet 4:17), but there is discipline as the out-working of salvation itself while we are grafted into the way taken by the Son (2:5–18; 4:14–16; 5:7–10; 10:19–25; 12:1–3) which was foreshadowed in Israel's history. Particular sensitivity is required if we are to translate this for individuals for whom parental discipline signifies abuse, or for cultures that reject the very idea of submission to authority. It will be important to communicate the history, character, and destiny of God's family.

3. Hardship easily reduces many to merely superstitious notions of a god's displeasure and of appeasement. The teaching of 12:4–11 kills all such superstition at its root.

4. In this we are made to see that we are not passive recipients of God's gift, but are made into flourishing humans who exercise freedom for obedience to the word spoken as did our Brother before us. With that comes the danger of forfeiting one's covenantal birthright, against which the entire sermon has been a warning. Moreover, this is an affair of our life together (vv. 12–17). We are not only personally strengthened but can take an active role in the strengthening of others, being fully invested in their well-being and success.

5. When we take together vv. 10–11 and 14 we are given a glimpse of the this-worldly life that Christians pursue as a matter of a faith centered on the approach to the divine throne. Either a theology of "saving souls" or one of "saving bodies" or "saving societies" can fall into the

---

12. We must avoid the swing from 1) humbly learning the grace of being made a member of God's family and embracing the enormity of that claim to 2) arrogance and presumption that turns in hostility against the Jews and/or unbelievers generally. This, too, belongs to the peace to be pursued.

13. Webb, *Corporal Punishment*; cf. Meadors, *Moving Beyond the Bible*.

trap of a soul-body dualism, simply choosing one of the extremes. As to the comment on sexuality in v. 16, if we reject the dualisms of "flesh and spirit" and allegorizing excesses we will have to accept the realism of the union of societal (bodily sexual) and covenantal (spiritual) infidelity that is chronicled in Scripture's history (see on 13:4). There is a spirit of faithlessness that has everything to do with our bodies and social existence and that is contradictory to wearing the emblem of this faith. This does not, however, justify all that has been taught in the name of "sexual purity" and the like, which is often as wrongly centered as a sexual libertarianism.

6. In Esau's bargain (vv. 16–17) is the whole history of apostasy in miniature. One meal (compare Matt 26:14–16; 27:9), the treasures of Egypt (11:24–26; cf. Rev 18–19), or the whole world (Mark 8:36; cf. Heb 13:14)—it is all one in that balance (Rom 8:18). Esau's despising of his rights as the firstborn is a singular warning for those who aspire to join the assembly of the firstborn (12:23). Hebrews does not dwell on a deficiency in Esau's subsequent efforts to bring about a change—a fair enough question in itself (e.g., Exod 9:27–35; Judges; Isa 1:2–31; 58:1–14; Matt 27:1–10; Luke 3:7–9; John 2:23–25; 2 Cor 7:8–13; 2 Pet 2:17–22)—but on the behavior that had brought him to this situation, and its permanence.

7. When all these things are brought into focus there are strains of robustness, stalwartness, strength, courage, and confidence that will be broadly appealing. The household of God is not a family of fear-ridden, guilt-stricken, cowering children. Its children are not marked by sloth, rebellion, presumption, waywardness, and stupidity. This is a good household. A joy-filled and thriving household. It is secure and permanent. It is a family formed and bound by the covenant that is the internal basis of creation itself, just as the creation of heaven and earth was the external basis of that covenant (1:1–4; 2:10; 13:20). It is a household celebrating because it is on the verge of coming into its inheritance. And it celebrates its life by gathering up its energies in filial reverence and sibling love, all bent on finishing the great pilgrimage together.

# 12:18–29

*"Our Father in heaven,
hallowed be your name.
Your kingdom come,
your will be done,
on earth as it is in heaven."*

## Context

1:1–4 Exordium: God has spoken in his Son

1:5—4:11 In praise of the Son who became high priest and the need to listen to what God says

4:12–13 Conclusion to first movement, reprisal of exordium

4:14—10:25 Christ as high priest and offering

10:19—12:29 Exhortations toward faith and progress (repeating 10:19–25 as transitional)

13:1–17 Peroration

13:18–25 Closing

AFTER THE ENCOURAGEMENT AND warning of 10:19–31 the focus shifted to the endurance of faith in the marathon that finds its goal in arrival at the great resting place, their inheritance (10:32—12:3). With 12:4–17 the "how" of following the preceding examples was considered from the perspective of living faithfully on the way of God as children of the covenant. Esau formed the counterpoint to the other examples and served as the quintessential case of apostasy through forfeiture of his covenantal birthright.

We are now at the grand finale, 12:18-29, which closes both 10:19—12:29 and the sermon as such, except for the peroration (13:1-17). With it we return to the theme of divine speech which began the sermon (1:1-4), closed the first movement (4:12-13), and bridged through everything along the way.

12:18-29 The grand finale: closing vision of the promised inheritance, the peril of refusing the promiser, and a final warning/exhortation

    12:18-24 The reason why they must endure in the great contest and as genuine children of the covenant

        12:18-21 Negatively: The mountain that pointed to the goal (old covenant and present age)

        12:22-24 Positively: The mountain that is the goal (new covenant and age to come)

    12:25-29 Final warning and exhortation

        12:25-27 Warning: Listen to the divine word for it has inaugurated the final judgment

        12:28-29 Exhortation: Worship God suitably in obedience to the word spoken in the Son

Hebrews' decision simply to describe the two symbolic mountains in 12:18-24 permits an openness to his argument that unites the *a fortiori* and imperfect-perfect strains of the exposition, as well as the assurance and warning. If the earlier covenant came with such power and threat of judgment, *how much more* does the new covenant (cf. 2:1-4; 10:26-31). In that vein, vv. 25-29 make explicit what was implicit in vv. 18-24. At the same time, see, they are told, how the earlier covenant came, how it actually held the people at bay so that even Moses trembled in fear at the wrath of God, for the law made nothing perfect (cf. 9:6-10). The new covenant, however, has opened the way and brought them together into the assembly of those who have been made perfect. Provocatively, the categories of *entering* and *approaching*, which the writer had kept somewhat distinct to this point (see on 4:14-16) blur, and with it the already and the not yet of arrival. There must be no mistaking as to where they stand on the great *camino* that has stretched through history from Abel to the present and continues on to this goal. They stand at the foot of the mountain! What folly to turn back! What wickedness to refuse the one who has declared himself! There must be no mistaking what "o'clock" it is. It is The Day (3:13; 4:7). In truth they already stand *inside* these future things (3:14; 6:4-5; 10:29; 11:1-2). That is enough to supply what is needed for the final, difficult steps. But by having got that far they have crossed the Rubicon. Should they sin willfully in the face of what they now know, there is no longer any sacrifice for sins (10:26-27); there is no turning back (6:4-6).

This collapsing of present and future continues into the final judgment scene of vv. 25-29. This is a difficult concept, but it has its precedent in 6:4-8; cf. John 3:18; 16:11. The "removal" (12:27) concerns what is already happening with the dawn of the new covenant—it concerns the subject matter of 8:2; 9:11, 24—during which we are already *receiving* the kingdom. Yet of course it primarily concerns what will happen at the second appearance of the Son (9:27-28; 10:13). The warning: The story has an end and this is it; for those who have rejected Jesus' offering there is no longer a sacrifice for sins. The encouragement: In what follows the end, there will be no more overlap, tension, need of endurance, or even faith. It is a vision that rivals that of Rev 21-22.

## Background

The preacher's rhetoric at this juncture is after effect even more than precise definition of ideas. This leaves the possibility of a range of differing, sometimes mutually exclusive, interpretations. Chiefly, vv. 25-29 are in need of background. The constraints of this volume do not permit a full account so we will cheat by beginning with a paraphrase that gives the sense, followed by a pointer toward the sources.

Paraphrased: Any opposition to the word spoken through Moses brought severe punishment so that we may be certain that a greater judgment awaits those who oppose the word spoken in and as the Son, particularly those who already share in its blessings (2:2-3; 6:4-8; 10:19-25). The God whose word "shook" his people at the time of Moses in ways that were a parable of what was to come— touching the form but not the substance of things (9:8-14; 10:1-10)—has made clear that his final word has brought and will bring the real "shaking" from which there is no going back. This "shaking" will leave in place only that which he himself has worked in his faithfulness to his promise. What he has promised is the possession of the great inheritance, the resting place, where nothing remains that is not within the sacred space of God's temple with God's throne at its center. All that is not of his promise will be removed, permanently. All that will remain will be, as the brother Paul would say it, incorruptible and immortal (1 Cor 15:50-57). But those who are of faith are already partakers of that reality

(3:14; 11:1-2) and so can and must endure in that very faith, lest they, too, be destroyed.

To get to that interpretation, in part we must refer back to the teaching on God's speech, his promise, the resting place and inheritance, the tabernacle and cosmology—all of which were treated in 1:1-4:16. It was not for nothing that the preacher covered that ground, and he brings it to its climax in 12:18-29. It was when God put his enemies under David's feet that the time of the tabernacle's journeys would end in God's choice of a place for his name, the inheritance of the resting place centered on Mount Zion (Deut 12:8-14; 1 Kgs 5:3-5; 2 Chr 6:41). The juxtaposition of Ps 110:1 (Ps 8:4-6) and Ps 95:7-11 anticipated this convergence (cf. Ps 132:7-8, 13-14). The cleansing of the people that would qualify them for their entrance came by God's speech in and as his Son. It was conveyed to them in a word of forgiveness, the gospel. Nor will Hebrews compromise on this point, offering rites and institutions for the church on which to pin hopes. It comes as a word of promise that must be heard in obedience; it is between God and his people directly without human brokers outside of Jesus the Son.

Hebrews signals arrival at this destination both by projecting Mount Zion onto the screen (12:22-24), and by the citation of Hag 2:6, a text that foretells God's judgment of the nations as he oversees the building of the temple to replace Solomon's.[1] The language of "shaking" used by Haggai had broader associations as well, signaling the sure standing and hope of those who stood with God and who would therefore not be shaken (e.g., the LXX of Ps 15:5; 16:8; 21:7; 46:4-6; 96:9-13; 125:1; Isa 33:20; 2 Sam 22:37); "shaking" is not a metaphysical concept but one of covenantal standing. The use of Hag 2:6 in Heb 12:26-28 aligns "earth" and "heaven" with the two mountains and their covenants (12:18-24). This allows the imagery of the shaking to do double service: If the shaking of judgment in connection with Sinai was serious, how much greater will be the shaking brought with the new covenant, sifting also the household of God (cf. 10:26-31; 2:2-3; 3:6, 14; 3:16—4:1; 6:7-8). And if the shaking of Sinai was a shadow of what was to come, the shaking to come will be final, leaving only the unshakable kingdom for eternity. The "removal" of "things that are shaken"—"things that have been made"—has frequently been understood to refer to the annihilation of physical reality but is more fittingly understood as the culmination of the entire history of the present creation which was bound up with the first covenant. The whole argument to this point has pivoted not on metaphysics but covenants, and the two covenants have been identified with the pres-

---

1. The following is indebted to Lane, *Hebrews*, 2:431-91, though freely modified where I have seen fit.

ent world and the world to come. As goes the covenant and its tabernacle/temple, so goes the world. As the story of the first covenant reached its end, so did the world for which it was the center and inner basis (see 8:13). This had been anticipated by 1:10-12. As for the future of the present world as creation, the preacher's positive estimate of it as God's handiwork (contrast systems based in metaphysical dualisms), his prioritizing of covenantal history over cosmic history, his hope of resurrection, and the broader apostolic traditions in which he stands (e.g., Rom 8) favor the assumption that he foresaw not its annihilation but its cleansing and reclamation as God's holy dwelling—freed of what is not of his word, and thus of what can be shaken.

Accordingly, the important "background" for these verses is contained in the preceding exposition of Hebrews coupled with the recognition that Haggai's context is about the new temple and that the language of "shaking" has wider OT associations unrelated to metaphysical dualisms.

This is not to say that other backgrounds are not informing. In the surrounding world of the time one finds the expectation that the present world would be destroyed or would "pass away" or "depart."[2] According to 4 *Ezra* 7:31, "And after seven days the world, which is not yet awake, shall be roused, and that which is corruptible shall perish." In the NT, one can point to 1 Cor 7:31; 1 John 2:17; Rev 21:1b, though this last explains the presence of a new heaven and earth. The Stoics believed in a regular cycle of cosmic dissolution and renewal with each cycle transitioning through a conflagration. Related ideas of recurrent cycles are found in Plato (*Timaeus* 22C-E) and elsewhere, involving alternate destructions by fire and water. Closer to home, however, were strains of judgment by fire possibly taking their lead from Sodom and Gomorrah and developing into an expectation of universal judgment (Deut 32:22; Ps 97:3; Isa 30:30; 66:15-16; Mal 4:1). This particular vision of a conflagration, which is found in a number of Jewish sources (e.g., 1 QH$^a$ 3:19-36; Josephus, *A.J.* 1.70), is expressed in the NT only in 2 Pet 3:7, 10, 12, though Hebrews points in the same direction (10:27; 12:29). Of course, in each case care must be taken to understand what is meant by "pass away," "depart," "consume with fire," and the like. In 2 Pet 3 the idea may finally be that the world is exposed to the judgment of God.[3] Or again, in Isa 51:4-6 the prophet declares, "the heavens vanish like smoke, the earth will wear out like a garment, [cf. Ps 102:26 in Heb 1:12] and they who dwell in it will die in like manner; but my salvation will be forever, and my righteousness will never be dismayed." And yet it seems

---

2. For the following, see the summary in Bauckham, *Jude, 2 Peter*, 299-301.
3. Laansma, "Heaven," 111-37 [128].

clear that the prophet expects that the righteous will go on inhabiting the land and indeed will flourish in it (Isa 51:3–5, 11, 16).

## Comments on Wording

12:18–21 See Deut 4:9–14; 5:22–29; Exod 19:9–25; 20:18–21.

12:18 *you have not come to what may be touched, a blazing fire.* The point of this is not tangible mountain vs. "spiritual." The contrast is between what was functionally a "shadow," on the one hand, and the actual atonement to which it witnesses, on the other; the latter marks the conclusion of the story.

12:19 *a voice whose words.* The sensory aspect is stressed. Cf. Deut 4:12; Israel did not see God, underscoring the limits of that theophany compared to the direct access of Zion. It also hints at the warning against the faithlessness of idolatry (Deut 4:15–31; cf. 12:15–17, 29).

*made the hearers beg that no further messages be spoken to them.* This inflects their response with tones of the rebellion that their subsequent history would uncover. See v. 25.

12:20 *For they could not endure the order that was given.* They had not yet been made perfect and so lacked the freedom to draw near (9:6–10; 10:1–4).

12:21 *so terrifying was the sight that Moses said, "I tremble with fear."* Cf. Deut 9:19; the OT context raises memories of Israel's rebellion because she had not yet been perfected (cf. 8:7–13).

12:22 *But you have come to Mount Zion and to the city of the living God, the heavenly Jerusalem.* See on 2:5; 3:7—4:11; 11:10, 14–16; 13:14. See also Ps 48:8–11; 87:1–7; Isa 14:32; 28:16; 54:11–14; Ezek 48:35; Gal 4:25–26; Rev 3:12; 21:1—22:21. Again: Ps 2:6; 74:2; Isa 8:18; Joel 3:17, 21; cf. Exod 15:17.

*to innumerable angels in festal gathering.* Cf. 1:5—2:16 on angels; we have now arrived where the Son is. The word for *festal gathering* echoes Isa 66:10 (cf. 66:1–2, 7–16, 22–23) and recalls the same reality anticipated in Heb 4:9.

12:23 *to the assembly of the firstborn.* Cf. Exod 4:22–23; Jer 31:9; also Heb 2:12. The word for *firstborn* is plural, referring to all members of the church. This is the assembly of the legitimate seed of Abraham, the covenantal family of God, to whom the inheritance passes (1:2, 6; 11:28; 12:16).

*to the spirits of the righteous made perfect.* See on 12:9. The word *spirits* indicates the completeness of their having-been-perfected; cf. 2:10; 4:12–13; 9:9–10, 14, 23–24; 10:1–18, 22. This description in particular is frequently taken as a reference to the intermediate state—believers who have died and are awaiting the resurrection—on which see 11:39—12:1. The language may, however, be looking to the final state.

*to the sprinkled blood that speaks a better word than the blood of Abel.* The sprinkled blood recalls 9:11–22; 10:22. For Abel, see on 11:4. The present reference has been taken as an allusion to Abel's blood that called to God from the earth for justice (Gen 4:10; cf. Heb 10:30) which is surpassed by the blood that speaks from heaven, the latter both announcing and making atonement and/or bringing final and permanent justice. Others take it as a reference to the entire history of animal sacrifice that began with Abel's offering as a witness to the effectual blood of the Son. Alternatively, the emphasis falls on the *speaking* that was inaugurated in 11:4 with Abel's faith and brought to its conclusion in God's speech in the cleansing blood of the Son (1:1–4).

12:25 *See that you do not refuse him who is speaking. . . . warns us from heaven.* Cf. 2:2–3; 3:16–18; 10:26–31. The same verb that was used for "begging" in v. 19 is used here for "refusing," implying that the people did something more or other than show a reverent fear of God in Exod 19–20. They resisted the whole goal of God's self-revelation when, according to Heb 12:19, they effectively asked that God withhold further speech. Verse 25 is also a critical pivot and transition to vv. 26–27, indicating how the words *heaven* and *earth* are to be understood. The imagery conflates spatial (earth/heaven), temporal (past/present), and covenantal (old/new) categories; cf. Gal 4:24–26.

12:26 *At that time his voice shook the earth, but now he has promised, "Yet once more I will shake not only the earth but also the heavens."* Cf. Judg 5:4–5; Ps 68:8; 77:18; further, Isa 13:13; 29:6; Ezek 38:19–23; Joel 2:10; Rev 11:13; cf. Matt 27:51. The meaning of the phrase *the heavens* is evident from vv. 22–25: The reference is to heaven as the abode of God *as it stands for* the promised city/new covenant/people of God.

12:28 *receiving a kingdom that cannot be shaken.* Against the backdrop of Ps 96:9–13 (cf. Ps 93:1; 46:4–6; Dan 7:14, 18)—not to mention Ps 110:1—the *kingdom* idea follows naturally. The *receiving* could be purely anticipatory but probably encompasses the present reception (3:14; 6:4–5; 11:1–2). Such a conception accounts for the way the future and irrevocable judgment of v. 27 can seemingly be operative among apostates in the present (6:4–8).

*let us offer to God acceptable worship, with reverence and awe.* Cf. 11:5–7; 5:7; 13:16. This faith-service (8:5; 9:9, 14; 10:2; 13:10; cf. 9:1, 6) involves both the "horizontal" (12:11, 14; 13:16) and "vertical" (4:14–16; 10:19–25) orientations that are always coordinated. The word *acceptable* is probably not at this point an implicit critique of "OT Jewish worship"; when offered in faith, that worship, too, was acceptable (11:6). The present verse is focused on faith's movement in the present; that said, it is, of course, a celebration of the divine word's arrival at the goal that was only anticipated in the earlier epoch.

12:29 *for our God is a consuming fire.* Cf. Heb 12:18; 10:27. The citation stems from Deut 4:24 and hints at the danger of idolatry.

## Comments on Theological Themes

Unlike some Jewish and Christian traditions but like Revelation, the angelic liturgy is given due mention without becoming a focus, still less an obsession. The wonder is not that we join company with angels, as much as that contributes to the glory of the reality, but that we as the people of God are made fit to enter beyond the curtain into the unveiled presence of God.

As for the juxtaposition of the two mountains in vv. 18–24, if Hebrews' intention had been to create a set of strict contrasts, then punctuating his exhortation at 12:29 with a line straight from Sinai—God is a consuming fire (Deut 4:24; 9:3)—ruins the effect. But this was not his intention, and likewise the assertion that they have not approached a mountain that can be *touched* (or seen, or heard) is not firstly a statement about Mount Zion being "spiritual" and thus immaterial. This detail is yet another way of underscoring that what lies before them in Mount Zion is not merely the shadow and pattern of the heavenly inheritance (cf. Heb 9:8–14), merely that which touches externals only, but the inheritance itself, the ultimate content of what was promised. What is before them in the Son is not the "sight" (v. 21) that points toward the goal and that bristles with testimony to its own incompleteness, but the Son himself and his great salvation. As to tangibility, at most v. 18 is indicating that Mount Zion cannot *yet* be touched, just as it cannot yet be seen; it lies beyond the present creation (2:5; 6:19).

Strictly neither Exodus nor Deuteronomy records the request attributed to the people in 12:19, but they did request that God not speak to them directly (Exod 20:18–20; Deut 5:24–27). At a pinch Hebrews' line could be characterized as a loose paraphrase of Deut 5:25 but it is loose to the point of altering the sense. In Deuteronomy their request is for a mediator. In Hebrews it is the request that God would stop speaking. In the original context the request seems to be an appropriate response of the people to the command of God given in Exod 19:20–25; cf. Exod 20:20–21; Deut 5:28–31. The idea that Hebrews has in mind is illuminated by the repetition of the allusion in the repetition of the verb *paraiteomai* in Heb 12:25. The implication is that Israel's was not a simple request but in its upshot something more like a refusal and resistance (cf. Acts 7:51). It would appear that Hebrews is compressing into Exod 19–20 the subsequent history of disobedience. It is superficially reading against the grain of Exod 19–20 but actually illuminating its true meaning. This, in turn, would imply that God's command in Exod 19:20–25 was itself a sign that the people had not been perfected and would not be perfected through that law (on analogy to Heb 9:8–10). This is what v. 20 goes on to clarify.

Looking back over vv. 25–29, a definitive conclusion to be drawn from this text is that history will not be cyclical. There is to be an end to the present history with its world-order and a new beginning that consists *only* of what is now a matter of faith. Here is in part the basis of the Christian hope that the age to come will be an age of eternal sinlessness and only eternal righteousness without the possibility of a reversal.

Finally, the claims made here demand an accounting of *who* it is that effects such a great salvation. Who possesses such authority and power? Such claims will not hang in the air. See on 1:1–4.

## Teaching Hebrews 12:18–29

1. Heb 12:18–21 does not cast the law in the role of a villain. The emphasis is on the positive, that toward which the law was always straining. What Hebrews is doing in vv. 18–21 is helping us to see how the law was preparing for what was to come. The accent of vv. 22–24 is placed on the celebration that *it has now come*.

2. Verses 18–24 are encouragement and warning, description and imperative. Authentic children own their identity and run the race with endurance. Jesus does not sit by our bedside and commiserate. He heals us and tells us to *walk* (12:1–17). We who inhabit the blessings of the last days are all the more clearly under threat of disaster in turning away, as 12:25–29 makes explicit.

3. In reaction to escapist ideas that have drifted away from the implications of faith for the promotion of justice and peace many moderns have become allergic to speaking of "heaven" and future salvation. Nevertheless, a sound faith requires conforming our own hope to Hebrews' vision. Understood in context this hope of heaven will fuel the promotion of justice in the present.

4. The difficult story of this world has an ending. It will not continue forever as it is at present, nor will it fall back into the past's cycles, nor will it fizzle into nothing. Both for a world that believes it has discovered the loneliness and the coldness of the physical universe and concluded

that this is all there is, and for all those occupied by the ceaseless hardships of their personal existence, this illusion of a story without a plot, endlessly cycling through the same patterns of death and renewal like a burned over grassland, needs to be and is shattered by the announcement of God's promise.

5. We must live a life that participates in what will last (3:14; 11:1-2). Though Hebrews does not parse out the removal of what is being shaken (e.g., 1 Cor 3:10-15), in keeping with everything said it is Christ alone and his great salvation that "remains" forever. All that is not participant in him therefore will not participate in the unshakable kingdom that remains. We are commanded to stake our lives on the promise by faith (10:32—12:3), to own our identity as new covenant children, actively submitting to God's discipline so that we might live and share in his holiness (12:4-17).

6. Perhaps in *carpe diem* defiance of the soulless death that seems to stalk the universe, perhaps in reaction to fear-mongering preaching, the command to "fear" has gone by the boards. Yet the gospel tells us that *our God is a consuming fire*. It is understood that it is the throne of this God that we are commanded to approach as the throne *of grace*. The fear of which Hebrews speaks is that which knows that a command is required if one is to dare an approach, that the command has been given, that faith must take hold of the word of forgiveness and obey, and that disobedience will not escape the wrath of the king. In that spirit alone it runs, it does not walk, to the throne of holy grace.

# 13:1–17

> "I do not ask that you take them out of the world, but that you keep them from the evil one. They are not of the world, just as I am not of the world. Sanctify them in the truth; your word is truth. As you sent me into the world, so I have sent them into the world. And for their sake I consecrate myself, that they also may be sanctified in truth."

## Context

THE WRITER'S EXPOSITIONAL EFFORT has rounded out with the thunderous conclusion of 12:18–29, taking us back to where things began in 1:1–4.[1] But the sermon is not over. 13:1–17 forms its peroration, a movement distinct from but continuous with the effort of what preceded.[2] Verses 18–25 contain the more typical closing features of a letter but also a benediction that closes both sermon and letter (vv. 20–21). Genre and structure were not straightjackets.

Internally, 13:1–17 outlines like so:

13:1–6 Specific applications on conventional topics

13:7–17 Restatement of the call to perseverance in connection with an endorsement of the church's leaders

  13:7 Recall the message of the former leaders

---

1. A compact listing of alternative theories of Hebrews' structure at this juncture is given with bibliography by Cockerill, *Epistle to the Hebrews*, 673–75.

2. Koester, *Hebrews*, 554–56, though he sets the peroration's boundaries at 12:28—13:21.

13:8 Recall who Jesus Christ is

13:9-14 Follow Jesus outside the gates

13:15-16 Render worship corresponding to faith

13:17 Submit to your leaders who share in your pilgrimage with special responsibilities

Verses 1-6 begin (v. 1, *philadelphia, sibling love*) and end (vv. 5-6, *aphilargyros, not loving money*) with love, a nod toward the Christian virtue. The admonitions of vv. 1-3 concern themselves with what upholds sibling love, and those of vv. 4-6 with what violates it.[3]

Why the writer bookends the summary of the discourse with the past (v. 7) and present (v. 17) leaders is not obvious. It is not necessarily the case that there would be comments *about* the leaders only if the congregation had been estranged from them, and we might have expected more hints of estrangement if that was a major issue. As likely, these verses betray the preacher's conviction that the fellowship he has been commending (3:13; 10:25) involves strong leadership. Further, he probably does mean to align his teachings with the church's leaders and they with it.

In this closing movement the telling of the story—one that has swept the readers *up* from their mean Roman streets to the Way of God on pilgrimage to the heavenly Jerusalem—now lands them back on their streets. It also forms a second closing crescendo. It is a new tapestry of the sermon's themes with fresh allusions to the OT; it raises to a new level the preacher's willingness to mash cultic images, bend figures, and work surprising twists on his argument. In vv. 15-16 we have the equivalent of Ps 150's trumpets and resounding cymbals. It is a fitting celebration for a pilgrim people standing at the gates of the heavenly city.

## Background

13:1-6 if not most of 13:1-19 is typical parenesis. Parenesis is a sometimes loosely strung series of familiar moral admonitions that bear on general expectations for conduct—they are not necessarily correcting specific shortcomings among those addressed—but which may also speak to the particular circumstances of the audience and the themes of the discourse in question.[4] Parenesis as such is not original to the NT but it was adapted by

---

3. Cockerill, *Epistle to the Hebrews*, 678.

4. Lane, *Hebrews*, 2:498-500, who also discusses "catechetical precept" as a literary form that accounts for 13:1-19.

NT writers (e.g., Rom 12:1—15:13) and frequently centered on the household (e.g., much of Eph 4–6; Col 3:1—4:6). By employing this genre the writer can in just a few words sketch in more concretely the form of life that is consistent with the gospel.

Hospitality (13:1-2) was a widely held value in the Mediterranean world, with a long tradition in Judaism (e.g., Gen 4:14; 18:1—19:29; 24:31-67; 29:13-14; Josh 2:1; Judg 6:11-18; 13:3-22; 19:1-30; 1 Kgs 17:7-24; 2 Kgs 4:8-37; Luke 16:4; cf. Homer, *Odyssey* 6.207-8). Inns (Luke 10:34), where available, were generally not a satisfying option.[5] Within Christianity hospitality became an essential way in which the mission of the church was supported, there being no dedicated buildings for their meetings and so much of the work being carried out by itinerants.[6] The exhortation of 13:2 probably has in mind especially the hospitality to be shown to traveling Christians, though the allusion to Gen 18 would suggest a broader practice.

For imprisonment, see on 10:32-29.

Verses 9–10 probably reveal little of specific misbehaviors in this church. They are ways of getting at the earlier admonitions (hold fast to the confession; approach the throne; eat the solid food; participate in the heavenly realities), in line with 1:1—12:29, as well as a transition to the argument of vv. 11–14.[7]

## Comments on Wording

13:3 *as though in prison with them* etc. Cf. Matt 7:12. Imitate your high priest (4:15; 2:14-18). This also involves some risk; see on 10:32-39.

13:5 *I will never leave you nor forsake you.* cf. Deut 31:6, 8 (1 Chr 28:20; cf. Gen 28:15; Josh 1:5). This is a promise made to people journeying to what was promised; it corresponds to the pilgrimage imagery of the earlier chapters (see on 3:7—4:11; 12:4-17).

13:6 *"The Lord is my helper* [cf. Heb 2:18; 4:16], *I will not fear* [cf. Heb 2:15; 11:23, 27]. *What can man do to me?"* Cf. Matt 10:28. The community responds to the words of God in v. 5 through the words of Ps 118:6, words sung by those in the festal pilgrimage to the temple.

13:7 *Consider the outcome of their way of life, and imitate their faith.* These leaders would appear to be the founders of the church, possibly

---

5. Rapske, "Acts, Travel and Shipwreck," 1-47 [15], noting as well other options for lodging.

6. Lane, *Hebrews*, 2:512-13; Riddle, "Early Christian Hospitality," 141-54; Arterbury, *Entertaining Angels*.

7. See Attridge, *Hebrews*, 394-96, for a survey and critique of the various theories.

those to whom reference was made in 2:3. They have apparently died by this time. The *outcome* must refer to the consistency, endurance, and fruit of their lives of faith in line with the examples of 11:1–40 rather than to martyrdom (cf. 12:4).

13:8 *Jesus Christ is the same yesterday and today and forever.* Cf. 1:12. This formulation sums up the content of the former leaders' faith (thinking of 1:1—12:29) and is the basis for the argument that the present readers can have the same confidence. In relation to what follows it is a call not to depart from what they had been taught.

13:9 *Do not be led away by diverse and strange teachings.* A teaching is *strange* relative to the stable center of v. 8 from which there may be a departure in any direction. No doubt there were many versions of the Christian faith floating around, tending either more toward the temple or toward some Roman philosophy or religion (e.g., Galatians; Col 2:6–23; 1 Tim 5:20–21; Jude). Stick to the confession as in 1:1—12:29 and as summarized afresh in 13:9b–14.

*It is good for the heart to be strengthened by grace* etc. Rather than be drawn from the straight path, move forward on the Way. Given the difficulties of that Way of obedience, *real* strength is needed. For *grace* see the introduction to this commentary; also 2:9; 4:14–16. The accent falls on the implied exhortation—Be strengthened by grace!—with the alternative of foods serving as a transition to the further argument of v. 10.

13:10 *We have an altar from which those who serve the tent have no right to eat.* Lev 7:5–6; Num 18:9–10. The idea of participating fully in grace is further developed through a new cultic image. In fact, the priests and worshippers did not eat any of the Day of Atonement offering (Lev 6:30)—to which v. 11 turns—but here as elsewhere (9:11–28) Hebrews is conflating different rituals which in various ways witnessed to the person and work of Christ. The metaphor of eating has already featured in the exposition (5:13; 6:5) and these earlier passages likely give the intended sense here. The principle of 1 Cor 10:18 (cf. 9:13) is presumably not wedded to the point Paul is making about the Eucharist and can inform Hebrews' argument. Thus Hebrews' desire is to draw them almost palpably into the sacrificial imagery to follow in vv. 11–12.

13:11 *For the bodies*[8] *of those animals whose blood is brought into the holy places by the high priest as a sacrifice for sin are burned outside the camp.* Cf. Lev 16:27 and the Day of Atonement. Though rhetorically it reads as if the OT ritual's pattern is controlling (v. 12 begins, *and so*), logically the

---

8. The reference to *bodies*, which departs from Leviticus's wording, takes us back to Heb 10:5–10; cf. 11:26; 12:1–3.

emphasis on this point about the bodies derives from the pattern of *Jesus' offering*, which was *outside the city gate*. In the light of Jesus' history, the law was once again quietly attesting its inadequacy by its own structure (cf. 9:6–10; see further below).

13:12 *So Jesus also suffered outside the gate in order to sanctify the people through his own blood.* Cf. 2:11; 9:1—10:18, 19, 29. In effect, the Most Holy Place has moved to Golgotha.

13:14 *For here we have no lasting city, but we seek the city that is to come.* Cf. 2:5; 3:7—4:11; 10:1; 11:8, 10, 13–16; 12:22–24, 27–28. The present wording is a restatement of these same ideas.

13:15 *Through him then let us continually offer up a sacrifice of praise to God.* Lev 7:11–18; 2 Chr 29:31; Ps 27:6; 44:8; 54:6; 50:14, 23; 107:22; 116:17; Isa 57:19; Hos 14:2. This wording recalls 12:28 and represents the swelling worshipful climax of the long pilgrimage of Abraham's seed. What is happening in this act of worship is the reality of 10:19–25; 12:22–24, 28.

13:16 *for such sacrifices are pleasing to God.* Cf. 5:11–14; 6:10–11; 10:24–25, 32–39; 12:11, 14; 13:1–6. The vertically oriented approach to the throne (v. 15) is coordinated with horizontally oriented fellowship (v. 16; cf. vv. 1–3), just as the whole covenantal world of Israel governing every aspect of life together found its center in the tabernacle.

13:17 *Let them do this with joy and not with groaning, for that would be of no advantage to you.* The Greek sentence phrases this as a purpose clause : *Obey your leaders . . . in order that they might do this* [= watch over your souls] *with joy.* 2 Cor 2:2; 1 Pet 5:1–4. The final words of this verse are an understatement as an endorsement of the leaders (they *are* providing sound leadership) and warning to the readers (to buck their leaders is to risk the judgment against which this entire discourse has warned; e.g., 2:1–4; 6:4–8; etc.).

## Comments on Theological Themes

The language of *grace* and *food* in 13:9 is finding a new way to urge these believers forward in grace. The heart being strengthened is a matter of faith taking hold of the promise, recognizing that what went before was a pointer and of no value in the removal of sin (10:1–4). The reference to "foods" does not need to be to "ceremonial foods" but can be as broad as Esau's meal (12:16)—the seeking of security in anything other than the promise—while making primary reference to the priests' and worshippers' share in the offerings (v. 10). The idea of being *strengthened, established* (3:14; 6:19), may echo 12:28.

In 13:10 the positive affirmation is the key: Just as we *have* a high priest (8:1–2; 10:21) so we *have* an altar.[9] An implied polemic against *those who serve the tent* would be an uncharacteristic triumphalism and vv. 11–14 suggest that the writer is once again marking out the *principle* of the full break between Moses and Christ (7:12, 18; 10:9), the exclusivity of the way of Christ, and the full membership in God's covenantal household granted to those of faith (see on 12:4–17). The triumphalism that is expressed is of a different cast: We have the grace given in the Son as priest and sacrifice. We have been granted the full privileges of God's covenantal children, the very thing on which all Israel's hopes had been bent. We—not even the sons of Aaron as such—*may* eat, and may eat of *this* altar. Make full use of those privileges so that you can finish the race (12:12–13). There is also the implied warning that to fail to do so is to forfeit everything.

The place outside the camp (13:11) was where the unclean were to be sent (e.g., Lev 13:46), where criminals were executed and where the leftovers of sacrifices were burned (Lev 16:27; cf. 4:12; 24:14, 23; Num 15:35–36; 1 Kgs 21:13)—for Hebrews it is the place of Christ's disgrace. This is seemingly Hebrews' allusion to the scandal of the cross and the curse of the law. It is also a correlation of Christ with the patterns that stretches the discontinuities almost to the breaking point: The new and old sacrifices are associated and correlated but only by locating Christ's offering where the Levitical offerings were disposed of. By this twist it succeeds in simultaneously signaling the covenantal move from the earthly to the heavenly Jerusalem (from which and for which the earthly had served), and the way in which the holiness of God broke free of the confines of the Most Holy Place to sanctify the people at large.

The writer lets this pregnant image of 13:12—the move from temple to Golgotha—do its own work. The Most Holy Place is the place where heaven and earth intersect. The place of slaughter is the place of the heavenly throne, the place the Christian is to approach, treading the same path of suffering that the Son blazed for them, approaching the throne of grace and mercy where he sits waiting for his enemies to be made a footstool for his feet. The earthly Jerusalem has played its part and been left behind. The holiness of God has broken out of its precincts, invaded the sphere of the profane, and has begun to sanctify the people at large. They are therefore to "leave Jerusalem" with him; *a fortiori*, they leave every earthly city, for here, like the Patriarchs, they have no lasting city. Moreover, his suffering outside

---

9. Both v. 9b and v. 10 lead with the positive, which is the writer's point: Be strengthened by grace! We have an altar! Some believe that the altar is a reference to the Christian Eucharist, but the writer's attention is on that to which the Eucharist points rather than the Eucharist directly.

the gate had a purpose: *to make the people holy*. So going out to him will share in the same purpose. It will be missional.

With 13:13 we are then commanded to follow Jesus out of the city to the place of the cross outside the gates. This call is not code, however, for a departure from Judaism, or the city of Jerusalem (e.g., because it is about to be overthrown), or, dualistically, the world of sense. This is a call to participate bodily in the movement of the Son's own obedience (12:1–3; cf. 11:26; 2:5–18; 5:7–10). Suddenly the direction of movement established throughout the book—oriented inward toward the heavenly throne (except 10:5)—is reversed: *go out* (cf. 11:8, 27). This marks a movement *forward* in history with God from his earlier speech through the prophets to his final word in and as the Son (1:1–2) in single-minded obedience. It is a movement *socially* in the willingness to live as a stranger in tents (11:9); to endure all insecurities to be suffered on that Way; to share in the opposition of sinners to the Son. It is also *missional* in sharing the purpose of the Son, namely, to sanctify the people (13:12), which is to do the will of God upon entering the world (10:5–10; cf. 10:36).

As a restatement of earlier affirmations 13:14 involves not just an urban image but the move from old covenant *Jerusalem* with its temple (Moses) to Mount Zion (Christ and new covenant) (12:18–29). On its face it stands in contradiction to the OT declarations of the permanence of Jerusalem (2 Chr 6:2; 33:4; Ps 48:8; 125:1–2; 132:1–18) but that tension is a summons to understand. This is a statement firstly about the covenantal history of the divine word toward its destination in the inheritance of the Son. But, as we saw with 12:25–29, because the tabernacle was the center of the world as goes Jerusalem so goes the world. If it is to be said of Jerusalem, *here we have no lasting city*, then *all the more* is this statement true of Rome and any other city, large or small, central or remote.

## Teaching Hebrews 13:1–17

For teaching on the leaders (vv. 7, 17) and on vv. 8–14, see what has already been said.

1. The OT allusions connected to angels in v. 2—particularly Gen 18-19—suggest that the visitation of angels was of no importance in itself but due to their divinely assigned role in the administration of God's purposes (Heb 1:7, 14). To receive angels, therefore, would be for faith to follow the leading of the divine word, in keeping with the whole thrust of 11:1–40. The expectation is of literal angelic visitations but

it is not a matter of showing hospitality to strangers in the hope of "winning the angelic lottery." It is a recognition of the way of God in and through "strangers." Cf. Matt 25:40, 45.

2. Regarding the typical pairing of sins involving sex and money (13:4–6), see Lev 19–20; Deut 5:18–19; also, e.g., 1 Cor 5:11; Eph 5:3–5. In sins of sex and greed people are not the object of love (13:1) but the means by which one attains his or her own desires. The argument of 13:4 is not that marriage is a particularly honored office—the unmarried are equally honored (see 1 Cor 7)—but that the institution and all marriage unions are to be protected, upheld, and supported not only by those who are married but all others in the community. The biblical conceptions of sex and marriage are owed firstly to the covenant with God which was the ordering center of Israel's and then the church's history. It is less a law of nature the violation of which carries its own punishment (Rom 1:24–27 follows from the fact that creation serves covenant) than it is a bond that depends on human obedience to the divine command, a command that is contextualized in and by the history of the covenant with God. Arguments for alternative sexual practices that are drawn from nature, genetics, social conditioning, and the like do not touch the heart of things. Because Christ and his church are one man and one woman, so is Christian marriage.

3. The range of NT teachings connected to wealth lurk behind vv. 5–6, but none of these exist as abstract principles; they are matters of personal and communal judgments to be made on the Way. In 13:6 the pilgrims, confessing that they have undergone severe chastening (Ps 118:18; Heb 12:4–11), enter the gates of the temple (Ps 118:19) and call others into the festal procession as it approaches the altar itself (Ps 118:27; cf. Heb 12:22–24). In what the faithful choose not to pursue, what they are willing to lose (Heb 10:32–34; 11:24–27, 35b–38), and what they freely share on that Way they seek their salvation solely in the Lord (5:7–10; 12:1–3), for here they have no abiding city but they seek the city that is coming (13:14). In a global economy there are new and unavoidable implications for obedience. In weighing responsibilities and the way of righteousness, it is instructive to observe the balancing perspectives of the wisdom (e.g., Prov 10:4–5; 12:11; 19:24) and legal (e.g., Lev 25:1–55) traditions of Israel, underscoring both responsibility for one's own situation and grace toward those who have ruined themselves or who have been ruined by others.

4. Though people of the gospel's faith frequently find that they are not wanted where they are (11:23–38), the gospel has not taught them to

abandon their cities in the sense of leaving them to their doom while pursuing a private or sectarian salvation. Christians are caught up in the gospel, and thus in God's mission *to* their neighbors and cities. Yet, in that same movement but on a different plane, the gospel has called them *from* their cities and homes, as was Abraham, on a pilgrimage to the city that is promised them. Their identity, in God's unrelenting mission, is that of a people that has here no abiding city, but that *seeks* the city that is coming. If they "have" here no abiding city, then, a fortiori, they can "have" (in the same sense) none of the political parties of those cities. To "seek" is not to pause to contemplate a future epoch of bliss, icing on the cake of a life lived on different terms, terms determined by what is seen *now*, what is the case *here*. If it is to be the faith that pleases God it must be a seeking that forms its present life, aspirations, and efforts to the promise—before it adopts, as it must, an economic plan or political platform. It refuses the illusion that God is silent and inactive now, and that we are left to ourselves to sort out the planet and our own lives this side of glory.

5. The sacrifices of praise (13:15) are the "real" (not merely "spiritual-metaphorical") sacrifices that were always waiting to be revealed in the Son, of which all the bulls and goats where shadows and patterns. They do *not* lack participation in a tangible and bodily offering; they participate in the bodily offering of the Son apart from which they are nothing; the phrase *through Jesus* needs to be given full weight as a summary of 4:14—10:25 (cf. 7:25). Moreover, in the Son—exclusively—God's true *name* is *professed* and praised. The OT sacrifices were offered perpetually because they were ineffective; these sacrifices of praise are offered perpetually because Christ's offering was effective.[10]

6. Life itself flows unidirectionally from the center of worship outward to service (13:15–16). Just as 13:13 already recalled 10:5–10, so 13:16's association of *sacrifice* and God's *pleasure* (11:5; 10:38; 12:28) all the more clearly joins their acts of obedience with the Son's bodily and *missional* self-offering in 10:5–10 (cf. 10:5–6, 8). The idea of Rom 12:1–2 is not far away.

---

10. Cockerill, *Epistle to the Hebrews*, 705.

## 13:18–25

*"I have said these things to you, that in me
you may have peace.
In the world you will have tribulation.
But take heart;
I have overcome the world."*

### Context

SEE 13:1–17. THE LETTER's closing falls out like so:

The letter's and the sermon's end are combined in these verses. The thought of vv. 18–19 might fall between the mention of their leaders (v. 17) and their great Shepherd (v. 20; cf. Matt 2:6) because the writer's heart is set on the care of this congregation. Nestled within these closing materials the benediction of vv. 20–21 serves for both the sermon and the letter. Even if the benediction was lifted from a liturgy the writer must have seen a thematic fittingness in its imagery. The elephant in the room of the entire book has been the wider mission of the church,[1] and it becomes more audible in the mention of those on the frontiers of the growth of the word, (vv. 18–19, 23), the unity of the recipients with the church in other regions (v. 24), and their investment in doing the will of God (v. 21; cf. 10:5–10).

The benediction (vv. 20–21) finds its force as much in the poetic association of ideas as in their logical arrangement. At its core it is the wish that God will equip them for the doing of his will; thereby he will be doing among them what is pleasing before him through Jesus Christ. The power and authority of God to do this as well as the character and goal of his work is what v. 20 indicates. It is the way in which the language of both verses lodges the blessing in a history-spanning drama of this God, his Son, and

---

1. Laansma, "Hebrews and the Mission," 330.

his family that both limits and frees our understanding: Limits it because this God and his will are known, and he is faithful, not capricious. Frees it because there are so many possible associations that are faithful to the benediction's language, and we are invited to embrace all of them as we move ahead in the drama itself.

## Background

The writer had a personal history with this church (vv. 18–19, 23–24), whether or not he had been or currently is a "regular member." The signals are mixed as to whether he had been one of their leaders. We might fairly guess that what has separated or kept him from them (v. 19) has something to do with controversy surrounding his teaching (whether it had to do with other church leaders, Jewish authorities, or Roman law). His reputation may have been placed in doubt, though this is not the only reason he might have penned v. 18. Taking together vv. 19 and 23, he is optimistic about visiting them soon. The Timothy mentioned in v. 23 is widely taken to be Paul's co-worker. Assuming this allows us to infer direct contacts with the Pauline mission and gospel. The allusion suggests Timothy has been imprisoned, but nothing more is known of the circumstances; v. 23 suggests that Timothy's situation is separate from whatever is detaining the author. Taking the apparent circumstances of the writer and Timothy together with other hints (10:32–24; 13:3; cf. 11:23–27) we may conclude that even if members of this church have not yet suffered martyrdom the wolves have been nipping at their heals.

It is likely (not certain) that the author is writing to a church in Italy, which may (possibly) be a specific house church (v. 24). If in fact this is a particular house church then we may imagine a group of at most 50 to 100 people but probably somewhat fewer.[2]

## Comments on Wording

13:18–19 *Pray for us* etc. The prayers are probably focused on the circumstances that are detaining the writer; the wording of *clear conscience* and *act honorably* (cf. 13:7) might suggest that he is viewing his own circumstances through the lens of the sermon's summons to approach the throne of grace and live in fellowship in a way pleasing to God (9:11–14; 12:28; 13:16). What is detaining him could involve, among other possibilities, work or

---

2. Blue, "Acts and the House Church," 119–222 [143, 175].

controversy with other churches or opposition from unbelievers. These verses reassure the church of his bond with them, invite them to share in his work (cf. v. 16), and indirectly commend his example.

13:20 *the God of peace*. Rom 15:33; 16:20; 1 Cor 14:33; 2 Cor 13:11; Phil 4:9; 1 Thess 5:23; 2 Thess 3:16.

13:21 *equip you with everything good that you may do his will* etc. In effect, the prayer is that God will enrich them with all the blessings of the new covenant (8:10–12). The connection between the two parts is in the verb for *doing*: God equips us for the *doing* of his will, God thereby *doing* (*work in us*) what is pleasing to him. The accent falls on divine initiative and the provision that is to be sought in prayer, the fruit of which is willing obedience.

*to whom be glory forever and ever*. This doxology is probably directed to Jesus, treating him as God, though it could refer back to God in v. 20. The ambiguity may reflect a lack of concern to assign it to only one or the other.

13:22 *bear with my word of exhortation*. Among the things the audience has to endure on the way of faith is this letter. The phrase *word of exhortation* in Acts 13:15 (cf. 1 Pet 5:12; Rom 15:4; 1 Tim 4:13; 1 Macc 10:24; 2 Macc 15:8–11) may have been a recognized expression for an edifying exposition of the Scriptures.[3] On brevity, see 5:11; 9:5; 11:32. There is no compelling reason to suppose that the writer is referring to a letter other than the present one.

13:24 *Greet all your leaders and all the saints*. See on 13:7, 17.

*Those who come from Italy send you greetings*. This phrasing could conceivably indicate that the writer is in Italy and sending greetings of those with him to the recipients in another region, or (more likely) that some from Italy are with him outside of Italy and are sending their greetings to the recipients wherever they are.

## Comments on Theological Themes

The *eternal covenant* of 13:20 is probably an *ad hoc* formulation that is firstly forward-looking (5:9; 9:12, 14, 15) but that assumes the history-spanning perspective of Hebrews' argument as a whole (13:8) which unifies around the one promise of God. It echoes the OT uses of the phrase "everlasting covenant" (e.g., Isa 55:3; 61:8; Jer 32:40; 50:5; Ezek 16:60; 37:26) though it is difficult to pin it exclusively to any one of them. Ezek 37:15–28 is particularly suggestive, however, with its references to the "one shepherd" (cf. Ezek 34:1–31; Jer 50:5–6) and the "everlasting covenant," its strong link

---

3. Cf. Griffiths, *Divine Speech*, 16–21; though Koester, *Hebrews*, 80–82, is properly reserved about how much we know about "sermons" in antiquity.

with resurrection (Ezek 37:1-14), and the associations of the resting place, temple, and family of God themes. Together with the other OT texts it represents the end of the movement of God's work.

The same verse makes the first explicit reference to the bodily resurrection of Jesus. Resurrection as such has been mentioned only a few times (6:2; 11:19, 35) but has been an active ingredient in the argument throughout, both in connection with Jesus (e.g., 5:7-10; 12:1-3) and as the hope of believers (e.g., 2:14-15). The phrasing used here (*brought, led* [*agō*]) verbally recalls 2:10 (cf. 8:9). By using the language of *leading* (vs. "raising") the writer intends the pilgrimage idea of the letter and the promise of the Lord to lead them to salvation, just as he did in the exodus and the return from exile.

With the *great Shepherd* (1 Pet 2:25; 5:4; Mark 6:34; Matt 2:6; 26:31; John 10:11, 14; Isa 53:6; 2 Chr 18:16; Mic 5:2-4; Zech 10:2; 11:4-17; 13:7) another new phrase is employed. One thinks of Moses (cf. Isa 63:11-14 and context; Num 27:17) and David (2 Sam 5:2), but also especially of Ezek 34, 37 (see above). God himself is Israel's Shepherd (Gen 48:15; 49:24; Ps 23:1; Isa 40:11), an almost certain implication being that Jesus is *that* Shepherd. Why would Hebrews use this designation for Jesus at this late point? Even if it is taken over from a traditional formulation it 1) recalls the royal imagery that has been laced through Hebrews (e.g., 1:3, 5, 8-9, 13; 2:7, 9; 7:2; 12:28); 2) picks up on the contextual imagery of Ezek 37 which is part of the "eternal covenant" allusion; 3) in effect, having already endorsed their current leaders in v. 17, commends the congregation into the immediate care of their Lord; and 4) provides yet further solace for a congregation by reminding them that the one who is their Shepherd himself succumbed to the suffering of death (2:17-18; 5:7-10) but now and forever "always lives" (7:25).

The reference to God's *will* in v. 21 (10:5-10, 36) is at one with what he did in leading out of the dead our Shepherd, why he did it, where he led him; likewise it is at one with his peace. Doing what is *pleasing* to him recalls not merely faith (11:5-6) but the missional example of the Son; there is more than one verbal link with 10:5-7. Those who follow the Son's example (2:10; 12:1-3) worship God acceptably (12:28), doing good and sharing, "for such sacrifices are pleasing to God" (13:16). They *go to him outside the camp and bear the reproach he endured*; see also on 13:15-16 and the association of that passage with Rom 12:1-2. That all of this is *through Jesus Christ* is not pious ornamentation but shows *how* God works in us and also *what* is pleasing.

## Teaching Hebrews 13:18–25

1. The theme of mission that we detected in these verses can be drawn to the surface. In the complementarity of gifts and roles within local fellowships and the shared identity across regions, the church is united as the *sent* church.[4] It is in this spirit that the lines of 13:18–19, 23–24 are written.

2. Verses 20–21 are rich in potential biblical associations. The best approach is to work with the grain of the preceding sermon's main themes.

3. By way of another possible perspective: Recent efforts in North American Christianity have been to prove—social media is where it is made real—that Christians can drink, cuss, sex it up, and hop activist bandwagons with the best of them. Some of this has been a necessary shedding of the now-moribund forms that a Christian subculture had taken in earlier years. The same wisdom that had adopted those forms for their time must advance to retranslate the gospel afresh for a new situation. The word moves on in this way too, always living and active. In some cases, however, such changes may represent the very loss of vision and faith that Hebrews moved to correct in its own time. In any event, whatever the merits, moves toward cultural assimilation are always relatively easy. Hebrews' call as summarized in this benediction is something else.

4. Again, all of v. 20 serves to indicate the power and authority of God to equip us, the way in which he does this, and its goal. The God who is the creator and source of peace (3:7—4:11; 7:2; cf. 12:11, 14), wholeness, security, fellowship, confidence (4:14–16; 6:13–20; 10:19–25), unshakability; the one who provides and promises these things for his people—all these things as seen in the history of Israel and now accomplished in the powerful leading out of Jesus Christ from the hitherto unbreakable bondage of death (2:14–15) and the establishing of that one as our Shepherd (Ps 23)—it is the God who represents and accomplishes these things who also equips us to be swept along in them unto salvation.

5. If we are looking for models of "biblical preaching," Hebrews likely affords us one example (13:22). There will have been other patterns and the one who composed this sparkling example of rhetoric will have

---

4. I am indebted to personal communication with Rev. Dr. David Zac Niringiye (Spring 2004) for his emphasis on this characterization.

favored substance over form in doing what he exhorted this church to do (3:13; 5:11–14; 10:25). Still, the pastoral passion and oratorical polish of Hebrews are a standing challenge for all who teach and preach.

6. The writer thinks of his letter as short (13:22) and manageable (5:11–6:12). Most readers ever since have found it a challenge and difficult. Yet even as their particular Christian world is crumbling around them many will rebuff calls to revisit their confession and to rethink all things from the ground up, preferring to repeat the same prooftexts and trust in their by-now instinctive grasp of what is true and right. Hebrews is a standing challenge to that mindset. The same gospel that can be grasped by a child is not nursery games after all (5:11–14). Hebrews, as the canonical voice of the Lord, has always stood in the midst of the church calling us to move "further up, further in," to grow up and grow strong in our identity as the seed of Abraham. We stand now in a place more dangerous than the children of Israel ever did, though she was confronted by the Nephilim, but a place more sure and with better promises.

7. The custom of sending greetings from one church to another merits attention. We need to realize in concrete ways our fellowship with the church in other parts of the world, deepening the realization of how interdependent we are and how through this fellowship the Lord provides the blessing of vv. 20–21.

# Bibliography

Allen, David M. *Deuteronomy and Exhortation in Hebrews: A Study in Narrative Representation*. WUNT II.238. Tübigen: Mohr Siebeck 2008.
Allen, Michael. "The Perfect Priest: Calvin on the Christ of Hebrews." In *Christology, Hermeneutics, and Hebrews: Profiles from the History of Interpretation*, edited by Jon C. Laansma and Daniel J. Treier, 120–34. LNTS. New York: Bloomsbury, 2012.
Arnold, Clinton E. "'I am Astonished That You Are So Quickly Turning Away!' (Gal. 1.6): Paul and Anatolian Folk Belief." *NTS* 51.3 (2005) 429–49.
Arterbury, Andrew. *Entertaining Angels: Early Christian Hospitality in its Mediterranean Setting*. New Testament Monographs 8. Sheffield: Sheffield Phoenix, 2005.
Atkinson, Rick. *The Guns at Last Light*. New York: Henry Holt, 2013.
Attridge, Harold W. "Epilogue." In *Reading the Epistle to the Hebrews: A Resource for Students*, edited by Eric F. Mason and Kevin B. McCrudem, 297–308. SBLRBS 66. Atlanta: SBL, 2011.
———. "God in Hebrews." In *The Epistle to the Hebrews and Christian Theology*, edited by Richard Bauckham, et al., 95–110. Grand Rapids: Eerdmans, 2009.
———. *Hebrews*. Hermeneia. Philadelphia: Fortress, 1989.
———. "Hebrews and the History of Its Interpretation: A Biblical Scholar's Response." In *Christology, Hermeneutics, and Hebrews: Profiles from the History of Interpretation*, edited by Jon Laansma and Daniel J. Treier, 202–12. London: T. & T. Clark, 2012.
———. "The Use of Antithesis in Hebrews 8–10." In *Christians Among Jews and Gentiles: Essays in Honor of Krister Stendhal on His 65th Birthday*, edited by George W. E. Nickelsburg and George W. MacRae, 1–9. Philadelphia: Fortress, 1986.
Barclay, John M. G. *Paul and the Gift*. Grand Rapids: Eerdmans, 2015.
Barth, Karl. *Church Dogmatics*. IV/1: *The Doctrine of Reconciliation*. Edited by G. W. Bromiley and T. F. Torrance. Translated by G. W. Bromiley. London: T. & T. Clark, 2009.
Bateman IV, Herbert W. *Charts on the Book of Hebrews*. Kregel Charts of the Bible. Grand Rapids: Kregel, 2012.
———, ed. *Four Views on the Warning Passages in Hebrews*. Grand Rapids: Kregel, 2007.
Bauckham, Richard J. "The Divinity of Jesus Christ in the Epistle to the Hebrews." In *The Epistle to the Hebrews and Christian Theology*, edited by Richard Bauckham, et al., 15–36. Grand Rapids: Eerdmans, 2009.
———. *Jude, 2 Peter*. WBC 50. Waco: Word, 1983.

Bauer, Walter, et al. *Greek-English Lexicon of the New Testament and Other Early Christian Literature*. 3rd ed. Chicago: University of Chicago Press, 2000.

Beale, Greg. *The Book of Revelation*. NIGTC. Grand Rapids: Eerdmans, 1999.

———, ed. *The Right Doctrine From the Wrong Texts? Essays on the Use of the Old Testament in the New*. Grand Rapids: Baker, 1994.

Betz, Hans Dieter. *Galatians*. Hermeneia. Philadelphia: Fortress, 1979.

Blue, Bradley. "Acts and the House Church." In *The Book of Acts in its Greco-Roman Setting*, edited by David D. J. Gill and Conrad Gempf, 119–222. Grand Rapids: Eerdmans, 1994.

Boyd, J. O. "What Was in the Ark?" *EvQ* 11 (1939) 165–68.

Bruce, F. F. *The Epistle to the Galatians*. NIGTC. Grand Rapids: Eerdmans, 1982.

———. *The Epistle to the Hebrews*. NICNT. Rev. ed. Grand Rapids: Eerdmans, 1990.

Buber, Martin. *The Later Masters*. Trans. Olga Marx. Vol. 2 of *Tales of the Hasidim*. New York: Schocken, 1948.

Caird, G. B. "The Exegetical Method of the Epistle to the Hebrews." *CJT* 5.1 (1959) 44–51.

———. *The Language and Imagery of the Bible*. Philadelphia: Westminster, 1980.

Calvin, John. *Institutes of the Christian Religion*. Edited by John Turabian McNeill. Translated by Ford Lewis Battles. LCC 20–21. Philadelphia: Westminster, 1960.

———. *The First Epistle of Paul to the Corinthians*. Translated by John W. Fraser. Calvin's New Testament Commentaries. Edited by David W. Torrance and Thomas F. Torrance. Grand Rapids: Eerdmans, 1960.

Carson, D. A. *Divine Sovereignty and Human Responsibility: Biblical Perspectives in Tension*. New Foundations Theological Library. Atlanta: John Knox, 1981.

———, ed. *NIV Zondervan Study Bible*. Grand Rapids: Zondervan, 2015.

Charlesworth, James H., ed. *The Old Testament Pseudepigrapha*. 2nd ed. 2 vols. Peabody: Hendrickson, 2011.

Cockerill, Gareth Lee. *The Epistle to the Hebrews*. NICNT. Grand Rapids: Eerdmans, 2012.

Conzelmann, Hans. *1 Corinthians*. Translated by James W. Leitch. Hermeneia. Philadelphia: Fortress, 1975.

Coogan, Michael D., ed. *The New Oxford Annotated Bible*. Third Edition. Oxford: Oxford University Press, 2001.

D'Angelo, Mary Rose. *Moses in the Letter to the Hebrews*. SBLDS 42. Missoula, MT: Scholars, 1979.

Dennis, Lane T. et al., eds. *ESV Study Bible*. Wheaton: Crossway, 2008.

deSilva, David A. *Despising Shame: Honor Discourse and Community Maintenance in the Epistle to the Hebrews*. SBLDS 152. Atlanta: Society of Biblical Literature, 1996.

———. *Honor, Patronage, Kinship & Purity: Unlocking New Testament Culture*. Downers Grove: IVP, 2000.

———. *Perseverance in Gratitude: A Socio-Rhetorical Commentary on the Epistle "to the Hebrews."* Grand Rapids: Eerdmans, 2000.

Ellingworth, Paul. *The Epistle to the Hebrews*. NIGTC. Grand Rapids: Eerdmans, 1993.

———. "Jesus and the Universe in Hebrews." *EvQ* 58 (1986) 337–50.

Ellingworth, Paul and Eugene A. Nida. *A Handbook on the Letter to the Hebrews*. UBS Handbook Series. New York: United Bible Societies, 1983.

Elliott, Mark A. *The Survivors of Israel*. Grand Rapids: Eerdmans, 2000.

Eusebius. *Ecclesiastical History*. Translated by Arthur Cushman McGiffert. In *The Nicene and Post-Nicene Fathers*, Series 2. Edited by Philip Schaff and Henry Wace. 1890. Repr. Peabody, MA: Hendrickson, 1999.
Ferguson, Everett. *Backgrounds of Early Christianity*. 2nd ed. Grand Rapids: Eerdmans, 1993.
Fletcher-Louis, Crispin H. T. "Jesus as the High Priestly Messiah: Part 1." *Journal for the Study of the Historical Jesus* 4.2 (2006) 155–75.
———. "Jesus as the High Priestly Messiah: Part 2." *Journal for the Study of the Historical Jesus* 5.1 (2007) 57–79.
Gager, John G. *Moses in Greco-Roman Paganism*. SBLMS 16. Nashville: Abingdon, 1972.
Greene, Graham. *The Power and the Glory*. London: William Heinemann, 1940.
Griffiths, Jonathan I. *Hebrews and Divine Speech*. LNTS 507. London: Bloomsbury, 2014.
Guthrie, George H. "Hebrews." In *Commentary on the New Testament Use of the Old Testament*, edited by G. K. Beale and D. A. Carson, 919–95. Grand Rapids: Baker, 2007.
———. *The Structure of Hebrews: A Text-Linguistic Analysis*. Grand Rapids: Baker, 1998.
Hay, David M. *Glory at the Right Hand: Psalm 110 in Early Christianity*. SBLMS 18. Nashville: Abingdon, 1973.
Hengel, Martin. *Crucifixion*. Philadelphia: Fortress, 1977.
Horsley, G. H. R. *New Documents Illustrating Early Christianity*. Vol. 1. North Ryde, N.S.W., Australia: Macquarie University, 1984.
Howard, Jeremy Royal, ed. *HCSB Study Bible*. Nashville: Holman Bible, 2010.
Hughes, Graham. *Hebrews and Hermeneutics: The Epistle to the Hebrews as a New Testament Example of Biblical Interpretation*. SNTSMS 36. Cambridge: Cambridge University Press, 1979.
Hughes, Philip E. *A Commentary on the Epistle to the Hebrews*. Grand Rapids: Eerdmans, 2002.
Jeremias, Joachim. "Mōusēs." In *TDNT* 4:848–73.
Jobes, Karen H. *1 Peter*. BECNT. Grand Rapids: Baker, 2005.
Josephus. Translated by H. St. J. Thackeray et al. 10 vols. LCL. Cambridge: Harvard University Press, 1926–1965.
Keener, Craig S. *The Gospel of Matthew: A Socio-Rhetorical Commentary*. Grand Rapids: Eerdmans, 2009.
Koester, Craig R. *Hebrews*. AB 36. New York: Doubleday, 2001.
Laansma, Jon C. "Heaven in the General Epistles." In *Heaven*, edited by Christopher W. Morgan and Robert A. Peterson, 111–37. Theology in Community. Wheaton: Crossway, 2014.
———. "Hebrews: Yesterday, Today, and Future. An Illustrative Survey, Diagnosis, Prescription." In *Christology, Hermeneutics, and Hebrews: Profiles from the History of Interpretation*, edited by Jon C. Laansma and Daniel J. Treier, 1–32. LNTS. New York: Bloomsbury, 2012.
———. "Hebrews and the Mission of the Earliest Church." In *New Testament Theology in Light of the Church's Mission: Essays in Honor of I. Howard Marshall*, edited by Jon C. Laansma, Grant R. Osborne, and Ray Van Neste, 327–46. Eugene, OR: Cascade, 2011.

———. *I Will Give You Rest: The 'Rest' Motif in the New Testament with Special Reference to Mt 11 and Heb 3–4*. WUNT 2. Reihe 98. Tübingen: Mohr Siebeck, 1997.

———. "The Living and Active Word: A Theological Reading of Hebrews." In *Listen, Understand, Obey: Essays on Hebrews*, edited by Caleb T. Friedeman. Eugene, OR: Pickwick, 2017.

Lane, William L. *Hebrews*. 2 vols. WBC 47A; 47B. Dallas: Word, 1991.

Lewis, Theodore. "Covenant and Blood Rituals: Understanding Exodus 24:3–8 in Its Ancient Near Eastern Context." In *Confronting the Past: Archaeological and Historical Essays on Ancient Israel in Honor of William G. Dever*, edited by Seymour Gitin, J. Edward Wright, and J. P. Dessel, 341–50. Winona Lake: Eisenbrauns, 2006.

Liddell, Henry George, Robert Scott, and Henry Stuart Jones. *A Greek-English Lexicon*. 9th ed. Oxford: Clarendon, 1996.

Lindars, Barnabas. *The Theology of the Letter to the Hebrews*. New Testament Theology. Cambridge: Cambridge University Press, 1991.

Llewelyn, S. R. "Changing the Legal Jurisdiction." In *New Documents Illustrating Early Christianity*, edited by S. R. Llewelyn, 45–53. Vol. 9. Grand Rapids: Eerdmans, 2002.

Lundin, Roger. "Interpreting Orphans: Hermeneutics in the Cartesian Tradition." In *The Promise of Hermeneutics*, by Roger Lundin, Clarence Walhout, and Anthony C. Thiselton, 1–64. Grand Rapids: Eerdmans, 1999.

Manchester, William. *A World Lit Only by Fire. The Medieval Mind and the Renaissance: Portrait of an Age*. New York: Little, Brown and Co., 1992–1993.

Marshall, I. Howard. *New Testament Theology: Many Witnesses, One Gospel*. Downers Grove: IVP Academic, 2004.

———. "Soteriology in Hebrews." In *The Epistle to the Hebrews and Christian Theology*, edited by Richard Bauckham, Daniel R. Driver, Trevor A. Hart, and Nathan MacDonald, 253–80. Grand Rapids: Eerdmans, 2009.

Mason, Eric F. *'You Are a Priest Forever': Second Temple Jewish Messianism and the Priestly Christology of the Epistle to the Hebrews*. STDJ 74. Leiden: Brill, 2008.

McCabe, Allyson. "Inspiration or Appropriation? Behind Music Copyright Lawsuits." *NPR*, September 5, 2015. Online: http://www.npr.org/2015/09/05/437598051/inspiration-or-appropriation-behind-music-copyright-lawsuits.

McGrath, S. J. *Through the Eternal Spirit: An Historical Study of the Exegesis of Hebrews 9:13–14*. Rome: Pontifica Universitas Gregoriana, 1961.

Meadors, Gary, ed. *Four Views on Moving Beyond the Bible*. Counterpoints: Bible and Theology. Grand Rapids, Zondervan, 2009.

Meeks, Wayne. *The Prophet-King: Moses Traditions and the Johannine Christology*. NovTSup 14. Leiden: Brill, 1967.

Mesa, Ivan. "Whom Do Tim Keller and Don Carson Look Up To?" *The Gospel Coalition*, August 1, 2015. Online: http://www.thegospelcoalition.org/article/keller-carson-tribute-alec-motyer.

Moffitt, David M. *Atonement and the Logic of Resurrection in the Epistle to the Hebrews*. NovTSup 141. Leiden: Brill, 2011.

Ngewa, Samuel. "The Place of Traditional Sacrifices." In *Africa Bible Commentary*, edited by Tokunboh Adeyemo, 1502–3. Grand Rapids: Zondervan, 2006.

*NLT Illustrated Study Bible*. Carol Stream, IL: Tyndale, 2015.

Orphan Hope International. "Facts & Statistics." Online: http://www.orphanhopeintl.org/facts-statistics/.

Pelikan, Jaroslav, and Valerie Hotchkiss, eds. *Creeds and Confessions of Faith in the Christian Tradition*. 3 vols. New Haven: Yale University Press, 2003.

Perrin, Nicholas. *Jesus the Priest*. Grand Rapids: Baker Academic; London: SPCK, 2017.

Peterson, David. G. *Hebrews and Perfection: An Examination of the Concept of Perfection in the Epistle to the Hebrews*. SNTSMS 47. Cambridge: Cambridge University Press, 1982.

Philo. Translated by F. H. Colson et al. LCL. 12 vols. Harvard: Cambridge University Press, 1929–1953.

Polkinghorne, John. "Eschatology: Some Questions and Some Insights from Science." In *The End of the World and the Ends of God: Science and Theology on Eschatology*, edited by John Polkinghorne and Michael Welker, 29–41. Theology for the 21st Century. Harrisburg, PA: Trinity Press International, 2000.

Potter, D. S. "Persecution of the Early Church." In *The Anchor Bible Dictionary*, edited by David Noel Freedman, 231–35. Vol. 5. New York: Doubleday, 1992.

Quinn, Daniel. *Ishmael: An Adventure in Mind and Spirit*. New York: Bantam, 1992.

Rapske, Brian. "Acts, Travel and Shipwreck." In *The Book of Acts in its Graeco-Roman Setting*, edited by David W. J. Gill and Conrad Gempf, 1–47. Vol. 2 of *The Book of Acts in its First Century Setting*. Edited by Bruce W. Winter. Grand Rapids: Eerdmans, 1994.

———. *Paul in Roman Custody*. Vol. 3 of *The Book of Acts in its First Century Setting*. Edited by Bruce W. Winter. Grand Rapids: Eerdmans, 1994.

Riddle, D. W. "Early Christian Hospitality: A Factor in the Gospel Transmission." *JBL* 57 (1938) 141–54.

Ross, Allen. "Introduction to the Study of the Book of Isaiah." Online: https://bible.org/seriespage/1-introduction-study-book-isaiah.

Schnabel, Eckhard J. *Early Christian Mission*. 2 vols. Downers Grove: IVP Academic, 2004.

Schürer, Emil. *The History of the Jewish People in the Age of Jesus Christ*. Vol. 2. Translated and revised by Geza Vermes, Fergus Millar, and Matthew Black. Edinburgh: T. & T. Clark, 1979.

Simpson, E. K. "The Vocabulary of the Epistle to the Hebrews." *EvQ* 18 (1946) 35–38, 187–90.

Smith, Ralph L. *Micah–Malachi*. WBC 32. Waco: Word, 1984.

Spiegel, Shalom. *The Last Trial. On the Legends and Lore of the Command to Abraham to Offer Isaac as a Sacrifice: The Akedah*. Translated by Judah Goldin. Philadelphia: Jewish Publication Society, 1967. Repr., New York: Behrman, 1979.

Svendsen, Stefan N. *Allegory Transformed: The Appropriation of Philonic Hermeneutics in the Letter to the Hebrews*. WUNT 2.269. Tübingen: Mohr Siebeck, 2009.

Swetnam, James. *Jesus and Isaac: A Study of the Epistle to the Hebrews in the Light of the Aqedah*. AnBib 94. Rome: Pontifical Biblical Institute, 1981.

Thiselton, Anthony C. "Hebrews." In *The Eerdmans Commentary on the Bible*, edited by James D. G. Dunn and John W. Rogerson, 1451–82. Grand Rapids: Eerdmans, 2003.

Torrance, T. F. *Atonement: The Person and Work of Christ*. Edited by Robert T. Walker. Downers Grove: IVP, 2009.

———. *Incarnation: The Person and Life of Christ*. Edited by Robert T. Walker. Downers Grove: IVP: 2008.

Turkle, Sherry. *Alone Together: Why We Expect More from Technology and Less from Each Other*. New York: Perseus, 2011.

UNICEF. *Africa's Orphaned Generation* (November 2003) 1–56. Online: http://www.unicef.org/sowc06/pdfs/africas_orphans.pdf.

Wallant, Edward. *The Children at the Gate*. San Diego: Harcourt, Brace & World, 1964.

Walton, John H. *Ancient Near Eastern Thought and the Old Testament*. Grand Rapids: Baker 2006.

―――. *Chronological and Background Charts of the Old Testament*. Grand Rapids: Zondervan, 1994.

Walton, John H., and Craig S. Keener, eds. *NIV Cultural Backgrounds Study Bible*. Grand Rapids: Zondervan, 2016.

Webb, William J. *Corporal Punishment in the Bible: A Redemptive-Movement Hermeneutic for Troubling Texts*. Downers Grove: IVP, 2011.

Westcott, Brooke Foss. *The Epistle to the Hebrews: The Greek Text with Notes and Essays*. 2nd ed. London: Macmillan, 1892.

Westfall, Cynthia. *A Discourse Analysis of the Letter to the Hebrews: The Relationship between Form and Meaning*. LNTS 297. London: T. & T. Clark, 2005.

Wildberger, Hans. *Isaiah 1–12*. Translated by Thomas H. Trapp. Minneapolis: Fortress, 1991.

Winter, Bruce W. *Roman Wives, Roman Widows: The Appearance of New Women and the Pauline Commentaries*. Grand Rapids: Eerdmans, 2003.

Woods, Christopher E. "The Sun-God Tablet of Nabû-Apla-Iddina Revisited." *JCS* 56 (2004) 23–103.

Wright, N. T. *Justification: God's Plan and Paul's Vision*. Downers Grove: IVP Academic, 2009.

―――. *The Resurrection of the Son of God*. Minneapolis: Fortress, 2003.

# Index

Aaron, 23, 128, 134, 177, 216. *See also* priesthood, Aaronic.
Abel, 265–67, 270, 317. *See also* blood of Abel *and* sacrifices of Cain and Abel.
Abraham
    faith of, 137, 150, 152, 157, 166–67, 169, 272–77
    promise to, 2–3, 13, 43, 53, 66, 75, 94, 99, 179
    seed of, 10, 14, 20, 22, 41–43, 52, 70, 166, 304–5, 308–9, 335
abuse, 136, 148, 309
access
    to God. *See* approach the throne.
    to Most Holy Place, 196–97, 200, 219, 244, 278
Adam, 43, 46, 57, 59
ages, end of. *See* last days.
allegory, 16–18, 120, 199, 276, 310
altar, 216, 326, 328
    of incense, 193–94
anchor, 65, 136, 158–60, 178, 225, 295
angels, 52, 56–62, 64–65, 71–73, 75, 78, 167, 172, 229, 318, 327. *See also* liturgy, angelic.
anthropology, theological, 74, 76–77, 235, 248, 254, 261, 271, 290, 296
apocalyptic, 29
apostasy, 65, 124–25, 140, 142–43, 146–49, 196, 250, 305, 309–11, 317, 326
    nature of, 147–49, 251–53, 310

of Israel, 15, 106, 189, 254
apostle(s)
    Hebrews' teaching has character of, 3, 10, 12, 17, 42, 128, 222, 315
    Hebrews' teaching in tension with, 143, 222
    Jesus as, 89, 100–101
    *See also* hermeneutics of the apostles.
approach, 37, 122, 124–25, 211, 245–46, 292, 312, 316
    of God, 254, 259
    of the Day, 48, 244, 246, 248–50, 254
    the throne, 11, 35, 45, 86, 91, 99, 107, 118, 137, 141, 149, 187, 189, 197, 239, 244, 260, 292, 297, 300, 303, 308–9, 320, 323, 325–26, 331
Ark of the Covenant, 29, 46, 192–94, 204, 216
assurance, 91, 144, 150, 174, 180, 267, 312. *See also* confidence.
athletics/race, 159, 256, 258, 294–96, 299–300, 305–6, 319, 326
atonement, 33, 153, 215–16, 232, 237, 240, 253, 264, 273, 277, 280, 284, 296, 316–17
    day of, 23, 32, 172–73, 195–96, 203–9, 213, 216, 224, 238, 324
    history of, 213
    Jesus', 31, 82
    location of, 120, 181, 183, 232

attentiveness/attention, 50, 65, 138, 142, 151, 246
author of Hebrews. *See* Preacher, the.

baptism, 38–39, 141, 196, 203, 245–46
Bible. *See* Scripture.
blessing(s), 22, 124, 132, 146, 149, 151, 153–54, 164, 166, 189, 234, 239, 254, 260, 270, 305, 308, 313, 319, 330, 332, 335
    experienced by non-Christians, 145, 148
blood, 46, 196, 207–9, 213–14, 216–19, 221, 232, 234, 264, 280, 284, 305, 317
    of Abel, 266–67
    of Jesus, 207, 209–10, 234, 244, 252, 278, 308, 317
    symbolism of, 46, 198, 207, 210
boldness, 93, 124, 244, 260, 292. *See also* confidence.

calling, heavenly, 88, 92, 98, 217, 222
Christ, 21
    body of, 228, 233, 235, 246, 308
    *See also* Jesus *and* sharing in Christ.
Christology, 20–26, 54, 61, 75, 108, 111, 113, 167–68, 234, 275, 284, 306
Church, 106, 248, 292, 316, 323, 328, 330, 332, 334–35
city, 40, 45, 75, 111, 214, 226, 261, 273–74, 276, 284, 326–27, 329
    heavenly, 284, 291–92, 322
    of God, 68, 94, 108, 141, 290, 317
    of God as resting place, 97
    *See also* Jerusalem.
cleansing, 14, 38, 41, 83, 175, 198, 210, 219, 222–23, 233, 237–38, 245, 273, 282, 284, 304, 314, 317. *See also* purification.
Communion. *See* Eucharist.
confession, 50, 90, 163, 229, 240, 246, 249, 260, 271, 289, 300, 323–24, 335
confidence, 66, 75, 90–91, 151, 180, 197, 210, 213, 261, 278, 291–92, 298, 308, 310, 324, 334

conscience, 187, 198–200, 203, 248, 306, 331
    cleansing of, 37, 40, 198, 200, 210, 237, 239
    perfection of, 197, 200, 237, 239
copies. *See* shadows.
cosmogony, 134, 274, 310
cosmology, 2, 41, 118, 120–21, 180, 266, 314
cosmos, 71, 74, 104, 111, 114, 118, 121, 180, 188, 207, 223, 230, 265. *See also* creation *and* world.
covenant(s), 41, 80, 171–72, 195, 213, 216, 261, 268, 303, 308, 310–11, 314, 328, 332–33
    and creation, 66–67, 90, 114, 188, 207, 234, 310, 315, 328
    change of, 175, 179, 187, 230
    community of, 95, 97, 150, 222, 303, 307–8
    continuity of, 175, 264, 276
    discontinuity of, 188, 197, 264, 326
    inauguration of, 213, 218, 244
    inauguration ritual of, 23, 213–16, 218
    Mosaic, 41, 43, 89, 141, 177, 247, 279, 303, 314
    new, 35, 43, 64, 85, 130, 141, 146, 152, 157–58, 173, 175, 179, 184–85, 188, 213, 218, 239, 244, 259, 283, 290, 303–5, 312–14, 317, 327, 332
    old, 173, 181, 186, 244, 267, 312, 314, 317, 327
    overlap of, 43
creation, 100, 109, 268, 270, 276, 315. *See also* cosmos *and* world.
    Jesus as goal of, 52
cross, 81, 120, 135, 148, 208, 217, 232, 282, 295–300, 326–27
crucifixion, 146, 148, 207, 295–99
cult, 33, 46, 67, 139, 172, 183, 198, 208, 216, 218, 265, 277, 322, 324. *See also* ritual.
curse, 148, 154, 214–16, 254, 296, 326
curtain, 29, 118–19, 156–57, 193, 223, 244–45, 295, 318

# INDEX

David
  history of, 15, 46, 110, 149, 233, 292, 333
  kingship of, 20, 58
  promise to, 60
Day of Atonement. *See* Atonement, day of.
death, 76, 81–82, 86, 136, 158, 160, 175, 198, 214–15, 224–25, 233, 267, 273, 274, 276–77, 285, 288–90, 293, 299, 320
  of Jesus, 73, 75, 77–78, 132, 210, 213, 217, 234, 240, 333–34
  triumph over, 73, 75, 82, 136, 265–66, 270, 280, 284
defilement. *See* impurity.
deliverance, 83, 229, 254, 260, 279, 283, 285, 289
descent of Jesus, 72–73, 75–76, 78, 85, 94, 234
Devil, 81–83, 85
discipline, 136, 139, 254, 302–3, 305–6, 309, 320
  church, 148, 252
  self, 258
disobedience, 46, 96, 187, 208, 273, 279, 283, 320
  of Israel, 209, 217, 234, 259, 319. *See also* apostasy of Israel.
drama. *See also* story *and* history.
  divine, 4, 265, 330–31
  earthly, 308
  heavenly, 2, 30, 308
  of history, 73, 80, 184, 190, 227, 272, 275
  of Scripture, 274, 303
  of the atonement, 231
  of the covenant(s), 139, 190, 213, 218, 224, 254, 283
  participation in divine, 4, 16, 184, 276, 278, 280, 283–84
dualism, 16, 120–21, 207, 210, 225, 265, 273, 283, 289, 309–10, 315, 318, 327

earth, 224–25, 317
education, 139. *See also* discipline.
election, 25, 38, 43, 145, 148, 254. *See also* God acts first in salvation.
encouragement, 60, 97, 160, 174, 177, 186, 248, 262, 278, 291, 295, 205, 311, 313, 319, 333
endurance, 118, 122, 152, 242, 256, 260, 277, 285, 295, 300, 302, 308, 311, 313–14, 319, 324, 332. *See also* perseverance.
enemies, 238, 241, 250, 253, 299–300, 314
Enoch, 266, 268–70
enter/entry/entrance, 13, 32, 39, 44, 94–95, 98–99, 102, 115, 117, 122, 156, 159, 168, 200, 208, 237, 245, 277, 312, 314, 318
  as the promise, 67, 135, 176
  of Jesus, 221, 223
enthronement. *See* exaltation.
Esau
  forfeits his birthright, 15, 36, 97, 145, 270, 302, 305, 310–11
  wives of, 307
eschatology, 105. *See also* last days.
eternal life. *See* life, eternal.
ethics, 140, 303, 322, 334
Eucharist, 186, 208, 231, 246, 324, 326
exaltation
  of humans, 71
  of Jesus, 14, 25, 57, 59, 72–74, 85, 94, 120, 132
exhortation, 100, 150, 237–38, 242, 261–62, 288–89, 295, 302, 307, 323
Exodus, 80, 85, 159, 304, 333
expiation, 33, 82

faith, 38–40, 48, 88, 92, 98, 101, 108, 121, 124, 127, 141, 153–54, 157, 160, 167, 175, 184, 199–200, 224, 233, 240, 246–48, 256, 259–62, 264–70, 272, 274, 276–86, 288–93, 295–300, 305, 308–11, 313–14, 317–19, 324–27, 333–34
  and obedience, 13, 38–39, 42, 68, 75, 92, 98, 138, 140–41, 154, 177, 190, 225, 228, 231, 261–62, 265, 268, 270, 277, 280, 283, 329
  as the whole life, 98, 145

faithfulness, 288
- of Christians, 152, 238, 242, 246, 255, 260, 283, 311
- of God, 52, 74, 138–39, 152–53, 158, 183–84, 265, 269, 313, 331
- of Jesus, 38, 90, 92, 176, 226, 233, 260, 284, 295
- of Moses, 88
- of the patriarchs, 154, 282

faithlessness, 47, 81, 248, 303, 307, 310, 316. *See also* unbelief.

falling away. *See* apostasy.

family of God, 80–81, 84, 90, 214, 248–49, 302–4, 309–10, 316, 331, 333. *See also* sons and daughters of God.

fellowship, 10–11, 97, 100, 109, 151, 153, 246–48, 255, 283, 297–300, 309, 322, 325, 331, 334–35

food, 36, 270, 323–25

footstool, 13, 110, 122, 190, 225–26, 237, 326

forerunner, 107, 158–60, 270, 291–92, 300

forgiveness, 38, 83, 85, 147, 149, 196, 198, 213, 218–19, 224, 226, 234, 238–39. *See also* word, divine, of forgiveness.

Gentiles and Jews, 37, 42–43, 82, 176, 279, 282

gift, 35–40, 141, 149, 245–46, 254, 276, 309. *See also* grace.

glory, 71, 131–32, 293, 295, 307, 318
- of the Son, 61, 89
- won for Christians, 85

God
- acts first in salvation, 38, 40, 132, 134, 141, 153, 156, 200, 332
- as creator, 153–54, 334
- as father, 306
- character of, 277, 289
- dwelling of, 273, 315
- existence of, 269, 271
- name of, 71, 269, 329
- nature of, 269
- power of, 268, 276, 206, 330, 334
- revealed in Jesus. *See* Jesus as revelation of God.

Gospel, 2, 25, 92, 116, 147, 175, 218, 225, 239–40, 253, 269, 272, 289, 299, 314, 322, 328–29
- as source of reality, 224–25
- confirmation of, 66
- for the present, 13, 106, 135, 147, 334
- tradition of, 51, 64, 280

grace, 36–37, 40, 109, 124, 184, 189, 244, 251–52, 300, 320, 324–26, 328
- as gift, 37
- as Gospel, 36
- undeserved, 37, 124

heaven, 181, 207, 215, 317
- Jesus as the pattern in, 27–30, 32, 119, 134, 182–83, 185, 189, 222, 231, 234, 272, 281
- joins earth, 181–83, 203, 224–25, 230, 232, 273, 299
- people of, 222, 245
- reality of, 27–28, 319
- structure of, 28–29, 119
- things in, 221–22, 225, 245, 267

Hebrews
- application of, 16, 68, 190, 253, 283
- canonicity of, 10, 11–12, 19
- date of, 9–10
- genre of, 4, 49
- influence of, 3
- logic of, 3
- purpose of, 4, 9, 12, 19, 24, 31, 46–47, 50, 63, 87, 97, 125, 170, 225, 330, 334–35
- retelling of history, 1, 12–15, 101, 177–78, 332
- sources of, 120, 129–30
- strategy of, 64, 127, 203, 318
- structure of, 4–8, 88, 117–18, 125–27, 138, 191, 201, 212, 220, 227–28, 236–37, 242–43, 249, 255, 263–64, 294, 303, 311
- theology of, 9, 10, 23–25, 86, 120
- use of OT Scriptures. *See* Scriptures, Hebrews' use of.

worldview of, 16, 18–19, 27–28, 32, 46, 119, 168, 180–81
heir(s), 215, 266, 268, 305
    Seed of Abraham as, 72
    Jesus as, 53, 77
Hellenism, 258, 287
hermeneutics, 18, 145
    imitation of apostolic, 26–27, 60
    of the apostles, 27
    of Hebrews, 18, 26–27, 57–58, 96, 99, 162–63, 165–66, 199, 230, 275
    *See also* Scriptures, Hebrews' use of.
history, 18, 117, 223–24, 226, 232, 246, 292, 319, 327
    church participates in Israel's, 14–15, 80, 85, 93, 95, 103, 189, 211, 304
    church participates in Jesus', 53, 85, 93, 217
    is covenantal, 2, 41, 181, 188, 207, 217, 315, 327
    is history of the promise, 13, 43, 53–54, 105, 184–85, 217, 223, 234, 265
    is Jesus' history, 14–15, 18, 23, 26, 54, 82, 118, 133, 160, 184, 203, 217
    of faith, 157, 282, 295
    of Israel, 1, 14, 43, 45, 80, 82, 84, 94, 101, 108, 141, 160, 209, 224, 234, 254, 303–5, 309, 316, 328, 334
    of Jesus, 170, 200, 210, 240, 277, 286, 289, 325
    of the church, 10, 328
    of the covenants, 2, 46, 181, 213, 249, 267, 315, 328
    of the promise, 13, 67, 75, 77, 95, 101, 105, 110, 114, 125, 137, 156, 160–61, 184, 216, 234, 259, 273, 277, 281, 290–91
    of the world, 2, 104, 223, 265
    *See also* drama *and* story.
holding fast, 92. *See also* endurance.

holiness, 45–46, 48, 119, 135, 246, 252–53, 298, 302, 304, 307–8, 320, 326–27
Holy Place, 33, 192
    architecture of, 192–95
    Most Holy Place, 33, 45, 87, 94, 99, 108, 119–20, 156, 223, 245, 325–26
    promised land as, 87
    whole world as, 15, 119–20
Holy Spirit, 58, 69, 83, 99, 112, 114, 116, 153, 196, 200, 203, 207, 209–10, 219, 231, 237, 239, 252
honor, 131–32, 257, 281, 292–93, 298
hope, 91, 93, 136, 149, 152–53, 246–47, 252, 261, 270–71, 275–76, 286, 291, 295–97, 314–15, 319, 333
hospitality, 257, 323, 328
house, 87–88, 90–91, 245, 266
household, 15, 44, 91, 246, 304, 308, 310, 314, 323, 326
humanity. *See also* anthropology, theological.
    as exalted. *See* exaltation of humans.
    insignificance of, 74
    Jesus as paradigmatic, 133
    promise to, 71–72
humiliation, 72–73, 81, 85
    of Jesus. *See* descent of Jesus.

imitation, 152
    of Abraham, 157, 159, 167, 169
    of the faithful, 140, 152, 154, 159, 167, 169
    of Israel, 99
    of Jesus, 77, 118, 135, 152, 234, 298, 323, 333. *See also* Jesus as example.
    *See also* hermeneutics, imitation of apostolic.
imperfection, 35, 99, 122, 290, 306, 312
imprisonment, 10, 257–58, 260, 278, 331
impurity, 33–34, 174, 209, 215, 234, 240, 252, 273, 326
inattentiveness, 50, 246

incarnation, 14, 25, 32, 82, 113, 228,
    231, 233, 296. See also Jesus,
    humanity of.
inheritance, 40, 45, 214, 267–68, 305,
    314, 318
  of believers, 60, 78, 80, 107, 152,
    260, 311
  of Jesus, 40, 72, 327
  promise of. See promise of an
    inheritance.
  receiving the, 13, 25, 39, 215, 219,
    264–65, 305, 310, 316
  won for believers, 71, 79, 81, 95,
    213, 234
intercession, 82–83, 161, 172, 176, 223,
    233, 244, 268, 291–92
invisible, 11, 17, 101, 114, 158, 224–26,
    265–69, 271, 279–80, 283, 291–
    92, 295–96, 318
Isaac, 161, 272, 274, 276, 305. See also
    offering of Isaac.
Israel, 82
  as temple. See Temple, Israel as.
  history of. See history of Israel.
  Jesus as ultimate, 81
  king of, 229
  plight of, 83

Jacob, 275, 277, 305
Jerusalem
  city of, 45, 64, 165, 192, 195, 290,
    326–27
  heavenly, 45, 222, 272, 274, 316,
    322, 326
  New, 102
Jesus, 21
  as (high) priest, 22–23, 35, 81, 84,
    87, 90–91, 94, 112–14, 124,
    130–32, 134, 137, 156, 166–68,
    170, 174–76, 180, 202, 219, 235,
    237, 245, 253, 277, 308, 326
  as example, 79, 83, 90, 92, 97, 132,
    159, 295, 300, 333. See also
    imitation of Jesus.
  as guarantor, 174, 177
  as king, 22, 32, 59–61, 253, 333. See
    also Kingdom of Jesus.
  as offering. See Offering of Jesus.
  as revelation of God, 19–20, 53, 269
  as Son, 51, 274–75
  death of. See death of Jesus.
  deity of, 2, 23–25, 51, 54, 57, 59,
    176, 332
  descent of. See descent of Jesus.
  eternality of, 57, 59, 74, 177, 297
  faith of. See faithfulness of Jesus.
  humanity of, 2, 23–25, 52, 54, 57,
    59, 74–75, 123, 125, 133, 161,
    166, 176, 207, 224, 233–34. See
    also incarnation.
  names of, 20–22, 71, 73, 92, 232
  perfection of. See perfection of Jesus.
  reign of. See Kingdom of Jesus.
  return of, 221, 224–25, 313
  work of, 80, 84–85, 297
Jews, 97. See also Judaism.
  exegesis of, 104
  literature of, 113
  teachings of, 140
Josephus, 65, 120, 146, 164, 216, 252,
    266, 280, 287, 315
journey, 45, 71, 80, 85, 87, 94, 107, 111,
    121, 144, 151, 178, 184, 196,
    200, 242, 248, 270, 277, 290,
    302, 304, 308, 310, 314, 322–23,
    325, 328–29, 333
joy, 68, 109, 254, 300, 306, 308, 310
Judaism. See also Jews.
  backgrounds from, 65, 88–89, 105,
    120, 128–30, 146, 164–65, 168,
    171–72, 186, 217, 221–22, 266,
    272, 274, 286–87, 295, 315
  history of, 129, 287
judgment, 66, 112–13, 144, 148, 151,
    224–25, 244, 249–52, 254, 260,
    265, 270, 288, 308–9, 312–15,
    317, 325
justice, 150, 267, 300–301, 317, 319

kingdom, 299, 313, 317
  of Jesus, 80, 93. See also Jesus as
    king.
  unshakeable, 314, 320

Land, 186, 275
Last days, 50, 53, 70, 87, 92, 100, 103,
    157, 189–90, 223–25, 241, 246,
    260, 292, 308, 319. See also
    Eschatology.

law
  change of, 130, 166, 170–71, 173, 175, 179, 183, 188, 192, 228
  eternality of, 171
  limitations of, 171, 177, 185–88, 196, 209, 219, 231, 312, 319, 325
  Mosaic, 44, 80, 114, 135, 173, 175, 185, 187, 229, 231, 250–51, 279
  new, 175
  on the heart, 187, 189, 199, 203, 223, 229, 237, 239
  pattern for the, 187, 189, 197, 199
  subservient to Jesus, 171
  uselessness of, 175
  value of, 168, 173, 175, 177, 184, 188–89, 197, 199–200, 207, 209, 219, 230–32, 319
leader(s)
  human, 154, 257, 322–25, 331–33
  Jesus as, 73–74, 81, 299
Levi, 129, 170
Levites, 91, 128, 129, 166. *See also* priesthood, levitical.
life, 198, 269, 289, 292, 301, 320, 322
  eternal, 166–67, 170–72, 174, 295, 333
  *See also* faith as the whole life.
liturgy
  angelic, 58, 129–30, 318
  Christian, 186, 222
  earthly, 30
  heavenly, 29, 119, 129
Logos, 20–21, 113
Lord, 21
Lord's Supper. *See* Eucharist.
love, 246–48, 253–54, 305, 310, 322, 328

Maccabees, 57, 129, 287–88
martyrdom, 267, 280, 288, 295–96, 324, 331
maturity, 10, 138, 140–42, 144, 308
mediator, 4, 16, 22–24, 134, 159, 172, 180, 182, 184–85, 188, 213, 215, 219, 318
Melchizedek
  compared to Jesus, 25, 120, 156, 163, 166–67
  figure of, 128, 137, 156, 162–68, 273

  order of, 22, 156, 162–63, 168, 179
  *See also* priesthood, Melchizedekian.
mercy, 36, 124, 244, 251, 300, 326
ministry
  better, 180, 182, 184–85, 218, 237
  of Christians, 152
  of Jesus, 87, 112, 122, 126, 156, 180, 183, 221, 268
  of Moses's priests, 182, 192, 213, 254
miracles, 66, 262, 289
mission, 10, 54, 111, 152, 226, 233, 235, 238, 246, 248, 260, 283, 295, 323, 327, 329–30, 333–34
modernism, 27–28, 135, 167, 181, 198–99, 218, 268
mortality, 174, 238
Moses, 89, 279–80
  as covenant inaugurator, 3, 23, 43, 89
  as priest, 89
  as prophet, 15, 18, 21, 43, 65, 67, 75, 93, 105, 125, 184, 281
  compared to Jesus, 88, 91, 131, 182
  faith of, 284. *See also* faithfulness of Moses.
  parents of, 280–81
  seeing the pattern, 27–28, 30, 32, 121, 134, 189, 222, 231, 272
mythology, 28, 45–46, 104, 181, 210, 221

Noah, 265–66, 268, 270

oath, 158–60, 171–72, 174, 177, 214
obedience, 39, 47, 91, 107, 124–25, 141, 153, 157, 167, 171, 184, 187, 189, 229–30, 232, 242, 246–47, 267, 276, 283, 288, 291, 297, 302, 309, 314, 320, 324, 327–28, 332
  and faith. *See* faith and obedience.
  of Israel, 199, 282
  of the Son, 13, 41, 74, 79, 111, 122–23, 132–34, 136, 198, 228, 231, 233–34, 298

offering. *See also* sacrifices.
   better, 179, 215, 268
   heavenly, 224, 232
   Mosaic. *See* sacrifices, Mosaic.
   of Isaac, 272
   of Jesus, 41, 113–14, 118, 124, 175, 182, 192, 224, 228, 231, 233, 239, 289, 308, 313, 325–26, 329. *See also* sacrifice of Jesus.
   once-for-all, 110, 192, 196, 202, 206, 210, 213–14, 217, 219, 222–23, 226, 232, 244, 250, 264, 282
   self, 14, 23, 99, 101, 198, 207, 211, 238, 244–45, 282

parenesis, 322–23
Passover, 89, 281
pattern, Jesus as the. *See* heaven, Jesus as the pattern in.
Paul
   as author of Hebrews, 8, 11–12
   similarity to Hebrews, 2–3, 10, 17, 36, 73, 147, 156, 159, 254, 260, 262, 279, 283, 305, 324, 331
   tension with Hebrews, 82, 176, 198, 239, 261, 269
peace, 247, 292, 300–302, 304, 307–8, 319, 333–34
people
   of faith, 105, 290
   of God, 280–83, 317–18
perfection, 33–34, 80, 166, 170, 175, 186–87, 197, 225, 230, 238, 266, 289, 297–99, 316, 319
   of Christians, 34, 38, 84, 118, 219, 237, 239, 306, 312
   of conscience. *See* conscience, perfection of.
   of faith, 34, 300
   of Jesus, 34–36, 79, 84, 94, 125, 229, 235
   of Jesus as priest, 132
   timing of, 132, 290
persecution, 11, 13, 86, 90, 210, 225, 229, 256–57, 269, 288, 295. *See also* trials.

perseverance, 10–12, 39, 68, 86, 118, 145–46, 150, 153–54, 246–47, 255, 257. *See also* endurance.
Philo, 16–18, 42, 120, 129, 158, 164–65, 273, 280
philosophy, 16–17, 139, 180–81, 273, 298, 324
pilgrimage. *See* journey.
Plato, 16, 121, 266, 315
prayer, 83, 132, 135–36, 145, 245, 331–32
preacher, the
   background of, 4, 8, 49, 331–32
   identity of, 8, 11–12, 63
presence of God, 13, 15, 33, 110, 113, 119, 192, 196, 200, 209, 237, 239, 247, 253, 260
priest(s), 238, 324–25
   expected, 222
   high, 129, 197, 223, 244
   Jesus as. *See* Jesus as (high) priest.
priesthood, 129, 134, 177
   Aaronic, 22, 35, 128–31, 133, 156, 166–67, 197. *See also* Aaron.
   and kingship, 128–29
   Jesus'. *See* Jesus as (high) priest.
   Levitical, 129, 170, 172–74, 180–81, 199, 202, 237. *See also* Levi *and* Levites.
   Melchizedekian, 22, 156, 162, 197. *See also* Melchizedek.
prison. *See* imprisonment.
progress. *See* maturity.
promise, 42, 47, 98, 102, 105, 108, 127, 137, 141, 154, 157, 161, 167, 177, 186, 217, 250, 259–61, 264–65, 267, 269–77, 282–83, 285, 289–91, 293, 304, 314, 320, 323, 325, 332–34
   as resting place, 101, 104, 237, 247, 286
   as secret of cosmos, 66–67, 75, 77
   better, 179–80, 182, 184–86, 189, 203, 218, 237, 289, 335
   for creation, 66, 273, 320
   obtaining, 159, 218, 289–90, 304–5

of an inheritance, 16, 39, 54, 67, 108, 152, 179, 184, 214, 219, 309, 313, 318
son of, 274
to Abraham. *See* Abraham, promise to.
to David. *See* David, promise to.
to humanity. *See* humanity, promise to.
prophet(s), 92–93, 111, 145, 231, 291, 304, 316, 327
propitiation, 33, 82, 205
punishment, 38, 67, 150, 209, 251, 289, 296, 313
purification, 33, 209, 304. *See also* cleansing.

Qumran, 42, 128, 164, 165, 186

Rahab, 279, 282
readers of Hebrews
    background of, 9–10, 44, 50, 139, 255, 281
    location of, 8–9, 129, 331
    problems of, 9, 10–11, 225, 261
rebellion, 96, 310, 316. *See also* apostasy.
reconciliation, 23, 33, 100, 124
redemption, 109, 123, 203, 207–9, 217, 219
repentance, 140, 146–48, 196
    impossibility of, 146–47, 253
    second, 253
repetition, 318
    of rites, 192, 195, 214, 222, 237, 329
rest, 15, 107, 110, 119, 238, 308
    sabbath, 13, 104. *See also* sabbath.
resting place, 13, 15, 44, 87, 92, 94, 96–98, 103–5, 109–12, 131, 156, 176, 196, 235, 245, 247, 286, 311, 313–14, 333
resurrection, 32, 38, 85, 119, 122, 132, 136, 157, 173–75, 188–89, 224–25, 229, 233, 246, 260, 264–65, 267, 270, 272, 274–76, 299, 315, 317, 333–34
    bodily, 121, 224, 273, 309–10, 333
revelation, 99, 135, 269, 277, 317
    nonexistent apart from Son, 31
    *See* revelation of the Son *and* Jesus as revelation of God.
reward, 39–40, 150, 153, 242, 261, 266, 268, 283, 289, 295
rhetoric, 313, 334
righteousness, 139, 149, 152–53, 241, 247, 260, 262, 265–68, 276, 289, 291–92, 295, 300, 306, 316, 319, 328
ritual, 179–80, 207, 240, 324

sabbath, 94, 105, 107–11, 200
    and resting place, 104–6
    celebration, 97, 99, 104, 106, 109
    of God, 109
    *See also* rest.
sacrifice(s), 45, 229, 235, 270, 277, 313, 326, 329, 333. *See also* offerings.
    and obedience, 232
    ineffectiveness of, 180, 195–96. *See also* law, limitations of.
    Mosaic, 121, 172, 182, 203–6, 229–31, 264, 267
    of Cain and Abel, 266–67, 317
    of Jesus, 156, 204–6, 228, 284, 326. *See also* offering of Jesus.
salvation, 32–35, 39, 54, 62, 67–68, 108, 145, 153, 168, 175, 195, 238, 244, 266, 282, 284, 290–91, 293, 299–300, 309, 318–20, 328–29, 333–34
    as accomplished, 41, 83–84, 223, 253, 265, 277, 290, 295
    as covenant, 32
    as future, 33, 39–40, 68, 91, 93, 99, 101, 107, 144, 151, 224, 230, 253–54, 267, 277, 290, 313, 317, 319
    as present, 33, 39–40, 83–84, 91, 101, 147, 168, 226, 230, 253, 313, 317
    as resting place, 44, 110, 261
    benefits of, 39, 85, 148–49, 176, 192, 202, 218, 247–48, 252, 270
    eternal, 174, 177, 208, 210, 221
    God acts first in. *See* God acts first in salvation.
    Jesus as, 31, 40, 245, 260
    story of. *See* story of salvation.

sanctification, 33–34, 38, 124, 197, 209, 234–35, 238–39, 326–27
sanctuary
　earthly, 89, 197, 207, 209
　heavenly, 197, 202, 207, 210
Sarah, 273, 276
savior, 35
Scriptures, 142
　as spoken by Jesus, 83
　as spoken now, 99, 101, 305
　God revealed by, 249
　Hebrews' use of, 25–27, 57–58, 72, 97, 106, 114, 134, 140, 161, 167, 187, 229–30, 232, 259, 272, 291, 304, 318
　Jesus as subject matter of, 52, 61, 68, 96, 113–14
　nature of, 17, 52, 97, 177, 199
　witness to Jesus, 32, 52, 135
seen. *See* visible.
Septuagint, 57, 104, 171–72, 258–59, 275
session of the Son, 22, 82, 119, 237–38
shadows, 30, 45–46, 96–97, 115, 130, 170, 177, 182, 197, 229–30, 247, 254, 303, 316, 318, 329
　Jesus as origin of, 14, 130, 163, 168, 182, 185, 213, 218, 222, 230–31, 237, 276. *See also* heaven, Jesus as the pattern in.
　Jesus revealed by, 26, 28, 44, 121, 134, 156, 162, 166, 172, 192, 200, 206, 225, 228, 230–31
　purpose of, 67, 121, 189, 209–210, 233
shaking, 14, 38, 115, 188, 313–15, 320
shame, 42, 81, 257–58, 282, 296–98
sharing in Christ, 100–101, 200, 222, 267, 308, 320
sin, 123, 140, 145–46, 172, 176, 221, 226, 251, 270, 300, 304, 328
　encumbering, 297
　intentional, 196, 251, 313
　of ignorance, 196
　prevents entrance, 13, 48, 94, 217
　Jesus as without, 121–23, 211
Sinai, 14, 23, 64–65, 88, 188–89, 247, 314, 318
Son, the. *See* Jesus.
　as name of Jesus, 20, 52–53
　of God, 166
　revelation of, 13, 240
　word centers on, 13, 172
sons and daughters, 61, 309, 311
　as siblings of Jesus, 73–74, 81, 90, 92, 245–46, 291, 295, 297–98, 300, 309–10, 322
　of Abraham, 176, 305, 309
　of God, 15, 139, 302, 306, 320, 326. *See also* family of God.
sonship, 132
speech, divine, 2, 18, 43, 49, 92, 99, 112, 203, 237, 312, 317. *See also* word, divine.
　as action, 25, 31, 54
　as salvation, 54
　as spoken now, 100, 103
　history of, 12–13, 54, 78, 83, 100, 108, 167, 240–41, 264, 277
　*See* word, divine, spoken in the Son
sprinkling, 89, 119, 204, 209–211, 216, 317
story, 319–20. *See also* history.
　of Israel. *See* history of Israel.
　of salvation, 85, 94, 98, 270, 304
　of the church, 2
　of the promise. *See* history of the promise.
　of the world. *See* history of the world.
　participation in divine. *See* drama, participation in.
strangers on earth, 273–74, 276, 279, 290, 327
substitution, 223, 234
suffering, 34, 41, 76, 79, 124, 224, 229, 235, 262, 268, 279, 282–83, 295–96, 298, 300, 302, 305, 326, 333
sympathy of Jesus, 70, 81–82, 84, 91, 112, 121, 123–24, 131, 135, 161, 176, 233, 244, 260

tabernacle, 94, 122, 230, 314, 325, 327
　heavenly, 119, 181, 187, 200, 215, 245
　Moses', 119, 121, 180–81, 192–93, 197, 254, 264, 274
　true, 179–80, 182–84, 218, 274

# INDEX

teacher(s), 141–42, 335
temple, 45, 98, 119, 145, 274, 287, 303, 313–15, 323–24, 326, 328, 333
   as center of the world, 104, 188, 247, 315
   church as, 31
   heavenly, 130
   history of, 192–93
   Israel as, 31
   Jesus as, 30
temptation, 13, 83, 86, 123, 125, 210, 225
testimony, 237, 296, 318
throne of God, 108, 119, 122, 295, 301, 303, 308, 313, 320, 326–27. *See also* approach the divine throne.
Timothy, 10, 331
tithe, 164, 168
today, 58, 95–97, 99–100, 103, 106, 110–12, 115
trials, 121, 123, 159. *See also* persecution.
Trinity, 69, 83, 136, 203
typology, 20, 119–21, 166, 196–97, 207, 222, 266, 268, 274–76

unbelief, 307, 310. *See also* faithlessness.
   as rejection, 47, 98, 245, 250–52, 269–70, 313, 317–18
   consequences of, 95–96, 99, 102, 105, 225, 250, 279, 283
   of the people, 187
   of the world, 10, 268, 282, 332
   warning against, 93
unblemished, 122, 208, 211
unfaithfulness. *See* unbelief.
unseen. *See* invisible.

veil. *See* curtain.
visible, 11, 53, 76, 91, 158, 181, 224, 265, 268, 270, 279, 283, 318, 329

wandering, 23, 47, 96, 247
warning(s), 2, 63, 91, 102, 138, 144, 148, 174, 238, 242, 249–50, 253, 261, 266, 289, 309–12, 319
way, 324, 327–28
   into Most Holy Place. *See* access to Most Holy Place.
   Jesus is the, 47, 100
   of faith, 13, 154, 298, 306, 308, 332
   of God, 47, 100, 307–8, 311, 322, 328
   of Jesus, 298, 300, 304, 309, 326
   of salvation, 42, 297
wilderness, 88, 95, 97, 99–100, 106, 204
will
   legal, 213–16
   of God, 61, 111, 228, 231–33, 235, 260, 295, 299, 327, 330, 332
wisdom, 86, 125, 253, 291, 293, 334
   literature, 1, 57
   personified, 14, 51–52
   tradition, 24, 113, 142, 328
witness. *See* mission.
word, divine, 113–16, 125, 127, 171, 229, 264–66, 268, 270, 279, 281–82, 285, 288, 293, 309, 317, 327. *See also* speech, divine.
   as director of history, 41, 52
   of forgiveness, 13, 19, 92, 237, 240, 314, 320. *See also* forgiveness.
   spoken as the Son, 41, 49, 75, 88, 108, 113, 199, 230, 237, 240, 291, 313–14, 327
   spoken in the Son, 13, 26, 31, 49–54, 75, 88, 99, 112, 199, 230, 237, 240, 291, 313–14, 327
   sustains faith, 159–61, 199, 269, 277, 279
works, 106, 111, 137, 149, 208, 247, 257, 259
   judgment according to, 151
   of God, 115
   salvation by, 38–39, 261
world
   and ecology, 77
   new, 265, 268, 270, 273, 292, 315, 319
   this, 226, 271, 273, 276, 281, 284, 292, 299, 309, 315, 318
   *See also* cosmos *and* creation.
worship, 208, 325, 329, 333

Zion, 15, 42, 108, 110, 314, 316, 318, 327

www.ingramcontent.com/pod-product-compliance
Lightning Source LLC
Chambersburg PA
CBHW020606300426
44113CB00007B/535